Brave New Mind

Brave New Mind

A Thoughtful Inquiry into the Nature
and Meaning of Mental Life

PETER DODWELL

New York • Oxford

Oxford University Press

2000

Oxford University Press

Oxford   New York
Athens   Auckland   Bangkok   Bogotá   Buenos Aires   Calcutta
Cape Town   Chennai   Dar es Salaam   Delhi   Florence   Hong Kong   Istanbul
Karachi   Kuala Lumpur   Madrid   Melbourne   Mexico City   Mumbai
Nairobi   Paris   São Paulo   Singapore   Taipei   Tokyo   Toronto   Warsaw

and associated companies in
Berlin   Ibadan

Published by Oxford University Press, Inc.,
198 Madison Avenue, New York, New York 10016

Oxford is a registered trademark of Oxford University Press.

Library of Congress Cataloging-in-Publication Data
Dodwell, P. C.
Brave new mind : a thoughtful inquiry into the nature and
meaning of mental life / Peter Dodwell.
    p.   cm.
Includes bibliographical references and index.
ISBN 0-19-508905-7
1. Cognitive science.   2. Creative thinking.   3. Consciousness.
4. Cognition—Social aspects.   I. Title.
BF311.D568   1999
153—dc21   98-31381

9 8 7 6 5 4 3 2 1

Printed in the United States of America
on acid-free paper

For Elizabeth,
companion in the
drama of life

Preface

This book is about cognitive science, a rather recent arrival in the pantheon of scientific achievement. What is it? A preliminary definition might be the study of mental phenomena via methods of rational and empirical research. A much fuller and clearer picture will emerge in due course, but for now we may note that a number of disciplines have contributed to the development of the modern scientific picture of mind, principally psychology, linguistics, neuroscience, philosophy, and, the latest but by no means the least, computer science in the form of robotics and artificial intelligence.

My original intention was to present a history of how cognitive science's roots were established as these contributory disciplines grew, and then to survey the contemporary scene and discuss current strengths and weaknesses in that light. But the project got out of hand and produced a manuscript of nearly twice the desirable length. What was originally one manuscript became two. This book, the second part of the original manuscript, carries the burden of my main message: a plea for the widening of the field of cognitive science to include some well-documented features of mental life that have suffered neglect over the past many decades but that are nevertheless valid topics of inquiry. I characterize these as the *drama* of the mind. They include such things as original creativity in mathematics, musical composition, and language; altered and changing states of consciousness; the history of cultural metamorphosis; and the development of novel ways of understanding the world, an understanding that is, after all, first and foremost a cognitive achievement. This last has been an abiding feature of mankind's journey over several millennia.

Widening the field of investigation necessitates a broadening and sharpening of the explanatory strategies we employ, and I shall have much to say about that. Asking what the next steps on this path might be is in some respects speculative but still a legitimate avenue of inquiry. Indeed, taking those steps provides a measure of the caliber of the times and is an important manifestation of the vitality of an intellectually motivated civilization. One of the greatest shocks to our cultural life imaginable would be the sudden cessation of new proposals about how to understand the world and our place in it, the taking of new *metaphysical stances,* as I shall call them. A principal theme of this book is that cognitive science, as presently practiced, is much in need of such renewal.

What do cognitive scientists themselves see as the future of their discipline? Many undoubtedly would opt for the further development of mechanistic analogies to mental, or at least cognitive, activities. Others will see the changing future of the modern mind as a function of its growing dependence on interaction with computers and other forms of "information" technology. Yet another powerful perspective views the mind as a simple outgrowth or emergent property of largish brains, so that cognitive science is claimed as mainly the province of neuroscience. Some brilliant and persuasive authors have argued for variations on these themes, and their views will be discussed. The writing of a book like the present one takes more than a year or two (at least it took me that long!), so one is continually being overtaken by new writing of others on cognate topics. Rather than try to capture the very latest flavor of this work, I have described the basic positions of many of the leading authors in their standard, or canonical, form. Hence, the ideas expressed in the latest writings of, for instance, Dawkins, Dennett, Hofstaedter, Searle, and Pinker, to mention some very prominent examples, are not directly addressed. Ingenious as these presentations are, they propose little that is fundamentally different—of new metaphysical substance, one might say—from views expressed earlier, so not too much is lost by passing over them lightly.

Some years ago C. P. Snow, a scientist as well as a prominent novelist (and powerful bureaucrat), wrote *The Two Cultures,* a book that achieved considerable notoriety. The burden of his message was that the hard-nosed world of science and engineering, exploiter of the natural world, is at odds with and perhaps basically incompatible with the domain of literary, humane creation and inquiry, as well as with the social and personal perspectives that flow from it. Perhaps, as he feared, the two cultures have grown too far apart to find common ground, although he was an advocate of seeking it. Moreover, with a foot in each camp, he was well qualified to adjudicate and seek reconciliation between them. Cognitive science, too, straddles the two cultures, because it seeks to study and explain mental life from a scientific perspective, yet its subject matter is obviously—to a great extent at least—in the domain that the humanities take to be their very own.

Here is the major question for cognitive science, and one with which we will eventually deal. Can mental life be exhaustively studied as a purely natural phenomenon, or must we go beyond the mundane, the merely physical, to grasp its reality? In other words, is cognitive science just a *natural* science, or is it, to use an older terminology, also a *moral* science? The weight of contemporary opinion accepts the former, but I shall argue strongly for the latter, more accurately, that we cannot dispense with either, that we need them both. It may be of importance for the cognitive scientist to be able (eventually) to give an account of the goings-on in the brain of Northrop Frye, the author of *Anatomy of Criticism,* for instance, but it would be a hard-bitten materialist indeed who would claim that those events are all there is of scientific interest to the creation of such a literary tour de force.

Cognitive science is now mainly concerned with the "grammar" of mental life. Important as this is, we should not let it blind us to the drama. Yet we cannot take the full measure of the drama without first apprising ourselves of the basic grammar. That is why I set out to give an account of the historical roots of cognitive science before embarking on discussion of the drama of mind. Much of that historical material, which has largely to do with the grammar of mind, had to be severely curtailed to produce a book of manageable length. Yet I feel the need to give a fuller account of that material. Some readers will find the historical cameos of the first three chapters all too sketchy, and some of my judgments of the movements that defined early (and even some contemporary) cognitive science not well supported by the evidence quoted. A much fuller account of these matters will appear in a second book based on the first half of the original manuscript. I refer to it in various places in the footnotes and trust that readers dissatisfied with the cursory treatment meted out in the early chapters of this book can find satisfaction of their interests (or grievances) there.

The gestation period for this book has not been short; in certain respects it goes back to the beginning of my academic career, over 40 years ago. During that time I have of course learned enormously from teachers, friends, colleagues, and others engaged in the great enterprise of studying the mind. It would perhaps be invidious to single out a particular few, and the depth and variety of my debt will be obvious as the reader progresses through the book. Great figures from the recent past who have influenced me strongly include William James, Bertrand Russell, Ludwig Wittgenstein, Karl Popper, Jean Piaget, Wolfgang Köhler, Donald Hebb, and James Gibson. I had the privilege of being educated at a Waldorf School, so the worldview of Rudolf Steiner, the originator of the Waldorf movement, also certainly played a role in my development.

I want to thank fellow inquirers and friends who read and commented on the original manuscript: Terry Caelli, Gus Craik, Merlin Donald, David Foster, Will Hoffman, Keith Humphrey, and David Murray. Selected chapters were also reviewed by Jim Cutting, Randy Harris, Hans and Pam Liebeck, and Roger Penrose. All of them made helpful comments and saved me from some faux pas, although of course I take full responsibility for the deficiencies that remain, particularly where I failed to heed their counsel! It is a real sadness to me that John Macnamara died at a tragically young age before I was able to show him my manuscript and get the benefit of his advice; our views on the nature of mind were remarkably close.

Thanks are also due to my editors at Oxford University Press: Joan Bossert (now elevated to higher responsibilities) for her initial enthusiasm for the project, and Philip Laughlin for efficiently seeing it through to completion.

Finally, I thank my dear wife Elizabeth for her constant patience, devotion, and encouragement. She has expanded my vision of what's important in life, as well as in the study of the mind. Without her enthusiastic support the book might well have faltered; to her I dedicate it with love.

Victoria, British Columbia,   P. C. D.
September 1999

Contents

Brave New Mind

1

The Scope of Cognitive Science

Man must cling to his faith that the incomprehensible is comprehensible, else he would cease to investigate.

JOHANN WOLFGANG VON GOETHE

Picturing the nature of self and mind has always been at the forefront of human inquiry, the earliest myths and legends gradually yielding to rational thought and eventually to scientific investigation. In its most recent version this enterprise is now called *cognitive science.*

Inquiries into the human condition have always been polarized into two camps. On the one hand are the passionate advocates of humanity's special status at the pinnacle of creation, seeing man as a being of freedom and unbounded creative potential—the idealistic view. This camp might borrow Hamlet's famous words, without irony, and pronounce:

What a piece of work is a man! How noble in reason, how infinite in faculty, in form and moving how express and admirable, in action how like an angel, in apprehension how like a god—the beauty of the world, the paragon of animals!

On the other hand are the more cautious, prosaic, and empirical thinkers, who view us as natural products of biological evolution, determined solely by heredity and environment, as free and independent spirits only in an illusory sense. This is a more cynical but, as many would have it, a more realistic picture. It is parodied elegantly in a ditty attributed to an admirer of Edward Lear:

There was a young man who said: Damn!
I find I undoubtedly am
A being that moves
In predestinate grooves,
In fact not a bus
but a tram!

The idealistic view was first expressed in fully intellectual terms in the Socratic dialogues. It is still one of the pillars of contemporary literary culture, with its heavy emphasis on the "daemonic," the "inspired" element of human creativity. The second view can be traced to Aristotle and his followers, a less flamboyant, more down-to-earth but no less potent way of accounting for humankind as a purely natural species. This perspective, which includes the claim that biology (including physiology) will yield the ultimate answers, has captured the allegiance of most contemporary scientists, who have elevated it to the status of official doctrine.

The modern study of brain and mind—cognitive science—is also based for the most part on unswerving loyalty to the second view. Cognitive science has proposed novel and incisive answers to many fundamental and long-standing questions about human mentation,[1] about why we are the way we are; yet in some cardinal respects it fails to give a satisfactory account of mind. One failure concerns how scientific thinking and methodology have been applied (or as some would argue, not applied) to just those elements that make us fully human and unique in nature's dominion, the elements that are most highly prized in the idealistic tradition. These elements include the creativity so abundantly found in music, language, and mathematics, for example—a matter I shall look into later—which opens up compelling new perspectives on the understanding of mind, in all its richness and variety. I will describe how the failure came about and evaluate the current situation, before proposing remedies that do not abandon the ideals of rigor and precision that are the hallmarks of good cognitive science.

What we know of ourselves, and of the world we live in, is deeply conditioned by our intellectual and social milieu. For contemporary educated mankind a predominant factor is the scientific outlook, the fairest fruit of what Jacob Bronowski[2] called the "Western intellectual tradition." The first great pinnacle in the scientific understanding of mind occurred, as I have already suggested, with the appearance of Aristotle's teachings in the fourth century B.C. They guided, and even largely controlled, the cognitions of humanity, including those it had about itself, for two millennia. Another great change came about with the beginnings of modern physics and astronomy some 500 years ago, culminating in "Newton's Century." Bertrand Russell remarked that in A.D. 1600 the educated European had an essentially medieval world view, epitomized for the English-speaking world in the dramas of Shakespeare. By 1700 the outlook was in most respects modern and centered on understanding the world in terms of natural law, an enormous step forward.[3] This overstates the case more than a little, because the accepted view humankind had of *itself* did not begin to change drastically until the middle of the nineteenth century, when Darwin came on the scene.

By the end of the nineteenth century, however, scientific knowledge really had profoundly affected mankind's understanding of itself,[4] but still at a fairly general level. Cognitive scientists today believe that yet another great turning point is upon us as the intellectual tools of modern research, and the technology it has spawned, are brought to bear in detail on the human brain and mind. This has been called the latest and most exciting, if not necessarily the very last, frontier of scientific exploration. Enormous advances in knowledge have certainly been made, but the technical and theoretical agents that brought them about have also in many ways restricted how we think about the frontier. I shall give a brief historical account of the field, to see what lessons can be learned there. I shall show, too, some of the conceptual limitations that have come to dominate the field. As we go about our main business, which is to gain an appreciation of the nature of contemporary cognitive science and the account it gives of mental life, I shall argue strongly that the current vogue for a reductionistic, materialistic concept of mind will never lead us to a proper understanding of the richness, variety, and creativity of human cognition that are so clearly apparent, even to the casual observer.

The triumphs of natural science have been so great as to make the desire to study ourselves from that same vantage point, and with the same methods, almost overwhelming. What has worked so well in the world of nature surely can be applied with equal success to ourselves, and specifically to mind. We are after all creatures of the natural world and as such are subject to its laws. Even so, the project of studying mental phenomena empirically, *experimentally,* and from a modern scientific viewpoint, is of comparatively recent origin.

Experimental psychology was the discipline that first attempted this. It is not much more than a hundred years old, a relative newcomer in science. Since about the middle of the twentieth century it has been joined in the scientific study of mind by researchers in other disciplines, notably linguistics, computer science (artifical intelligence and robotics), neuroscience, and certain branches of philosophy. Collectively the researchers engaged in this enterprise call themselves *cognitive scientists,* and the reasearch they undertake *cognitive science.* This is a joint venture, often undertaken cooperatively, to understand and explain mental life; although experimental psychology was the first in the field, many would argue that it should no longer be thought of as the core—and certainly not the only—discipline committed to the enterprise. That is a point we shall only be in a position to evaluate in a later chapter.

Science's Picture of Human Nature

Let us consider more closely the history of science's contribution to the understanding of mind. Implicit in the new "natural philosophy" of the fifteenth century was the idea that truth is to be read only in the book of nature and attained by the power of human reasoning, rather than to be found in the writings of Aristotle, Galen, and the Church Fathers, so far as the earth, its physical laws, and the "Great globe itself" are concerned. Galileo's quarrel with the Church had everything to do with whose authority was to hold: that of the ecclesiastical establishment or that of the evidence of the senses as interpreted by the free intellect and proclaimed by the new discoveries of natural science. It had little to do with the question of man's origin in the divine world, which was not under dispute. Even in Newton's day the permeation of civilization by new ideals of scientific knowledge that would redefine the image of man—the appearance of a new orthodoxy concerning his natural origins as opposed to the theological doctrine of his supernatural creation—lay somewhere in the future.

Descartes (1596–1650) was the first scientist of the top rank to qualify as a leading philosopher since Aristotle, and he played a pivotal role in this drama. For Descartes the mathematician and scientist, the position was clear: The world is a machine. As philosopher, however, he had to wrestle with problems of a different order, especially with theological doctrine concerning the human soul. Moreover, his celebrated *cogito, ergo sum* could not easily be reconciled with a purely mechanical view of the world. This led him to postulate a profound division between mind and body, between cognition and matter, between the psychical and the physical, a division that still dominates a great part of our theoretical discussion of mind. Cartesian dualism, as it is called, is with us still.[5]

It is wrong to think of Descartes as the sole originator of the concept of dualism; it thoroughly pervades the scholastic debates of the Middle Ages, for example (to say nothing of the Socratic dialogues), but he is certainly the first great proponent in the modern era of the concept of strong dualism, the thesis that there are only two different substances or essences in the world, the "stuff" of matter (*res extensa*) and the "stuff" of mind (*res cogitans*). By means of this postulate he was able to evade, or at least postpone, the application of the new scientific methods of inquiry to the human being, and specifically to mind.

The personal philosophy of scientists—with the notable exception of Descartes—was scarcely decisive in the evolution of ideas about nature and humankind's place in it. Scientific *discovery* was what mattered. So it was with Galileo, Kepler, and Newton; so it was in supreme measure with Darwin and his theory of evolution. More than any other new scientific conception about the essence of the world we inhabit physically, biologically, and culturally, the Darwinian theory of evolution by natural selection of the fittest affected the civilized world's image of itself. *The Origin of Species* was published in 1859. For the very first time here was a scientific theory, well grounded in extensive and meticulous observation, that offered a self-contained and ostensibly complete account of the appearance of the human race on earth, without recourse to any "special effects" in the way of divine intervention, singular acts of creation, and the like. It was the ultimate victory of materialism, one might say. Newton's magnum opus, "Philosophiae Naturalis Principia Mathematica," was addressed exclusively to the world of physics and astronomy. Human life and mentality were, as Descartes had insisted, still the concern of the deity and its earthly representatives, not directly affected, much less challenged, by the new discoveries. Darwin changed all that, because the bastion of theological dogma was again breached, not just in terms of the physical world, as in Galileo's time, but now for everything in the biological world, too.

Cognitive scientists have gone the further step to argue that everything of a psychic nature, such as consciousness and the mental activities that accompany it, whether in us humans alone, or in all the animal kingdom, is to be studied and understood under Darwin's rubric. In this sense Descartes' doctrine is put aside: There is no dualism; only matter, not mind, matters. Yet there is a paradox: Materialism has something of a stranglehold on us, and the form of materialism to which cognitive scientists subscribe is one that has changed very little *since* the nineteenth century. This, despite the fantastic advances that have been made by science in its understanding of the physical world in the mean time, and despite the many pronouncements from a variety of leading scientists that might lead us to question our adherence to the old doctrines of materialism.[6] In later chapters we shall find good reason to question the necessity, and a fortiori the completeness or validity, of this materialistic worldview.

Science and Metaphysics

Natural science has over the past few centuries forced us to make profound changes in our metaphysics. What does that mean? Baldly stated, metaphysics is the attempt to discover *from first principles* the nature of *reality.* Philosophers, especially in the English-speaking world, tend to evade metaphysics, or at least treat the topic with extreme caution. The fact cannot be denied, however, that most thinking people, scientists included, experience a strong need to entertain thoughts about the grand scheme of things, about metaphysical questions; they are, in a rather strong sense, what we live by. Natural science has made us change our claims about what there is in the world (also called our *ontology*) as well as to review our ways of justifying what we claim to know about that world (called *epistemology*), a world that includes ourselves as one of its not unimportant ingredients. Science has thus made metaphysicians of us all!

Does that remark apply to cognitive science, too? It certainly does. We shall see later how modern scientific knowledge, in neuroscience and "artifical intelligence" (AI) in particular, have greatly influenced, if not overwhelmed in many cases, philosophical debate about the mind. Here, too, it is what the scientists do and discover that has been decisive, rather than what they discuss in an abstract way about the nature of the mind. Cognitive philosophy (that branch of philosophy that aligns itself with cognitive science) is a separate discipline, but its practitioners pay very close attention to what is going on in other fields of cognitive science.[7] Probably nowhere else is the philosophical scrutiny so detailed and close, or the belief of philosophers that they have cogent contributions to make to science stronger. Yet philosophers of cognition have an approach to unraveling the mysteries of mental life very different from that of their more empirically driven colleagues. Newton's science caused profound interest and a new ferment of activity among professional philosophers, as did Darwin's two centuries later. Is that happening again today? If so, what are the recent scientific findings and ideas about cognition that are motivating the new activity in philosophy?

The driving force in cognitive science, including the scrutiny it receives from cognitive philosophers, now is not so much the emergence of new *scientific ideas,* leading to the discovery of new scientific laws and principles, as in earlier times, as it is the introduction of *technological innovations* that allow for the posing of previously unaskable questions. The distinction between science and technology is very difficult to draw and is seldom clear cut, but the distinction does make a difference. Whereas in the earlier revolutions of the seventeenth and nineteenth centuries science eventually made a huge difference to the images of nature and of humanity that became dominant in the civilized world, today's technological novelties rather reinforce and radicalize already well-established doctrines. These include the ontologically exhaustive conception of a purely material world, and an entirely "natural" evolution of humanity within it. As I said, philosophical systems, broad and ingenious though they may be, generally do not *lead,* they *follow* what science postulates. A very influential stream of scientific thought promulgates the metaphysics of materialism; that is where philosophers have in the past tended to place their bets, and mostly do so still.

Philosophers have tended to eschew the field of metaphysics, and under the influence of positivism—the claim that only physically observable and measurable quantities are real and worthy of scientific attention—even went so far at one time as to declare all metaphysics to be nonsense.[8] This followed from the principle of verification, first promulgated by the philosophers of the Vienna Circle, which claimed that all meaningful statements are either factual/*synthetic* truths, to be verified by empirical observation, or else *analytic,* logical, or linguistic truths that are true "by convention," that is, because of the ways we have decided to use words and other symbols. The verification of analytic truths consists in establishing that the way they are being used does indeed follow the prescribed rules; such truths, however, have no empirical content. In this view all other statements—including metaphysical ones that may have the appearance of being factual—are unverifiable, and hence, literally, nonsense.[9]

Unfortunately for philosophers of this persuasion, the principle of verification turned out to be a self-defeating ordinance. Why so? The principle is certainly not factual; it states no verifiable fact about the world. Nor is it a logical certainty; to deny it is not self-contradictory. The uncomfortable truth for one of this persuasion is that the principle is just what it says it is: a *principle!* In that sense it is itself metaphysical, because it proclaims a fundamental method for the accumulation of empirical knowledge (an unexceptionable one at that); indeed, it propounds the metaphysics of modern natural science. Yet according to the strict verificationist, it must be counted as nonsensical. The obvious, and commonsense, solution to this dilemma is to realize that we cannot do without metaphysics. We need principles of procedure to guide our progress in life, in the scientific enterprise no less than in the pursuit of personal, social, political, and ethical goals. To that extent, verificationism was certainly far too narrow a view of what can meaningfully be said. Nevertheless, the debate over verificationism has left its mark, and philosophers still tend to be uncomfortable in the metaphysical arena. Insofar as they do embrace, or at least acknowledge, a metaphysical stance, philosophers of mind (and other philosophers, too), accept the position of natural science and therefore are in the main materialists, as I said. Having otherwise largely renounced the field of metaphysics of their own volition, philosophers are in a weak position when it comes to making pronouncements on the big questions. But they are in no position to deny that luxury to others, and the need to find answers to the big questions is evidently at the base of our culture, indeed at the very heart of the human condition itself. Notice too that there is no principle of science or logic (or of metaphysics for that matter) that can prove the metaphysics of materialism to be the only game in town.

Does the flight from metaphysics mean that philosophers have given up the attempt to tell us what we should think of the mind, of where human understnding of human life is headed? Far from it. Cognitive philosophers are only too ready to tell us to pay attention to their views on such topics. As suggested above, they have a widely accepted, although seldom explicitly expounded, metaphysical position, namely the metaphysics of materialism, plain and simple. Although there is nothing novel about this, the power of the position gains immeasurably from the success of modern neuroscience in unraveling many of the mysteries of the brain and linking them in important respects to psychological function.

Who is to say the philosophers are wrong? My purpose right now is not to argue whether they are correct but to make clear that theirs *is* a metaphysical claim. It feeds on the success of science rather than leading scientific inquiry in a novel and principled way. It plays a very central role in how we discuss and, in particular, how we try to limit discussion on matters pertaining to the understanding of mind. As a metaphysical claim, however, it has scarcely been open to the same sorts of skeptical debate and empirical challenge that a scientific theory faces.

The natural world has yielded its secrets increasingly to successful theoretical and experimental investigation based on mechanical and materialistic premises.[10] Although the "clockwork" view has only been applied radically and systematically in psychology in this century, its philosophical antecedents go back a very long way. It only became a dominant theme among Western philosophers following Hobbes (who was mightily impressed by Galileo's discoveries and theories), and with the later strong boost given by Darwin's science.[11] It culminated in this century in positions such as Armstrong's,[12] in which the mind is conceived of as a straightforward function of brain processes. Most cognitive philosophers now embrace this view in one form or another, as we have already discussed. The vast majority of other workers in cognitive science are of the same persuasion, even if they seldom pause to think critically about the matter; it is a deeply rooted conviction, almost an axiom of their faith. This is really not too surprising, given the many outstanding successes of neuroscience and neuropsychology, which will be discussed in the following chapter.

Cognitive science is really behind the times, however, in two respects. First, in subscribing to a view of the material basis of the world (or what we mean by *matter*) that was abandoned by physics no later than the 1920s, and second, by refusing to face the question of how fully a physics-only conception of the cosmos can deal with the facts of mental phenomena, including consciousness. It is quite remarkable to realize that well over half a century go, many of the leaders of the scientific community were questioning in one way or another the adequacy of natural science's view of science itself, including its understanding of mankind. Exploring the question of whether that view is necessarily all there is to understanding the world, whether it captures all the essentials, is certainly a metaphysical enterprise, but not, as we have just seen, therefore to be scorned as idle speculation. Some of the most urgent and provocative statements of this sort were made in the 1930s, when the triumphs and prestige of natural science were at their zenith. The clockwork view of the universe was still firmly in place, although no longer universal and unquestioned in physics and astronomy, and the technological terrors and abuses of science with which we live today had scarcely been imagined.[13]

The general tone of those pronouncements was to strike at natural science's epistemological foundations, to question the necessity of metaphysical materialism. But more was involved. A major attempt to position science within the general stream of modern culture was Whitehead's *Science and the Modern World*,[14] an essay that by no means subscribes to a simple conception of mind as an easily comprehended natural phenomenon. For him there is an ever present danger of missing the essentials of human culture, as well as many of the greatest secrets of nature, in the development of an austerely materialistic-mechanical-clockwork view of the world. He was not alone. Some of the world's most eminent scientists, including many of the leading theoretical physicists such as Heisenberg, Schroedinger, Eddington, and Jeans, questioned in one way or another the adequacy of science's view as a comprehensive perspective on the universe and, specifically, its understanding of humanity's place in the natural order.

Heisenberg put it this way in 1949 at the bicentennial celebration of Goethe's birth: "Almost every scientific advance is bought at the cost of renunciation, almost every gain in knowledge sacrifices important standpoints and established modes of thought. As facts and knowledge accumulate, the claim of the scientist to an *understanding* of the world in a certain sense diminishes." We should not forget, he continues, that the attainments of science are bought at a cost, the cost of "renouncing the aim of bringing the phenomena of nature to our thinking in an immediate and living way." This aim was of course at the heart of Goethe's own beliefs about what the goals and methods of science should be. A bit further on, Heisenberg gives us this extraordinary statement: "If one should wish to reproach Goethe, it could only be for not going far enough . . . [by] declaring the whole of Newtonian physics—Optics, Mechanics, and the Law of Gravitation—were from the devil."[15] Without doubt only a physicist of the very first rank could vent an opinion like that! What did he mean by it? Surely not that Newton had any evil intention; rather that, although Newton had set science on an immensely fruitful path, this should not be allowed to swamp our sensibilities to other perspectives on the world. Natural science is in danger of losing, or at least neglecting, vibrant, vital, essential aspects of life. There is absolutely nothing inherent in the scientific worldview, Heisenberg maintains, to justify that neglect. Once in a while it behooves us to stand back, to pause and ask whether the neglect is leading us astray.[16] In recent times similar considerations have been raised by other eminent theoretical physicists, including Stephen Hawking and (of especial interest to our inquiry, as we shall see later) Roger Penrose.

Science has thus not failed entirely to face those ultimate, metaphysical, questions, and among philosophers too there has been concern about how they can be posed in a meaningful way within the orbit of science.[17] Among such questions, those concerned with the nature of mind must surely hold a prominent place. The belief is sometimes expressed that new developments within natural science itself will eventually give us the answers. In one celebrated essay along these lines, for example, Penrose has proposed that the key to understanding consciousness lies in the discovery of a new quantum theory of gravitation.[18]

Science and the Mind

In earlier times it was science itself, rather than the metaphysical musings of its practitioners, that made inroads into the generally accepted world view, as we saw. That has changed in an important respect, because many of the findings of modern natural science, and more especially the mathematical theories in contemporary physics and cosmology, are no longer accessible to the very great majority of the educated laity, not even to those with expertise and understanding in other branches of science. The findings sound bizarre and the theories in particular are too recondite, too technical, for others to comprehend fully. To a very great extent therefore we are now dependent on the packaging of those findings and theories by the experts in forms that are accessible to the nonspecialist. Moreover we are for this reason almost entirely dependent on those same experts for *interpretation* of modern physical theories, and especially those in cosmology, in terms that address our need for answers to the big questions.[19] So, in contrast to earlier times, it is now not the science itself so much as the views and beliefs of a rather small group of specialists with particular skills and interests that have the potential to influence the general consciousness of what the mind is all about. Of course *they* are deeply influenced by their science, both as to their own ideas and in the ways they attempt to convey them to others. Many of them, with Hawking and Paul Davies close to the forefront, have attempted to explore the territory beyond the precincts of simple materialism, thereby following in the steps of a noble tradition described earlier. But it is debatable whether the recipients of their ideas (the rest of us) are in general capable of interpreting what they have to offer from any but the materialist stance to which modern culture has inured us.

With very few exceptions, the newer natural science itself—starting, say, at the turn of the twentieth century—has had no discernible effect on the ways our cultural leaders (apart from those experts) pose and answer the big questions; in particular, its influence on cognitive science has been minimal. The fact is that the science that has filtered into the general metaphysics and culture of our times is, in its essentials, the science of the 1850s or so (perhaps we should say the 1860s, thus making sure that Darwin gets his due). To take a major example: In the early days of general relativity very few scientists, let alone laymen, thoroughly understood the theory and its implications. Despite a great literature of popularization, including Einstein's own essays, it is no doubt still true that few outside the circle of professional mathematical physicists have a deep appreciation of the theory or its significance for cosmology. It is even more evident that any possible implications the theory may have for the world of human culture outside science are largely unexplored. We can express doubts about the ability of the nineteenth century's clockwork worldview to provide an adequate concept of mind, but there are singularly few proposals about how to replace it. Whitehead, Heisenberg, Eddington, Hawking, and the rest (Penrose, as we shall see, may be an exception) do not get us very far in the matter of finding a positive alternative to the materialistic image of man, the clever, lopsided,[20] naked ape.[21] Recent moves in biology have not done much in that regard either.[22]

Can cognitive science, out of its own resources, so to speak, come to the rescue? To answer that, we need to get a much closer understanding of what cognitive science, and psychology in particular, has to say about the explanation of mental phenomena. What, if anything, is its *theory* of such explanation? How does the belief in materiality, the conception of something we call *matter* as the ultimate bedrock of all that is real, enter into the explanatory process?

Explanation in Psychology

The broad aim of cognitive science is to explain the workings of the mind. What would constitute such an explanation? How is it different from the commonsense explanations that are the meat of gossip, school reports, assessments of character, justification of promises made, excuses for failure, and the like? How can it improve on the insights of the great essayists, novelists and playwrights? What of Montaigne, of Shakespeare? What of Steinbeck, Camus, or Brecht? We claim that our psychological explanations are scientific, but what does that mean? Clearly there has to be something different, something that goes beyond what common sense—or the insightful playwright or novelist—has to offer if it is to be claimed that a scientifically valid psychological explanation is worth having. Yet it is not easy to identify what that something is. Here are some questions that point us on our way:

(1) Can we *give* a useful but still general definition of psychological explanation? In our everyday lives we have an excellent grasp of what it means to explain someone's moods, ambitions, beliefs, desire to please the boss, understanding of a legal contract, and so on. There is an elaborate language, tied to a well-articulated set ot concepts concerned with needs, hopes, plans, ideals, and social responsibilites, that is the common property of every minimally educated person. This set of concepts, and the sorts of explanation that flow from them, are unproblematic to the layman; we can call them the "practical wisdom of common sense." We also know them as *folk psychology,* a term used condescendingly, not to say pejoratively, by some cognitive scientists. The conceptions of folk psychology seem to be altogether too familiar, just too simple and well understood, to be the linchpin of scientific theories of human behavior. If that is true, what do we need to replace, or perhaps to supplement, folk psychology? Should it indeed be replaced? What does the cognitive scientist want that the layman can evidently so well do without?

(2) If there is a schism between what satisfies the workaday needs of everyone else, and what the scientist sees as necessary to give adequate heft to his explanations of human behavior, can the difference be captured? Is it more apparent than real? What exactly is the relationship between the two?

(3) Even if the relationship turns out to be too elusive to capture fully, is it nevertheless possible to give an adequate meaning to the notion of scientific explanation in psychology?

(4) Many cntemporary psychological theories rely on biological—most often physiological—processes as underpinning to give them plausibility and punch. Is knowledge of the physiological basis for a psychological activity such as living, perceiving, or thinking *necessarily* involved in its explanation? It is almost universally agreed that there is a close connection between the physiology of the brain, especially, and cognitive activity, but is the connection such as to *require* that the physiological process be identified before the psychological function can be understood?

(5) It is well established that there are strong *correlations* between certain sorts of activity in the brain and psychological events related to them: Sometimes if you know that a given activity occurs in the brain, you can predict with confidence that the psychological event will occur (the subject under investigation will report anxiety, or seeing the color red, for example). Does this

mean that the brain activity explains the reported sensation? Some psychologists, and virtually all neuroscientists, believe the answer is yes. But it is an open question whether the prediction of one thing from another justifies the claim that this is an explanation of the one thing by the other. In general we can ask: What is the relationship between prediction and explanation? Are they essentially different, or merely expressions of differing degrees of uncertainty about the relationship between two (or more) occurrences in the world?

(6) What has the newest member of the club, the field of artificial intelligence (AI), to offer? The amazing feats of computation, the mimicking of human cognitions, simulation of the world in "virtual reality," and so on, are common knowledge. You can read about them every day in the newspaper. Researchers in AI claim that their computers can outperform humans in many ways, which is obviously true. What of the further claims, however, for instance that in its most advanced versions AI is a form of *real* intelligence, that by studying it we can learn important things about human cognition? Or, an even more radical view, that it is in essence a form of mentation exactly like our own? There are many advocates of such a position,[23] but to be sure plenty of skeptics too.[24]

(7) Cognitive science is highly specialized, and its practitioners use a multitude of different research techniques. Despite this diversity, there is a unity of purpose, a focusing of effort to understand the mind in a particular way. It seeks explanations that are consonant with the rest of science and in particular (for by far the majority of its practitioners) with the natural sciences of physics, chemistry, and biology. But there are also thinkers who believe such an enterprise is incomplete, if not basically flawed. They would claim that literary and artistic insight into human nature and the achievements of mankind do not seem, at first blush, to owe anything at all to natural science. Nor is it apparent how knowledge of natural science's view of the world will intensify or enlarge our appreciation of literature, art, music, or any other cultural activity. The opposition in goals and outlook between the "two cultures" is now an oft-told tale,[25] nevertheless they both seem to be, or would claim to be, addressing the same question: How do we understand the mind? There must be at least a border territory between the culture of humanistic insight and scientific explanation that is worth exploring.

My point of view on these questions owes much to the thought and empirical investigations of others; yet some of the important elements have not (so far as I am aware) been put forward before. In the course of my 40 years of research there was plenty of opportunity to observe how one discipline can be greatly enriched by contributions from others.[26] At the same time questions and lack of clarity about the nature and role of theory in contemporary psychology (especially in cognitive psychology) have obtruded themselves with ever greater insistence. With the advent of cognitive science in recent decades, unease over such questions has been expressed ever more strongly, especially among cognitive philosophers. Much of the discussion of psychological explanation has been conducted with passion and acumen, if not always with perfect insight. Some questions have received undue amounts of attention, whereas others of equal if not greater importance have been ignored or misrepresented. The situation cries out for redress.

Prediction and Explanation

Neuroscientists, AI and linguistic researchers, philosophers, and psychologists all have their own, different, standards of inquiry and theoretical tools. Despite such diversity they share the belief in a corpus of phenomena to be studied that is *regular* and *lawful;* that it is possible to discern the regularities and exploit them to discover the laws. That is the way science works, and belief in the lawfulness of mental life, at least in most of its manifestations, appears to be well justified. The salient characteristic of regularity is that it permits the prediction of one event from another. All cognitive scientists are good at describing such regularities and making predictions about mental consequents. To some degree the regularities they work with are the same in each discipline; certainly there is much borrowing of data from one field to another. No surprise there, as they are working at the same topic from different viewpoints.

When it comes to *explaining* the phenomena, however, the matter is quite otherwise. Explanation involves *theory* (a matter we shall have occasion to discuss in great detail) and there the opportunities for disagreement are almost without limit. I have often been amused to see the self-same information in the form of perceptual demonstrations, figures, or dataplots used to support diametrically opposed, and often mutually contradictory, theoretical arguments in perceptual psychology, for example. One should not press the matter too far; in broad terms there is agreement among cognitive scientists about what needs to be explained, even on the type of explanation to be sought. That does not mean, incidentally, that the consensus is correct in all its assumptions! Disagreements about particular theories are of course commonplace, indeed are frequently and properly the engines of new research and discovery; as such they go well beyond the mere description and analysis of data. Constructing explanations is the scientist's stock-in-trade; as the philosopher E. Nagel points out: "It is the desire for explanations which are at once systematic and controllable by factual evidence that generates science; and it is the organization and classification of knowledge on the basis of explanatory principles that is the specific goal of science."[27]

One of our primary tasks will be to characterize the commonly accepted paradigm of explanation in cognitive science and to see how it relates to—even perhaps supplants—the explanatory canons of folk psychology as well as the mere cataloging of correlations between this and that. Then we shall be in a position to tackle some of the age-old problems such as the question of mind/body dualism, materialist doctrines generally, the psychology of scientific discovery,[28] mathematical invention,[29] consciousness, and other ambitious topics, to see what the new science has to offer. Examining current ways of explaining mental phenomena will lead us to recognize how far we fall short of the goal of an adequate theory of mind. This in turn will fuel the campaign to reach a better understanding of the nature of human knowledge (the epistemological goal) and a fuller appreciation of its objects, the furniture of the world (the ontological objective). In that sense, my enterprise is fully and unashamedly metaphysical, addressed to the nature of the great universe itself and how we can know it.

Our culture has a well-developed conception of the adult human being as an agent responsible for his or her actions that is made explicit in our legal and political institutions and pervasively present in literature. It is also of the essence of folk psychology; I called it the practical wisdom of common sense. Cognitive science appears to challenge all that, to the extent that it claims a level of insight into human action and the lawfulness of behavior that is inaccessible to the laity. The grounds for this challenge will be examined in due course; to the extent that it claims to *displace* what folk psychology (and common sense) has to offer, it must be able to give us something more powerful, more precise, and just as practical as what serves to guide us in our day-to-day actions and in our evaluation of the behavior of others. Can it possibly do that?

Not only should cognitive science, to be worthy of the name, go one better than the practical wisdom of common sense, but it also must be very much more cognizant of its conceptual and practical debt to that wisdom. Could there possibly *be* a cognitive science if it were not constructed, in a very real and intimate way, on that foundation? Far from belittling folk psychology, it behooves us to examine carefully the roots from which our science grew, and grows yet. We should honor the debt to what our culture has evolved over the centuries as a way of comprehending the mind and, as a fundamental component of that understanding, the language by means of which we talk about mental phenomena. At present the debt is honored far more in the breach than in the observance.

George Wald, Nobel laureate in biology and an outstanding humanist, noted that the fundamentally important questions about science and life are those asked by intelligent young children who, getting no clear answer, stop asking. It is timely to return to some of those questions, to pose them for cognitive science, and to see how adequate the answers may turn out to be. The culture of a civilization is grounded very strongly on the image of man it embraces. The one we promote must not be too crude, too pale, too mechanical; yet the current worldview of cognitive science, if taken literally and seriously and widely applied, leads exactly in that direction. Is there an alternative that is richer, less rigid, more open to a true appreciation of the high quality and dignity of the human condition, but still able to claim the merit of scientific sobriety and sensibility? In later chapters I shall propose an answer—although without doubt not the *final* answer—to that question.

2

The Psychological Underpinnings of Cognitive Science

It is the theory which decides what we can observe.

ALBERT EINSTEIN

Five Paths, One Goal

Five main paths of inquiry, developing sometimes in isolation but often connecting in strong and useful ways, define the discipline of cognitive science: (1) the experimental psychology of cognition; (2) neuroscience, particularly its application of sophisticated new techniques to the detailed study of the anatomy and physiology of the brain and the rest of the cental nervous system; (3) those fields of computing science that study artifical intelligence (AI) and robotics in relationship to human thought and action; (4) linguistics, especially in its imaginative treatment of language competence and in its biological and developmental aspects; and (5) the philosophy of mind, insofar as it concerns the study of the ontogeny and epistemology of cognition. In this chapter I shall survey briefly the presuppositions, methods, and findings of the first of these paths. In the next chapter I shall do the same for the remaining four, and show how, despite their differences, the five paths have each come to embrace a common view of the mind. I call this the *standard model* of the mind. Their assumptions about the nature of the subject of inquiry—in fact, their metaphysics—have steered the sorts of investigation to be undertaken, and the success of those investigations has for the most part heavily reinforcd the perspective of the standard model. So, despite the diversity of their starting points, we shall find a surprising degree of concordance in what the five paths of inquiry have to say about the nature of mind.

Experimental Psychology of Cognition

Although research in experimental psychology started somewhat earlier, its formal beginnings are identified with the establishment of a research laboratory at the

University of Leipzig in 1879 by Wilhelm Wundt. In Wundt's laboratory, and in a number of other departments that sprang up in Germany soon after, the study of mental phenomena proceeded apace.[1] Keen as they were to prove the scientific bona fides of their new discipline, the early researchers concentrated on the careful description and analysis of simple phenomena of sensation, memory, judgment, and decision. The studies of memory by Herman Ebbinghaus, and of relations between sensory stimulation and reported sensation (psychophysics) by Gustav Fechner, for instance, stressed the importance of careful control and replicability of results. They worked in the laboratory with simple materials—nonsense syllables for memory, variation of simple sensory qualities like auditory pitch or visual brightness in psychophysics—and constrained their subjects to make only plain responses that could be recorded accurately. This started a commendable tradition of methodological purity and caution that still informs virtually the whole of experimental psychology to this day.[2] These methods were in tune with the prevailing view of mental life, which owed much to the *constructivist* theories of philosophers like John Locke, David Hume, and J. S. Mill. Mentation was held to be elaborated by the "association of ideas," the ideas themselves being the basic units, the "atoms" one might almost say, out of which more complex mental phenomena are built. The first of these atoms to be explored would, of course, be the elementary units of sensation and memory.

The successful study of lawful aspects of such units led to more ambitious efforts in the study of thought and imagery. Elementary units of mental life, "ideas," were still at the basis of all mentation, but the possibility of finding and analyzing them in an "internal" field of observation was accepted. The methods of detection and report already successfully applied to sensations were held to be the right way to proceed here, too. *Introspectionism* was thus born, the idea that one can inspect and report on mental goings-on in much the same way as for the effects of external stimulation. It was the high point of the attempt to treat what has been called the "Cartesian theater,"[3] the inner arena, as if it were just another place for making scientific observations, albeit in a peculiarly private and inaccessible sort of laboratory. This line of work was also centered in Germany, and its most influential practitioners formed what was known as the Würzburg school.[4] Things did not work out too well, as sharp and irreconcilable differences concerning what could be observed and reported from the Cartesian theater soon surfaced. This led to a radical reassessment of the scope and proper field of investigation for scientific psychology that resulted in *behaviorism,* a topic we shall revisit shortly. So introspectionism can be counted as an early, and perhaps the very first, casualty in the campaign for hard-nosed scientific rigor in cognitive psychology.

In the meantime the new science had spread abroad, particularly to the Anglo-American world. Students from Britain and the United States, having flocked to the feet of the masters, carried the new ideas far and wide. A strong tradition of experimental psychology was started at the universities of London and Cambridge in Britain, and at Clark and Harvard in the United States. William James at Harvard became the leader of an influential generation of psychologists known as functionalists. Eschewing the Hegelian "big sweep" of nineteenth-century philosophy, and with a typically American flair for the pragmatic, they inquired into the practical uses of psychology rather more than into abstract theory. Even so, to read James today is to be astounded at the range and variety of topics that engaged his giant intellect, in both psychology and philosophy.

In Britain, too, a more pragmatic approach to psychology had emerged, actually somewhat earlier, in the studies of Frances Galton on mental imagery, the varieties of human ability, and the attempt to measure them with precision.[5] Galton's own efforts at this were not particularly successful, but across the channel in France Alfred Binet[6] made great strides in mental testing and laid the foundations for what is now perhaps the most widespread and useful technology of applied psychology, the assessment of aptitudes and abilities by standardized tests. Along with this has developed an elaborate methodology and body of theory called *psychometrics*. The underlying thought here is that human abilites are somewhat fixed (there is continuing, and often acrimonious, debate about just how fixed) and can be sampled by appropriately designed instruments. There are usually in the form of quite short problems with well-defined answers, and are commonly known as *mental tests*. They are typically verbal and numerical in character but often, and increasingly, involve nonverbal items like the solving of pictorially presented puzzles, even for the assessment of cognitive functions like intelligence.[7] The psychometrician would argue that you can't get a handle on mental phenomena unless you can measure them accurately, and that is justification for mentioning the field of mental testing. This type of psychological work has, however, played but a minor role in the development of cognitive science.

Another slant was also given to cognitive psychology by the experimental and theoretical research of F. C. Bartlett at Cambridge. His seminal work on memory in action, as we may call it, that stressed the importance of social and motivational factors in cognition, set a standard that is still emulated. Bartlett, like James before him, was not afraid to leave the laboratory and study human thought and action in its normal context but without forgoing the scientific rigor taught by the German pioneers. The result was a robust attempt to grapple with the real world, apply psychological understanding to the solution of practical human problems, and demonstrate that the new science had some clout on the street as well as in the ivory tower. One immediate application was to personnel selection and training and later to the design and use of military equipment in World War II.[8]

Behaviorism

A different and very radical development had occurred meanwhile in the United States. The ideal of an ever more strictly scientific psychology was widely debated early in the twentieth century, largely as a response to the failures of introspectionism and without doubt under the strongly positivistic influence spreading from the Vienna Circle (see chapter 1). It gave rise to the doctrine that only what is publicly and openly observable can be the subject matter of psychology. J. B. Watson argued this most forcefully and successfully, so that for many years the behaviorism he championed became the leading theoretical stance of American psychologists.[9] There were of course some dissenters, but behaviorism was certainly the order of the day in the 1920s, 1930s, and 1940s.

Behaviorism in its strict form asserts that factual statements can be made only about physically observable entities, such as body movements and the recording of physiological states by appropriate instruments. Nothing else can be observed directly, therefore nothing meaningful can be said about it (verificationism at work), so it can certainly play no part in science. Watson also accepted the position of Thorndike[10] that the essence of psychology is to provide an explanation of the phenomena of learning, and made brilliant use of the then-recent discovery of conditioned reflexes by the Russian physiologist I. P. Pavlov. It will be recalled that Pavlov was able to produce a form of anticipatory learning in dogs by repeatedly pairing a neural stimulus (a bell, the conditioned stimulus) with a motivational signal (food, the unconditioned stimulus) to provoke a new but appropriate response (salivation, the conditioned response) when the bell was presented alone. Here was a publicly observable, reliable, and easily executed paradigm for producing behavioral change—a form of learning.

Watson claimed that the conditioned reflex is the *only* form of learning. So he thought he had in his grasp all that was needed to implement the full program of behaviorism, namely, to explain the behavior of organisms in terms of learning, by fully observable and quantifiable processes that function with imperturbable efficiency through all the vicissitudes and in very possible situation in life.

The program was carried to what we would now consider extreme lengths by Watson's followers, in particular by C. L. Hull,[11] who dreamed of creating a comprehensive theory of psychology, or at the very least a general theory of learning, based entirely on behavioristic principles. Hull's main idea was that learning occurs as the result of "drive reduction," "drives" being for him, in the main, simple biological appetites, as in the Pavlovian paradigm. They could be defined ("operationalized" was the standard jargon) in terms of observables, usually the number of hours of deprivation to which the animal had been subjected. Hull aimed to follow the "hypothetico-deductive method"; hypothetical entities were allowed but only insofar as they led immediately to the deduction of testable (publicly observable) events in behavior. The goal of the theory was to generate meaningful behavior of organisms from "colorless movements," to use Hull's own phrase. He produced an amazingly complex system of equations, and deductions from them, aimed at giving a principled account of the laws of learning. The testable products of these equations were mostly in the form of predicted "learning curves," or rates of learning, usually for simple types of response such as running without error through a maze (the preferred subject in these experiments was the white rat).

An extraordinary amount of effort was put into testing supposed deductions from Hull's theory, many hundreds of papers were published, and not a few careers floated on the strength of his work. Yet that elaborate production all came to naught.[12] Looking back 50 years and more, it is sobering to realize that what was taken with all seriousness at the time as the very pinnacle of psychological science turned out to be largely an unsustainable fad and a huge waste of effort and resources. Nevertheless, at the time it defined a whole generation of Western, and especially American, psychology.

Hullian theory had its champions even in cognitive psychology. One of the ablest and best known of these was the British psychologist D. E. Berlyne.[13] He sought to interpret cognitive activity of every type within the framework of Hull's system, including esthetic judgment, children's learning, concept formation, and language. To do this he postulated a number of nonbiological drives; the best known of them was the *epistemic* drive, the drive for knowledtge, or what we would probably just call *curiosity*. He attempted to derive laws that would not just apply to laboratory experiments, but also be useful in the classroom and atelier. He was another example of the urge to take experimental psychology out of the research arena and make it more useful, more relevant. At the time (the 1950s and 1960s) Berlyne's work was highly regarded, even influential in many circles. Yet today he is scarcely remembered, even in the field of cognitive development where he made his best contributions. Where Berlyne was a leader, many others followed: All have been forgotten. *Sit transit gloria Academiae!*

What led to the collapse of Hull's elaborate house of cards? A number of things were responsible. There was revolt from within the "rat-running" tradition, led by E. C. Tolman, based on the finding that even that lowly rodent is capable of far more insightful and flexible action than the Hullian theoreticians gave it credit for; some of its behavioral repertoire turned out to be quite sophisticated. Hull's system was anchored in the belief that the general laws of learning must apply to all organisms, rather like the universal laws of physical action discovered and so successfully exploited in other fields. Most of the research on Hullian and similar systems, however, was done with rats and pigeons, mainly for reasons of tradition and economy. Hull's psychology was in many ways quite abstract, to be applied with equal potency to all biological creatures. It was found, however, that what was true of rat learning was not true for other species. Largely under the influence of the new discipline ethology, founded by Lorentz and Tinbergen,[14] psychologists began to realize that rats and pigeons are indeed biological organisms, have a natural habitat, and can only be studied fruitfully and comprehensibly in the context of their normal environment. The contemporary field of study called animal behavior, which now even includes a field identified as animal cognition, has far more affinity with biology and ethology than with physics, the science that Hull had tried to emulate.[15]

What has Hullian learning theory to do with cognitive psychology? Quite a lot. Apart from its considerable value as a cautionary tale, the contemplation of Hullian behaviorism is important for other, quite different reasons. Hull would have argued that it is appropriate to study and try to understand learning in simple organisms first, because it is necessary to understand the simple before tackling the complex (reminiscent of the strategy of investigating simple "ideas"); after all, his goal was to find a unified theory of learning, so the understanding of the complex in terms of the simple seemed a reasonable enough strategy. Yet, as Bertrand Russell remarked, even Newton could only learn to solve a maze by trial and error! That is to say, if you define your learning task in a sufficiently narrow way, you may find laws that express the rate at which simple learning occurs, but you do so at the risk of eliminating from consideration most of what should interest the cognitive scientist. Research limited in this way is called "paradigm driven"; it still constrains many varieties of psychological theory and experimentation.

So strong was the influence of the behaviorist tradition that for decades experimental psychologists, even those purporting to be cognitive psychologists, were inhibited from studying the domain that is rightfully theirs. Or if, like Berlyne, they attempted to do so within the Hullian framework, they ended up with theoretical tools and insights that bore little fruit in either the academic or the secular world.

Just as the attempt to derive universal laws of learning that could be applied without favor or distinction in all situations was unfruitful, so the attempt to treat cognizing humans as homogeneous "subjects" that were to be studied in isolation from the world of their social, educational, and cultural milieu proved to be in vain. Yet so strong was the hold of Hullian behaviorism that psychologists were loath to strike out into more fertile fields of inquiry. In particular the behaviorist crusade to rid psychology of "unobservables" like thoughts, images, beliefs, and even emotion and motivation (except insofar as the latter could be defined in terms of physiological deprivation) lay like the Ancient Mariner's albatross about the neck of the young science. What is orthodox at one time may, within a comparatively short period, come to be seen as little more than boastful posturing, but in that meantime can still exert a very deleterious and deadening influence on scientific creativity.

History's judgment of Hullian psychology (mine, too) has been harsh, but it would be wrong to conclude that nothing worthwhile issued from his work. A few technical terms retain their usefulness (reinforcement by drive reduction, habit, the distinction between learning and performance), and the cautionary attitude that prevents flights of theoretical fancy and speculation from wandering too far from the hard rock of experimental evidence remains strong. But considering the effort, time, and resources expended, the harvest was meager.

Bartlett's Approach: Memory

It was largely social psychologists and cultural anthropologists who led the way out of the desert of Hullian "dustbowl empiricism," as it has been called, and for much of psychology F. C. Bartlett was the inspiration.[16] Even as the behaviorists in America were procaliming the faith in the 1920s and 1930s, Bartlett was demonstrating, in his groundbreaking studies of memory, that they had followed far too narrow a trail, although perhaps he was not quite ready yet to proclaim that their path was a dead-end.[17]

Bartlett started with rather straightforward questions like: What happens if you ask someone to recall a simple story after a period of several days or weeks? What happens to a story if it is retold serially, passed from one listener to another? That's an old party game called "gossip" or "telephone"; the end result is often hilarious. Bartlett showed that it also can throw light on the psychological processes of acquisition and recall. Memory he showed, is essentially reconstructive: It can only be understood in its particulars if the personal and social characteristics of the recaller are known. Just as, to use a familiar example, a botanist, an engineer, and an artist will observe and describe a country walk taken together in very different terms, so, too, the recall of any but the most rigidly learned or stereotyped material will be affected by one's interests, expectations, and social conventions. Central to Bartlett's concept of memory was the idea that memories are typically laid down in schematic form, or *schemas* in his jargon, to be elaborated at recall in a more or less creative manner; in fact, they change in very systematic ways. This is a far cry from the at-

tempts to study memory in the straightjacket of the recall of lists of nonsense syllables advocated in an earlier tradition.[18]

In that tradition it had been accepted that "pure" memory was the object of
study, and to get at it one would have to remove the personal elements, the manner-
isms, the unscientific, idiosyncratically colored penumbra of memory to expose its
untainted essentials (Locke's "simple ideas" again). Just like Hull with his rats,
however, such an approach misdirected its efforts by taking an abstract ideal to be
the proper object of scientific study, rather than real people living in a social and intellectual environment that motivates and guides memory. Following the line of
work started by Bartlett, a rich field of investigation into how memory operates has
emerged that now includes many areas of practical significance.[19]

Perception

Somewhat similar developments occurred in the field of perception. The study of the
senses, particularly of seeing and hearing, was one of the pillars of the earliest experimental laboratory work in psychology, as we saw. Gustav Fechner, in particular,
pioneered methods of studying the responsivity of the senses (so-called sensory
threshold measurement) that are still in use today. Again the ideal was to measure
"pure" sensations, unencumbered by personal preference, expectation, or motive. A
long and distinguished history of sensory psychophysics could be told: It is one of
the proudest accomplishments of experimental psychology.[20] Yet even here the tendency to abstract, to theorize in a formally proper way that nevertheless fails to
grapple with the realities of perception, laid its heavy hand on the young discipline.

Traditional psychophysics reinforced the analytical approach to perception, that
is, it fostered the belief that the sense organs detect only elementary sensations
(patches of color, simple tones, fragments of contours and shapes) and are capable
of nothing more. The richness and variety of the world we experience, therefore,
would require that something be *added* to the elements provided by the senses. This
"something" had to be supplied not by the senses themselves, but by other mental
powers in the form of memory, habit, inference about what the sensory elements
imply or mean—in general, a "cognitive" component of perception that allows us to
derive meaningful events and objects from the "raw" stimulation to which we are
subjected. This view of perception attributes a great deal to nonsensory events, and
emphasizes the importance of a *constructive* component in *perceptual learning*. It is
indeed an enriched version of the philosophers' "association of ideas," albeit
couched in new language, that was strongly defended in the first 100 years of
experimental psychology. The position has since generated vigorous antagonism
from at least two directions.

In the early 1900s the German psychologist Max Wertheimer demonstrated
some very striking perceptual phenomena that cannot be explained just in terms of
physically stimulating conditions that excite "elementary sensations," as these were
identified in the traditional empiricist theory, but equally do not seem to be attribut-
able to the results of learning, habit, or memory. His experiments were on apparent
motion. We are all familiar with the advertising displays that flash lights in sequence
to give the appearance of movement. The effect can be studied in the laboratory and

gives rise to a number of laws that relate the spacing, timing, and brightness of the lights to the appearance of apparent motion. We are not so concerned here with what the laws are but with the fact that the phenomena themselves are lawful. What is seen when two separated light spots are alternated at the right speed is a *single* point jumping from one position to the other. What is physically present is a *pair* of lights in alternation. How do we account for the very real difference between what is seen and what (physically) is present? Wertheimer (who used bars, as well as spots in his groundbreaking experiments) reasoned that the difference had to be a function of the way the visual system—the eye and brain and the neural connections between them—processes the incoming stimulation from the two successive stimuli.

The details of the mechanism Wertheimer thought was responsible for the transformation from physical signal to perceptual event need not concern us; it was faulty, as might be expected, since exact knowledge of how the physiological visual system operates was scanty in his day. The importance of Wertheimer's theorizing lay in his recognizing the principle that to understand perceptual phenomena requires invoking the mechanisms of visual processing in the brain. The marriage of this concept with the careful experimental investigation of perceptual phenomena to be elucidated by its means, sparked a brand new school, originally in Germany, that became known as Gestalt psychology. It had its heyday in the 1930s and 1940s.[21]

The German word *Gestalt* means "configuration"; the Gestalt school claimed that all natural perceptual events are inherently organized. We don't after all see patches of disembodied color or hear isolated acoustic events, we see apples and oranges and hear music, as many a philosopher has pointed out. The Gestalt psychologists discovered a number of laws that characterize perceptual organization and attributed them specifically to processing in the visual brain; the perceived organization *had* to be the way it is, because the organizing mechanisms of the brain so dictated. Although they were wrong as to the details, the Gestalt point of view has a very modern stamp to it, insisting as it does that psychological phenomena require a knowledge of the physiological substrate in the brain if they are to be understood scientifically. In particular the emphasis on the coding functions of the brain (as we now call them) assumed vast significance in subsequent developments, both in the hands of neuropsychologists like Karl Lashley and Roger Sperry,[22] and later in the applications of electrical recording to the activites of single cells in the visual system in response to external stimulation. We shall take that story up shortly.

The Gestalt psychologists held that their principles of organization apply to *all* forms of psychological activity, including thinking, language, problem solving, and memory, but their research in those areas was less extensive and has had far less impact than in the field of perception.[23]

A different but related attack on the "perceptual atomism" of empiricist theory was mounted somewhat later by the American psychologist James Gibson. Gibson came to his fresh insights into the nature of perception in a very practical way. As a young Air Force psychologist in World War II he had the task of assisting in the training of pilots. He found that the currently accepted theories of perception were of no help to him. Taking "frozen sections" of the visual field and gluing them together to construct a coherent visual world, as the traditional empirical theory required, was not helpful. He discovered that what pilots used in controlling their planes, when landing them for instance, was the whole "optic array," as Gibson called it, the changing, dynamic large field of visual stimulation impinging continuously and (in the case of landing) very rapidly on the eyes. Response to this stimulation seemed to be immediate and required no interposition of other psychological activities such as the traditional theory demanded. From this insight Gibson went on to create a wholly novel approach to the study of perception, in terms of what he called *global psychophysics,* the study of optic arrays and the "gradients of stimulation" they contain.[24] From this he subsequently developed a new theory of perception that relied far more on the careful analysis of the information contained in optic arrays, and far less (in fact practically not at all) on the intrusion of habit and memory as prescribed by traditional empiricist theory. In this he was close to the Gestalt psychologists, although in other respects his approach was diametrically opposed to theirs.

Gibson argued that to attend too closely to the physiological substrate of vision (as the Gestalt psychologists did) is misleading, because it steers us away from the important questions we should be asking about perception, indeed about cognition generally. Gibson's views were controversial but have played a leading role in the development of recent perceptual theory. His theoretical position is sufficiently important to justify devoting a large part of chapter 6 to it.

Another, contrasting, major strand in the development of cognitive theory, also starting from the perceptual side, occurred almost simultaneously with Gibson's early research. This was the work of the Canadian psychologist Donald Hebb, whose magnum opus appeared in 1949.[25] Hebb was a student of Lashley, steeped in the neuropsychological tradition of seeking brain mechanisms that would account for psychological functions. He was influenced by the Gestalt school's demonstrations and their insistence on the importance of organization, not just in perception but also in thinking and memory, in fact in all of psychology.[26]

At the time very little was known about the innate *connectivity* of cells in the brain cortex; connections were held to be essentially random at birth, only becoming organized as the organism develops and acquires experience. Hebb's theory was therefore couched in terms of early perceptual learning, which would give rise eventually to a full measure of cognitive functions: memory, attention, language, and so forth. In the mature organism these were held to be controlled by the concerted activity of *cell assemblies* in the brain and their extended operation over time, called *phase sequences.* The development of these cortical structures was said to be controlled by the oft-repeated sequences of stimulus events occurring as the organism moved about its normal environment.

Hebb remarked that his theory was too general to be useful and too specific to be correct. Nevertheless it exerted an enormous influence, first in perceptual psychology, spawning a huge amount of research on learning in young organisms (both human and animal), and then in other branches of psychology and cognitive science. It captured in ample measure the Zeitgeist of psychology of the midcentury. It was already widely believed that neural function, and organized activity in the brain in particular, had to be of basic importance to the understanding of psychological processes. It was generally held that learning had to play a prominent role in the organization of those processes, and some mechanism was needed to explain how such "neural learning" could be implemented. That mechanism would of course have to be compatible with what was then known about the anatomy and physiology of the brain. In all this Hebb succeeded brilliantly; his synthesis of neurophysiology and psychology seemed at the time to be entirely plausible, so much so that a new term, *neuropsychology,* became popular; the power and influence of his theory was unparalleled. We shall leave it at that for the moment but return later to the question of "Hebbian learning," as it is now called, which plays a prominent role in some other recent developments in cognitive science.

The Search for Precision

A new level of sophistication in psychological theorizing came about with a proposal by J. A. Deutsch[27] in response to some of the questions raised by Hullian and Hebbian theory. Without going into details we can call his work a landmark, because he introduced to psychological theorizing, for the first time, the concept of a well-formed procedure for coding stimulus information—what we now call an algorithm—and related this to specification of plausible (if still speculative) brain mechanisms for their implementation. These are two of the hallmarks of modern psychological theory; we call it *computational* theory.[28]

I have spent some time describing the development of theories about pattern and object perception not just because of their historical precedence but also because they give the most direct approach to understanding how cognitive scientists go about studying brain and mind. Starting from such crude and elementary (as we now see) models as Deutsch's, contemporary work has achieved rather sophisticated conceptions of the computational relations between brain and behavior. Perception has played a major role here, compared to the study of memory and thinking, for example, because there has been much greater success at linking neurophysiology to phenomenology and behavior in perception than in any other field. We shall take a closer look at that in chapter 3.

Another major contribution to the search for precision in cognitive psychology occurred at about the time Gibson's and Hebb's ideas had their major impact. It is called *information theory,* and came to prominence in psychology with the publication of a paper by George Miller in 1956 with the intriguing title "The Magic Number Seven Plus or Minus Two: Some Limits on Our Capacity for Processing Information."[29] Information theory as such originated in electrical engineering; it is a formal mathematical theory of the informational content of "events" (signals), something that is vital to measure precisely for the theory and practice of electronic signal processing. Miller showed how the theory of information measurement, abstract and extremely general though it is, can be applied to the ways in which, and the means by which, we humans cope with the complexities of our life and environment. Dealing with this "information flow" has both an active and a passive component, the first having to do with the emission of "signals," judgments, or the making of decisions, the second with the receiving of "signals," that is to say, with perception. (I have put items here in quotation marks to emphasize that they are new and unfamiliar uses of common words.) Despite the totally abstract nature of the original theory, its application to psychology has proved to be fruitful; it is another early, but prime, example of how computational ideas entered the field.

A general problem that has dogged psychological theorists from the very first attempts to apply quantitative ideas to the study of cognition is addressed by information theory. Here is a straightforward example: Since the earliest experiments on recall of verbal items, it has been obvious that the quantity of material that can readily be committed to memory is highly variable. You can easily remember a sentence like, "the maximum number of people that can sit in this restaurant is set by law," but it would be impossible to recall, after one brief exposure to them, an equal number of unrelated words. In fact, you might be able to recall about half as many (seven). You can try it with a set of words like, "Toes indeed to behind furnace wool voting extra seek wander." What's the difference? Clearly one set of words constitutes a sentence, the words have grammatical form, meaning, and perhaps conjure up a coherent image that helps in the recall, whereas the other set is unrelated, has no simple interpretation, and does not readily attach itself to a visual image (although a useful ploy is to try to construct an image as a mnemonic aid). How is one to explain this large difference in recall capacity? Is it just a result of factors like meaning and grammatical coherence? These do play an important role but do not supply the whole answer.

There are also big differences in perceptibility and recall capacity for other word-like materials that do not have the obvious difference in meaningfulness of our example. The problem is to find a way of quantifying such differences that is both exact and has some psychological relevance and plausibility. Information theory supplies one solution to the problem: It states that the difference in quantity of material, while not irrelevant, is not the major factor because it does not take into account the *amount of information* that each message (word string or letter string) contains. Messages having greater informational content will be more difficult to recall than those with less information. That sounds promising, but is it not merely redefining the meaning of information in terms of ease of recall? Moreover, is it not obvious that the sentence, which is the easier material to recall, contains *more* information than the unrelated string of words? The sentence states something that has meaning, contains some usable information, whereas the string of unrelated words is meaningless, and in that sense carries no information. If the theory states the opposite— that the randomly chosen words contain *more* information than the sentence—is there not surely something wrong with trying to apply the theory to psychology?

It all depends, as the BBC's Professor Joad would have said, on how one defines information. Information theory does so, to simplify somewhat, in terms of the *redundancy* in a message. A message of high redundancy, that is, one whose components do not all have to be received to get the meat of it, has less information *per symbol* than a nonredundant message. The latter is one in which each symbol has to be correctly received to get the message in full. Information theory has ways of independently measuring such redundancy, so the definition of information content is not circular. To go back to our example: The message in the meaningful text could be reconstructed even if we missed seeing (or hearing) some of the words or letters in it. This would not be true of the string of unrelated words in the second message; missing even one symbol would prevent a full reconstruction of the message. So, there are no redundant symbols in the second message, whereas there are some in the first.

To cut a long story short: It has been found in many different situations and re-search paradigms that human observers do, as Miller surmised in his paper of 1956, respond as though they are sensitive in very specific ways to the nature and rate of flow of information—information as measured by information theory in terms of re-dundancy. More precisely, it has been proposed—and much experimental evidence on language, perception, and memory supports the proposition—that humans be-have like *limited-capacity information channels.* This position has been championed by many leading theoreticians, one of the first being Donald Broadbent.[30] I shall not go into details but merely note that the information processor's model of cognitive functioning strongly supports the notion of an algorithmic base for mental life. The ideal here is to specify effective procedures for the quantification and processing of all stimulation, whether in language, memory, or perception: procedures that yield verifiable predictions of the outcomes of experimental tests. Naturally the models so postulated become more plausible, the more their implementation can be envisaged in terms of known brain functions. But like the models of Deutsch, their main ex-planatory power derives from the behavioral predictions that flow from them.

The theoretical perspective of humans as basically processors of information is in any case a strong affirmation of the metaphysical conception of the human being as a species of, admittedly very refined, machine and, as such, a supporter of the metaphysics of the clockwork universe.

Humans as Control Systems

Information theory exerted two quite distinct influences on cognitive psychology, the first bringing a new technique of measurement to bear, the second and more fun-damental proposing a new paradigm of man as information processor. There is probably no one place to be identified as the origin of this second influence, but an important strand can be traced to Bartlett's laboratory in Cambridge, where in the 1930s Kenneth Craik as a very young man started to explore the analogies between human skilled performance and the behavior of "intelligent" machines. This was of course long before computers were invented, so "intelligent machine" meant some-thing far more primitive than what we currently mean by those words. Nonetheless, such thinking was anything but primitive and was destined to shape a major branch of cognitive science.[31]

Craik was much struck by the fact that certain machines are designed to evince "goal-directed" behavior, so that, for example, the governor on a motor controls the speed at which it works, the goal being the steady target speed set by the human supervisor (an early device was the Watts governor for controlling the speed of his steam engines). Even the simple thermostat of a space heater can likewise be thought of as "seeking" the goal of a preselected temperature. Such machines work on the principle of "error feedback." For the thermostat, the target temperature is set and the heaters turn on until such time as the desired temperature, the target, is reached. The heaters are then turned off until the temperature drops below the target, and so on. The "error," plus or minus, is the difference between the actual and de-sired temperatures. Naturally many refinements are possible, even in this simple mechanism, such as arranging for the heat to be shut off early so as not to overshoot the target. Feedback of information and control of this sort is called *negative feedback* because it reverses, or negates, the direction of deviation from the target.

Elementary examples of mechanical feedback control, some of them known for centuries, seem hardly the stuff out of which a new cognitive psychology could arise. They remind us more than a little of the hydraulically controlled statues at Versailles that gave Descartes his model for the control of organisms by the "animal spirits" flowing through the bodily conduits of the nerves. But more sophisticated examples of feedback control came to Craik's attention. The Cambridge laboratory was engaged on military research during World War II, and relatively new systems were under investigation; for instance, a control system to keep the turret-mounted gun of a tank "on target" as the vehicle maneuvered. This was achieved by a negative feedback mechanism that compensated for the tank's movements. An elaborate theory of information and control started to develop, later known as cybernetics, a word derived from the Greek *kybernetes,* meaning "steersman."[32] At about the same time new concepts of motor and sensory control in animals based on the principle of *reafference* were under development in Germany.[33] What is the principle of reafference? It is the principle that self-produced stimulation in the organism is used to control (and stabilize) its activity—the very same concept of negative feedback we have been discussing.

Another very influential conception of feedback control was introduced by Walter Cannon in *The Wisdom of the Body.*[34] He demonstrated how widespread the principle is in the regulation of vegetative functions such as temperature and hormone balance; he called it *homeostasis.* A principle of such great importance in physiological activity in the body could surely be applied fruitfully to the control of behavior? Something along these lines had even appealed to Hull in his theory of drive reduction as the motivating force in learning.

In several different places and in various fields of application, the same idea thus took root, namely that biological organisms can be studied as control systems, and even that much of the abstract mathematical theory of control could be used, at least in an informal way, to help grasp the nature of biological, including human, behavior. Here again we may be struck by the analogy with Descartes; concepts derived from control theory, a theory developed in the first place to guide the design and understanding of machines, is applied to human and other biological action. In a not-so-subtle way, although more subtly than for Descartes, this promulgated strongly the concept of man as a species of machine. A wonderful and mysterious one, certainly, but nevertheless a machine. Once again, welcome to the clockwork universe!

Craik and his successors applied these ideas to human skilled performance. Von Holst and Mittelstaedt in Germany used them in their analysis of the behavior of insects and the lower vertebrates. In North America they paved the way, following Norbert Wiener's pioneering work, for the application of machine concepts to intelligent action, leading eventually to robotics.

I shall not pursue further at this point the growth of theories of information processing and control; we shall meet them in another guise—or perhaps several of them—in due course. As in other fields of cognition, the question of the relevance of this brand of psychology to the real world has been raised. For memory studies this was done most forcefully by Neisser,[35] who, interestingly enough, was a colleague of J. J. Gibson at Cornell University and much influenced by him. It is remarkable that Neisser's book *Cognitive Psychology,*[36] of the mid-1960s, is credited with launching the modern discipline of cognitive psychology, at least in North America, and of doing so very much within the information-processing tradition just described. The 1982 book is not a repudiation of the earlier one, but it does strike at the root of the assumption that all of man's cognitive functioning can be encompassed and understood within a quasimechanical idiom.

The New Mental Mechanics

Earlier I described how the dead hand of behaviorism had stifled much intellectual inquiry about the nature of mind. The perceived sterility of introspectionism, too, had for many decades held at bay the study of what goes on by way of conscious accompaniment to thinking, remembering, problem-solving, and similar mentation. In the nineteenth century images and imagery had been investigated quite successfully by Gustav Fechner, Alfred Binet, and Francis Galton, but their methods and findings did not remain in the mainstream of psychological research. Experimental psychologists had become convinced that the study of cognition could be adequately pursued without venturing again into that murky Cartesian theater, where the study of events only privately observable all too easily lured the investigator along false paths and into blind alleys. And yet it surely must be the case that those private events can tell us much that is interesting, perhaps vitally important, about the way cognition works. Something radical seemed to be needed to get us back on track with the study of conscious experience, to—as one might say—set the imagination free again. That was certainly the point of view of Hebb, whose incisive contributions to neuropsychological theory we met earlier. His ideas about the study of imagery were equally important, but not as immediately effective in generating research. But following Hebb's lead, Alan Paivio initiated, over a long and distinguished career, many simple but insightful ways of studying imagery and the role it plays in mental life.[37]

The study of "internal states" such as images only became respectable again when techniques were devised that cause observable, and measurable, effects in behavior, such as the study of how "mental maps" are elaborated and used. The single most dramatic, even spectacular, demonstration of this sort, and the one by which the study of imagery was truly seen to be fully rehabilitated, was an experiment by Shepard and Metzler on "mental rotation."[38] These authors obtained unambiguous evidence that "internal states"—mental images—can be handled in ways that are surprisingly analogous to the manipulation and measurement of external objects. In their experiment observers had the task of deciding whether two presented (abstract) shapes, displayed in different orientations, were identical. To decide, yes or no, observers imagined rotating one shape into alignment with the other before making a judgment. Not only can the act of mental manipulation (in this case an imagined rotation of a shape) be timed, but also the mental "action" appears to have a characteristic we usually associate with a certain class of physical motions under a well-specified set of mechanical constraints, namely rotation at a constant angular velocity. Yet this is not a mechanical system. There are no mental strings and pulleys to control the action. There is no object actually (physically) in a state of rotation, there are no mental images moving about in the brain; there is the imagination of real objects being rotated, moved into alignment.

Well, well: A measurement system devised for strictly physical-mechanical theory and application turns out to be totally adaptable to, and appropriate to, measurement of a purely mental event! Has the problem of "mental measurement" been solved? Hardly, because although from one point of view this experiment succeeds brilliantly, from another—the epistemological point of view—it offers less than at first seems to be promised. It shows how to measure the *consequences* of a mental operation, and proves how robust and quantifiable this can be. From the other point of view, it (and the host of similar experiments that have followed in its steps)[39] raises many more questions than it answers. For instance, we must understand that it is not the mental operation as such that is observed. We don't even know quite what it would mean to make such an observation—a matter we shall raise in detail later— yet it is also undeniable that *something* is going on that has observable and highly regular consequences. This experiment and its derivatives are probably among the most replicated findings in cognitive psychology. Yet there is an important sense in which we are no closer to grasping what it means to observe a "mental event" or "act" or "operation" (and each such characterization has its share of problems and critics) than were the introspectionists 100 years ago.

In assessing the achievements of contemporary cognitive psychology one needs to be very careful not to confuse the important new methods of experimental study of mental phenomena, which without question have had great impact on understanding of mentation (or, if you prefer, on how cognitive processes do their job), with the question of how to grasp the real nature of those phenomena. That is a deep, indeed a metaphysical question, perhaps not amenable to the sort of inquiry and research with which psychologists feel comfortable. For the moment I will rest content with the observation that if we aspire to creating a rich and full picture of humankind, we cannot avoid the obligation, at some stage, of making such inquiry. Some would argue that modern cognitive psychology supplies all that is needed, indeed all that is *possible* in this field. Others, myself included, feel that to take that stance is to abdicate our responsibility to the science of the mind.

The Shape of Contemporary Cognitive Psychology

This chapter has been a very brief and selective tour through some of the major fields of cognitive psychology and their history. I have not been at pains to describe the very latest in current developments (we shall get to some of them in due course), but have rather concentrated on giving a picture of how psychologists have arrived at where we are in the study of mind. There are two reasons for this: First, as Smitty Stevens used to say,[40] following the "cutting edge" too closely can get you caught up with the fads of the moment, to the detriment of a proper perspective on the subject and a sober assessment of lasting progress. Second, observation over several decades has convinced me that to understand a corpus of scientific (or any other) inquiry at any depth, and to see where it may be leading, it is vital to have a grasp of where it came from and how it developed. Who was it that remarked that those who fail to learn the lessons of history are doomed to repeat its mistakes?

To understand what cognitive psychology has achieved, but also where it may have fallen short, we need to have a solid understanding of how it arrived at its present beliefs, theories, and, yes, prejudices about the nature of the mind. Nearly all the important elements of the image of the human mind in current vogue in cognitive psychology were introduced and elaborated in their essentials in the 1950s. Some of them, certainly, are of much earlier vintage, especially the Darwinian view of the human species as a purely natural phenomenon (chapter 1), and a few are of course quite recent. But the fundamental notion steering modern cognitive psychology is that the human being is a biological entity to be understood completely in terms of its genetically given substrate and the effects that a particular environmental history has had in molding it as an individual. That, too, is quite an old idea, but it is expressed forcefully in modern form in Hebb's theory of the determining influence of the individual brain and its physiology on what makes a cognizing (perceiving, thinking, language-using) and distinctive person. From Gibson we have an elaboration on the evolutionary theme, and the insistence that there is nothing mysterious about "information pickup" and the veridical, fully informing, life-steering relationship between the individual and its environment. In his view they are a mutually interacting and beneficial dyad, the product of aeons of biological metamorphosis under the pressure to adapt to the exigencies of terrestrial life. According to Gibson, that is sufficient for an understanding of what we are.

Looking at the seemingly goal-directed action of even some quite simple machines led a number of psychologists to postulate that the principles on which they work might be applied to human behavior. Walter Cannon's conception of homeostasis, the self-regulating wisdom of the body that maintains all the vital functions in harmonious balance, was also applied in psychology and was instrumental in furthering the notion of the mind as a very elaborate control mechanism. The advent of information theory, and the related conception of man as information processor, has, perhaps more than any other single idea, shaped the current conception of *Homo cogitans.* Not only do we get the picture of man as a species of subtle machine, but in particular most cognitive psychologists have also come to think of him as a very well-articulated subspecies of that type, a *computational* machine.

If there is one single characteristic that most clearly identifies contemporary cognitive psychology, it is the insistence that everything is to be understood computationally. *Computational* is very much a buzz word in cognitive science, but we have not yet really tackled its meaning seriously. That must wait until we have looked at other contributions to cognition, especially those in machine vision and artificial intelligence. But the general idea is clear enough: Man as computational being is a biological machine, one that is driven by homeostatic principles and shaped by environmental pressures to deal efficiently with the information that impinges on him. In other words, a prime specimen in the nonhumanistic, determinist tradition! That, at least in the view of some critics, is a pretty gloomy view of what we are,[41] and a challenge to be taken up at a later point in our story.

3

Other Paths in Cognitive Science

I do not know what makes a man more conservative—to know nothing but the present, or nothing but the past.

JOHN MAYNARD KEYNES

Of the five strands in cognitive science, I give the most attention to experimental psychology, not just because I know it more intimately but because historically it has been dominant. Not only was it "first in the field," but many of its basic ideas initiated and informed the development of the other four. In examining these four remaining strands, little more than a series of sketches is possible. I shall outline the core assumptions, history, methods, and findings of each, providing landmarks and signposts rather than maps of the territory. All these topics are discussed in much greater detail, but from the same point of view, in another place.[1]

Neuroscience

Modern science has been dependent for its development, even in some cases for its very emergence, on new instruments and technologies such as the microscope and telescope. Nowhere is this dependence more evident than in neuroscience, one of the hottest areas of research of the late twentieth century. Neuroscience encompasses the study of all life systems of such complexity as to require neural tissue—sets of functionally interconnected neurons (nerve cells)—to "work"; that is, to live, grow, reproduce, and behave.

In earlier centuries a surprising amount was learned about the structure and function of nervous systems, including the central nervous system (CNS) of humans, using rather crude methods. But the success of modern research on the CNS (the brain and its neural appendages) hinges on two major technical advances. First was the discovery of dyes that selectively stain nerve cells in tissue slides so that their detailed anatomy becomes visible under the microscope. This made possible the detailed tracing of neural pathways and interconnections in the CNS. The second breakthrough came with the development of sufficiently fine electrodes, and sufficiently sensitive methods of detection and amplification, to make possible the recording of the electrical activity of nerve bundles, then of the individual fibers within a bundle, and eventually of the single nerve bodies themselves. The early use of these techniques was pioneered by Ramón y Cajal about 100 years ago and by E. D. Adrian (Lord Adrian) in the 1920s, respectively.[2] As the techniques have been refined they have provided ever more profound insight into how neural tissue works. Most of the major characteristics and concepts of neuroscience were, however, discovered and defined quite early on.

Paramount among these was the detailed description of the structure and function of the neuron, the highly specialized type of cell that is the basic unit of neural tissue. Neurons connect together via synapses, chemical-electrical junctions that ensure that electrical action flows unidirectionally from one neuron to another. The electrical activation itself consists of spike potentials (so called because of their appearance on a recording oscilloscope), generated in one neuron and transmitted to one or, more likely, very many receiving or host neurons. The spike potentials vary in frequency; the more highly activated a neuron, the higher the frequency of spikes it generates. The spikes themselves, however, are of constant form and amplitude for any given neuron. We thus arrive at the conception of communication between neurons as being essentially a frequency code, somewhat like the discrete dots and dashes of Morse code.[3] Neurons can thus be thought of as one-way gates that both initiate and control the flow of activity through the networks of which neural tissue is composed.

Interconnection between neurons can be exceedingly complicated. In the cortex of the brain (the gray matter comprising the outer covering of the brain) a single neuron may receive signals via 60,000 or more synapses impinging on it from many other neurons! No wonder the early researchers despaired of ever making sense of the connectivity of neural tissue, let alone the part played by individual cells in the processing of neural signals.

One of the most astounding findings of modern neuroscience is the fact that the coding function of single neurons, even in that densely connected cortical layer, can often be discovered by relatively simple means. For example, single cells in the visual areas of the brain have retinal receptive fields, which means that such a cell responds only to stimulation of a very restricted area of the retina of the eye to which it is connected. The retinal receptive field has a particular shape and position, so that its appropriate stimulation "tells" its host cell in the brain what visual feature is present at that position in the visual field. This gives rise to the concept of visual neural coding, the notion that discrete "packets of information" are preserved and transmitted from the receiving sense organ (here, the retina) and delivered intact to the cortex. From there it is not a big step to conceive of a neural image, the elaboration in the brain of a "representation" of some external, perceived feature.[4] Receptive fields are found in all sensory systems; they are a general feature of the "input" areas of the brain.

Activation of neurons—the generation of spike potentials—can occur spontaneously without external stimulation, or by synaptic transmission from other neurons, or by the activity of end organs that are themselves further specialized neurons designed to detect external energies like sound (in the inner ear), pressure (on the skin), and light (on the retina). Incidentally, some of these specialized cells detect internal states of the body, as, for instance, the balance organs of the inner ear and the muscle tension detectors in the skeletal musculature of arms and legs. The distinctiveness of the messages appears to reside in the routes they take, and their places of origin and destination. Electrical activity in the optic nerve, from eye to brain, would thus not be detectably different from activity in the auditory nerve. Nevertheless, one is intrinsically concerned with visual events, the other with the world of hearing. This is known as the law of specific nerve energies, and is one of the most salient, as well as one of the most puzzling aspects of neuroscience. You might wonder why it is called the law of *specific* nerve energies, as the doctrine says that all nerves have a common energy (and form), but that is the name tradition has prescribed for it.

Architecture of the Brain

The cerebral hemispheres, which overlie the older structures of the midbrain and hindbrain, are the seat of all the capacities that make us distinctively human, especially those of language, thought, the sense of identity, and long-term memory. The cerebral hemispheres are divided into two rather symmetrical halves (the by now too familiar left brain–right brain), each being further divided into a number of lobes that have distinct functions.

Localization of function in the brain was initially just an assumption, but it has been amply borne out by more than a century's empirical investigation. Logically it is not impossible that the representation of psychological function in the brain would be widely dispersed and thus mixed together in diverse ways—but that is not in fact the way things are. The basic layout of the brain is extremely orderly and well articulated. The optic nerve conveys messages to a part of the brain that is specialized for vision, the auditory nerve communicates with another part that is organized for hearing, yet another distinct area subserves language, and so on. Of course this is a great oversimplification for the purposes of exposition, but it is not a distortion. The basic plan really is straightforward, and thus affords more possibility for understanding the principles of the brain's operation than we might otherwise reasonably hope for. That is indeed lucky, because otherwise teasing out the way the brain works would be a vastly more difficult enterprise. Localization of function is the second overarching principle of neuroscience, the first being the principle of electrical transmission of discrete signals (information) between individual neurons; together they anchor our conception of how the brain operates to subserve psychological functions and phenomena.

One of the most remarkable findings about neural coding, investigated in great detail and with consummate skill by the Nobel laureates David Hubel and Torsten Wiesel, is that to a large extent the coding is innate. It exists in kittens at birth, for example, and even before they have had any normal visual experience. Certainly the system is not exactly like an adult's, and the coding becomes sharper with maturity; nevertheless in most essentials it is present in the newborn, so must have a genetically programmed basis. Does this mean that it is fixed for all time? Not at all; we cannot go into the details, but suffice it to say that neuroscientific research has established that a high degree of plasticity—the ability to alter the coding system as a function of externally imposed sensory stimulation—exists in the mammalian brain. Investigating this matter, again pioneered by Hubel and Wiesel, has opened up the most exciting possibilities for understanding the development of the brain and its relation to concomitant changes in behavior.

A third set of new techniques now supplements the tissue staining and single cell recording methods already described. It is called *metabolic imaging,* comprising ways of detecting and recording the metabolic processes that support all neural action. They are basically techniques for pinpointing "where the action is" in the brain, allowing the investigator to identify not only the general area in which neural activity is occurring (during recall or speech, for instance) but also in many cases giving an indication of the detailed functional anatomy of a region of the brain. The so-called laminar and columnar organization of most primary sensory areas in the cortex has largely been mapped out with the aid of such techniques (see, again, note 4).

One further quite remarkable aspect of cerebral organization demands mention. It has been found, in the visual system especially, that the external field of view has multiple representations in the brain, multiple *maps,* as they are called. The whole of visual space is separately coded in a number of different locations—in the human brain more than two dozen times! One might think it wasteful of Mother Nature to provide such redundancy, but the various maps are generally concerned with different aspects of visual stimulation and hence presumably with the processing of different sorts of visual information. Some specialized maps contain neurons that code only for color; others are concerned with movement of various types; others respond to visual "texture" or other, less easily specified, characteristics of the sensory input. The brain has evidently traded global processing of sensory stimulation for the advantages of detailed work on a single aspect of that stimulation in separate structures. We are already familiar with this design feature between modalities in the law of specific nerve energies, so perhaps we should not be too surprised that such a piecemeal method of handling information is found intramodally as well. It makes the unraveling of the ways the brain processes sensory stimulation easier than it would otherwise be, but it does raise some serious questions about the coherency of experience. How could a fractured cortical representation of this sort underlie, fully represent, or even be the essence of our experience of the visual world, which, beyond any shadow of a phenomenological doubt, is vividly unified and, as the Gestalt psychologists insisted, intrinsically holistic and organized?

We'll consider that question in due course. For now it is sufficient to emphasize that neuroscientific research strongly supports a particular conception of the brain as processor of sensory information. It performs its task by routing information from the various sense organs to different cortical areas, and even different classes of attribute (color, shape, texture, for example) to specific sites for further analysis. The evidence suggests, and is certainly interpreted to mean, that the neural codes discovered for single cortical neurons are the basis for the elaboration of "neural images" that fully represent features of the environment that are perceived by the organism. Whereas this interpretation is well founded in the research on sensory systems, it is generally extrapolated to the view that all cognitive activity is similarly coded and represented in neural terms.

Brain and Mind

I have taken evidence from research on the mammalian visual system to present an overview of what neuroscience contributes to an understanding of the brain in its relation to psychological—in this case perceptual—activity. But similar principles lie behind work on all aspects of the relations between brain and behavior. Even this is but a small segment of what is now a vast and hugely successful research enterprise. It would be impossible to give here even a hint of the ways many disciplines contribute to neuroscience, from molecular biology to ethology. What I have described, however, is enough to characterize the general stance of neuroscience and especially its distinctive contribution to our present inquiry: how understanding the brain furthers our grasp of mental phenomena.

The position of virtually every neuroscientist is simple enough: The brain (with its various "peripherals") is the seat of all behavioral action and control; also of all mental—including conscious—phenomena. To understand those activities and phenomena it is sufficient to have an exhaustive knowledge of how the brain works. The position is completely reductionist; that is, it states that once all the processes that go on in the brain have been investigated and understood, there is nothing more to know. The processes themselves may be studied at various levels of complexity, and with many different theoretical and experimental techniques. At bottom, however, it all comes down to accepting that the brain is a material organ, subject to all—and only—the laws of physics. Every event in it can ultimately be understood as a physical process, even if we do not as yet know in detail how to state (reduce) knowledge couched in a biological, chemical, or psychological idiom in terms of physical processes. In principle, so the neuroscientist claims, it is possible to do so without remainder. Most neuroscientists would be quite surprised that this stance would even be questioned. It is not just that it is an article of faith; the evidence seems overwhelmingly to support it.

Not that many decades ago, it was common to relegate activities of which we were confident in principle, but unable to observe in practice, to "higher cortical processes." Since the advent of single unit recording and image processing, matters have come into much sharper focus, and that need to relegate has shrunk enormously. And as it shrank, what did we find? Exactly what scientific intuition, or shall we say even a robust common sense that has faith in the fundamental simplicity and comprehensibility of the world, would hope for, even expect: A system that selects, codes, and elaborates sensory information into neural representations of those external features that are in fact perceived. The neural codes, and the cytoarchitecture, are in general outline fixed at birth, but in some respects are plastic in the sense of being modifiable by specific types of stimulation, especially early in life. Such modifications affect both brain organization and representation as well as behavior, and make sense from the point of view of biological utility for the organism.[5]

Neural codes of a far more complex type, indeed of a new order, are starting to be found that correspond to biologically salient aspects of the organism's environment, such as faces, hands, and limb movements. They tend to be found in areas known to be concerned with the more abstract and general cognitive functions of attention and memory such as the inferotemporal cortex, and are so dramatic as to lend even more substance to the neuroscientist's faith in the power and potential comprehensiveness of his or her methods of inquiry.[6]

Scope of Neuroscience

Spectacular success has occurred over a relatively short time, essentially not much more than 40 years. New findings appear that reinforce and extend the present knowledge but do not challenge it in any fundamental—that is, metaphysical—way, so it is hardly surprising that neuroscientists should be satisfied with their conception of brain and behavior. The brain demonstrably does compute many things. Is there any reason to doubt that eventually everything known about visual perception, cognitively and phenomenologically, will yield its secrets to neuroscientific investigation? Can we doubt it for the rest of cognitive psychology, even for cognitive science as a whole?

Neuroscience says no to those questions. This should not, however, be accepted without reservation: The program of neuroscience is self-proclaimed, and there are questions about cognition that its methods are simply not designed to answer. Its successes in vision are brilliant, but what about memory, thought, and language? Here it has less to offer in terms of representation, organization, or the details of neural coding. A good deal is known about localization of function, but the level of knowledge is perhaps no greater in general than what was known about the visual and other sensory systems in the early 1950s, that is, before the advent of electrical recording from single neurons within the brain. It is not that the capacity for making similar recordings in brain areas known (or thought) to be concerned with language or memory is lacking. The problem is that there is not the same sort of conceptual scheme to guide research as there was for vision, nor the help provided by knowledge of the anatomical arrangement of the sensory pathways. In vision it was to a great extent obvious where to look, and even what to look for, before the search began in earnest. The terminus of the eye's input to the brain was known, the existence of at least a crude cortical map of the retina had been demonstrated, and the catalogue of sensory elements and qualities well established and in many respects exhaustively studied in experimental psychology and psychophysics. Much of that conceptual infrastructure was missing outside the field of perceptual inquiry.

There have been some conjectures, but nothing like a coherent theory to explain how what happens at the sites identified with memory or language can give rise to mental life, or why particular mental events are associated with one part of the brain rather than another. This is in contrast to the knowledge of sensory pathways that indicate the routes to the relevant areas.[7] But even the wonderful insight into sensory processing in the brain provided by neuroscience does little more than the research on localization of attention and memory to create an understanding of the genesis of mental life, of consciousness. To ask, What's the neuron doing? is to refer to some physical-visual event out there, whose occurrence is a sufficient condition for the neuron's firing. It does not explain how the neuron comes to code a particular feature, nor does it explain how that neuronal activity fits into the grand scheme of cortical representation of vision that we assume must be at the heart of all the coding activity we now so readily take for granted. So, contrary to the general consensus that this work "cracks the code" for visual analysis and representation in the cortex,[8] in reality it just identifies sites of activity. The "language of the brain," the propagation of Morse code–like trains of discrete pulses along neuronal axons from one place to another, can be said, at a very abstract level, to "convey information" (chapter 2), but to make any biological or psychological sense of them we have to know where the trains originate, where they terminate, and how those sites are related to the outside world or to psychological function. To make this work coherent and comprehensible we already have to know a great deal about the nature of sensation, perception, and memory. There would be no point in recording from the visual cortex if we had no model or plan to guide the investigation. This point will receive detailed analysis in later chapters.

I have simplified to make a point, but the simplification is not one of principle. There are many ways in which neuroscientific research has enriched our understanding of visual and other processing, enlightened us on the relations between neuroanatomy and physiology, and expanded our understanding of the innate mechanisms and plasticity of the brain. It has led to new methods, ideas, and experimental investigation in cognitive psychology, but the fact remains that its contributions are only valid and exciting in the context of an already fully developed conception of the behaving, cognizing organism. Lacking that, we would have little incentive to investigate, and no notion of what to make of neuroscientific data. We only make headway by force of our ideas, something that may appear paradoxical to the "bottom-up" approach to cognition favored by current orthodox neuroscience.

There are many aspects of neuroscience, even in its application to perceptual phenomena, that we have not touched on.[9] Much of this work is insightful and brilliant, but it does not alter the fundamental argument I have just been making. The stance of neuroscience is: Know the brain, and you know all. It accords well with the general conceptions espoused by experimental psychologists (chapter 2), as well as the biological account of the origins of mental life. The establishment of many correlations between brain function and psychological process has been brilliant, but such correlations are not in themselves explanations of mentation.

In summary, those parts of the neuroscientific "program" that aim to relate neural function to psychological process, especially to cognitive process, have had far more success in perception, and especially in vision, than in any other field. So I have presented the strongest possible case for neuroscience's contributions to cognitive science, but it does not give the full picture. Neuroscience cannot define or explain mental phenomena, reasoning, attention, perception, memory, and the rest out of its own resources, but it can help in their understanding by discovery of the necessary conditions of brain activity that make mental development and activity possible. This is less than the metaphysics of materialism would have us accept as the absolutely central role of neuroscience in the understanding and explanation of cognition.

We turn now to a third path of investigation in cognitive science: artificial intelligence.

Machine Visions, Artificial Dreams

The idea that mechanical devices can lend aid to mental work has been around for many centuries, from the counting sticks of prehistory to the digital computer of today. The idea of mechanical simulation of human movement and action is also of ancient origin, although successful examples of robotic and similar mechanical devices are more recent.[10] Notice that in the handling of routine information, as in the use of the simple handheld calculator, the effectiveness of the machine depends on its control by a human operator, whereas the power of the digital computer, the mechanical extension of purposive movement, depends on the aims and objectives of the human designer that are implemented in the machine. These are aids to, or extensions of, human intentionality, and as such present no problem of justification or explanation to philosophy, science, or common sense.

This all changed, however, when the power and speed of computers began to challenge the intellectual supremacy of the human being. Raw computing power and speed were not decisive. What changed the nature of the game was the invention of new ways of using computing machinery and the deliberate attempt to ape human intelligent action, especially in pattern recognition, logical and mathematical problem solving, and verbal behavior. A machine can do better than merely store data and respond to explicit instructions from the operator. It can be made to store its own instructions and to respond to them in ingenious and novel, often apparently even in creative, ways. These instructions typically embody goals to be achieved and decision criteria that determine when the goals have been met.

The history of computers is a key ingredient in the story of modern culture.[11] We shall limit consideration to aspects that affect cognitive science most directly, namely those that gave rise to, and currently support, the belief that designing, studying, and exploring the uses of computers can add to our understanding of cognition. The term *artificial intelligence* (AI) has long been used to honor the remarkable feats of computation that can be achieved, such as solving logical puzzles and playing chess, but also in the belief, in some quarters at least, that this computational virtuosity is just the realization in a different medium of the sorts of mentation that are traditionally reserved to the powers of the human brain.[12]

A distinction is often drawn between strong AI and weak AI. The latter asserts the relevance of AI to the study of human thought, intelligence, and action by making possible the modeling and simulation of complex behavior, including certain aspects of mentation. Strong AI, on the other hand, claims that the behavior of the computer is much more: It is an embodiment, or instantiation, as philosophers like to say, of those very mental powers we are bent on studying. This is much more than a theoretical hunch, it is a very strong metaphysical claim.

Weak AI allows that some mental operations can be adequately represented in a computational system. Strong AI claims, however, that this formalism is, at least in principle, all there is to mental activity. How did that belief come about, and can it be justified? For an answer we must turn, perhaps rather surprisingly, to a different discipline and field of inquiry: mathematics and the formalization of logic and language.

Symbols and Representation

In the nineteenth century a revolution occurred in the understanding of the nature of mathematics, spearheaded by the realization that geometry is not what, from antiquity, it had been assumed to be. Euclidean geometry had a dual character. It was an axiomatic system, with postulates and rules of inference, but it also was held to be the uniquely correct means of codifying the properties of the physical space we inhabit. This gave rise to the comforting thought that we can know the real space of which our senses inform us in a quite special way; we can know it with certainty. Why? Because its geometry is based on the "necessary truths" of an axiomatic system. This again is a strong metaphysical position, and one that played a prominent role in nearly all epistemological debate over the course of the nineteenth century (see chapter 7).

The realization (at about mid-century) that there are other geometries, based on a different set of axioms and just as valid mathematically as Euclid's, imported a wonderful freedom into the realm of mathematical thinking and a new sense of the power of human thought generally. This new insight had two major effects on the understanding of the relations between mind and world, on epistemology. First, it undercut belief in the certainty that Euclidean space is the absolute and only foundation of all empirical knowledge. Second, it led to the examination of the foundations of the whole of mathematics. Mathematics, it was realized, is what we decide to make it, so its ground must be made logically secure.

What has all this to do with the question of the mechanized mind? As it happens, a great deal. Bertrand Russell's groundbreaking formulation, early in the twentieth century, of the relations of mathematics to symbolic logic, language, and the nature of knowledge had a profound impact on the epistemology of his day. Together with Ludwig Wittgenstein, he set the stage for a new brand of philosophy. In their joint work they propounded a powerful, if restricted, conception of how language can represent the world. According to that account, all facts about the world are singular, limited to a particular time and place, and have no generality; they called them *atomic facts.* Such facts can be stated in *atomic sentences,* similarly basic and limited, thereby yielding a pleasingly simple and direct match between world and word. No matter that this conception, popular early in the century, was soon decisively rejected as a general theory of knowledge; it had injected into the realm of epistemology a powerful tool, and gave logicians the necessary impetus to continue their efforts to formalize language.[13]

An atomic sentence can be expressed in a string of symbols having a common form, such as subject-verb-object. It can thus be written as a formula containing variables that, when given appropriate values, yield factual (verifiable) statements. This is, in an obvious way, much like an algebraic formula that is interpreted in terms of the values of its separate components. To take a simple example: Subject-verb-object is the formula, with the substitutions of "I" for subject, "see" for verb, and "chair" for object. This is a very crude outline of the doctrine, but sufficient for an understanding of a groundbreaking new idea, the possibility that the formulas can be fed to a machine, appropriate substitutions for the variables inserted, and empirical (fact-stating) sentences thereby generated. To the extent that language can be so restricted, it can be made machine compatible. Moreover, the rules of logical substitution and implication, even of simple grammar and verbal inference, can be translated into the rules of operation of a computing device.[14]

All this is getting a bit ahead of the game; the philosophers of language, again led by Wittgenstein, soon abandoned the idea that all useful knowledge can be captured in the narrow net of the theory of atomic facts and sentences. For one thing it resembled too closely the old idea that a special geometry (Euclid's) gave privileged access to the nature of the world. Logicians, psychologists, and those who were later to be known as computer scientists, however, kept going. For them the ideals of rigor and formality motivated the search for new ways to capture thought and language in a manner amenable to explicit computation, and so ultimately to implementation in a machine. This conception of language fits rather well with the information-processing model of mind described in chapter 2, which was under development at about the same time.

Another avenue, mathematical computing theory, was opened up by the English mathematician Alan Turing. He made explicit the notion of an *algorithm,* which is a procedure (known in another context as an *effective procedure;* chapter 2) for breaking the solution of a computable problem into discrete steps.[15] Properly stated problems in logic, mathematics, and (some restricted forms of) language certainly qualify for algorithmic solution.[16]

We shall have to skip further details, including the parallel development of formal neurons and modular nets by Pitts and McCulloch in America.[17] Their research laid the foundations for formal modeling of brains, the precursor of the now very active research enterprise concerned with neural networks.[18]

The character of AI has changed enormously since its inception. This has happened in all fields, but can be well illustrated by work on modeling perceptual processes. The best computer pattern-recognition system of 1959[19] has a character totally different from suggested general models for perception based on machine vision of more recent vintage. Much of the meat in the 1959 system of Grimsdale et al. consists of detailed descriptions of how visual patterns can be transformed into "machine-readable" form—not unlike the problem of the machine representation of words and sentences. Great ingenuity was expended on transcending the limitations of the then-current technology. Today these efforts seem as primitive as, say, the first efforts at powered flight appeared to the fliers and aeronautical engineers of the 1940s (that is, about three or four decades into the new technology).

In sharp contrast is Feldman's perceptual model of 1985, which still has a contemporary flavor. There the matters of interest all have to do with what one may call the logical structure of perception, with what are primarily psychological questions. Feldman's model is a typical example of how a computer scientist now tackles a topic in cognitive science. Technical hardware limitations are practically nonexistent, or at least do not limit the virtuosity of the modeler, and so allow freedom to concentrate on the solution of scientific questions. This he does by the implementation of his ideas in programs that are designed to simulate human or other biologically based (in this case visual) performance.[20] The same can be said for creators of natural language simulations.

Computational Theory in Cognition

The change from concentrating attention on the machine as simple recognizer to using the computer, employing exclusively computational techniques to model cognitive processes, was brought about principally by David Marr.[21] Once again, the field of action starts in perception. By introducing a biological perspective to the application of computing techniques in the 1960s and 1970s, he gave a great impetus to research on machine vision and made respectable the notion that progress in visual science is possible, indeed inevitable, along these lines. He was largely responsible for introducing the term *computational theory* to cognitive science, and for popularizing the aims, terminology, and methods of computational work.

What is the computational theory of vision? It is the theory that all we need to know about visual perception, everything of scientific importance in the field, can be captured by defining sets of algorithmic processes that describe how input variables (the physically defined stimuli to which we are sensitive and to which we respond) are transduced and transformed to produce the output categories that we recognize as the true phenomena of perception (static and moving scenes and objects, people, events). It is thus much broader than the approach introduced by Deutsch (chapter 2) but champions the same ideal of logical rigor in terms of defining fully effective procedures for perceptual processing. Marr's work can also be seen as the natural successor to the models of Pitts and McCulloch, but again broadens the approach to apply to all of visual perception, not just some special problems in pattern recognition.

The computational theory of vision is much more than a model of how the visual system (human or other) might work; it is a prescription, or blueprint, for what any model of the workings of a visual system should be like.[22] While Marr's influence was felt most strongly in vision research, the same basic ideas about computation and machine implementation of cognitive functions were enthusiastically accepted in other fields like language, memory, and thought.

The distinction between cognitive psychology and this branch of computer science is now quite blurred; there are many psychologists who make free use of computer simulation in their work, and borrow from the concepts (and jargon) of computer science with enthusiasm. Few psychologists would agree with the argument, however, made quite early on by Uhr,[23] that modeling in vision (or any other cognitive field) should now be exclusively in the province of computer science. As a source of rigorous techniques, computer science and machine vision have much to recommend them, but as fountainheads for new ideas or arbiters of what constitutes good science, they need to be viewed circumspectly. The caveat is the same as the one directed at neuroscience: Computational modeling won't help much unless one already has a well-formulated set of concepts about the phenomenology and logical "space" of cognition. If one has that, computational modeling can do much to formalize, to lend precision and clarity, to one's ideas.

Not surprisingly, most of the earliest successes of AI occurred in the field of symbolic logic and mathematics, where the development of theorem-proving programs held great promise for the future.[24] Far less successful were attempts to deal with more natural language and language-like behavior. After 40 years of intensive effort, some useful machine translation systems are now available, for example, but the road to the goal, let alone to the perfection of such systems, has been far longer and rougher than was originally thought.

Why should that be? The early belief that most of the subtleties of language can be captured in straightforward symbolic formulas, and therefore readily translated into symbol strings easily manipulated by machine, was of course naive. It reflected a view of language that was crude, insensitive, and outdated. It was in fact the residue of the "atomic" theory of facts, language, and knowledge propounded early on by Russell and Wittgenstein and so soon abandoned by them. The lesson of its inadequacies should have been learned by the machine translators, one would think, because language was found to be so recalcitrant to the sort of manipulation that, had the theory been even approximately correct, should have been routine and yielded usable translations of text. That did not happen, yet the idea that thinking, and the language in which it is expressed, can be captured in discrete symbolic "molecules" has a grip on the imagination of computer scientists. That is not to say that the computer implementation of logical, mathematical, and other "articulated" symbolical systems is open to any general objection; it is, rather, that this view of language as such is too crude and simplistic to get a handle on its everyday manifestations, let alone its imaginative, poetic, or even scientific uses.[25]

Enormous effort has gone into the creation of interactive programs that "understand" language—verbal instructions, questions, commands and the like—and that respond appropriately.[26] Language simulation shares the advantages and confronts the same difficulties as machine vision: careful analysis of the features to be simulated, the need for exact specification of the processes (the algorithms) that implement the simulation, and an unforgiving criterion of successful achievement in the actual machine output. It is often, and correctly, claimed that the relentless honesty of the computer output leaves no room for the sort of ambiguity, not to say fudging, that can occur when the predictions of a verbally stated model are evaluated.[27]

Criteria for the "Mental"

On the other side of the ledger is the danger of letting the startlingly realistic effects now possible obscure the essentials of what is going on in communication with a computer. The essential properties do not include the medium in which the activity occurs, the time scale of operation, or the type of language (artificial or natural) that is used to communicate. It also emphatically does not include the peripheral mimicry involved. Doubtless the more "natural" the appearance and behavior of the computer, the more we shall be inclined to imbue it with human-like motivation and skills; that, however, is a human weakness, not a rational or defensible attribution. At Disney World you may be intrigued by the ingenuity of the high-level mimicry achieved, but if you return next year and find it even more impressive, that is not going to persuade you (I hope!) that the figures of fun are in any important sense more real as people or animals than they were before. What is it then that makes the claim of strong AI in any way plausible? What are the essential properties shared by man and machine that could possibly justify such an apparently bizarre identification of the two?

Much ink has been spilled over this matter; the debate has been fast and furious, but we have no space to follow it in detail. There are actually two issues: First, is a behavioral criterion for ascribing mentality sufficient? Second, is the ascription of consciousness in the agent necessary? The answer to the first question is no; a detailed analysis and criticism of the claims made for the behavioral criterion of the so-called Turing test can be found elsewhere.[28] Let us turn to the second question: Is consciousness a defining property of mentation? Closely linked with that question, indeed an alternative way of putting it, is to ask whether understanding of what the agent is doing is a necessary condition for applying the term "mental" to cognitive (or seemingly cognitive) behavior, whether in man or machine. We have few ways of trying to grasp the nature of consciousness (which has not stopped many a philosopher from trying to explain it[29]), so the debate in the AI context has proceeded mainly on the basis of whether having understanding, or insight, into what one is doing is a defining property of the mental.

The best known modern discussion in favor of a positive answer to the question, indeed now something of a classic, is the Chinese Room thought experiment of John Searle.[30] He compares the case of a nonspeaker of Chinese who is taught to manipulate symbols to give "correct answers" in Chinese, without understanding their meaning, with the performance of a knowledgeable user of Chinese. Although their behavior may be identical, there is an obvious difference between them, although to pinpoint it with precision may be difficult. Searle claimed that it is the very same difference as that between the way a computer handles the problem and the way a knowledgeable human does so. He argued that however skilled and versatile a computer simulation of mental activity might be, it is still only a simulation, and is more like a map of the terrain covered than an embodiment of the real thing. Contrary to the claims of strong AI, the running of a program on a computer does not display one of the characteristics that must necessarily be present if we are to apply the term "mental" to an activity. It does not understand what it is doing, so cannot be a true form of mentation. A simulation is not a remanifestation, nor even a full-blooded representation in all relevant respects, of the event simulated. No one expects a simulated rain shower to cause a real flood, for example, and just so one should not expect a simulated mental event to display all the properties of human mentation.[31] The details of this insightful thought experiment can be found elsewhere.[32]

Many AI practitioners have claimed that existing programs understand stories, solve logical problems, and generally display mental states and activities like ours, so not surprisingly Searle's paper elicited vigorous and often hostile debate from the AI community.[33] His Chinese Room fantasy has been a focal point for discussion of the issue of awareness and understanding in machines for nearly two decades. The issue is by no means settled and has led to some interesting speculations on the relations of cognitive activity to its underlying brain activity, not least by Searle himself.[34] He insisted that whatever it is that distinguishes the mental accomplishment of understanding from the mere manipulation of symbols according to the rules of a program must depend on the "powers of the brain." These are evidently a biological "gift" in his view, but something that, we should note, itself requires explanation as obviously as the mental powers it is supposed to support. We shall have to postpone discussion until later chapters.

Artificial Intelligence and the Mind

For most AI researchers any cognitive question can be posed and answered in terms of (a) specific inputs, whether suitably transduced words, visual patterns, logical or mathematical formulae; (b) effective procedures (algorithms) for processing them; and (c) the resultant well-formed (categorized) outputs. Conceptually, all this was known to Pitts and McCulloch, and exploited in their brilliant work of the 1940s and 1950s on modular nets, symbolic logic, Universals, and pattern recognition. To the extent that questions of psychological interest can be posed in this way, there is no question that AI, computer vision, and cognate disciplines have made large contributions to cognitive science. What have they contributed to our understanding of mind? Has our conceptual clarity about the broader issues concerning machine "cognition" advanced at all beyond what was understood by Pitts and McCulloch?

It has done so in several ways. It is now realized that the sort of program sophistication needed to simulate even simple cognitive activities is far greater than the early enthusiasts believed. Second, it is understood that to be effective, such programs often need to be tailor-made to fit specific situations and types of problem solving, as in their application in so-called expert systems, but it is also well recognized that the way in which the computer solves problems (based, let us not forget, on the conceptual insights and programming skills of its operator) need not be, and generally is not, the same as the way humans do so. The computer may have access to a huge and essentially faultless database, which can be searched reliably at enormous speed. That is not the way humans develop great skill (in chess for example), although a good memory is generally needed. But what constitutes a good memory in a person is again orders of magnitude less than the capability of the biggest and fastest computers. A highly skilled chess or bridge player does not have available the "memory" resources of the best computer so how does he, or she, demonstrate comparable abilities (which in the computer depend on that superlative memory) even at the very highest level of achievement, as in the recent contests between Gary Kasparov, world chess champion, and "Big Blue," the very best in computer play? The human player seems to depend on "intuition," but what's that? Briefly, part of the answer is that humans "chunk" information into usable large patterns, and somehow are able to grasp how they can be marshalled for effective deployment. This is surely not the whole of what we mean by human intuition, but discussion of that topic must again be deferred to a later chapter.

The drive to provide computer simulations of human mentation is strong. Take, for example, the ambitious attempt to create a "general purpose cognitive machine" of Alan Newell, a leader in the AI field almost from its inception. His SOAR system aims to simulate a wide variety of human cognitive performances, and claims its justification precisely in the extent to which, by a variety of criteria, it succeeds in doing so.[35.] But one has to ask what the motivation for such an enterprise is. Does it lead to general insight into human behavior? Does it do anything useful, as an expert system for traffic control or inventory management might do? Does it lead to new hypotheses about how machines might, for example, lead to better understanding of muscular control, on the one hand, or the guidance of speech by internal constraints like grammatical rules, on the other? Does it help us to understand mind? In every case the answer is No. Evidently the real motivation for producing SOAR, and for similar systems, is metaphysical. It is the desire to show in principle that machines can do everything minds can do.

Newell (now unfortunately deceased) took the basic AI stance for granted, perhaps was even a champion of strong AI, but did not address the question of how far this sort of enterprise can yield a satisfactory explanation of cognition.[36] To that extent he was quite typical of computer scientists who work in cognition; demonstration of cognitive-like behavior in their machines is sufficient justification for what they do.

The same remarks apply to the newer work on *parallel distributed processing* and neural networks, which aims to implement computation on hardware that shares many more features in common with the "wetware" of the brain than does the classical digital computer. One might say that in this field the spirit of inquiry and the explicit motivation for biological relevance found in the early research of Pitts and McCulloch and of Hebb have resurfaced quite strongly. This approach, despite many impressive practical successes, still adds little that is new to the metaphysical debate concerning strong AI.[37]

The computational approach of AI fits well with the information-processing models of cognitive psychologists, as well as the hope of neuroscientists that studying the machinery of the brain is going to reveal the desired answers about the nature of mind. In all three cases mind is conceived of in the deterministic, clockwork tradition, and has little to contribute to the creative, idealistic, humanistic view of human nature.

Language and Mind

We turn now to the study of language, one of the oldest themes in the quest to understand the mind. Again we can afford but a brief review of its contribution to cognitive science. As with most things in Western culture, the origins can be traced to the thinkers of classical Greece; the Socratic dialogues are one of the first systematic explorations of the uses of language of which we know.[38] In modern times the general study of languages—linguistics as it is called, to distinguish it from more specific matters like the investigation of the grammar and vocabulary of a particular language—has undergone a true revolution (see below). The study of language within psychology paralleled the work going on in the broader field of linguistics, but only since the time of the revolution have the two converged strongly.

The first linguistic inquiries started with the cataloguing of facts about how language is used, and especially with reports of how it develops in the young. For many decades there was little in the way of what today would be recognized as a theory of language and language development in either linguistics or psychology; everything remained at a descriptive stage. The first theory to make much impact was the behaviorist theory of learning by classical conditioning (see chapter 2) applied to word learning; the further development of language then proceeded by an admixture of classical and "instrumental" conditioning, the latter being a version of the theory of learning by "drive reduction" (only those responses are repeated that in the past led to reward in terms of the satisfaction of a drive like hunger).[39] There is no doubt that the acquisition of single words and sentences may occur in this way, but that is a far cry (punishingly so, one might say!) from the question of how language as such is brought to life in the individual child, as we shall see.[40]

The behaviorist tradition became strong in linguistics at the same time it was dominant in experimental psychology, accompanied by a cautious, but still valuable, comparative study and taxonomy of many of the world's languages.[41] Linguists and psychologists, far from holding their collective breaths in anticipation of new ideas, were perhaps rather complacent. They certainly were unprepared for the tidal wave that was to break over them in the revolution that engulfed linguistics and had such a profound effect on cognitive science generally.

In contrast to the behaviorist position, the layperson's view is that language is at once a most precious spiritual heritage, our chief instrument of communication, the very basis of culture, as well as a tool of workaday life. We tend to feel that if we really knew what language is we would be closer to understanding ourselves. The traditional linguist's approach was more prosaic, as embodied in the dictum: Language is a path running from sound to meaning, and linguistics is the exploration of that path. Even on this view, linguistics should eventually give us a true window on the mind, and that is what the revolution aimed to do.

The Components of Language

The following are accepted linguistic categories, the stepping stones on the path:

Phonetics studies the sound signals that are the acoustical carriers of spoken language.

Phonology studies the aggregating of phonetic elements into linguistically proper units. The phoneme is the smallest cohesive unit of speech; it consists of what we commonly understand as a single speech sound, like the different vowels and consonants.

Morphology (the study of form) describes and catalogues the clustering of phonemes into meaningful units—syllables and words. It is remarkable that from so small a set of phonemes (there are about 40), thousands—indeed hundreds of thousands—of words can be generated in English, although any individual will know (that is, recognize) only a moderate fraction of them and use even less.

Syntax studies the way words are strung together into "correct"—that is, allowable and expressive—sequences. These are typically sentences that obey the conventional rules of grammar; but the category includes other sequences that are meaningful even though they do not exactly fit the definition of a fully grammatical sentence—the language of young children is a case in point.

Semantics is the study of meaning: how words and sentences are used to convey meaning, how intended meaning determines the form and interpretation of an utterance. Semantics as a discipline, however, is not limited to questions of verbal definition but encompasses also questions relating form to substance, symbol to symbolized, syntactical species to intended meaning.

Through its early behavioristic phase linguistics had little to contribute to the "fuzzy" far end of the path from phonetics to semantics. In attempting to be hardheaded it ignored many of language's most distinctive features. This was, as we now see, at the cost of losing all that is most exciting, most intimate, and above all most insightful about this putative window on the mind.

The Revolution

The tidal wave that swept away the positivistic attitudes prevalent in linguistics (and experimental psychology) hit in the mid-1950s and was caused by one man, Noam Chomsky. He alone can be credited with starting the revolution in linguistic science that in turn played a leading role in the development of cognitive science. As he put it, he wanted to grasp the nature of meaning—the exciting stuff that had been ignored for so long.

Before him the successes in linguistics had tended to be comparative, technical, and unexciting, however promising as empirical science. Chomsky's success in standing linguistics on its head consisted in demonstrating how to bring the good stuff in again, not just as an adjunct to the structural description of language, but as a set of principles at the very heart of what language is. He proposed the concept of a transformational-generative grammar, a system from which correct English (for example) sentences and their allowable transforms can be obtained. The idea of transformations and transforms as such were not novel in linguistics,[42] but Chomsky's insistence on their central role in understanding the very basis of language—of all languages—was. Especially compelling was the notion that there is a core structure for every valid sentence; the hope was that the core structure could somehow be identified with the meaning of the sentence. Here was the enticing prospect of getting a handle on the meaning of meaning and thus, it seemed, opening up a powerful avenue for exploration of mind, no less. One needs to be careful about putting words into Chomsky's mouth in the expression of these ideas, to go beyond what his theory claimed, yet it is clear that even if this is not quite what Chomsky had in mind, it certainly is what—even if by a process of creative misunderstanding—shot him to the forefront of cognitive science.[43]

Was all the excitement justified? Consider first a simple sentence like: *The dog sees the man.* Then consider an alternative sentence that "says the same thing": *The man is seen by the dog.* These are like the atomic sentences discussed earlier and, like them, express elementary facts about the world (true or false). In this case they express the same fact, so there must be a core meaning that is being expressed in different ways. The task, and the challenge, was to find a grammar that will generate all correct sentences, and only correct (allowable) ones, and their valid (equivalent) transforms. Chomsky proposed a set of rules that (we shall take here on trust) really do this job of generation and transformation. The hope was, certainly among many of his followers, that further investigation of the system, and especially of the concept of "deep structure," would lead to new and illuminating results concerning language as a window on the mind.

A pivotal feature of Chomsky's grammar is that since it is an "open-ended" generative system, an effectively infinite number of valid sentences can be produced. Despite such multiplicity and diversity, native speakers of the language (and others sufficiently well versed in it) can tell without hesitation or detailed scrutiny whether a sentence is valid or not; valid, that is, as a correct grammatical sequence. Hence, "The storm promulgated the foetid prevarications of the incontinent amanuensis," is recognized as grammatically correct and thus allowable, even if the hearer does not know the meanings of half the words. The sentence is indeed pretty much nonsense. However, "Without by bone interference blocked inside gut found," is seen to be nongrammatical, although the words are familiar and even suggest a topic to which they might refer. We are adept at recognizing grammatically correct sentences and are good at producing them too; in many cases (I hardly believe in most cases, as some linguists suggest) they are entirely novel productions. We produce them effortlessly, and correctly; we are extremely good self-monitors in most situations. Winston Churchill's (good) advice to speech-givers is said to have been: "Open your mouth and start speaking. As soon as you recognize that you have completed a sentence grammatically, sit down."

What is the mechanism of this effortless recognition and production? How is it done? Chomsky makes a sharp distinction between competence and performance in language, and his main, indeed almost his exclusive interest, is in the former. The structure of language, he claimed, is not contingent, arbitrary, or determined in its deeper properties by local cultural and educational custom or precedent. The structure of language is the same in all human communities, and evidently has always been so since the appearance of *Homo sapiens* on earth. There is a universal grammar to which the varieties of language in the world are as the branches and twigs on a tree. What gives them life and substance is the fact that they are derivative from that one source, which is innate, preprogrammed, and a common heritage of all human beings and societies. It is a property of mind. Let us be more careful; it is the propensity, the disposition to acquire and use language—actually an aspect of competence—that is inborn. Obviously the particular language or languages an individual learns depends on contingencies of time and place of rearing. These determine performance. But all normal human infants, given even a minimally helpful environment, learn to use and understand language, and do so with incredible facility.

If there is this universal disposition to language, it seems that it must be part of our biological heritage.[44] Chomsky argued that language competence is a functionally discrete entity, like a limb or a lobe of the brain, but this is too coarse an analogy. It is true that parts of the human anatomy and physiology are highly specialized for the recognition and production of language, so the more apt comparison might be to a sensory-perceptual system like vision or hearing (see earlier section on neuroscience). In those systems it is not sufficient to know what the anatomical and physiological support for them may be; to understand them requires a conceptual, functional understanding that goes well beyond knowledge of the substrate. The same is true of language.[45]

Well, one might ask, what's all the fuss about? Chomsky's ideas on syntactical structure and transformation are an improvement on what went before—but are they revolutionary? We surely didn't need Chomsky to inform us that all human societies have language, or that all children learn their mother tongue with facility and accuracy. Cogent arguments about the special properties of language as a unique human attribute can be found in the writings of the early Greek philosophers and in more than a few places thereafter. Nativism, and rationalism, have a long and proud record in the Western intellectual tradition. So why have Chomsky's ideas had such a profound impact, not just in linguistics, but in cognitive science generally? The promise of "deep structure" as the key to unlock the magic world of mind has gone largely unfulfilled;[46] there must be other reasons for the ideas to have proved so compelling, so fruitful. Perhaps the main one is that he, like Hebb before him, hit upon a conceptual scheme for which the academic world was ripe and waiting. He was influential because he forged a new path in somewhat familiar, but still inadequately charted, territory. While doing this he demolished the conventional account of language and language acquisition with formidable power.[47]

Effects of the Revolution

Chomsky's fresh approach caught the imagination of a number of younger psychologists. His theory cried out for detailed empirical confirmation and pointed the way to promising new fields of investigation. Finding out how well the new transformational-generative model fit the data (or was it the other way 'round?) presented a great new opportunity; revising accepted views of human mental capacities was another, as was the search for the biological foundations of language. Investigating the development of linguistic skills was a fourth, and in some ways the most compelling. It was certainly one of the most successful in terms of empirical investigation giving support to Chomsky's ideas. The research brought out, in an entirely new way, the sheer creativity and virtuosity displayed in the way language drives human cognition when the opportunity arises in early development.

Startlingly supportive evidence was found especially on the way children first begin to speak. They do so with extraordinary speed within a fairly narrow window of opportunity; there are naturally individual differences, but the consistencies are much more impressive than the differences. Children grasp the inner form of language, as von Humboldt called it, in a far from haphazard way, and very early on show signs of shaping their utterances in conformity with structural principles of great sophistication. It is also certain that this language is not learned by rote. Novel word combinations and attempts at generalization appear, such as the use of plural words and the wrong construction of irregular forms (*mouses* for *mice* and *goed* instead of *went,* for example).[48]

All this happens with immense speed and panache, like a tropical storm flooding the infant's budding cognitive world, and it does so all over the Earth in much the same way, in nations with high and low educational and intellectual standards, in every stratum of society and level of intelligence within them. Getting language is, indeed, a universal gift, the true mark of humanity. What a far cry from the old notion that it's all done by a grinding process of conditioning! That is not to say that reinforcement is unimportant, only that it is but a small part of the total picture.

There are other ways to observe the wonders of the creative capacity for language, such as in the appearance of pidgin, or even more remarkably the creation of a creole, a "new" but fully fledged language created by children (initially) out of the elements of other existing languages to which they are exposed. The new research on language is a cornerstone of cognitive science, and makes for fascinating reading; we have scarcely skimmed the surface. An engaging, although hardly dispassionate, tour through the territory by a follower of Chomsky can be found in Pinker's *The Language Instinct.*[49]

A very important facet of psycholinguistics is the concern to understand the relations between language and thinking. Most people express their thoughts to themselves in a sort of private discourse that has been called *mentalese.* But to conclude that language is the necessary and only vehicle of thought would be wrong; several lines of evidence deny it. There is a vigorous and well-documented domain of studies of nonverbal thought processes in which mental imagery (visual, auditory, tactile) plays a dominant role.[50] We cannot pursue the matter here but will return to it in later chapters.

Assessing the Effects of the Revolution

Pinker claims that the Chomskian goal has been reached: The modern field of linguistics has given us new tools to dissect, reconstruct, and thus comprehend the nature of mind. If all the answers are not yet in, we are assured that in principle they certainly can be found by methods presently available to the research community. It is a faith reminiscent of some of the bolder claims of neuroscience and AI research; as in those cases, we should inquire whether the faith is justified.

There can be no question about the impact of Chomsky's ideas on the study of cognition; "arresting," "insightful," "ground-breaking," even "thrilling," are words that have been used to convey some of the flavor of his revolution. Yet a revolution seldom meets all the expectations of the faithful; some accounting of where it has succeeded, where it may have fallen short, is needed. This exercise does not address the merits of Chomsky's linguistic theories as such; that is a technical matter to be settled by experts in the field.[51] We are concerned with a more general question: Have Chomsky's ideas solved any fundamental questions in cognitive science, in the sense of breaking new ground in our understanding of mind?

The first beneficial effect, as we have seen, was to undermine the powerful habits of thought promulgated by behaviorism and other "peripheralist" schools of thought about mental life. Chomsky's insistence on the innate properties of language, and thus of mind, together with the facts of the universality and generativity of language brought to light by him, provided the demolition team.

Second, the new rationalistic account of language encouraged a generation of psycholinguists to investigate language from a fresh point of view. One major aspect of this new work was that it turned from the laboratory back to the field; it looked (as had an earlier tradition) at the actual ways language is learned and used, by children, in different social and cultural contexts, in novel milieus. This is not to say, of course, that experimental studies in the laboratory were lacking—far from it. But the most forceful discoveries (discoveries, it must be said, that were under our very noses and there for the taking) were made in natural settings. Language is universal, has a remarkably complex but well articulated structure, and is wonderfully creative and spontaneous.

Third, Chomsky's views gave encouragement to research on the innateness of language production and thus on its biological-physiological substrate, also on the question of origin in terms of evolutionary adaptations. This in turn brought further respectability to research on the question of language, or language-like behavior, in subhuman species.

Has all this helped us to understand what language is? The new Chomskian perspective lends insight to the study of language, but does it in any sense explain it? The answer is the irritating fork—both Yes and No. In this case, however, the emphasis is on the negative reply. The fact is, we already have to know the essentials of what a language is before we can identify and describe one, let alone study it in detail or from a particular theoretical viewpoint. In that sense the study, even the Chomskian study, of a language or of linguistics presupposes a conceptual framework presently existing in our cognitive, cultural—yes, even our linguistic— heritage. Seen from that angle, we don't discover from research what a language is, we must know the answer to that question before we start; research enlightens us on some of the properties of language and how it does its job. That is no mean feat, but it does not shake the bedrock of our understanding of language nor our faith in what our folk psychology (the practical wisdom of common sense) tells us about the mind. Rather, it supports and extends that understanding and our faith in our intuitions about language.

To make this point clear, consider the study of language in chimpanzees. There would be absolutely no point to such study, indeed we could scarcely conceive of it, if we did not already know pretty clearly what a language is. Studying the behavior of chimpanzees will never throw light on the nature of language as such, however much it may enlighten us about chimpanzees and their ability to manipulate symbolic tokens. The same is true of infant studies; unless we have the right categories and the relevant conceptual framework in place, such study would be fruitless, indeed meaningless. Take one step further; *any* sort of linguistic study would be impossible without that requisite minimal background. Do Chomskian studies expose cracks in the bedrock? To continue the metaphor, do they expose fault lines or rattle the furniture in the house of words? I think not.

Modern linguists have argued for the importance of the study of the biological substrate of language, a matter of undoubted importance. But the only theoretically strong pronouncement to have come from that corner is the insistence that, because it is (by definition) a biological-physiological matter, that substrate must be a product of Darwinian evolution. This scarcely rates as a hot new item of information or insight. It is also not without problems, but we shall defer discussion of them to chapter 8.

So, despite all the enthusiasm and partisan arm-waving, I conclude that linguistics in its modern Chomskian form, although it has revealed many a treasure, has not brought about any profoundly new understanding of mind. It has brought in more than a whiff of fresh air, but it has not fulfilled the early promise that many a cognitive psychologist expected of it, of being a stiff and steady breeze by which to sail into new mental territory. Whether Chomsky himself had quite those same high expectations, or whether he considers them met, are questions we do not need to answer.[52] To the extent that his followers espouse the biological-evolutionary thesis of language origin, they are following the near-universal trend in contemporary science toward material and physical explanations. Nothing new there.

To sum up: There is nothing in the new linguistic doctrine to question, much less to challenge, the established orthodoxy of science, the metaphysics of materialism. The discovered *facts* of generative language, the sheer creativity and virtuosity that its study have revealed, do demand some radically different ways of thinking about mind, some as yet unmanifested, novel perspective. Linguistics presents an unfulfilled promise, but also an as yet unanswered challenge.

Cognitive Philosophy

Our look at the fifth and final strand in the fabric can be brief. The stance of modern Western philosophy is predominantly analytic:[53] To follow up on an earlier theme, philosophers in general, and philosophers of science in particular, tend to be systematizers, analysts, guardians of consistency and clarity. As to the metaphysics of science, they have seldom been innovators, tending to follow what the science itself promulgates.

The generally positivistic trend in the science of the early twentieth century had its counterpart in philosophy. The very influential early work of Russell and Wittgenstein on logic and language gave rise to logical positivism and accompanied promotion of the principle of verification, described in chapter 1. Their metaphysical conception of atomic facts and sentences was soon thrown out as being much too narrow, to be replaced, largely under Wittgenstein's leadership, by a far more complex and subtle school of philosophy known as linguistic analysis. In a nutshell, this brand of philosophy is based on the idea that most philosophical puzzles are generated by the idiosyncrasies of our use, and misuse, of language. Applied to science, it appears in the thesis that scientific language, and the concepts it generates and applies, is similarly subject to misuse and misdirection, which it is the job of philosophy to correct and clarify. It is the self-selected task of philosophers of cognition, too.

Russell and Wittgenstein made profound discoveries, especially early on, that have influenced cognitive science in many ways. We have already discussed how the formalization of logic and language affected the development of AI. The distinction between fact-stating sentences and rule-giving (definitional) sentences, together with the development of so-called truth-functional logic, was also seminal in providing fruitful insight into the philosophical analysis of language. Unfortunately we can do no more than mention such matters here.[54]

Three Cognitive Philosophies

To illustrate cognitive philosophy's approach, we shall review briefly in chronological order the contributions of three outstanding but very different individuals in the modern era: Gilbert Ryle, Mario Bunge, and Daniel Dennett.

Ryle was an English philosopher whose magnum opus was published in 1949,[55] interestingly enough the very time at which other landmark contributions in cognitive science such as Hebb's and Gibson's appeared (chapter 2). Ryle was essentially a defender of behaviorism, albeit behaviorism of a particularly clever and subtle variety. His avowed aim was to exorcise the Cartesian view of mind—Cartesian dualism—and to replace it with a different, less misleading form of discourse, an aim very much in the then-dominant tradition of linguistic analysis. His main positive thesis was that psychological statements are basically dispositional. For example, the statement that Fred is ambitious can be analyzed into a set of statements about what Fred is disposed to do under various circumstances. Ryle's book contains much of interest, and many enlightening distinctions and comments are made on memory, perception, and language. Nevertheless his systematic treatment of psychological concepts in dispositional, behavioral terms was a failure; it confused the issue of what a claim about mental phenomena means with statements about the evidence that supports the claim. Despite this, Ryle's thesis did an admirable job of bringing to the fore many conceptual confusions about how we use psychological terms and provided some useful recipes for avoiding them in future. Rather influential at the time, Ryle's program now receives scant attention. It illustrates perfectly, however, the sort of conceptual contemplation, analysis, and clarification philosophers can provide in cognitive science.

Second, we have the philosophy of Mario Bunge. Physicist turned philosopher of science, he represents the hard-nosed biological approach to psychology, and is in particular a champion of the brand of physiological psychology associated with Donald Hebb and McGill University. His stance is forthright, brisk, and somewhat dogmatic. It has been presented often, and in many different guises; one of the most accessible, most general, and most readable is his *Philosophy of Psychology.*[56] He contrasts neuropsychology, as he terms this brand of biologically based psychology, with other theoretical systems, ending up with the assertion that it is the only truly empirically based scientific psychology. I shall not go into the details, which have been debated at length elsewhere.[57] The major theoretical stance is the one we came across in discussing the merits of neuroscience, namely that the necessary and sufficient conditions for understanding psychological functions and capacities is the identification of brain processes associated with them. In one very characteristic passage Bunge states: "We also wish to know what pain, love, and thought are, that is, what are the neural processes we call pain, love, and thought. " As I pointed out in rejoinder, this surely is begging the question: Unless we already know what pain, love, and thought are from personal experience—interpreted and labeled within the categories of folk psychology—there would be absolutely no way in which any neuropsychological correlate or theory of those states would make sense. If we wish to redefine pain, love, and thought in purely neuropsychological terms, as has indeed been proposed, that is another matter; it is logically possible, but does nothing to enlighten us on the nature of the psychological attributes in question.

Third, I shall touch on the work of Daniel Dennett. In a long series of publications he has addressed the problem of intentionality.[58] It is the problem of dealing with concepts like belief, reason, mood, motive, and foresight in a scientific manner. Others, like Ryle and Bunge, attempt this head-on by redefining intentional concepts in terms of something else (dispositions and brain states, for these two) but Dennett takes that to be too crude a tactic. Instead, he argues that in giving scientific explanations of psychological matters we cannot avoid using intentional concepts and language, but to do so does not commit us to any particular view of the mind as mysterious agent, or to the tenets of folk psychology either. Instead, he argues, we commit ourselves only to the intentional stance. What does that mean?

When a behaving system is very simple, be it machine or biological organism, it is possible to describe its structure and function by enumerating the basic elements and finding how they interact. Talk of neurons and synapses, or physical switches and their connections, is all that's needed. As soon as things get a bit complicated, however, we start naturally to adopt a sort of generalizing shorthand in which those individual elements no longer figure. Instead we "chunk" the activity into "modules" and talk of "higher level" processes of storage, sequential operation, and control. Machines as well as biological organisms display goal-directed activity, storage of information, and utilization of rules. Why not shortcut to the *natural categories* (a useful term coined by Eleanor Rosch [1973]) that obviously apply equally well to both? This means that we attribute in either case aims, memory, and thought—the categories of the discipline of psychology. To use such language is to adopt the intentional stance. It commits us to nothing metaphysically; it is merely a convenience, employing a useful feature of our linguistic heritage, nothing more.

One might say, then, that rather than try to refute the conceptual apparatus of common sense (folk psychology), Dennett deconstructs it into a harmless species of convenient fiction. Real people, and modern computing machines (among others) are just too complicated to deal with in terms of their low-level components, so we invent ways of capturing and describing their behavior that do not refer, except very indirectly, to those components. The physical substrate is divorced from what the system is designed to do, and intentional language is both the tool and the result. The analogy between brain and mind, on the one hand, and computer hardware (the nuts and bolts of the machine) and software (the programs that run the machine), on the other, has been a favorite among cognitive scientists from the beginning. Dennett is thus following a well-worn tradition when he invokes the distinction, in a rather roundabout way, to justify the intentional stance, whether applied to man or machine.

This is a bald summary of Dennett's position. He is a master of expository innuendo and subtle argument—of humor too—but *au fond* this is the meat of his message: When you ascribe intentionality, you are using a serendipitous feature of language that implies no metaphysical overtones; it is merely a convenience. Having said that, Dennett leaves little doubt that he believes the future of cognitive science belongs to AI.[59]

Here we have three philosophers who base their positions on what three distinct branches of cognitive science have achieved. They analyze, clarify, and reconcile, but without making the attempt to forge new substantive theory (or metaphysics) in any of them. Each is dazzled by a different facet of cognitive science—behaviorism, neuroscience, and artificial intelligence, respectively—but no one of their philosophies affords any new insight into the nature of mind, which is what we are after. Rather, they polish and reinforce different aspects of what is really a single metaphysical position, the absolute belief in materialism as the sole basis for understanding and explaining mind.

This is a blunt, even peremptory and dismissive assessment. The arguments needed to bolster it adequately and to justify it in detail can be found elsewhere.[60]

Language as Agent

There have been other philosophical contributions of greater originality and of more help in coming to an understanding of mind, contributions by philosophers not usually identified with cognitive science. We shall encounter some of them later; for now I shall mention just one, whose insights on language point very strongly in the direction we need to go. In 1975 J. L. Austin published a book called *How to Do Things with Words*. Following (like most twentieth-century English-speaking philosophers) in the footsteps of Wittgenstein,[61] Austin argued eloquently and persuasively that we (philosophers that is, as well as psychologists and others concerned with language) have been far too timid in describing the functions of language and ascribing to them a role in human affairs. Fact-stating discourse is important, even of pre-eminent importance for creating and disseminating the works of science, but there are other uses of words that have suffered neglect. Words are used to issue instructions, command attention, make a promise, indulge a fantasy, plead an excuse, express eternal love, and so on. These are language acts. They guide, motivate, actively promote change and response, as well as communicate facts and opinions; generally they are the agents of expression and transfer, not just of information, but of intentions, of purposeful behavior. They are indeed the primary tools of our personal and cultural life. Without language acts, could there be such a thing as cognitive science? Well, once again, is that not just a rather pedantic statement of a question whose answer is obvious? Once presented, it seems obvious enough, but it was not obvious to the forerunners of cognitive philosophy nor apparently to its contemporary exponents. The consequences for the way language should be treated in cognitive science, however, are drastic, if not revolutionary. A heady word that; we shall get to attempt its justification in chapter 9.

Austin's thesis can be stated as the claim that words are the vehicles of human intention and action; when used by individuals they define social as well as personal character, ingenuity, and obligation, dominance and acquiescence, freedom of action, moral tone, legal status, and so on. These matters are only understood when we see them in the rich social and personal context of what Wittgenstein characterized as life's games. As he insisted, language is one of the major instruments for carrying out moves in the game. Perhaps Austin did not quite put it in this way, but one can even think of words as servants of the will, an unpopular—indeed an almost nonexistent—concept in cognitive science. But the will is what's important in human practical and social life, and the will is conditioned by thought and belief, as an earlier breed of psychologist well understood; we cannot dismiss it lightly. This also sustains the idea that words and language—the vehicle for the expression of mood, intention, and action—are much nearer the source of human creativity (as the newer research on language indeed demonstrates), even the feeling of identity that is so strong in the normal individual, than is given credence in the dissection and re-definition of concepts that is the stock-in-trade of modern analytical philosophy. To get closer to that source is the object of our inquiry; to form a picture of man that, as Koestler would have it, is decidedly less limiting and drab than the one traditional cognitive philosophy has to offer. This is the way he put it in one of his most famous essays on the predicament of modern man:

> And I do not believe that we can formulate even the simplest questions, much less arrive at a diagnosis, without the help of the sciences of life. But it must be a true science of life, not the antiquated slot-machine model based on the naively mechanistic world-view of the nineteenth century. We shall not be able to ask the right questions until we have replaced that rusty idol by a new, broader conception of the living organism.[62]

In the following chapters we shall attempt to take some steps in that direction. Up to now we have followed, however briefly, a path that outlines the grammar of mind. It is time to go beyond this to enquire into the drama of mind.

4

The Science of Mind

O, do not lose the drama of knowledge
In striving after the grammar of knowledge.

RUDOLF STEINER

Cognitive Science's Mind

So far I have sketched the established disciplines of cognitive science, in brief out-line only, to give the flavor of their separate claims to the understanding of mind. Each has its distinctive approach, but with a good deal of mutual borrowing and in-teraction. Together they have converged on what can be termed the *Standard Model of Mind* in cognitive science, or the standard model, as we have called it. We can characterize the convergence on that model in terms of its most basic features, ones that are accepted pretty well without question in the cognitive science community as being both necessary and sufficient for an understanding of mind. We might even call them *axioms* of cognitive science, given their dominating place in the thinking of cognitive scientists. Collectively they define the metaphysics of cognitive sci-ence. The ones that hold unquestioned sway are the axioms of

(a) Neural substrate. Mental activity of every sort is a function of brain processes (that is, primarily the interactions of neurons and their supporting structures).

(b) Reducibility. The physiology of the brain (i.e., all observable processes in the brain) will eventually be understood in terms of chemical and physical laws, so that ultimately statements about mental activity will be reducible without remainder to statements couched in physical terms.

(c) Unlimited access. Conscious activities are mental processes, but do not exhaust that category. Cognitive science is concerned with mentation (all "mental activity") and is not limited to investigation of conscious states.

(d) Biological evolution. The brain is a product of the natural biological world, developed under the same evolutionary pressures as the rest of the body, and is to be understood in those terms.

(e) Biological emergence. When brains (under the pressures of evolutionary change) became large enough, and complex enough mental activity—including consciousness—emerged as a means of coping with an increasingly diverse and demanding environment.

(f) Mental emergence. Mental activity, a product of brain activity, is also to be understood *solely* as a product of the natural history of that development.

These seem to be the core statements of the standard model, but the recent computational trend in cognitive science adds a few more that are very widely accepted, the axioms of

(g) Machine architecture. The goal of cognitive science is to determine what sort of machine the brain is, and what the design principles are that underlie its components and their mutual interactions—that is to say, to discover its correct functional architecture.

(h) Mental architecture. In view of axioms (a) and (b) above, axiom (g) implies that the successful conclusion of (any part of) its program ensures that the relevant *mental* architecture will also be revealed thereby.

(i) Computability. New and existing theory must meet the goal of being explicit enough to be expressed in terms of *efficient procedures* for implementation (i.e., as algorithms), either in abstract, formal terms, or as simulations on a suitable machine. Theory must be *computational.*

The axioms stated so far by no means limit the methods of empirical search and discovery available to cognitive science; but we have the important ancillary, the axiom of

(j) Respectability (or pragmatism or orthodoxy). The criteria for acceptable investigation are pragmatic: Are the results public, reliable, and repeatable? Are they intrinsically interesting and do they jibe with the generally accepted canons of research and theory in the field?

In summary: The orthodox view in cognitive science, the standard model, treats the mind as a product of brain function and of the evolution of that wonderfully complex organ under the demanding priorities of natural selection. All mental activities, whether conscious or not, can be understood in principle on that basis, and the job of cognitive science is to find appropriate explanations in those terms. In recent decades the aims and methods have become more and more "computational," to the extent that this is now something of a slogan, even though often there is no clear denotation for the word. It is certainly obvious though that computers have become an increasingly important item in our box of research tools. So, on the one hand, we have a consensus that mental activity is no more than the expression of particular biological exigencies, on the other, that it is just a machine-like phenomenon. In all this, have we perhaps lost the mind?

Nowhere in the standard model is the mind identified as a *thing,* or a *substance,* but rather as a set of functions or activities. The tendency to *reify* is ubiquitous in our attempts to understand a "something" that we can name but that is not itself a thing (*res*); consider the widespread use of the term *intelligence,* as if this were a commodity to be measured and assessed for quality like a bag of beans. It has often enough been pointed out, per contra, that intelligence is an abstraction, a shorthand way of referring to the demonstration by individuals of skilled performance, usually of an intellectual or abstract problem-solving variety. Those can of course be measured and assessed, without implying any particular theory as to what intelligence may be. It is likewise so in the standard model; mind is the congeries of functions and activities that by common consent (more or less) are agreed to manifest mental attributes like "goal directedness," "inner control," and, most generally, "intentionality." But remember that naming those attributes does not in itself explain them.

That stance allows one to evade the awkward but tenacious question of *substance dualism* (the ghost in the machine), a matter to which we shall return, but precipitates another equally difficult problem, namely the question of the experience of the self, the I, and how it can be handled within the standard model. This seems to be inextricably tied up with the question of consciousness, how to define it, and what role it plays in mental activity. Is it in the driver's seat, as some have argued, or does it play some lesser part, even down to the possibility that it is a mere epiphenomenon, an illusory and narcissistic accompaniment to the real work of the brain? The standard model, as we have seen, adopts an uncompromisingly materialistic view of things, if by materialistic we mean the view that the mental can all be accounted for by the brain's physiology. That, however, begs a very fundamental question. As Lockwood puts it:

> Regarded from the standpoint of physical science, the most puzzling thing about consciousness . . . is the fact that it exists at all. There is on the face of it absolutely nothing in the laws of physics and chemistry, as currently understood, that is capable of accounting for the extraordinary capacity of that lump of matter that we call the brain—once likened by Alan Turing to "a lump of porridge"—to sustain an "inner life." This is not to deny that some progress has been made in explaining how the brain encodes and processes the information that arrives from the sense organs, and how it controls behavior. What remains mysterious is why this complex *physico-chemical* activity should be associated with any subjective states at all: why, in Timothy Sprigge's memorable phrase, there should be a "what it is like to *be*" you or me.[1]

Even within the context of a materialist view of mind there is little agreement among cognitive scientists on these matters, let alone an accepted single doctrine of the self. But the questions raised by the plainly evident fact of the occurrence of consciousness, awareness, sentience, and the importance we impute to them, can scarcely be avoided, and cognitive philosophers have tackled them in a number of different ways. One influential but currently unpopular view, espoused nevertheless by two very eminent leaders in their respective fields, a neuroscientist and a philosopher of science, actually argues for a form of dualism, despite the anathema in which that idea is generally held.[2] In their view the self is a "given"; we know it and many of its properties, by immediate acquaintance. That much is unproblematical.

Difficulties only arise when we try to relate that immediate and intimate experience of the self to what modern neuroscience tells us about the brain.

At the other end of the spectrum of positions are the "bundle" theorists who claim (following the Scottish philosopher David Hume) that the concept of the individual self, or ego, is a simple delusion; all the evidence we have about continuity of self is due to memory:

> According to the Bundle Theory, we can't explain either the unity of consciousness at any time, or the unity of a whole life, by referring to a person. Instead we must claim that there are long series of different mental states and events—thoughts, sensations, and the like—each series being what we call one life. Each series is unified by various kinds of causal relation, such as the relations that hold between experiences and the later memory of them. Each series is thus like a bundle tied up with string.[3]

It is true enough that we can't point to a single *thing* that holds the bundle together, and cases of evidently separate streams of mutually unaware consciousness in split-brain persons complicate the story, but it is also true that ordinary consciousness occurs by the grace of brains, and both present awareness and the awareness of things past do require an intact brain. Brains alone (or more generally, bodies) will not suffice on their own, however. What do we make of the discontinuous nature of self-awareness, as evidenced in sleep and general anesthesia? The problems pointed out by bundle theorists are real enough, but their proposed solution really does nothing to resolve the question of the unity of consciousness. Split-brain cases, where one may have to account for two bundles rather than one, do not point to a solution or bring the problem into sharper focus; the problem becomes far more tenuous and ambiguous. There *are* in certain respects two separate brains rather than one when the corpus callosum is not functioning (the split brain), but the sense that there are two separate personalities, two selves, is by no means as clear.[4] If two pieces of string rather than one are required for the split brain patient, according to bundle theory, that merely lays emphasis on the fact that the nature of the string, simple brain function or not, remains yet a total mystery that cries out for explication.[5]

Other notions are not so radical as the bundle theory, or so crude. Many find the somewhat deconstructive arabesques of philosophers like Dennett more to their liking; the I is not a single "thing," nor is the mind for that matter, but we can weave patterns of ideas around them that will allow their properties to emerge, as it were, like a sort of bas-relief against the background of more conventional conceptions drawn from neuroscience and AI.[6] We shall have occasion to review these matters more fully in later chapters. For now we make note of the fact that I, self, and consciousness are unresolved problems, not to say embarrassments, for cognitive science; most of its practitioners deal with them by neglect or other forms of denial ("pseudo-problems" comes to mind—it's difficult to avoid the word and what it connotes, is it not?)

Where the mainstream of cognitive science fears to tread, other thinkers, at times brave, on occasion brilliant, have been willing to venture beyond the pale of the established wisdom. I shall describe two of these essays and the ways in which they can extend our concepts of mind, self, and consciousness. Their perspectives are different, and the extent to which the axioms of the standard model are accepted, challenged, or ignored, is certainly different. But they do tend to hold in common, along with the layman (and, I believe, all but a few of the most ruthless of hard-nosed cognitive scientists), a firm belief in the vivid reality of the phenomena of which they treat, and a strong desire to do them justice both scientifically and in accord with the dictates of the natural wisdom of our history and culture, folk philosophy and psychology included. They hold fast to that "robust feeling of common sense" that Bertrand Russell so strongly commended to us when dealing with philosophical questions, especially those concerned with the analysis of mind.

Popper's Three Worlds

As I mentioned, two of the most eminent elder statesmen of cognitive science made a strong case for a form of dualism some years ago.[7] This was greeted with skepticism, if not scorn, in many quarters, and has not by any means held center stage in recent discussions of the "mind-body" problem.[8] Nonetheless their case was attractive, intriguing, and in some important ways rather compelling; they tackled issues that have suffered general neglect, despite their central importance for understanding cognition.

The main cooperative work of Popper and Eccles is presented in their book, *The Self and Its Brain.* The first part is a philosophical discourse on the nature of self and brain, the work of Sir Karl. The second is a review of neuroscience by Sir John, and the third the presentation of a series of dialogues between them. We shall discuss the first part only, as the review of neuroscience, good as it was at the time, is now seriously out of date; the dialogues, a sort of self-congratulatory celebration of their defiance of the orthodox antidualist positions in philosophy and neuroscience, have few new points of interest.

Popper's thesis cuts a wide swath. Its central thesis is contained in the strong distinction he makes between three worlds, a threefold ontogeny (an *ontogeny,* remember, is a statement, a theory, a metaphysical position, concerning what there is) that encompasses everything in our universe, or at least all that human knowledge can comprehend. The first of these is $w1,$ the physical world of material objects, natural laws, the occurrences that are investigated by physics and its cognate disciplines. The second, $w2,$ is the world of mental phenomena, of consciousness; memories, thoughts, beliefs, passions, hopes, and fears—all that we understand as the goings-on that grab our interest because they are the essential attributes of human experience and motivated action (all that—as the quotation from Lockwood above reminds us—seems totally mysterious and incomprehensible from the viewpoint of $w1$.) The third, $w3,$ is the world of cultural—that is to say social, intellectual, legal, moral, and spiritual—products: literature, science, art, architecture, religion, social and political structures, etc., insofar as these are to be found in continuing records of human achievement. Such records may be in books, buildings, films, scientific models and theories, political, social or economic organizations, philosophical systems, metaphysical extravaganza, and the like—a rather mixed bag. The contents of $w3$ are distinguished from $w2$ by the fact that they exist, or can exist, independently of any immediate human conscious effort or experience; their *genesis,* or *discovery,* however, is an altogether different matter, because that in an obvious sense is a creative process involving $w2$.

Popper's purpose is not merely to catalogue the contents of the three worlds as the exhaustive description of an ontology, it is to analyze their properties, characterize the relations that hold between them, and thereby establish a coherent view of mind and brain. This project is to stand as a microcosm of the wider matter of understanding humanity's place in Mother Nature's bosom. His primary question, and the one on which all else hinges, is this: Is $w1$ *closed,* that is, are all the properties of the universe of which we know, or of which we might entertain scientific questions, contained in $w1$? Are those other two worlds simply ephemera, if not figments of the imagination, to be dismissed as convenient fictions, if not outright dissemblers and generators of troublesome philosophical puzzles? The answer we find to this question will have a very powerful influence on the rest of our metaphysics. It is widely maintained, by orthodox cognitive science for instance, that $w1$ *is* closed, that all we know and all we need to know (of the mind, among other things) is within the province of material existence, and will ultimately be explained by the correct application of the (perhaps in some cases as yet unknown) laws of physics.

Interaction between the Three Worlds

That opinion may currently be the most popular answer to the traditional plain question that asks whether the mind is something *more* than a congeries of brain activities, but Popper disagrees with it. He takes the contrarian and definitely controversial position of denying the closedness of $w1$. In other words he rejects the first two axioms of the standard model, the axioms of neural substrate and reducibility. He surely must need powerful arguments to do so. He starts by considering the nature of $w3$, the realm of cultural and specifically of intellectual products. He argues that the existence of such $w3$ products cannot always be correlated with, or tied to, or explained by events in $w1$, that there are cases in which the reality of those products must necessarily be admitted to exist as entities *quite independently* of $w1$. Nonetheless, there are instances in which those $w3$ products can, and do, react on and influence events in $w1$. Moreover, this is not a rare or isolated phenomenon. In that sense, therefore, $w1$ is *not* closed. He gives as his most solid and salient example the circumstances surrounding Frege's attempt to provide a logically unimpeachable foundation for arithmetic.[9]

Frege's intellectual work, one might argue (accepting the axiom of neural substrate) is a product of his brain, and expressed in words written on paper, so still safely in the closed realm of $w1$; his monograph was accepted as a sound piece of groundbreaking scholarship (an acceptance for which the existence of brains was a necessary condition, so still arguably in $w1$) and initially maintained this honorable position. There was, however, a flaw in Frege's logic, which Bertrand Russell soon uncovered. Not only did this exposure challenge the status of Frege's system, it engendered much discussion and markedly affected the development of ideas about the logical foundations of mathematics; it also led directly of course to the revision of Frege's work. Although a diehard might argue still that this was all going on in brains and on paper, and so still comfortably in $w1$, what are we to say of the flaw in the original work before Russell exposed it? And, what is also very important, what of the correct account before Russell discovered it? These most certainly were *not* in *w1* within any conceivably acceptable meaning of the words, but they were also not *nonexistent.* They were, it seems clear, *waiting to be discovered* (and thus unlike the unicorns and other mythical and imaginary entities that cluttered the philosopher's cupboard before Russell's theory of types rendered them innocuous). The correct account was a relevant "fact of the matter" so far as Frege's system was concerned, and very real. We would have to say that it is (or was) in *w3;* no two ways about it. Once discovered it reacted on (influenced, generated effects in, controlled) aspects of *w1,* in terms of what went on in brains and on paper, and also *w2,* in that interest, argument, passion, and ambition were undoubtedly generated and had to be dealt with. So, here is a case in which *w1* clearly is *not* closed; it is subject to influences from and interactions with things outside itself, things not definable or nameable within it, and existing independently of it.

If *w1* is not closed, there is no a priori reason to argue that *w2* necessarily exists only as an epiphenomenon of *w1,* or in parallel to and without interaction with *w1,* and, according to Popper, no reason to deny its reality as a world worthy of exploration and explanation in its own right and on its own terms. In fact, as he argues, *w2* is the very medium by means of which, in the normal course of events, the other two worlds influence and respond to one another—as is obvious in the case of Russell's exposure of Frege's folly. It was Russell's hard, conscious, intellectual work that did the trick. This much seems incontestable.

The point that a *w3* event (the hidden flaw, subsequently revealed) can govern directly goings on in *w2* (the world of conscious experience, where hard mental work was required to expose the flaw) merits further discussion. The influences are more extensive than is first evident; they occur not only in the thoughts of philosophers and logicians—the sorts of thing we are inclined to believe might be usefully duplicated in some artificial way, for instance, by simulation on a computer—but they also result, as I mentioned, in feelings of pride, envy, admiration, thwarted ambition, and all the other accompaniments of a conspicuous scholarly coup. It would be difficult to see what insight might be gained by *their* artificial replication, as by computer simulation. Successful simulation characteristically encourages belief in the possibility of reducing the mental to the mechanical, as in the development of programs to prove theorems in logic, but the passions are just as real in their own domain as the more readily formalized intellectual processes are in theirs. We experience, if not a compulsion, then at least a strong urge to find out whether the latter can be simulated, and if they can, to feel that in some sense the simulation helps us understand what a thought process is. Even if one could simulate an emotion in a computer, one would have to be relentless indeed to claim that the simulation in any realistic way duplicated the real thing; it is even difficult to imagine what additional insight into an emotional state might be provided by its simulation.

Any difference in principle between the two cases is not easy to discern, yet it is only the former (the intellectual simulation) that has been claimed in strong AI to reproduce the real thing. Thinking about the limitations of simulation in the latter case (the emotions) thus may give us further grounds for skepticism with respect to the uses of AI, especially strong AI, as a path to the understanding of mind. Only the

THE SCIENCE OF MIND **65**

routine, *mechanizable* constituents of mental action are amenable to such treatment, and that leaves out a lot! In any case it seems clear that the effects of *w3* on *w2,* and vice versa, cannot be limited arbitrarily to any single domain or process.

Russell's exposure of Frege's mistake is but one dramatic example out of the boundless number that could be given to illustrate how widely and powerfully items and events in *w3* can exert effects on conscious activity. It can happen equally well through the discovery of historical records (think of the Dead Sea Scrolls, for example), the transmission of knowledge and culture in books and other media, and in many other less striking ways. Moreover the influence on *w1* is obvious, too, in the very production of novel physical objects like books and CDs. To the extent that what you read in this book (made possible by black marks on a page, assuredly things in *w1*) provokes dissent or agreement—even enjoyment or anger—we have an example of *w1* reacting directly and forcefully on *w2,* unless of course you insist on refuting the existence of one of the two worlds in favor of the other. In that case I would give you the response of Samuel Johnson to the more extravagant of Bishop Berkeley's theories regarding the nonreality of the material world. Kicking a stone (and feeling, if only momentarily, a pain in his toe) he said: "Sir, I refute it thus!" The philosopher G. E. Moore made much the same point by sticking up his thumb. Both were asserting the plain man's privilege of deciding what is a clear fact of the matter, in this case that something "out there" can and does affect directly something in one's immediate experience, whether as a pain or as a visual perception. In Popper's terms this is the direct action of *w1* on *w2*.

Popper stresses the point that the contents of *w3* are very often (but not always, as I shall argue in detail later) the products or artifacts of human exertion and intention, that is, of *w2*. The interaction of *w1* and *w3* thus occurs most naturally through the mediation of *w2,* as we noted in the case of Frege and Russell. It is necessary, nonetheless, to emphasize the fact that *w1* is open directly to influence from "somethings" in w3, which are outside human awareness and have no physical existence, as forcibly and rigorously as possible. We need to do this to dismiss the argument, with which we are already very familiar, that *w2* and *w3* are merely constructions from *w1,* their apparent independent status being no more than an illusory consequence of our persistent unwillingness to grant the hegemony of *w1*. The importance of Popper's illustration is that it shows, beyond any reasonable doubt, that *w1* is not closed in the required sense. We shall find the point further reinforced when we get to discuss the nature of mathematics first in chapter 7 and again in chapter 9. The first statement of this paragraph should be put more exactly, because it is the *discovered* contents of *w3* that owe their transduction into the "public domain" to human effort, which leaves the notion of *undiscovered* contents of *w3* as a thought tantalizingly ripe for investigation and exploitation, which we shall start—if only with a few rudimentary moves—in chapter 9.

It is necessary to emphasize that Popper in no way belittles the importance of neuroscience for an understanding of mental and cultural life, quite the opposite. His arguments, and his philosophical position, are based on his analysis of what we can in principle know and state about the three worlds as he defines them. That is why his discussion of the non-closedness of *w1* is so central to his position, and what ultimately makes him a dualist; the sorts of brain activity studied by neuroscience (in *w1*) on his view strongly interact with conscious mental goings-on (*w2*), which are not reducible without remainder to *w1*. Given that *w1* is not closed, there is no principled way to restrict the influence of one on the other, or on *w3*. One of the most important of these influences is, in Popper's view, the interaction of brain and self, which forces on our attention the thorny issue of choice, the obverse of determinism. We will get back to that shortly.

Although Popper can be scornful of some metaphors for the powerful experience that sudden scientific intuition can bring,[10] he nevertheless accepts creativity as a mighty riddle of cosmology, thus reminding us of Einstein's dictum that the greatest mystery of the universe is its comprehensibility. Much of that creativity and mystery belong, of course, to *w2* where, for the dualist, the sharp leading edge of scientific inquiry lies. Even if one wanted to claim that such inquiry has no observable effect in *w1*, it would be hard to maintain that it was irrelevant to our *understanding* of *w1*, and, dualist or not, that is a matter which cognitive science cannot ignore.

Origins of the Three Worlds

Given the joint authorship of *The Self and Its Brain* it is no surprise that Popper gives serious consideration to the question of the origins and evolution of his worlds. He accepts the axioms of biological evolution and even those axioms of biological emergence and mental emergence in a limited sense, although we shall see that his treatment of the latter is not satisfactory. He enunciates four principles of natural selection that are needed to account for—we'd have to say—everything! In that sense Popper hews to the standard Darwinian line of argument, of which the axiom of biological evolution is a cardinal part. His four principles are

(i) Natural selection is purposive and progressive.

Comment: This can be read to mean no more than is contained in the concept of survival of the fittest, although it is not certain that is all Popper had in mind.

(ii) Natural selection is the instrument of survival, and is therefore, paramountly a factor in *w1*.

Comment: Whether natural selection is exclusively a matter of *w1* is not made clear, but in view of the next principle we should have our doubts.

(iii) Natural selection must explain the emergence and evolution of *w2* and *w3*.

Comment: How are we to know that the selection pressures for these other worlds are *natural;* in other words, to know whether they belong in *w1?* If not, the concept of natural selection itself is compromised.

(iv) Any explanation (e.g., of the emergence of all three worlds) in terms of natural selection is

Comment: This is unsatisfactory; whenever an unanswerable question about origins arises, the easy

THE SCIENCE OF MIND

incomplete, because we do not know what all the selection pressures are.

answer is always available: It is the result of unknown, or incompletely known, selection pressures. But Popper is not alone in his evasive action; it is quite common throughout the life sciences.

We see that Popper's ambiguous treatment of the evolution of mind within the confines of the biological world is unsatisfactory, but he is hardly alone in this.[11] His derivation of a dualist position on the basis of natural selection is hardly watertight, but Popper had to make the attempt in order not to flout yet another of the sacred cows of contemporary science: How could we be respectable cognitive *scientists* if we questioned the solid ground of Darwin's account of evolution, and the emergence of mind that seems to follow naturally (excuse the word!) from it? Yet Popper seems at times to be close to doing so. He calls his stance "promissory materialism,"[12] although it would be at least as correct to call it "evasive materialism."

Mind, Brain, and Machine

The dualist perspective more readily accords with two other arguments Popper makes, concerning the relations between logic and neurophysiology, on the one hand, and concerning logic and machine (or more generally physical) manipulations and interpretations of symbols, on the other. As to the first point, he quotes a well-known comment of J. B. S. Haldane, to the effect that he could not accept the idea that his thought processes were subject to regulation by the chemistry of his brain rather than to the dictates of logic (yet that, after all, appears to be the position of most contemporary neuroscientists). One is reminded of the statement of Moritz Schlick, leader of the Vienna Circle (chapter 1), to the effect that if a person insisted to him that $2 + 2 = 5$, he would engage him in argument, not send him to be operated on by a brain surgeon.[13] The point of both these remarks is to emphasize that what is a logical (or linguistic, or mathematical, or philosophical) claim or matter of dispute is resolved not by what the physiology of the brain dictates, but by the exigencies of rational debate. An intact and well-functioning brain may be an empirically necessary condition (the well-functioning vehicle) for such debate to take place, but it is scarcely logically sufficient to ensure its proper outcome. Whether the outcome *is* proper is decided on rational, logical, linguistic grounds, and on those grounds alone.

As to the second question, of the machine representation of logical, linguistic, mathematical, and other symbolic systems, Popper argues that such representations can never take precedence over the abstract science of logic. He considers the matter of *logical proof.* It is a fact that machines are capable, under appropriate programming and supervision, of producing acceptable and indeed superior logical and mathematical proofs. There are now plenty of instances, and ones that are far more impressive than in Popper's day, in which computers play an important and even essential role in providing such proofs;[14] the speed and accuracy of their computations, the size and accessibility of their databases, far exceed anything of which an unaided human is capable. Sheer speed and efficiency are, however, no criterion by which to judge the adequacy of a proof. Popper rightly maintains that when a machine does the work, it is certifiably correct only under the condition that the machine did not break down or show some other physical/mechanical fault. And that itself is not a matter of logic, but of engineering. Logical adequacy still is a concept that transcends the domain of the machine. Logical proof can be implemented mechanically, but the implementation itself is subject to scrutiny over and above, and independently of, the *prior* question of logical sufficiency. To see why this is so, imagine a faulty machine that happens to implement a faulty step in logic that, by happenstance, cancels the logical fault, thereby producing—serendipitously but still incorrectly—a correct logical result; a true theorem for example. No one would accept that as a *valid* logical procedure. Malfunctioning computers can produce false results, just as can malfunctioning brains, but the *criterion* of correctness is not to be found in the "wetware" of the brain, as Moritz Schlick knew, any more than it is to be found in the hardware of the machine. To argue that it is in the computer's *software* is to concede the point, given the ultimate origins of the software, that the criterion is a matter of logical propriety, force, and consistency.[15]

So, once again, Popper asserts the primacy of the conscious mind (*w2*) in the enterprise of science, in the furthering of our logical, mathematical, and linguistic activities, as well as in the more commonplace understanding of the world(s) we inhabit.

True to his earlier philosophical work on the nature of science and his doctrine of falsifiability as the hallmark of a genuinely scientific theory, in *The Logic of Scientific Discovery* (1934/1959) and *Conjectures and Refutations* (1969), Popper denies that there is anything absolute about his conceptions of mind and matter or about the relations that hold between them. He is, to use his own word, against "essentialism," the strategy of trying to winkle out the essence of things, to tie them down with a definition, to hold a glittering but dead prize up to the mind's relentless scrutiny, like a butterfly impaled on a cork under the lepidopterist's revealing eyeglass. Far more fruitful, in his view, is to advance our understanding incrementally, a step at a time, by conjecture and refutation. This, according to Popper, is the way of all good science, indeed of all genuine empirical investigation, whether the steps be great or small. So, for him it is a mistake to attempt sweeping definitions of mind and matter; far more fruitful is the trail of hypothesis (conjecture) and experimental test (refutation, or the opposite) that advances understanding against the background of previously acquired knowledge, but knowledge that is itself always subject to revision in the light of new evidence. Maintaining this stance, he points out that we have little knowledge of the essentials of matter—that is, what matter *is* (assuming this is even a valid question to ask)—but we know much about its structure and peculiar properties (e.g., as advanced in theoretical and experimental physics).[16] The same is true of mind. It is not pertinent, or even rational, according to Popper, to ask or expect more.

Interaction of Brain and Mind

One might think that such a cautious stance is at odds with the rather sweeping claims of Popper's three-worlds doctrine, an exposition quite in the tradition of grand metaphysical philosophy. I shall not dispute that point, but rather take a look at the proposed mechanism of dualistic interaction that Popper and Eccles had in mind. Eccles in particular has searched earnestly for evidence, even hints, in recent discoveries in neuroscience and developments in physical theory that might support the notion of dualistic interaction between mind and brain. In this he is not by any means alone, as we shall discover in the next section of the chapter. Other scientists have followed that scent, too. The idea is to find in the submicroscopic world, even in the subatomic world of quantum physics, processes that do not obey the classical principle of the conservation of energy and so might be a ground for allowing the "mental" to interact with and control the "material," in this case the material processes of the brain that subserve thinking and action. I use quotation marks advisedly in the previous sentence, because many philosophers (and no doubt many natural scientists, too) find such a bald notion of mental events influencing, or being influenced by, material events (brain processes here) is an anathema.[17]

The search for those physical events in what Eccles has called the "liaison brain" is at a level that defies the classical materialist views on which orthodox theories of brain physiology are based. Consider the problem of choice, of free will, as it has traditionally been posed. If we have freedom of choice, and much in *w2* leads us to believe that we have, how can that be reconciled with the doctrine of control by brain processes? Eccles proposes mental-neural event neurons (MNEs), which in contrast to neural event neurons (NEs), which have inputs only from other neurons, also have inputs from mental events per se.[18] It is these neurons that make possible the dualistic interactions that Eccles (and Popper) claim *must* occur and have to be accounted for in any comprehensive theory of cognition.

How are MNEs supposed to work? Eccles's basic idea, which has gone through a number of modifications and revisions, is that the mind influences cortical events at the level of synaptic activity, where one neuron impinges on and interacts with another (chapter 3). Each end bouton of a synapse holds about 20,000 synaptic vesicles, minute pouches that contain a high concentration of a specific neurotransmitter substance. The contents of a vesicle is ejected quantally (all-or-none) into the synaptic gap where its action brings about the depolarization that, if strong enough, leads to the generation of a spike potential on the host neuron (neural transmission; see chapter 3).

We must note that the idea of a quantum emission from a vesicle is not the basic entity named in physical quantum theory; nonetheless Eccles seeks support from developments in that discipline, and especially in the writings of the quantum physicist Henry Morganau:

> In very complicated physical systems such as the brain, the neurons, and sense organs, whose constituents are small enough to be governed by probabilistic quantum laws, the physical organ is always posed for a multitude of possible changes, each with a definite probability; if one change takes place that requires energy, or more or less energy than another, the intricate organism furnishes it automatically. Hence, if there is a mind-body interaction, the mind would not be called upon to furnish energy.[19]

The idea is that the MNE intervenes at the level of synaptic transmission to bias, steer, or govern an otherwise purely physiological event. Here the mind, or the will, or whatever other nonphysical agent one may propose, has its site of action. Here indeterminacy of the sort required to break the stranglehold of physiological causation asserts itself, leading to the possibility of freedom of choice, the primacy of logic over brain chemistry, etc. For Eccles the problem of breaking the law of conservation of energy is thus solved.

There are two major problems here, one empirical, one theoretical. The empirical problem is to know how such things as MNEs could be identified; the mere possibility that they exist, or circumstantial evidence about where they might be located (and Eccles has some speculations about this) is not sufficient. We would need to know how and where they operate and how to identify them. New hypotheses about these matters are proposed from time to time as neuroscientific discovery and physical theory advance (see following section), but nothing so far has enjoyed anything close to wide acceptance.[20] The theoretical problem is that even if these magical units were to be identified, and a plausible mechanism for their operation proposed, the major question, the question of their magic, remains unsolved. Their magic is just the fact that they transmute the neuroscientist's dross into the philosopher's gold—the electrochemical goings on in $w1$ into the conscious mental acts of $w2$. We still do not have, and would not have even if the MNE were discovered, any notion of how or why the magic happens.

To summarize the position of Popper and Eccles vis-à-vis the standard model: They accept the importance of the biological substrate, but strongly deny the axiom of reducibility (all mental activity can be understood in physical-chemical terms). They accept the axiom of biological evolution, but are ambiguous, even evasive, on the questions of biological and mental emergence. They gloss over the inherent contradiction between the paramountcy of mind, which they champion, and its emergence as a natural product of evolution according to the standard biological model. They are not opposed to the axiom of machine architecture (as long as "machine" is interpreted generously) but strongly oppose the axiom of mental architecture, the principle that mental structure will be clearly revealed when brain structure is fully known. Although the issue is not addressed directly in their writing, one can readily infer that Popper and Eccles would deny the axiom of computability because it is far too confining: It dictates a priori what can, and what can not, be acceptable as cognitive theory. For the same reason they might be hesitant to embrace the axiom of respectability, and certain to resist it in the form of adherence to present orthodoxy in cognitive science. Quite apart from their own unorthodox views, especially on dualism, they would question anyone's right to dictate a priori what can, and what cannot, be considered respectable or even plausible in a discipline as young as cognitive science. For this they are to be applauded.

So we have a view of the mind/body question that in some respects reasserts a very traditional position, arguing (to put matters rather coarsely) for the primacy of mind over matter. If the mind cannot be reduced to $w1$ (Popper) and the mind, via the MNEs, controls at least some events in $w1$ (Eccles), that thesis seems to follow. The account of the genesis of mind is also quite orthodox, but now claimed from a different tradition, namely that of neo-Darwinism—the assertion that it's all come about (emerged) through natural selection. But as we saw, there is ambiguity, if not outright fudging, in the account of this given by Popper.

The Emperor's Shadow

Several recent attempts to tackle the unresolved problems of mind and its place in the natural order have been mounted by thinkers not owing their primary allegiance to cognitive science. The solutions they propose may not be cut from the cloth of current orthodoxy, but nonetheless are of fundamental relevance and interest to our inquiry. Among the foremost of these is Roger Penrose, distinguished mathematician and seeker for the truth about the mind, the role of consciousness in thinking, and the sources of mathematical inspiration. In two books he has made a detailed study of these matters, in many respects challenging the established fashions. He has dared to ask many of those awkward questions cognitive science tends to dismiss and has formulated a powerful and original conception of mind.[21] It is not possible to do full justice to Penrose's position in a short summary, nor am I qualified to comment on much of what he has to say about modern mathematical physics. But we can gain a clear picture of his central themes concerning the nature of mind; we can see how they relate to the standard model, and what lessons can be learned from them. The latter are of two types: lessons about the shortcomings of the orthodox views, and lessons reminding us of the sorts of unanswered questions about mind that need resolution, whether or not we accept Penrose's own answers.

Penrose's position is as follows in terms of the axioms of the standard model: He accepts the core position of the first six axioms, but with certain reservations and modifications. The axiom of neural substrate must be altered to allow that the relevant brain processes are not all, or mainly, to be identified at the level of individual neurons, such as the units having specific "mental" attributes (the MNEs) postulated by Eccles. The axiom of reducibility to the realm of physical law is accepted, indeed enthusiastically, but with definite restrictions on the sorts of hypotheses about the physical events in terms of which mental events will be explained. The axioms of unlimited access, biological evolution, biological emergence, and mental emergence are all accepted without serious question—but, as we shall see in chapter 9, not all of this is consistent with some of the doctrines propounded in his second book. Penrose's sharpest divergence from the standard model comes with his strong rejection of the axioms of mental architecture and computability. Together the two axioms embody the doctrine that human cognition is comprehensible, at least in principle, as machine-like activity capable of capture in the algorithmic net, in other words the doctrine of strong AI.

The main thrust of Penrose's argument against the claim that brains and their minds are in all relevant respects like computers and their programs is that mental activity—in particular the processes of mathematical invention and comprehension, demonstrably dependent on the brain though they be—is not only, not even mainly, algorithmic. Some of the arguments are very technical, and I shall only give their general outline. A second salient feature of his position is that the attempt in AI to capture the essentials of mentation, whether or not it is algorithmic, ignores (or in even the kindest interpretation evades), the question of consciousness and how it is to be treated in scientific terms.

Thinking: Competence and Performance

To a psychologist any debate over whether human thinking is always, and only, algorithmic has a bizarre dimension, because it has been so clearly established experimentally that in the vast majority of cases it is not. Humans, even adult, highly educated, and articulate ones, are seldom totally rational. They rarely can make correct logical inferences, except in rather simple cases or under special circumstances, and are easily misled (as any pollster well knows) by the context and format within which questions and problems are posed.[22] Our thought processes typically lack organization, often are not even coherent, and are subject to bias and prejudice; in fact they are generally the antithesis of algorithmic. Why, then, has so much (mostly rational and coherent!) thought been given over to attempting either to prove or disprove the algorithmic conjecture? Part of the answer is to be found, without doubt, in the fundamental distinction between competence and performance so insightfully invoked and exploited by Chomsky in linguistics and by the behavioristic learning theorists before that.

What humans are capable of and what they actually do are all too often quite different. You may know how to play a Beethoven piano sonata and while practicing have done so perfectly more than once. That is no guarantee of perfection, however, when performing it for others. You may be a great speller (or logician, calculator, conversationalist, actor, baby-sitter, racing sailor, etc.) in terms of your competence— what you know how to do—but whether you can cut the mustard on a particular occasion, or even on most occasions, is another matter, as Chomsky emphasized. Cognitive scientists who argue the two sides of the strong AI debate are concerned much more with competence than performance. (It's those dreary experimentalists who keep muddying the debate with awkward and, according to some, irrelevant data on what human subjects actually *do* in the laboratory and on the street). That is to say, on this view, despite all the vagaries and shortcomings of human attempts at rationality, it still makes sense to ask whether, under something more like ideal conditions and at the highest level of competence, the pinnacle of human thinking can be captured in the net of the formal algorithm.

An analogous situation in developmental cognition can help us see the theoretical importance of the question. Before the advent of the great Swiss psychologist Jean Piaget, the study of children's thinking was largely anecdotal and biographical; there was little in the way of theory. Piaget made it clear, by observation in more or less natural conditions, that there is a great gap between what small children normally comprehend and what they can adequately communicate. Moreover their comprehension can be of a kind quite foreign to the adult mind. The genius of Piaget's insight allowed him to discern some of the patterns in this different form of understanding and to design methods of probing it.[23] He claimed to savor the essence of the child's competence, thus leading him to propose an elaborate theory of "genetic epistemology" by formulating the structure of thinking in terms of a sequence of biologically determined stages of assimilation (of sensory-motor "schemas" and then of concepts) and their adaptation to the existing environment. This theoretical structure, according to Piaget, is the way thinking really *is,* and governs how it develops in the child.[24] Experimental work soon showed that things are not as neat and tidy as the theory suggested; the appearance of the capacity to understand and manipulate numbers, to take one of the clearest examples, does not follow the clear sequence of stages predicted in the theory.[25] No matter, was the response; that's just the way children perform on a given test. The *real* question is whether the child's competence, the ideal of what's actually available to him as a means of coping with the concept of number, is properly captured in the theory of logical stages.

Piaget postulated an *ideal* of rational observation, description, judgment, and argument that incorporates what we find to be important in mature intellectual activity; in time it is arrived at naturally by the child. This ideal, a sort of "model mind," is approached by a sequence of developments in the child that is very similar to the maturation of any other biological system developing toward a stable, orderly, and well-articulated structure. It is this end-product that defines the true measure of mind (of human rational behavior), and it is therefore the proper object of scientific scrutiny. If *that* could be fully described and understood, all the idiosyncrasies and obscurities to be found in actual childish thought and speech would be of little real account, according to Piaget, except to document progress toward the ideal. They would be mere surface characteristics to be swept aside as the true model of mind emerged in all its pristine elegance.

It is just so with the debate over algorithms. Defenders of strong AI, and Penrose, too, for that matter, take it for granted that an important aspect of logical, consistent, rational thinking is captured in the concept of the algorithm. They are surely correct in this, but we need to put the matter in proper perspective. A *very small* proportion of all human mental activity, even of that in which mathematicians and scientists engage when they are "doing their thing," consists of following procedures that are strictly algorithmic.[26] Why then should we be so concerned about the matter? The Piagetian example provides part of the answer, and Popper's concern over the primacy of logic in human thought completes the argument.

Ideals of Rationality

Both Piaget and Popper in their very different ways are concerned with the *ideals* of human thinking, with how to describe their full and perfect form, with how they would appear in the guise of pure competence. If there are such ideals, the fact that human thinking seldom lives up to them is a side issue. The ideals are there to establish the criteria of correct thinking. Without such ideals, we would be at a loss to justify *any* procedure as basis for a satisfactory epistemology, as the foundation of scientific method, or as the justification of rationality itself. Ideals are a sine qua non of our culture, at the very heart of the Western tradition of civilization.[27] From this point of view one could say that proponents of AI are simply legislating a particular form for the ideals, not questioning their general validity. It is obvious enough that the proponents of AI *rely* on rational arguments to make their case! The arguments in favor of the AI postulate of algorithmicity are not, however, themselves purely algorithmic. If they were, they surely would have been resolved by now. For Popper the philosophical tradition and the ideals of rational competence are manifested not in algorithms as such, but in the canons of logical theory (whose primacy over the brain and the machine he argued for so passionately), in the desiderata of plausible argument, and in the procedures of conjecture and proof that he held to be the only acceptable method of progress in science.

Given that the algorithmic argument is concerned with only a tiny segment of what actually happens when thinking occurs, what reason is there to get excited about it? The reason has to be, surely, that the laws are there to ensure that the generation of ideas, arguments, proofs, and the like happens correctly. They are the *prescription* for thinking. If that small but vastly important ideal portion of human intellectual activity can be captured in algorithmic form, the rest can in one way or another be derived, deduced, or dragged out from it. It ought to be like the situation regarding the laws of classical physics; no one doubts that physical phenomena at the macroscopic level, like the waters pouring over Niagara Falls or the flight of a flock of geese, are subject to Newton's laws of motion. In some cases it would be possible (if we took the trouble) to demonstrate the fact, but in general it would be impractical. Still we are comfortable with the idea that *in principle* the laws are obeyed, even when, as is now evident, in many large-scale phenomena like weather systems, prediction over anything other than a short time scale is not possible and never will be.[28] Nevertheless we do not abandon belief in the orderliness, let alone faith in the lawfulness of the phenomena; we accept that some systems are too complex, intricate, or cover too great a time span to allow for prediction or control. It is just so, one might argue, with thinking. In any particular case it may be impossible to discern, much less to prove, that well-specified logical laws (ideals) underpin a person's discussion or line of reasoning, but we may still take comfort from the thought that they're nonetheless present, doing their job of monitoring and mentoring the thought processes. That begins to look very much like the grammatical competence underlying all language use of which Chomsky and his followers persuade us. Aristotle argued from the same perspective; it is doubtful that he would have claimed that all the actual forms of discursive argument of philosophers and lesser mortals could be captured in the syllogistic typology, only that it represents the ideal kernel from which they are derived and to which we should aspire.[29]

That still doesn't quite seem to get at the root of the matter, because the strong AI thesis maintains not only that thinking is steered in a specifiably lawful way, but also that its very nature can be grasped in only one possible way. Critics of Penrose's first book were quick to take him to task for a purportedly mystical streak in his claim that thinking cannot be captured in the algorithmic net (the algorithmic *vice,* I would say; a pretty little double entendre that the algorithmic conjecture might have difficulty capturing in its simulating net). But surely the boot is on the other foot: Claiming that the essential nature of thinking is algorithmic is, if not exactly mystical, without doubt a deliberate metaphysical stance. The proponents of strong AI do not argue that their claim is empirical and thus open to observational confirmation (or otherwise). It is certainly not a logical truth, because to deny it (that is, to deny that all human thinking is algorithmic) is not self-contradictory. Like the principle of verification (chapter 1) it enunciates a method of procedure, and like the principle of verification, the strong AI claim falls victim to its own sharp weapon. The arguments that have to be used to establish the claim *are not themselves algorithmic.* If they were, there would be no dispute over the strong AI claim, because by their very nature algorithmic arguments yield unambiguous answers in a finite number of steps. That has not happened, nor is there any prospect that it will happen. Taking the self-reflexive stance can have radical consequences for cognitive science, as in many other fields!

In the history of cognitive science an arresting comparison to the algorithmic doctrine of AI comes to mind; it is the theory of atomic facts and atomic sentences of Russell and Wittgenstein discussed earlier. That theory was strong medicine and fell by the wayside to philosophical linguistic analysis and common sense. The algorithmic doctrine of thinking appears to be headed in the same direction, and for very similar reasons.[30] But more of that later.

Algorithm and Intention

The discussion so far is not intended to minimize the importance of the debate over AI. It has been pointed out that there are several different forms of the strong AI argument,[31] and that the simple identification of thought process with algorithm may not be the most plausible or defensible of them. But it is the one that has attracted all the attention, and the one that most clearly challenges our conceptions of what mind, consciousness, and self are all about by proposing strict limitations on the ways they can be studied scientifically. In that sense Penrose is right on target with his attacks on the doctrine of (very) strong AI; that is, the form of the doctrine which asserts that all useful thinking can be reduced to algorithmic form without remainder.

As a mathematician, Penrose would be the last to make light of the importance of formal steps in an argument. A mathematical *proof* relies on, indeed consists in, the demonstration that a *conclusion* can be reached by a sequence of sound logical moves from a given set of *premises* or *axioms*. The conclusion is shown to be a logically (mathematically) necessary conclusion from the premises, and that is an algorithmic procedure. The argument is over whether that's *all there is* to mathematics. To that question Penrose gives a resounding no. He is not alone in this by any means. Very many, perhaps the majority, of great mathematicians and mathematical physicists, Poincaré and Einstein among them, have testified to experiences of a clearly nonalgorithmic nature when creative new ideas were stirring in them.[32] There is much variety in how these experiences are described, but what is common to them all is that they do not have the clear stepwise sequence of logical statements and propositions leading inexorably from premises to conclusion that characterizes the algorithm. "Moods of anticipation" and "flashes of inspiration" seem to capture the nature of the experiences better, although such words are not common currency in cognitive science. New conceptions and theorems, however they may first announce themselves, have subsequently to be properly established as respectable mathematical truths by constructing adequate proofs, which is the kingdom where algorithm rules.[33]

There has been much discussion and disagreement among mathematicians about the nature of their discipline. At one extreme are "conventionalists" claiming that all mathematical knowledge is a matter of formal procedures and structures that may or may not have relevance to other forms of knowledge and understanding, but that in any case are creations resulting from human ingenuity rather than being "about" anything, at least until they receive an interpretation at the hands of their creators or other interested parties.[34] At the other extreme are "idealists" who find it natural to think of the truths of mathematics as being discoveries from a realm of pure ideas that transcend our mortal coils. Since the time of Pythagoras this has been a dominant theme, speaking of which Bertrand Russell says:

> Mathematics, in the sense of demonstrative deductive argument, begins with him, and in him is intimately connected with a peculiar form of mysticism. The influence of mathematics on philosophy, partly owing to him, has, ever since, been both profound and unfortunate.[35]

Most mathematicians, naturally enough, fall somewhere between these extremes, but nonetheless it is not unusual to find them espousing the idea that Mathematics (the whole body of that august discipline, as opposed to the particular mathematics that may be known at any one time) exists as something to be discovered, to be known but imperfectly or indirectly in many instances, and in a universe of ideas that is timeless and has no spatial location. In other words, they subscribe to some form of the Platonic world of ideas. Penrose argues for something like this,[36] and it is the ground for the charge against him of a mystical streak in his position. The strong AI claim is, of course, directly opposed to such a view, and can be thought of as a modern form of the conventionalist position: Mathematics, logic, and hence all forms of rational thinking, are products of human invention and convention, and are to be understood solely in terms of, can reduced to, a prescribed set of man-made formal procedures (in this case, algorithms). If such a claim could be rigorously established,—that is, proved to every mathematician's satisfaction—it would undermine the Platonic view of mathematics without question.

What are the prospects? Penrose treats the question with utmost seriousness, and devotes a good portion of the early chapters of both of his books to dealing with it. He was preceded in this enterprise, albeit on another tack, by Alan Turing, the originator of the whole conception of algorithmic procedure (see chapter 3). He, too, was concerned with the question of the completeness of the approach. He showed that there is no algorithmic solution to the *halting problem,* that is to say, there is no way to prove in general that an algorithmic procedure will always and necessarily yield a solution and come to a stop. In that sense there may be algorithmic procedures that are indeterminate—an anathema to the formalist! A more spectacular and much better known roadblock is thrown up by the work of Kurt Gödel, whose celebrated theorem has been a thorn in the flesh of formalists since the 1930s.

How important is this theorem? Penrose has this to say about it:

> What did Gödel's theorem achieve? It was in 1930 that the brilliant young mathematician Kurt Gödel startled a group of the world's leading mathematicians and logicians, meeting in Königsberg, with what was to become his famous theorem. It became rapidly accepted as being a fundamental contribution to the foundations of mathematics—probably the most fundamental ever to be found—but I shall be arguing that in establishing his theorem, he also initiated a major step forward in the philosophy of mind.

There can be little doubt, then, as to the importance of Gödel's work. What does his theorem state? Penrose continues as follows:

Among other things that Gödel indisputably established was that no *formal system* of sound mathematical rules of proof can ever suffice, even in principle, to establish all the true propositions of ordinary arithmetic. This is certainly remarkable enough. But a powerful case can also be made that his results showed something more than this, and established that human understanding and insight cannot be reduced to any set of computational rules. For what he appears to have shown is that no such system of rules can ever be sufficient to prove even those propositions of arithmetic whose truth is accessible, in principle, to human intuition and insight—whence human insight and intuition cannot be reduced to any set of rules.[37]

Penrose rests the main weight of his thesis on these statements, but they have not been accepted without challenge. Before going into that matter, it behooves us to look a bit further (but still only at the most elementary level) into what Gödel's theorem says. Another way to state it is this: In a formal system rich enough to generate simple arithmetic, it will always be possible to deduce statements that are in principle *undecidable,* that is, whose truth or falsity cannot be established. This seems to run counter to all that we know about arithmetic, so just what does it signify? What the logician means by arithmetic is of course not a little different from what we need to know to balance the checkbook or tip the waiter. Nevertheless it seems quite bizarre to think that this seemingly simple and stereotyped (algorithmic) system of counting should need so powerful an underpinning as to threaten the very foundations of logical reasoning!

Several "layman's proofs" of Gödel's theorem have been offered,[38] but we shall not contemplate them in detail. Something of the flavor of the theorem can be gleaned by considering the concept of a *set.* Everyone is familiar with this idea, even if they may lack a precise definition of what a set is. A set is simply a collection of items, be they objects, numbers, names, or even sets (that is, a set of sets). If a set is to be useful, one needs to know which items belong in it and which do not. For example, in the set of odd numbers (an infinite set, incidentally), the numbers 3, 11, 101, etc., are members, and the numbers 6, 42, and 1000 are not. That seems clear enough, and one would think it should be true of any well-behaved set that there is a criterion for deciding which items belong and which do not. But Gödel's theorem asserts, and indeed he proved, that in a formal system of the required sort, sets will always be found whose membership, for some items at least, is essentially undecidable. Said another way: There will be sets whose membership cannot be established by an algorithmic procedure. That seems rather counterintuitive when the talk is about arithmetic, but there is no dispute about the accuracy and rigor of Gödel's work; the controversies it has spawned in the philosophical community have been about its interpretation—including what it means for our understanding of mind.[39]

Here are the main themes: Does it force upon us a view that opposes strong AI? Is it applicable to only a very limited form of thinking, or are its implications wider? Is this piece of abstract mathematical logic even relevant to the concerns of cognitive science? Penrose's answers to these three questions are, obviously, yes, yes, and yes. As the above quotations make clear, it is the fact that mathematicians (and, one would have to concede, others, too—although the case might harder to make!) can correctly apprehend truths that have not been formally stated or proved that, in his

view, demonstrates the total inadequacy of the strong AI thesis and its cognate derivatives. Gödel's results just make the case that much stronger and more explicit.

Specialists in the field are not in good agreement on the importance—even the
relevance, in some interpretations—of Gödel's work for understanding the formal
aspects of human thinking. To me the importance is obvious, at least in this sense:
Logical and mathematical proofs, like any other procedure of formal verification (in
a legal dispute over title, for example) have very much the character of trail *marking,* in clear distinction to trail *blazing,* to adapt a useful metaphor from Ryle.[40] The
metaphor points up the difference between an original line of thought or investigation that covers novel territory—blazing the trail—and the process of following that
line (and perhaps improving on it, solidifying it)—marking it after the fact. Gödel's
theorem states that in trail blazing there cannot in principle always be markers to
guide the way, to define the steps on the path with logical certainty. That does *not*
mean that the trail is necessarily obscure, or that subsequent marking is impossible.
To follow the metaphor one further step: A trail can be marked by a set procedure,
making it fully secure, perhaps even while in the process of blazing it, but there is no
sense to the idea of marking a trail until it has been (perhaps simultaneously) blazed.
That is true, no matter how simple and obvious the trail may be. Creativity, even
trivial creativity, is not to be confused with routine, even insightful routine and sub-
stantiation. So far as mathematics is concerned, the majority of us are constrained to
be satisfied with the latter, but that should not prevent us from taking to heart the
lessons of those who have the talent to practice the former.

As should by now be abundantly clear, mathematical proof is not the whole of
mathematics, nor the most original, engaging, enthralling, aesthetically pleasing, or
creative part of what mathematicians do or experience. In Popper's terms, we could
say that the creation of new mathematics involves access to, and contributions to,
w3, because what is discovered and what is recorded both transcend the level of individual experience (*w2*); the validity of a new theorem or proof is unaffected by the
death of its discoverer, for example. Events in *w2* are, however, a necessary condition of access to *w3,* which is another way of expressing Penrose's insistence on the
importance of individual intuition and understanding in bringing to fruition new
mathematical knowledge.

So much for the testimony of a leading practitioner of creative mathematics. We
shall find other, less recondite, reasons for rejecting the claims of strong AI, whether
in its most radical form or not, in later chapters.

The second major theme of Penrose's books is to inquire into the relations between brain events and mental events. This is the philosophical minefield we have
already encountered, a version of the mind-body problem that has challenged our attempts at comprehension not just since the time of Descartes, as is usually claimed,
but throughout the era of self-conscious inquiry that stems from the earliest Greek
philosophy. Perhaps the most salient and durable version is Plato's metaphor of the
cave, which pops up in one form or another throughout the Western intellectual
tradition.[41]

Penrose argues, and is by no means the first to do so, that developments in
physics in this century, and especially the amazing changes in our understanding of
matter and energy forced on us by the general theory relativity and quantum theory,

must have profound effects on the way we view the relations between mind and brain. The orthodox cognitive scientist claims that mental function can be reduced to brain function (axiom b), but generally has in mind the comfortably "solid" sort of brain activity envisaged in the clockwork universe version of reality, a physiology that conforms to the laws of classical chemistry and physics. But, as Lockwood put it:

> The scientific picture that emerged in the seventeenth century has . . . been effectively shattered by Einstein, Bohr, Heisenberg, Schroedinger, and Dirac. And philosophy needs to come to terms with this scientific revolution.[42]

Not just philosophy must make this accommodation, I might add, but biological science, too, and cognitive science in particular. Eccles, in the quotation given earlier, can be seen to be moving in this direction in attempting to reconcile his dualism with the major objection that it violates the principle of conservation of energy. But Penrose goes much farther than Eccles in invoking not just the facts of wave-particle activity at the quantum level to break the notion that mental and material are irrevocably distinct and incommensurable; he shows how the facts discovered in particle physics, and the theories that have been developed to account for them, call for a comprehensive reorientation of our cognitions about mind and matter. Arthur Zajonc has even termed it the need to develop new organs of cognition.[43] However that may be, it is certain that the traditional notions of ping-pong interaction in the clockwork universe, with the mind relegated to the position of a ghostly puller of strings and pusher of levers, is not part of Penrose's universe. Nor should it be part of ours.

A New Physical Basis for Mentation?

Penrose devotes a great part of both his books to expounding the theoretical marvels of modern physics and cosmology. Remarkable though the exposition is, we need not spend time contemplating it, because its relevance to our inquiry is limited to the two main claims it is designed to support. That relevance can be assessed without detailed scrutiny and evaluation of the physical theory. His first claim is that an understanding of consciousness, and therefore eventually of mentality, will arise out of a development in physical theory that has not yet occurred but that can be anticipated with confidence.

It is postulated in *The Emperor's New Mind* that a correct theory of quantum gravity (CQG) will supply the hoped-for breakthrough; this claim is modified in *Shadows of the Mind* but with essentially the same motivation:

> In my opinion it is not very helpful, from the scientific point of view, to think of a dualistic "mind" that is (logically) *external* to the body. . . . I cannot believe that such a picture can be close to the truth. To have a "mind-stuff" that is not itself subject to physical laws is taking us outside anything that could be reasonably called a scientific explanation. . . .[44]

Nevertheless Penrose rejects the notion that computation, even *quantum computation,* will achieve what is required to understand consciousness as a physical process (or, if one insists, as a "something" that is still subject to physical law in the strictest sense).[45] Instead he opts for a sort of (as yet undiscovered) noncomputational physics to save the day. Whether this will be the postulated CQG is, as yet, undecided.

In the search for structures and functions that might link physical processes with consciousness, Penrose makes much of new work in microphysiology that describes the *cycloskeletons* and their *microtubules* that are essential parts of all eukaryotic cells (the cell-type of all but the most primitive life forms). He shows that they have many properties that might qualify them to be the vehicles of *quantum coherence* effects that, he argues, must bridge the gap between the quantum and classical levels of physical action, the place where the mysteries of awareness and conscious understanding may, it is conjectured, be unraveled. This is powerful stuff, and no doubt many new wonders of nature will be uncovered in microphysiology, but we need not follow them in any detail. The reason is that, logically, this (admittedly highly speculative) conjecture about where neuroscience may have discovered the requisite substrate for consciousness is of *exactly* the same type as arguments we have already rejected. Even if the closest association could be established between microtubule process and consciousness, it would not *explain* consciousness; it would simply give us a closer and more detailed understanding of the physical conditions under which consciousness occurs. We still have the problem of explaining the magic of spinning the neurophysiologist's dross into philosopher's gold.[46]

Although Penrose challenges the AI conception of how consciousness is to be handled scientifically, he still adheres to the spirit of three of the primary axioms of the standard model, those of neural substrate, reducibility, and mental emergence. Let us remind ourselves of them: The axiom of neural substrate states that mental activity is a function of brain processes; that of reducibility states that those processes will eventually be understood in terms of physical laws; and that of mental emergence states that mental activity, a product of brain activity, is also to be understood solely as a product of the natural history of the brain's evolutionary development and emergence. Penrose does not question that mental activity is a function of brain activity, nor should we. But that does not entail that mental activity can be completely *understood* in terms of brain activity, something that Penrose accepts implicitly, but which we shall find good grounds to challenge later. A fortiori we shall therefore not accept without question the idea that mental activity can be fully explained, even in principle, when the applicable physical laws (CQG, or whatever else) have been formulated and proven. And I shall challenge the notion that the natural history of the brain (its evolutionary story) can yield sufficient harvest to satisfy our desire to understand and explain mental activity, consciousness.

Explanation and Mind

These are rather large challenges to the position of so eminent a thinker as Roger Penrose, and to substantiate them will take more than a paragraph or two. The burden of my argument will be to show that we need a far clearer conception of what it means to explain a natural phenomenon than has up to now been deemed satisfactory. To give a hint of this, consider the question of mental emergence. It seems certain that minds as we know them would not exist if brains had not developed over a long evolutionary course whose physical and paleontological conditions are, at least in broad outline, reasonably well known. Does anything in that course presage, much less entail, the emergence of the conscious mind? No. Does the idea, even the intimation, of the conscious mind obtrude itself anywhere in the history of evolution before its actual appearance? No. One might want to challenge that assertion, but the only reason for doing so is that we are quite uncertain about how to decide what would constitute evidence for the first appearance of conscious mind. Viewed by the proverbial Martian, we would have to admit that the conditions that would be sufficient to entail the emergence of mind (*prior* to its emergence) are totally unknown, and to that degree the grounds for the *explanation* of mind, of consciousness, are missing.[47] That we now have minds capable of contemplating this question does not seem to lend much comfort when the question at issue is, how did minds originate?

The generalization to be made from these considerations is this: There is a distinction to be made *in principle* between the conditions that are sufficient to display a relationship, even a close and intimate relationship, between two kinds of event, and the conditions that are logically sufficient to explain the connection between them, or one in terms of the other. Finding that two things are correlated, perhaps in the tightest imaginable way—which is the forte of neuroscience, for example—is not equivalent to *explaining* one in terms of the other. This is true universally, be it in physics, physiology, psychology, philosophy, or mathematics. It is a metaphysical claim, if you like, no less so than the principle of verifiability or Popper's criterion of falsifiablity, but one that I shall be prepared to defend in some detail.

I intend to mount an even more radical challenge to the standard model than Penrose. In many respects I believe he is on the right track, and one has to admire his courage in bringing to the fore questions about the emperor's new clothes that badly needed airing. I am certain, however, that the answers will not emerge from the shadows but will flash forth, like darts of sunlight on the surface of the stream of consciousness, indeed in the very same manner in which creative new ideas themselves are first apprehended. Penrose himself, in the last pages of *Shadows of the Mind,* comes close to such a view by espousing a version of the three worlds doctrine, albeit with somewhat different emphasis than Popper's. I shall aim to show that this doctrine (which in principle I accept), if consistently maintained, opens up a far richer and more exciting set of perspectives on the mind than either Popper or Penrose have presented. That is the drama to which I now turn, and the burden of the remaining chapters of this book.

5

Brain and Mind, a Many-Layered Enigma

Once we have decided that the law of causality is by no means a necessary element in the process of human thought, we have made a mental clearance for the approach to the question of its validity in the world of reality.

MAX PLANCK

Ways of Studying Brain and Mind

A number of disciplines contribute richness and variety to the development of cognitive science. I want now to structure and refine the ideas to show more clearly how their different methods and findings complement one another. The protagonists of any one discipline often give the impression that it alone has a handle on the truth—not just *a* handle, but *the* handle—with sole possession of the skills and intelligence needed to uncover all the mysteries and marvels of mind and brain. Such confidence is certainly present in the newer fields of AI and neuroscience, where the propensity to reinvent the wheel is common, but it is also found at times in much of cognitive psychology, linguistics, and cognitive philosophy.

Yet, this coat of ours is cut from cloth of many colors, and it would be unreasonable to see the enterprise of cognitive science as a race (to change the metaphor yet again) in which there are winners and losers. It is far more fruitful to look at the special and sometimes unique contributions of each discipline, and to see how they mutually support and reinforce one another.

There is a scheme that occurred to me in stages over a number of years; it applies principally to psychology,[1] and in particular to the field closest to my own research interests, visual perception. I do not hesitate to use it here for illustrative purposes, however, because the lessons it teaches certainly can be generalized to all of cognitive science. Moreover, perception has always occupied a central place in cognitive science, for several reasons. In the first place, there would be no such thing as cognitive science if perception were not there to supply the "front end." An important legacy of the British empiricist tradition in philosophy is the insistence that the analysis of perception must precede any further inquiry into the nature of cognition: *nihil in intellectu sed praeter in sensu,* as the good Bishop Berkeley said. Moreover the major early leaders of cognitive science all did much of their principal work in perception: Adrian, Lashley, Sperry, even Sherrington (neuroscience); Wertheimer, Hebb, Gibson, Craik (psychology); Pitts and McCulloch, Rosenblith, Marr, even Wiener (machine simulation of cognition). Perhaps the linguists are a bit of an exception, although they would not deny the central part perception plays in the study of language.

The perceptual theorist has to be concerned with the brain and nervous system, especially the receptors and their connections to sensory areas of the brain; with the actions of neurons and populations of neurons in those places; with the phenomenology of perception; with its development; with how perception relates to thinking and language; and so on. It is a veritable microcosm of our science. So why not claim, like some other ambitious cognitive scientists, that perceptionists have all the answers? The response is straightforward: The field is just too big and complex to be comprehended in one discipline, too rich to be captured within a single perspective. Even within perception itself single perpectives are far too limiting to do justice to the richness of the field, as we shall see. So, this is not an attempt to grab priority for perception, rather it is using perception as a model of that to which explanation in cognitive science must aspire.

Three Levels of Perceptual Function

There are three quite distinct ways of trying to understand what visual perception is all about (or four, if one includes the understanding and analysis of the physical energies that give rise to perception, but this is generally external to the perceiving organism and not a part of our study). Starting at the bottom, as it were, we can ask what the physiological basis is. We need an intact brain, good eyes, proper connections between them, well-functioning neural channels, and so on. This is the domain of *sensory physiology*. A great deal is known about these matters, how physical energies are transduced at the receptor surfaces into physiological response and neural code (the action of photoreceptors and their photopigments in the retina is a prime example), how the coded information is relayed to the visual cortex and further sorted and elaborated within the brain. Psychophysical as well as physiological research has thrown much light on the basic question at this level, which is: How are signals received and detected against a "noisy" background of irrelevant and interfering physical and neural activity? Let us call this level of investigation and understanding *level 1*.

Level 1 by no means exhausts the questions we want to ask about perception. Visual signals from the external environment are received and detected, but this is not just a passive process, as the Gestalt psychologists were the first to demonstrate in a totally convincing way; remember the experiments on apparent movement and their interpretation (Wertheimer) that were described in chapter 2. There are questions about *perceptual awareness and organization* that certainly transcend the question of mere detection. They are concerned with matters of coherence, what has been called cooperativity and figural synthesis (how signals interact to compose more global, distinct and interpretable events in the brain), and with investigating the neural substrate for this more elaborate type of perceptual processing.[2] Let us call this *level 2*.

Why should it be claimed that this level is any different from sensory physiology? There are several reasons, to be discussed shortly. Here is just one: The phenomenon of perceptual organization in some cases, and probably in very many, requires that the organism be subject to particular sorts of experience and interact with its environment in particular ways; in other words it depends on perceptual learning of specific kinds. (Remember the theories of Hebb, discussed in chapter 2.) That is not just a matter of sensory physiology, but of the flow of information between organism and environment, in both directions. It also involves, among much else, understanding afference, reafference (the feedback of self-produced stimulation to the organism as it locomotes) and exafference (the discrimination of world-produced as distinct from self-produced movement),[3] and how they affect behavior—a logically new and different set of factors in the equation. We also have to recognize at this level that perception involves, with rather few exceptions so far as we know, *conscious processes*. That will loom large as the discussion progresses.

Our perceptions are organized, but again that is not the end of the matter. Perceiving *serves* cognition, and the organized forms of our perceptions are but a means to the achievement of cognitive goals. The fact that objects, people, events, and actions appear as organized "wholes" is basic to the world we live in, but our understanding of that world, our ability to describe and control it, to monitor our behavior, most assuredly does not depend only on the fact that perceptions are the way they are. It depends on grasping the world in thought, on comprehending and having insight into how and what we perceive, on using our percepts for *cognitive* ends. Let us call this level of *cognitive use* of the products of perception *level 3*.

This threefold division appears at first quite innocuous, but it has enormous consequences for our understanding of the nature of perception, even of cognitive psychology as a whole and a fortiori for our ability to grasp the strengths and limitations of cognitive science.[4] The reason for saying this is that the three levels of activity—sensory physiology, perceptual organization and awareness, and cognitive use—each has its own proper level of research methods and discovery, its own distinct lexicon and sort of discourse and, most important, its own models and conceptual schemes that entail its own idiosyncratic ways and means for the *explanation* of the phenomena with which it deals.

Just as the different disciplines of cognitive science tend separately to the view that they alone provide the key to truth about the mind, so too each of the three levels of investigation of visual perception has a propensity to trespass on the turf of the others. Neuroscientists typically believe that all questions (or, perhaps, all the *important* and *worthwhile* questions) can be answered by research in their domain, that is to say, at level 1.[5] Gestalt psychologists and later theorists deriving from that school, such as J. J. Gibson, likewise argue that *theirs* is the only appropriate level of analysis—that is to say, level 2.[6] Many cognitive psychologists, though not totally dismissing the relevance of the other levels (particularly the physiological) nonetheless insist that all the truly interesting ideas and telling research findings are at the cognitive level, that is, at level 3.[7] It will shortly become abundantly evident that this sort of arrogation of all the important matters to a single discipline, or to a single subspecialty within a discipline, is insupportable, not to say narrow-minded. Here, too, we need to sort out how the different specialties contribute to the understanding of mind, and how they complement one another.

To say that there are three distinct levels of perceptual function does not imply that the levels are insulated from one another. Quite the contrary. To live successfully in the world obviously requires that all three levels are functioning smoothly, interacting cooperatively and coherently. You won't be able to read a book or answer the phone if the black marks on the page or the pressure waves emitted by the receiver aren't properly organized by your nervous system, any more than that organization can occur if the sensory signals are too low in intensity or distorted to be correctly detected. You won't *understand* what you read or hear unless language is in place, and not just language in general but the particular language that is relevant to the passage, and unless that was acquired to an adequate level of competence by virtue of your surroundings, upbringing, and education.

We can't just say, "The three levels must interact smoothly," and leave it at that. We need to discover what the principles of interaction are and how they arise, but that does not vitiate the strong claim that there are major thematic differences, and distinctions of great theoretical import between the levels, that require analysis. To lay out the sensory physiology of the eye and its connections to the brain, for example, is a wonderful scientific achievement, but no amount of investigation at this level can lead to a full understanding of the principles of perceptual organization and information flow referred to above. The point is often overlooked because, of course, the latter does depend in a principled way on the former. That is to say, no perceptual organization can occur in the absence of underlying sensory activity that in important respects constrains it. In like manner we could not "pick language from the page," *use* the written word, if the organization into letters, words, and sentences did not occur more or less automatically and without effort. We can characterize the dependence by this general principle: The lower level activity, whether from levels 2 to 3, as in fluent reading, or from levels 1 to 2 in recognizing single letters and other symbols (or perhaps even from levels 1 to 3 in perceiving single words), is a *necessary condition* for the higher level process, the cognitive activity of reading in our example, to occur. Later this will need to be refined somewhat.

Theme and Variations

The reasons for making the division into three levels run deep and deserve very close analysis. I have sometimes used an analogy with art to clarify the matter, as follows:[8] There are many instances in science and in life where the distinction into levels is accepted and used unself-consciously, because it is obvious, unproblematical, and well understood. The differences between levels in these instances are not unimportant, or thought to have no theoretical relevance; they pose no difficulty of principle because the relations between the levels are clearly recognized. Consider the wonderful world of classical music—or indeed of nonclassical music if your taste runs in that direction. One can comprehend the beauty and majesty of a Brahms symphony in many different ways, but let us consider just the most direct and accessible one, its performance by a fine orchestra. Your appreciation of the symphony will certainly depend on your level of musical sophistication. You may just enjoy the (mostly) cheerful and concordant melodies and harmonies you hear, but you may also appreciate the structure of the composition and savor the subtle use of rhythm, modulation between keys, the many typical "Brahmsian" touches. You may be interested in the sound quality produced by the players, the interpretative ideas of the conductor, the general feeling of inspiration—or lack of it—that the performance manifests. You may have an interest in the history and development of symphonic writing, be particularly on the lookout for the ways in which Brahms pays his respects to Beethoven in this work, and so on. How do we love the music? Let us count the ways!

To be more specific: The basis for the music we hear is, of course, the sound waves generated by the various instruments as they are bowed, blown, plucked, or thumped. These purely physical events are studied and explained in the science of *acoustics*. The dimensions of the acoustic signal (wavelength, amplitude, phase, the mixture of these variables in a given sound source, their interaction at a receptor site in space, the effects of reflecting and absorbing surfaces, etc.) are well understood, as is their relation to the sound-producing instruments (in terms of materials, shape, source of vibrational energy, and the like). However completely the generation and propagation of acoustic signals is understood and explainable in physical terms, it would take a truly monumental Philistine to claim that this is all that can be known, or all that we need to know, about the symphonic performance.

The next level, related to level 1, defined above, is concerned with the immediate sensory effects of the acoustic stimuli produced by the instruments. These may be simple, like the detection of the tone produced by a flute, which is characterized essentially just by its frequency and amplitude (a simple sinewave). The frequency and amplitude (physical acoustic measures) are tightly correlated with the *perceived* sensory qualities of pitch and loudness of the tone. The physical and perceived events, however, *are two different things*. The relations between them are studied in the science of *psychoacoustics*. We accept the strong relation between the sets of variables in the two domains (frequency and amplitude in the physical, pitch and loudness in the psychological) to such an extent that we often *overlook* the fact that they are empirically and logically distinct and, indeed, quite separate entities. It is a fact of the world that as frequency of a sinewave increases, the perceived pitch goes up so long as the frequency remains in the audible range, but it is a bare fact. It invites explanation, but is not itself more than the description of a relation between a physical and a psychological event; the same goes for the relation between amplitude and loudness. Frequency does not explain the *quality* of perceived pitch. It is just one term in the dyadic relation, a relation that is extraordinarily tight and predictable, between the two variables. A change in frequency is a sufficient condition for a change in pitch, but equally a change in (perceived) pitch is sufficient evidence for a change in frequency. Likewise with the mutual relation of amplitude and loudness.

All this may seem like straining at a gnat, so what is the point? Consider a more complicated psychophysical relation, that between the frequency components of a tone and *timbre*. The difference in sound quality between, let us say, a flute and an oboe is obvious even to a naive listener; one is "pure," the other is "plaintive," to put it simply. The sound produced by the steady blowing on a flute is pretty well a pure sinewave, as I mentioned—that is, a waveform of a single fixed amplitude and frequency. The oboe's note, however, has a number of components, each expressible as sinewaves of different amplitudes and frequencies, that are related to each other in complicated but perfectly well understood ways. One can synthesize the sound of an oboe, or a French horn, a trumpet or clarinet, if one knows the relevant frequencies and amplitudes of the "simple" component tones, a fact first demonstrated by Helmoltz a century and half ago.[9] Again, the correlation between the physically complex waveform produced by each instrument and the resulting *tonal quality* that a listener experiences is very tight, very regular; it is a fact of the world, but it does not *explain* how or why the complex waveform gives rise to the particular perceived quality of timbre that is characteristic of a given instrument. We can say that (under normal circumstances) the physical event of a particular sound pressure waveform is a sufficient condition for some specified auditory quality (the sound of a trumpet, for instance) to be heard, but that merely asserts the empirical regularity that is discovered between them. It is not at all an explanation of the relation.

So, the point is this: We find that the physics of acoustics needs to be supplemented by the empirically discovered correlates in what is heard, if we are to make sense of the psychophysical and sensory basis of music. Is that the end of the matter? Most certainly not! We could go into the question of how the ear and brain sort out the most incredibly complicated acoustic waveforms generated by an orchestra in full flight, into the individual instruments and different orchestral sections that the listener (if properly schooled and paying attention) can readily discern. That in itself is an astounding achievement, indeed one that seems impossible of accomplishment in terms of what we know of the detailed action of the inner ear, the cochlea, and its basilar membrane, which are the medium of transduction of the physiological auditory system.[10] We shall not pursue the question, because it is in most respects still unanswered (truth to tell, it is still scarcely ever asked). There can be no doubt that these astounding feats of perceptual organization occur, because we *experience* them, despite the fact that they are beyond the competence of basic auditory psychophysics to explain! We can be confident, however, that the functions relating relatively simple acoustic signals to their perceived correlates, as described in psychophysics, are a necessary foundation for the more complex perceptual events that we experience in the sounds of musical instruments and their playing together in ensemble.

Does the discovery of auditory perceptual organization settle the matter? Again, certainly not. There is more to music than just organization of sounds into pleasing patterns. As the renowned conductor Sir Thomas Beecham put it: "The English don't appreciate good music, they just enjoy the noise it makes!" In other words, the appreciation of music goes well beyond the pleasures produced by the triumphant resonance of a full brass section playing *fortissimo,* or the silky ease of the perfectly attuned *legato* of the twelve cellos of a great orchestra like the Berlin Philharmonic. Those sounds may be necessary components of a good orchestral performance, but they hardly begin to manifest on their own the hallmark attributes of the great symphony of Brahms with which we started, let alone those that characterize a musically outstanding rendition of the work. To savor those qualities, a whole new universe of discourse and sensibilities must be brought, as we may say, into play.

Not to belabor the matter unduly, this would include the formal basis of classical music; the diatonic scale, harmony, rhythm, meter, tonality, sonata form and its development in the romantic and post-romantic eras; aesthetic appreciation of music and its changes over time; the influence of leading composers on contemporary taste, and the steady flow of the "radical" into the "mainstream" of musical culture; the training of musicians in the skills required to play or conduct; and so on and on.

Other aspects of musical performance and appreciation could be raised, but my point is now obvious: There is no one level of knowledge or expertise, no single universe of discourse, that suffices to describe, much less to comprehend, the complexities of executing or appreciating that symphony of Brahms. We understand quite well how the different levels of acoustic, perceptual, cognitive, and esthetic phenomena feed into the total complex that is music, and we have a good grasp, on the whole, of how the different levels relate to each other. In particular we can see the sense of the claim that "lower" (or at least empirically "prior") levels of activity are the necessary foundation for "higher" or subsequent occurrences. This is clear in the case of acoustic signal and perceived tone, or the relation between single tones and their function as building blocks for a tonal or harmonic sequence—much as single letters are related to words and sentences. These sequences are themselves the basis for the cognitive-cultural realities of music appreciation. In every case the antecedent precedes and in a sense mediates, but does not foretell conceptually, forestall, or *embody* its sequelae. You cannot *explain* musical taste in terms of the organization of heard notes, much less in terms of their underlying acoustic signals. They certainly "go together," but one does not *follow from* the other in a logically necessary or consistent fashion. No amount of study, experimentation, or theorizing in the domain of physical acoustics, pure and simple, could ever, even in principle, lead to the recognition and knowledge of sensed tonal qualities,[11] and similarly with the other levels. A full comprehension of the musical domain requires us to recognize the existence of these different levels (a matter of principle) and to be willing to explore their properties and interrelations. One hugely important matter is the question of whether, and to what extent, events at one level can ever be invoked to *explain* those at another. This is distinct from the question of the discovery of tight correlations between events, or classes of event, at two levels.

We have barely skimmed the surface, but the lesson is now obvious: Levels of function, discourse, and explanation are at the heart of our knowledge and understanding of music. The same is true of many—perhaps most, or even all—complex domains of interest in science and in life. Back to cognitive science: It is true of visual perception, indeed of perception in general and of cognition in its broadest sense. Three levels of function in the mature perceiver were identified earlier: the levels of sensory physiology, perceptual awareness and organization, and of cognitive use. At each separate level there belong distinctly different and well-recognized research methods, concepts, explanatory models, and theories of function,[12] so what is properly an explanation at one level is not likely to be appropriate at another. The failure to recognize this can lead to great confusion in our attempts to understand perception.

In music it is rather obvious that what is acceptable as discourse and explanation in the realm of musical esthetics is generally quite remote from bare questions of physical acoustics. That is not to say that the latter are *irrelevant;* not at all, but they are not the ground on which to establish a high-level discussion about musical taste. Similarly the appropriate level at which to tackle research on social communication by means of facial expression is not likely to involve in any direct way questions to do with photoreceptors or the retinal receptive field properties of rods and cones. The latter are by no means irrelevant, because with very few exceptions the recognition of facial expression involves visual detection as a first step, and in that the retinal receptors play a pivotal role. However, to get to a useful discussion of social communication, that role, and many others, has to be assumed as necessary background, so to speak, to the task at hand; it scarcely enters the pertinent phases of the discussion. In both these examples it is clear that reference to some other level of function would be incongruous, inappropriate, even misleading, although not in principle wrong. I shall argue later that we need to encourage similar sensibilities in cognitive science, where things may not be so obvious, so caution is needed lest we be led astray by loose thinking about what constitutes a level, what is allowable as theoretical debate both within and between levels, and especially about the explanatory moves that are permissible and fruitful within this framework. Before doing that, there is a very important distinction to get straight: the distinction between a *cause* and a *reason,* something that is intimately related to the difference between a matter of *fact,* and a matter of *logic.*

Prediction and Explanation

In previous examples I have emphasized that although certain events might be a necessary groundwork for some other occurrence, such groundwork need not be, and in fact frequently is not, a part of the *explanation* of that occurrence. To make this fully transparent, we need to look closely at what is meant by an explanation and to distinguish this from some other sorts of claim that are often confused with it.

Let us start by making a sharp contrast between a reason and a cause. These terms, and the concepts they purport to identify, have given rise to endless philosophical debate and a great deal of erudite research among philosophers of science on the nature of explanation.[13] I shall skirt most of that, and only consider the distinction between reason and cause that is needed to further our understanding of explanation in cognitive science. The contrast I have in mind is hardly new,[14] but it has not had any discernible impact on the way most cognitive scientists go about attempting explanation of their findings. This must change, because the difference between a reason and a cause plays a central role in the analysis of what it means to give an explanation. In fact, failure to make the distinction has led to all manner of mistakes in presenting what purport to be explanations in cognitive science, and indeed elsewhere too.

We think we know pretty much what it means to say "A causes B," but the matter is not as simple as we might want to believe. B may in fact always occur after A, but we tend to mean more than this; we imply that there is a necessary connection between the two. Where does the idea of necessary connection come from? David Hume (1711–1776) argued that the notion is essentially psychological, a habit of mind induced by the frequent association or constant conjunction of two things. Having been indissoluble in experience, they are conceived by the mind as necessarily connected.[15] However, that necessity is illusory; it is induced by mental habit; it is certainly not the logical necessity we are familiar with in other contexts, such as in drawing the conclusion of a syllogism. Hume's ideas have been very influential, although without doubt more among philosophers than practicing scientists. Nevertheless in modern science we can readily find examples of experimental work that illustrate and reinforce this "empirical" view of causality. Here is a favorite of mine, if only because its simple clarity struck me so forcibly as a young man.

In the 1950s it was discovered that the shapes of snow crystals, remarkably symmetrical and surprisingly individual in pattern, can be strictly controlled by the ambient conditions at the time they are formed. A nylon thread suspended in a supercooled vessel of water vapor is all that's needed for a demonstration. Snowflake crystals start to form that are either plate-like or needle-like; the two types are readily distinguishable, and which type is formed depends only on the temperature and pressure of the vapor. Given the antecedents, a specific temperature and pressure, the consequents follow with perfect regularity. We would be strongly inclined—and correct—to say that the given temperature and pressure *cause* the formation of crystals of a particular type, either plates or needles. Is this an explanation of the difference in patterns? Of course not! All that has been demonstrated is an empirical regularity, but it is so strong and tidy that we are convinced something further remains to be discovered. This may be described as "the underlying cause" or "the *real* cause"; but what is really being asked for is not a cause at all, it is a *reason* for, or an *explanation* of, the relations between antecedent conditions and consequent crystal form. At the time of this discovery no explanation was in fact offered. It would be extremely surprising if, after 40 years or more, no explanation has been forthcoming. And what would such an explanation be? Most assuredly it would *not* consist in the mere reiteration, or even the further exploration, of the antecedent conditions that ensure the phenomenon's occurrence. No; it would consist without doubt in the elaboration of a model of molecular dynamics, probably mathematical in character, from which the differences in crystal formation can be deduced, a model that entails those differences *as necessary consequences*. That, we would no doubt all agree, gives a *reason* why the phenomena occur.

We see then that cause is related to prediction; the type of crystal to be formed is perfectly predictable if the antecedent temperature and pressure are known. The reason for an occurrence is quite different, has a logically distinct character, and occurs (if we use the concept correctly) within a certain theoretical context. The context may be poorly articulated, even undiscovered or totally misconstrued, but that is a contingent matter. The essential character of a reason is that it has theoretical substance, has some—perhaps even quite tenuous, but nonetheless present—explanatory power. It is important to realize that this is true not just of physics, or of sciences only, but is a universal feature of how we express and analyze our thoughts about the world. It is a basic endowment of our language and the cognitive powers it mediates.

The intrinsic contrast between reason and cause can be further clarified by examining a situation in which giving a reason (or reasons) is right and proper, whereas to talk of cause is not. Our example comes from mathematics; examples in logic or formal modeling could also make the point. The branch of mathematics called *analysis* progresses by following accepted rules of inference to show that if a mathematical expression (called a *function;* say F) has some property or properties, $a,b,c,$ . . . , then it must also have the property X. This is called a proof that F is (or has) X. To complete a proof it must be shown first that $a,b,c,$ . . . are *necessary* conditions for F to have $X;$ that is, unless the properties $a,b,c,$ . . . are true of F, it cannot (*logically* cannot) have the property X. Secondly it must be shown that $a,b,c,$ . . . are *sufficient* conditions for F to have $X;$ that is, that $a,b,c,$ . . . on their own guarantee, or entail, that the property X is true of F. These elementary conditions of necessity and sufficiency are universally recognized canons of logic and are accepted criteria for a valid proof, but they have nothing to do with *causes*. It would be a strained use of language indeed to say that $a,b,c,$ . . . *cause* F to have $X!$ They are, however, the reason why—as was to be demonstrated—F has X. Or we could equally well say, they are an *explanation* of why F has the property X.

The concept of prediction is thus intimately associated with the concept of cause, and the concept of explanation with the concept of reason. We could as well put the matter the other way around; saying you know the cause of something is implicitly claiming that you can predict the conditions under which it occurs (the type of snowflake crystal in our example). When you say you know the reason for something, you mean—or should mean if you use the words correctly—that you have an explanation for it (the reason that F has X in our mathematical example). The former is basically empirical, the latter essentially theoretical, conceptual. One has to do with facts, the other with ideas.

To find the cause of something, really all you need do is observe, remember, and recount the facts. But to find the reason (or, more properly *a* reason) for something, you need an explanatory context, a theoretical position, even one that's only implicit or vaguely formulated (the typical situation outside science, and even within it on occasion), to justify your claim. Much effort has gone into trying to analyze the concept of explanation in the philosophy of science, some considerable amount of which could have been saved if this simple distinction had been born in mind or better understood. We see immediately, for instance, that the concept of a "causal explanation" is misleading and unfortunate; it hopelessly obscures the distinction. Admittedly my point goes against a strong tradition in the philosophy of science;[16] too bad! It is an unfortunate tradition.

The reason, or rather *a* reason, for the muddle is the prominent role the concepts of necessary and sufficient conditions have played in the debate. But two meanings or interpretations of necessity and sufficiency have been badly confused here. When we talk of the necessary and sufficient conditions for predicting something, as in the snowflake example, we are talking of empirically discovered conditions that are necessary and sufficient (or in many cases, just sufficient). There could be other conditions, but that would be a matter for further experimental investigation. The researcher may have hunches about what these conditions might be—after all such discoveries are seldom made in a complete theoretical vacuum—but at this stage of inquiry that's what they would be: hunches. Of course many important scientific discoveries have been made by following up such hunches, but we must be clear that this is in principle different from the experimental test of a specific theoretical deduction.

Unfortunately, the waters are further muddied by the fact that the word *prediction* is also used in the theoretical context. We do talk of experimental tests of theoretical predictions; that is, of predicting factual outcomes on the basis of a specific model, hypothesis, or theory. That usage is well-sanctioned by tradition, too. If we had the presence of mind always to call them theoretical, or theoretically based, predictions (which they are) in contradistinction to practical or pragmatic (that is, Humean) predictions, we would not go astray. It would be an excellent and confusion-killing change if we could find different words to identify the two very distinct meanings of the word *prediction;* perhaps *entailment* (theoretical) and *forecast* (empirical) would fit the bill? When both very different types of prediction are called by the same name, and more often than not confounded conceptually as well, it is small wonder that we run into serious trouble. This is particularly a problem in cognitive science, as we shall very soon see.

Back to the matter of necessary and sufficient conditions: In the mathematical, logical, or *theoretical* arena, these conditions have nothing to do with practical necessity, sufficiency, or the prediction of factual outcomes. They have the force of *logical* necessity and sufficiency; that is, they follow from the ground rules of logical discourse and procedure. You have to accept them if you adopt those ground rules and want to remain consistent; that is, want to avoid self-contradiction. And what is the nature of those ground rules, of the logical theory that dictates the correct rules of argument, inference, and entailment? They are certainly not empirical generalizations. We do not decide on whether a rule of logic is correct or not by a democratic vote, or by going out into the world and finding out how the rule is in fact applied! No, the way to decide whether a logical argument, or a mathematical proof, is watertight is to find out what the accepted rules are, and whether they have been properly followed. And that itself is a wholly conceptual, theoretical, thought-dependent process. To reiterate the point: The reason why an argument is logically acceptable is not that it has been popular in the past, nor even that astute people have accepted its validity, nor yet (the modern guise of its misapprehension) that a computer/calculator made use of it. The reason for acceptability is that the rules were correctly followed, and that constitutes an *explanation* of why the conclusions follow from the premises of the argument. Empirically necessary and sufficient conditions are, as we have seen, fundamentally different, and have to do with regularity in factual occurrences.

To summarize this centrally important section: Empirical predictions (forecasts) are in principle different from theoretical predictions (entailments), and the two should never be confused. The difference is closely related to the distinction between a cause and a reason. We can follow Hume in identifying causes as empirically observed sets of circumstances that always precede some particular result;[17] the observation is essentially atheoretical. In claiming to have discovered a cause we are claiming that some given set of antecedent empirical conditions are necessary and/or sufficient to predict the consequent (the stated outcome), but nothing more. It would be excellent if we could get into the habit of always calling these *empirically* necessary and sufficient conditions, and what follows from them *empirical* predictions, if we must continue to use the word *prediction*. In contrast, making a *theoretical* prediction is to claim an entailment; the predicted outcome follows necessarily from some given scientific model or theory. Again, it would be good to be rid of the word *prediction*, although the sanctions of tradition make this unlikely. The word *forecast* sits awkwardly in the present vocabulary of science, so I shall continue to use the word *prediction*, but now only in the first, Humean, sense of empirical prediction.

Armed with knowledge about the difference between a cause and a reason, between empirical prediction and theoretical explanation, we can proceed with the dismemberment and reorganization of cognitive psychology, using as our guide and key perceptual psychology.

Levels of Function and Powers of Explanation

We have distinguished three main levels of function in the cognitive-perceptual organism, those of sensory physiology and analysis, perceptual awareness and organization, and cognitive use. It was argued, as in the analogy with music, that each level has its own characteristic motifs, data forms, methods of research, and explanatory principles. No one level is more important than any other, and for a comprehensive understanding of perception it is without question necessary to take into account all three. To develop this theme satisfactorily we have to apply the distinction made in the previous section between cause and reason, between (empirical) prediction and explanation, to the multilayered enterprise before us.

Recall the argument that to understand the nature of a sensed quality of a tone (of the oboe, say) it is not sufficient to analyze its acoustic waveform. However, if we know that the given waveform meets a (properly functioning) human ear, we can predict—*forecast*—with confidence that a tone with oboe timbre will be heard. The statement is completely atheoretical, and simply expresses that intimate empirical relation known to exist between waveform and tonal quality. We would be comfortable too, saying that the acoustic wave *causes* the sensed tone. What about an explanation? It should by now be abundantly clear that so far we don't have one. We are in the same position as the physicists of 40 years ago when the snowflake phenomenon was discovered. And yet, not quite so. Why not? Because we are rather inclined to believe that, having found the acoustically necessary and sufficient conditions for the oboe tone, we *have* explained it. If so, we are wrong. Moreover, a persistent sensory physiologist or psychologist, even if the point about mere prediction from acoustic signal to sensed tone were accepted, might very well counter that of course there is an explanation; it is to be found in the way the inner ear transduces the energy in the acoustic wave into neural signals in the auditory nerve pathways, which then transport them to the relevant cortical centers in the auditory cortex for further analysis. That is a complicated but relatively well-known story, so it is in the details of this transmission that explanation should be sought and can be found.

What should be made of that argument? Simply that it embodies that very same confusion between prediction and explanation that I have been at pains to exorcise. How so? All our sensory psychologist is able to establish, beyond the admittedly very important and fascinating details of transmission of nerve pulses from ear to brain, is that, on arrival at the appropriate place in the auditory cortex, those signals are sufficient to give rise to, to *cause* the tonal sensation. That is all. The statement is atheoretical; it does no more than establish yet another, although an even more intimate, correlation between one event and another, between brain event and sensed event. It gives no hint of an *explanation* of why one is associated with, causes, the other. It just moves the site of uncertainty, of bewonderment, one place further up, or into, the mysterious regions of the brain where conscious experience is, apparently, "generated." I use this word advisedly because, as is now very obvious, we have no theory of how consciousness arises, of whether "generation" is an appropriate descriptor. It is perhaps just as misleading as any other word, because it seems to hint at a mechanism or mode of genesis, but the hint is an empty promissory note.

In going from physical signal to sensed quality we have gone "up" a level, from level 1 to level 2. Within the first level we obtain accounts of how one form of energy is transformed into another, from acoustic wave into nerve signals and cortical activity. At this level our sensory psychologist would be quite right to claim understanding and explanation of the physiological happenings, because there are relevant models of neural and chemical processes that underlie them and from which, if they are correct, the facts of neural transduction and transmission can be deduced. What is wrong, *in principle* wrong, is to claim that these models give us any theoretical handle on the leap between levels from neural action to awareness. The matter is complicated by the fact that, in psychophysics especially, reported sensations are used as the basis for developing models of neural action, for inferring what the underlying physiological processes must be like.[18] A little thought will show, nonetheless, that sensations are here being used merely as evidence for occurrences at a lower level, not as terms in a theoretical account of that level—which would be the converse of the situation we have been discussing.

Let us agree, then, that at level 1 we can comfortably accommodate all that lies within the province of physiology and its relations with the "external world," the world of physics and chemistry that supplies the energies to which the receptors respond. Physiological and chemical models, explanations, deductions form the necessary and sufficient conditions of a mechanism's postulated mode of operation, entailments of experimental outcomes, all are allowed and give no cause for concern. It is when we want to gear up from this level to the next, "extrapolate" as some theorists like to say (although it will become clear, if it is not already, what a misleading and dangerous word that can be) to a higher level, that the difficulties start.[19]

At level 2 there is a dual concern: We need to deal with awareness, conscious perceptual experience, as the fundamental fact of perception, and at the same time with the unquestionably organized character of that experience. The major champions of that dual aspect of perception in this century were the Gestalt psychologists and their followers. The "mature" or later Gestalt psychologists, led by Köhler, were caught in something of a bind, because they insisted on the primary importance of their phenomenology (the way things *look* is the royal road to understanding the nature of perception), on the one hand, but on the other were determined to find physiological, brain-based principles by which to explain the appearances. That is why their theory of isomorphism (roughly the theory that patterns of activity in "cortical fields"—probably electrical in nature—determine what is perceived) achieved such dominance and, when shown (by physiological experiment) to be wrong, led to the eclipse of the Gestalt movement for several decades.

The Gestalt *phenomena* are, without question, at level 2. The first Gestalt psychologist, Max Werthiemer, and latter day followers on his path like J. J. Gibson, have stressed that the way to understand perception in the first instance is to investigate it *sui generis,* that is to say, to study it on its own terms, without preconceptions about any mechanisms or physiological substrate. All the brilliant perceptual demonstrations of the Gestalt school, and of the transactionalists and Gibson, owe their success to this fact.[20] They are essays in phenomenology, exploiting what the nature of a perceptual system (usually vision) has to offer, and they assume that their effectiveness is principally a function of what the attentive observer actually perceives. No problems there. Things only start to go amiss when the question of explanation is raised.

The later Gestalt psychologists went astray by misidentifying what the underlying physiology might be, as already noted. We should not castigate them for that, but for the much more serious fault of thinking that the underlying physiology would *explain* perception. The point is subtler than at first appears. They were within permissible bounds in asserting that the organized quality of perceived events and things is mediated by organized brain fields. It could well be that one is correlated with the other; that is an empirical matter, and open to investigation. We might thus find grounds for claiming that those brain fields *cause* the perceptions to have certain properties (remember the snowflakes). But to say that the organized brain fields *explain* perceptions as such is to fall into the trap of confusion between cause and reason, a case of failing to make the distinction between two meanings of the word prediction described earlier. Showing that two things are correlated in no way constitutes an explanation of one by the other. We have no model, no theoretical mechanism, no modus operandi, by means of which to deduce from brain states anything essential about what is *consciously perceived,* but that is exactly what we would have to have in order to explain the perceptual facts uncovered by the Gestalt psychologists in the way they advocated.

To return to an important point, I must insist that what is true of the Gestalt account of the relation between brain and perception is equally true of all contemporary accounts of that same relation. What is the current view (I refuse to call it a theory—that is just what it is not) and why is it so popular? The current view is that perceptions are due to the activation of particular neurons in the visual system, or populations of such neurons, their mutual excitatory and inhibitory interactions, and that perceptual organization can be accounted for in terms of the receptive field and architectonic properties of those units (chapter 3). Its popularity stems from the hugely successful research into those properties, following the pioneer studies of Hubel and Wiesel.[21] Not only does that research convey a sense of incredibly detailed and complex, but delicately balanced, order and stability in the visual system, it also shows that many of the systematic features of vision discovered in its pure phenomenology and in psychophysics have remarkably exact counterparts in the receptive field organization and the multiple mappings of the retina (and hence the visual field) onto different divisions of the cortex. So, for example, the separation among color, texture, and contour boundary found in normal vision is reflected in the separate "processing channels" and "maps" for these attributes in the neurophysiology and anatomy of the brain.

We are greatly impressed by all this, and rightly so, but let it not blind us to the fact that we are still talking of discovered correlations, empirical parallels between the two domains. Conceptually it brings us no farther forward than the theory of isomorphism. That theory had some merit, as we saw, in that it proposed a way for properties of one domain to be reflected in the other, and exactly the same is true of the current view. It would be strange indeed if the micro- and macroscopic principles of organization found in the retinocortical pathways had no bearing at all on what is perceived, and I think no one believes that to be the case. But we must not ignore the fact that, however much we discover about the physiological substrate of vision, those discoveries do not *in themselves* entail anything at all about perception per se, perception in the ordinary phenomenological sense of the word. That is, they do not afford explanations of the qualities of perceptual awareness. To think otherwise is to fall into the cause/reason confusion.

It is difficult to "think away" the cognitive components of the perceptions we normally experience. The distinguished perceptual theorist Irwin Rock stated: "Perception is shot through with intelligence," and he is right. Nevertheless it is possible to strip those components away, to think of "stimulating information," as Gibson called it, information that elicits perceptual responses as it were automatically, one might say instinctively, in the manner of the "sign stimuli" described in ethology. We can do the thought experiment of seeing a circle pure and simple, without naming it or thinking of its geometrical properties or any of its uses; it would still be that characteristic, well-organized shape. The same would be true of a tree, a bird, or a log of wood. Any one of those would provide an "affordance," to use Gibson's term, invite a response (to seek shade, shoot it, or sit down) without the intercession of thought. That we could say is perception "pure and simple"; let us call it for convenience perception (a).[22] This is what we mean by the level 2 phenomena of perception. Contrast it with the full panoply of cognitive activity into which perception (a) feeds in activities such as reading, cheering on a favorite racehorse, or—as one insightful pair of commentators put it—recognizing the North Star *as* the North Star, that is, recognizing a specific "raw feature" of the perceptual manifold (a point of light in the night sky) as a pivotal component of the cosmological model espoused by Western science. We can call this activity, shot through with intelligence as Rock said, perception (b). It is perception serving cognitive ends, which I described earlier, and is clearly at level 3. It is, as a matter of fact, the "knowledge saturated" perception of normal experience, and what we have in mind and refer to when we mention seeing, hearing, etc., in everyday talk.

So, just as the goings-on in the physiological visual system fall short of the requirements for explaining conscious perception [in the first instance this is perception (a), we may note], so, too, the occurrence of perception (a) does not in any way explain activities at level 3, however strong the correlation between events at the two levels may be. You may have a perfect [perception (a)] description of the men on a chessboard, to take a striking example, but that in no way ensures that you see them *as* the pieces in a game of chess.[23] Over time you might work out the allowable moves empirically by watching the game being played, but that, too, is far from gaining an understanding of what it means to play a game, what strategy, attack, defense, castling, pawn promotion, and all the rest connote, what it means to compete against another player, to contest a championship, etc. To return to a familiar theme, occurrences at level 2, the "stripped down" sort of perception [perception (a)] may yield empirically necessary and sufficient conditions for the game to be played, but it certainly does not supply logically necessary and sufficient conditions for the complete analysis of what chess is all about.[24] It does not, in other words, lead to an explanation of chess as a cognitive skill. To think otherwise is to fall once more into the cause/reason trap; if you say that in a given game moving the rook to e7 causes the king to be in check, you are asserting that, empirically, that's what the move of the rook brings about. You could eventually discover the fact by observing a lot of games; the outcome is predictable. To give a reason why the move puts the king in check, however, cannot be done except by invoking the rules of the game. That way you can *explain* why the move must result in check, *logically* must do so, because of the rules, not just as an empirical generalization.

It should now be clear that reasons, explanations, because they occur in a context where rules are invoked—that is, within certain logical and/or linguistic conventions—can only be given when there are valid conceptual connections between explicans and explicandum. The antecedent and consequent terms of the relation must be logically congruent; this has sometimes been known as a *nomic connection*. Philosophers used to talk of the "logical geography" of a word or expression. I find that a very useful, although no longer a popular, image. We can say that explicans and explicandum must share the same logical territory in order for an explanation to be well-founded. In the case of syllogistic reasoning (All men are mortal, Socrates is a man . . . , etc.) this may seem pretty obvious, but the subtleties and intricacies of the conceptual and linguistic presuppositions that make for valid syllogistic reasoning have only recently been properly investigated.[25] If this "territorial imperative" is true of the syllogism, we can be fairly sure it is equally true of other, less tightly categorized, forms of reasoning. Neglecting this matter will always land us in danger of falling into the cause/reason trap, the trap of confusing empirically necessary and sufficient conditions for an event's occurrence with the logically imposed (nomic) necessary and sufficient conditions that support an explanation.

The previous paragraph is not getting as far away from our main theme as might be supposed. To return to the Gestalt psychologists, it seems that they made a second major logical blunder. Not only did they fail to appreciate that brain states can never (logically, never) explain conscious experience, they fell into the cause/reason trap a second time by assuming that their organized perceptual fields [perception (a), be it noted] could explain cognitive phenomena.[26] But to put it briefly, no perceptual field, however highly organized, entails anything at all about cognition as such, about the thinking needed to solve a geometrical problem, for instance; recall the chess example. Perceptions may be effective *preconditions* for cognition; indeed most of our talk of perception is about perception (b) ("shot through with intelligence"), so much so that we fail to make the distinction between it and purely cognitive activity.[27] The latter has its own distinctive characteristics, and invites explanation in its own terms. You can't explain thinking in terms of perceptual activity or imagery that may accompany it any more than you can explain seeing blue by pointing to tightly correlated activity in the cortical substrate. Just as in going from level 1 to level 2 we have to be watchful and not fall into that familiar cause/reason trap, so too we must distinguish empirical predictability from logical entailment in going from level 2 to level 3. In this case it is more difficult to find a pure and convincing example, but here's a suggestion of what's involved: Consider the congruence of two triangles (they are "exactly the same" in normal parlance). You could demonstrate that they are congruent by cutting out two replicas and placing one on top of the other to show that their edges coincide exactly at all points. With the help of graphics technology, you could make this coincidence as precise as you please (or as the technology will allow), but however exact the fit, this does not have the same conclusiveness as *proving* congruence from Euclid's postulates. The former is an event at level 2, the latter of level 3, a cognitive act par excellence. The example is not perfect, because the technology that allows one to make the perfect fit certainly will involve elements of level 3, and the "purity" of the Euclidean proof—freedom from contamination by perceptual elements—might be questioned, and indeed has been in the history of mathematics.

What would it mean to explain "pure" cognition, to treat it completely on its own terms? Well, to take one easy example, it can mean to demonstrate that an argument is faulty because it fails to live up to the canons of rational inference, misuses a concept, or misconstrues a perceptual cue.[28] Perceptual confusion, brain malfunction, faulty memory, poor instruction, etc. may be relevant factors, but they are not themselves in the position of explaining what poor reasoning is. They certainly might, however, be cited as causes for poor performance!

To summarize: The three levels of function (sensory physiology and analysis, conscious perception and organization, cognitive use) are accompanied by three levels of different explanatory principles. Each level has its own appropriate theoretical constructs, specific models and mechanisms of operation. Each level has its own set of pertinent questions and answers, and these are relevant only *within* that level. Necessary and sufficient conditions for an explanation have validity only *within* a level. *Between* levels the relations are often close, even intimate and necessary, but the flavor of the necessary and sufficient conditions is now quite different. They are the *empirical* conditions that are relevant to Humean causality and are essentially atheoretical.

Explanation and Machine Vision

In case you are still not convinced, here is a very similar argument about levels given by David Marr, one of the most hard-nosed of AI researchers and a founder of modern research on machine vision. His argument and mine were arrived at independently, and from quite different points of view, so it is gratifying to find them converging on the same conclusion—different paths to the same destination.

Marr also argues for three logically distinct levels of understanding and explanation in cognitive psychology. They are (c) computational, (b) algorithmic, and (a) physical. Starting from "above," level (c) is needed because, without a good idea (model, or theory) of what the computations under consideration are designed to achieve, no adequate scientific explanation is available or even logically possible. Marr believed that everything in cognitive science (in fact, it seems, everything of any interest whatsoever) is computational, or rather is to be explained in computational terms. That to me is far from evident. In fact the word *computational* is a gross misnomer for level (c); it should be called the *conceptual* level. In any case Marr's point is that, without a good conception (idea, model, or theory) of what the computation (or, less tendentiously, the activity) under consideration is designed to achieve, no explanations are in principle available. Level (b), the algorithmic level, is the one where the actual processes (the *effective procedures,* as we earlier called them) designed to execute those computations are defined. The third, physical, level (a) is the one at which the specified procedures, the algorithms, are implemented in hardware or, if we are talking of biological systems, in "wetware," the physiological basis for implementation. Marr stresses the vital point that different sorts of question are asked at each level, so different sorts of answers (that is to say, explanations) are appropriate to each one.

He illustrates his basic argument by way of a simple example; the handheld calculator. The point, or purpose, of such an instrument can only be grasped given prior understanding of arithmetic (or statistics, algebra, trigonometry, etc., depending on what the calculator was designed for) and the ends that calculation within the relevant domain serves. This is the conceptual level (c). At the second, algorithmic, level one asks—and answers—questions about the routines, rules, and conventions (e.g., of binary representation) by means of which the calculator functions; one might say, by means of which it achieves the desired outputs. Questions about the physical nature of the device, whether it is mechanical, electronic, etc., are asked at the "lowest" level, level (a), and physical explanations are appropriate. This division is clear enough for a simple device like a handheld calculator. Marr asserts that the three levels apply to any cognitive activity and the brain that implements it. I think he is basically correct.

Notice that while explanations are in principle different at the three levels (about the concepts to which computation will be applied, the procedures for achieving calculation, and the physical implementation of the procedures) and are level-specific, there are nonetheless intimate relations between occurrences at the three levels. A lower level provides the empirically necessary and sufficient conditions for the activity at a higher level, as is particularly obvious in the case of hardware implementation. If you know what is going on in a bit of the hardware you can perhaps predict that a particular calculation is in progress, but that is far from furnishing an explanation of the nature of that calculation, let alone of calculation *tout court.* So it goes in general; the situation is directly analogous to the one I discussed at length for perception, with level (a) corresponding to my level 1, etc. What is admissible as explanation at one level is not applicable as explanation at a different level, but the occurrence of an event at one level can still have causal consequences for what occurs at another.

To pursue the comparison a bit further: Level 1 in my scheme is the one at which questions about sensory physiology and neural coding are asked. Appropriate answers (explanations) will in principle be in physiological and biophysical terms, just as in Marr's case questions about the physical properties of the hand-held calculator are answered in physical terms [level (a)]. Level 2 is the level at which organization (memorial, perceptual, linguistic) occurs. Such organizational phenomena—in some respects algorithmic, but certainly psychological processes par excellence—are the vehicles of (or, as some contemporary theorists put it, provide the support for) true cognitive activity, just as in Marr's example the algorithms of level (b) supply the necessary support for achieving correct calculations. Understanding what these calculations are, however, is not to be confused with stating the algorithms. Just so, at level 3 things such as language (speech acts) object and event recognition occur, but their occurrence is not simply a restatement of the level 2 processes of organization and routine. No amount of modeling at level 2 entails any statement about the use of such organization for cognitive ends—that is, for mental acts. Even though the level 2 processes provide a causal context, a necessary effect of which is the level 3 phenomenon (just as the calculator's algorithm leads to a correct calculation), the relationship between the level 2 and level 3 events is more complex, and more subtle, than cognitive theorists typically admit. To say that the level 2 activity *explains* that at level 3 is not merely simplistic, it is wrong, and does less than justice to our knowledge of cognition as well as our understanding of what an explanation is. It confuses causal context with nomic connection.

It is important to realize that the influence from one level to another goes in both directions but has an entirely different character when it is from "above down" compared to the empirical-causal influence we have identified from "below-up." This can be explained in terms of Marr's calculator example. Hardware activity at level (a) causes certain algorithms to be implemented, but those algorithms themselves were the *reason* that the hardware was put together in the way it was in the first place! Without the design features deliberately built into the hardware, the latter would simply lack point. So in this case the intentions of the designer play a crucial role in the "above-down" control and that seems to be a general characteristic of such influences. For the calculator this degree of teleology is necessary, comprehensible, and perfectly acceptable.[29] Whether it will be convincing when we come to talk of cognition is a difficult matter we shall have to defer to the final chapters.

There are many long and erudite treatises by philosophers of science on the nature of explanation, and the distinction I have made between reason and cause has been debated in various guises. I do not mean to suggest that what is here proposed exhausts all there is to say on the topic of explanation.[30] What does seem to be clear is that cognitive scientists have not been aware of the weighty consequences that must follow if the distinctions between reason and cause are accepted. This applies most particularly to the age-old mind/body problem and the question of the evolution of consciousness. These matters are further explored in chapters 8 and 9. Our next task is to complete the taxonomy of the research endeavors that constitute the core of cognitive science.

Carving at the Joints: Vertical and Horizontal Slices

Many other attempts have been made to characterize psychology that make fine distinctions between different schools and methods that do not seem to fit comfortably
into the threefold division described above. The point of this scheme is, however, to
make broad logical and practical distinctions that are relevant to any and every form
of cognitive inquiry. The levels identified may seem too coarse, but they do start the
task of carving the research material at its natural joints.

A refinement of the scheme may be suggested that does not increase the number
of levels, but rather cuts across them. Some years ago, in response to the imperial
ambitions of AI (that sometimes unstated claim to have all the answers to cognitive
questions) I suggested a taxonomy which takes into account the three levels already
discussed, but also seeks to do justice to the many different methods and techniques
for studying brain and mind that have legitimate claim to the title of "science of cognition."

These also fall conveniently into three classes, called *stages of analysis*. The
first, or "lowest" of these—low only in the sense of a scale of abstractness—is the
study of the brain itself, its detailed anatomy, physiology, biochemistry, and so
on. The second stage investigates what may be called *working models* of the brain.
An example is the artificial neuron. The aim is to abstract from the known anatomy
and physiology of the brain the formal principles that determine its operating
characteristics and to design artificial brains while sticking closely to the known
biological features and constraints of real brains. The third stage is *abstract modeling*. Here logical, mathematical, and other abstract theory (what Campbell calls
the "uninterpreted calculus"[31]) is applied to cognitive science; an example is the
attempt to apply the mathematical theory of Fourier analysis to visual and auditory
perception.

When these three stages of analysis are combined orthogonally with the three
levels described earlier, that is to say when the horizontally layered conglomerate is
sliced vertically into three, a neat taxonomy arises to encompass just about all the
enterprises recognized as components of contemporary cognitive psychology. This
is shown for the subspecialty of perception in table 5.1. I give this perceptual version for two reasons: First, and of lesser importance, it is the part of cognitive science I know best, so feel most comfortable about assigning categories. Second, and
much more important, perception is (as I argued earlier), far and away the best-de-
veloped and most sophisticated discipline within cognitive science as far as the detailed and mature study of its physiological substrate and formal properties are concerned. Other fields of cognitive psychology such as memory and thinking can be
accommodated within the same taxonomy without strain. The same is true in principle of other fields of cognitive science, too, although some of the cells of the table
might be quite empty, as for instance in cognitive philosophy and AI.

The point of the taxonomy is not to be exhaustive, or exact. In some instances
the correct categorization is open to debate, and some fields of cognition have not
been accommodated; development stands out as an obvious example.[32] The point is
to show in broad terms how wide-ranging and diverse cognitive science is, even in

TABLE 5.1. Taxonomy of the Study of Perception

Levels of Function	Stages of Analysis/Models		
	Brain	Working Models of Brain	Formal Approaches
"Sensation"; sensory coding functions	Sensory physiology, neural transmission and coding (single cells)	Biophysics of sensation logical networks, spatial frequency channels	Elementary coding principles, Fourier analysis, holographic and stochastic models
"Perception"; organization, perceptual categorization	Macroscopic coding, binocular congruence, cortical maps	Gestalt processes, alogrithms for edge/ shape detection; vector fields, cooperative and global processing	Optic arrays (Gibson), Lie transformation groups (Hoffman), information theory, geometry of space (Helmholtz, Luneberg)
"Cognition"; use of level-2 processes for cognitive ends (thought, event perception, language)	Neuropsychology of cognition, animal studies of higher brain functions	Perceptrons, machine simulation, semantic networks, scene analysis, PDP (part of)	Catastrophe and Chaos theory, symbolic logic, computation theory

the subspecialty of visual perception. For a single discipline to claim to encompass all the important questions and provide all the answers concerning mind, when viewed within this larger frame, is manifestly absurd. Another point to be emphasized is this: One might suppose from table 5.1 that all cells, and the contents of all cells, are equally important in the conduct of cognitive science. That is not necessarily true, and indeed there would be violent disagreement about it between, say, a neurscientist and a cognitive philosopher. The table is not intended to be evaluative, it simply describes the congeries of methods, interests, perspectives, and models to be found in cognitive science. In chapter 9 I will get to the point of evaluating what's important, and what needs to be done to bring it to prominence.

Perceptual psychology has traditionally been divided into the three categories of sensation, perception, and cognition, and the three levels of table 5.1 are somewhat similar to this. Notice, however, that logically speaking the division between sensation and perception comes not at the point where "raw sensation" branches out into perception proper with the addition of new elements based on memory, anticipation, interpretation and the like, as the empiricist doctrine insists is the way things are (and with which I do not quarrel). It is made between what we know about the substrate in the brain, on the one hand, and the appearance of the totally new quality we experience as conscious awareness, on the other, as was expressed earlier in the chapter. The traditional division between perception and cognition, however, does square quite well with the division between levels 2 and 3 of table 5.1, although the traditional division is perhaps not as well marked and secure as one might like it to be.

The taxonomy should certainly not be taken as an attempt to cast the outline of perceptual psychology, much less of cognitive science, in a single definitive structure, valid for all time. Moreover, it is a taxonomy of *methods of research* in perception (and cognitive science) as much as a denotation of its substantive fields. It would take a bold person indeed to attempt to limit the methods of research on mind and brain that may, in time, come to be accepted as valid and fruitful. A brief account of the contents of each cell of the table will give an indication of how well they cover the field as currently understood, relating them to the earlier discussion of topics in cognitive science.

Starting in the top left-hand cell of the table, study of basic sensory function (level 1) in terms of the brain itself, it is fairly obvious that the topics covered will be the functions of sense organs as transducers of physical energy, neural transmission, the coding functions of single cells, synaptic transmission mechanisms, and metabolic support for those activities in terms of biochemical action and physical energy transfer. The next cell in the top row covers research on working models of the brain: biophysical models of nerve-signal propagation, synaptic action, and models for elementary stimulus analysis. The third cell, abstract models at level 1, comprises those systems that have been applied in attempts to capture the most general and formal properties of the visual brain. They are the theoretical systems that guide the modeling at stage 2. The four systems named are the main abstract frames that have been fruitful in studying the brain, but certainly not the only ones.

The second row of the table contains the topics we think of as eminently "psychological" in character. In the first cell are all those wonderful findings on the organization of the visual brain that stem from the pioneering research of Hubel and Wiesel described in chapter 3. A great deal was known about retinal-cortical mapping and the gross layout of the visual system before their time, but the extraordinarily fine, systematic, and stable properties of macroscopic coding, binocular congruity, multiple visual channels and maps were only to be discovered after the basic organization of simple retinal receptive fields (level 1) had been established. They are placed at level 2 because the evidence for this organizational structure depends explicitly on the stimulation of the organism with complex displays derived from knowledge of perceptual behavior: We certainly would not have discovered these properties of the visual brain nor have had any motivation to explore them without a detailed prior knowledge of perception and perceptual categories.

The central cell of table 5.1 (level 2, stage 2) represents the heart of perception. Remember that organization in vision is in the first instance a matter of phenomenology. What we *see* (or hear, smell, etc.) is the ground on which we develop conceptions about the nature of perception, whether in the tradition of the Gestalt school, Gibson, or from some other point of view. Its research and discovery methods are rooted firmly in what observers perceive and report. These are used as evidence for working models of the brain, including algorithmic and vector-like mechanisms, ideas about the roles of edge detection, shading, perspective, movement, and other physically definable variables in visual pattern recognition. The physiological proposals about how these mechanisms might be implemented are concerns of level 1, and as such do nothing to explain organized perception *per se*. They can, however, yield useful explanations of how perception comes to have some of the organizational properties it does in fact have.

The third cell in row 2 of the table is where the most general theories about the nature of perception belong, insofar as they are couched in abstract, formal terms. Hence we find Gibson's theory of the optic array and the role it plays in vision, Hoffman's theory of fiber bundles and Lie transformation groups in pattern and object recognition, Helmholtz's and Luneburg's conceptions of the geometry of visual space. Again, these feed back into theories of how perceptual phenomena arise, as is the proper domain of the central cell of the table. Gestalt theory perhaps also belongs here, but we have seen that its proponents mixed their levels of explanation so mightily that it is difficult to confine them to a cell! Some other theories, such as Hebb's, do not sit comfortably here because they are lacking in formal elements. Hebb's ideas constitute a working model of the brain rather than a formal theory of brain function.

Now to the third row, level 3, the use of level 2 structures for cognitive ends. One might think that the possibilities are somewhat limited as far as stage 1 (study of the brain) goes; I have been arguing that what goes on in the brain is in certain respects "blind" with respect to higher mental functions. That does not, however, make such brain activity *irrelevant* to those functions; the former may well provide basic (empirically necessary) support for the latter. There is a flourishing field of cognitive neuropsychology that relates brain function to memory, language, problem-solving, and so forth. There is also a very influential research field on higher brain functions (perception, memory, learning), using animal models, that feeds directly into the search for brain correlates of human cognition.[33]

The second cell of row 3 in the table identifies working models of the brain, most of them currently arising in the context of computer modeling of brain function. One of the earliest of these was the perceptron, an abstract machine for pattern classification, initially inspired by Hebb's ideas about neural cell assemblies (chapter 2). Perceptrons have many of the characteristics of the modular nets of Pitts and McCulloch, and it is debatable whether they belong here or at level 2. I classify them here because they were held explicitly to model cognitive functions. Recent networks of similar logical type, the parallel distributed processing (PDP) networks, have been applied to most other cognitive capabilities. One of the most vigorous contemporary research fields in cognitive science, the study of neural networks (NN), is an outgrowth of PDP combined with the ancient game of neural modeling.[34]

The final cell of table 5.1, the bottom right-hand corner, represents the most abstract and formal theories so far applied: symbolic logic, category theory, along with catastrophe and chaos theory. All have suggested new avenues of inquiry, although often only at the level of loose analogy or metaphor. An exception to this is computation theory, in Marr's sense. He attempts to bring things down to earth, but one needs to be aware that "computational theory" may just be a misnomer for conceptual analysis, a danger that was pointed out earlier. Perhaps everything in this final cell should just be called conceptual analysis, which as we know is the job of philosophy. Cognitive philosophers, however, would be unhappy to have their inquiries confined by fiat in this way. They regard the whole contents of the table as the legitimate field of their inquiry.[35]

So we acquire a feeling not merely for the breadth of the science of perception, but also for the extraordinary depth and variety of research techniques and conceptual boxes out of which to conjure the essence of the subject. What is contained in table 5.1 does not by any means exhaust the legitimate ways of studying perception. I already mentioned the matter of development; there are likewise social, comparative, cultural, and anthropological aspects that do not appear (the same is true of any other branch of cognitive science). For the main core of experimental research on perception, however, the table does encompass nearly everything of note.

Relations between Stages and Levels

The importance of the independence of levels so far as explanation is concerned was emphasized earlier, but the *influence* of one level on another, or of one stage on another, cannot be stressed too strongly. It is just that we need to be careful to identify what the *nature* of the influences may be. The main point about explanatory independence between levels does not apply in quite the same way between stages. In the stages of level 1 for instance, knowledge about the "wet" brain does *shape the way* working brain models are devised, and these in turn feed into ideas about what abstract and formal models might be relevant. In that sense they help explain why *this* working (or formal) model is chosen rather than *that* one to represent brain activity. Conversely a formal analysis may suggest what specific attributes to look for in the working model or in the real brain, thus feeding back information from a higher to a lower stage. The interplay can be suggestive, rich, and subtle, even powerful, but it does not constitute the sort of logically strong bond that exists between premises and conclusion in an explanatory model within a level, as discussed earlier. It is much more of the nature of what lawyers call *plausible argument,* which also has a big role to play in science.

Nearly all the moves made in trying to understand perception (and all other cognitive activity for that matter) occur under the aegis of the standard model, and the goal of plausible argument is then to show that a particular piece of theory, or batch of experimental data, is congruent with the model. Such an argument can be made with respect to the whole of table 5.1, incidentally, although the taxonomy does not itself embody or demand any particular theory or model of mind (see the following chapter). Its job is to pigeonhole and describe the data, ideas, and research methods that are fruitful in the study of perception—or of any other branch of cognitive science. It would certainly be of interest to examine how exactly the taxonomy can be applied in other branches, but that lies somewhat outside the scope of our present inquiry.

To some practitioners the taxonomy may seem too cut and dried. In the real world of research the understanding aimed for, and the allowable moves, are implicitly understood and the methods flexible and eclectic. Many would argue that it is not necessary to bother with this sort of logic chopping; the standard model is a sufficient guide. The counter argument is that too easy an acceptance of the standard model can lead astray, particularly when it comes to tackling the most basic questions, the metaphysical questions, concerning brain and mind. We have already seen (chapter 4) that there is not universal agreement about the standard model, nor is it prudent to accept all of its assumptions without further ado. The aim here is not to repudiate the standard model, however, nor even to modify or excise its vital parts. It is to elicit greater sensitivity to the logical, linguistic, and conceptual desiderata of any descriptive and explanatory approach to mind. The goal is not to attempt to demolish the standard model, but rather to raise the level of awareness of the consequences of holding to it.

6

New Perspectives on Representation and Reality

In philosophizing we may not *terminate* a disease of thought. It must run its natural course and *slow* cure is all-important.

LUDWIG WITTGENSTEIN

Monolithic Theory in Perception

How does all this jibe with modern theories of cognition? Despite the great variety of research techniques, levels of study, and explanatory ideas, as expressed in table 5.1, there is a striking and apparently anomalous characteristic of most cognitive theorists, especially those who initiate major "schools." They tend toward profound commitment to a single particular conception of the nature of their field. Perhaps some minor variance is allowed, but still there is only one central way to approach the important questions, one valid principle of explanation. Indeed, that principle is what makes the theory unique. Theories of perception, in other words, like most other theories in cognitive science, always have a strong metaphysical message to convey. Köhler in Gestalt psychology, Hebb, Gibson, and Marr in their perceptual theories, all insisted that everything, but *everything,* is to be classified and explained in terms of a single overriding principle.

This single-mindedness seems truly remarkable once we have recognized that the study of perception, and perception itself, are intrinsically multifaceted and varied. The unswerving dedication to a single principle of explanation of its major theorists seems to belie the very nature of their subject. Or does it? Let us consider in more detail the views of one of the century's most influential theorists, James J. Gibson. As stated in chapter 2, Gibson was a fiercely "antiphysiological" theorist who swam against the very strong current of orthodox opinion, then as now, basically the standard model. Far from denying the ubiquity and importance of organization in perceptual experience, where he was at one with the Gestalt school, Gibson insisted that the understanding and explanation of such organization was not to be sought in the mechanics of the brain, a position diametrically opposed to theirs.

To Koffka's innocent-seeming question "Why does a tree look like a tree?,"

Köhler gave the standard Gestalt answer: "Because that is what, given a particular sensory input, the constraining brain forces cause to be seen." What is seen is simply isomorphic with the brain field resulting from that particular instance of stimulation (chapter 2). Such an answer, as we saw, is not satisfactory. Without more specific hypotheses about what those forces are and how they work, it is dangerously circular. ("What you see as a tree is what your brain produces when a tree is in the field of view. How do you know? Because a tree is in the field of view!") According to Gibson the question should be posed differently, namely: "What information does the observer pick up from the optic array that identifies for him the presence of a tree?" That is to say, the organization is *out there,* and the observer's perceptual task is to discover, or *discriminate,* those already present features of the array that are relevant to the identification of a certain object or happening. There is no problem about identifying types of object (object categories) or classes of perceptual event. That, too, is a matter of discrimination learning, of which *generalization* is a well-known attribute.

To the question, "Why does a tree look like a tree?" the Gibsonian answer is: "Because the optic array carries information of 'treeness' that is correctly discriminated." So the identification of a tree has nothing immediately to do with a brain process (or, more accurately, is not *identifiable* in terms of what happens in the brain); rather it is a relation between an object and an observer that is characterized only by the way we carve up the arena of stimulation (the optic array) in order to garner usable information. You could object that this does not tell us why a tree *looks* the way it does, appealing to the intuitive sense that there has to be a truer, more *phenomenalistic* and profound answer to such a simple but basic question. But the fact is that neither the Gestalt theory of isomorphism, nor any other extant perceptual theory actually answers that question. Most of the attempted answers about "representation in the brain" boil down to the idea that treeness is somehow reflected in the brain—an idea that founders on the point that to *know* that it is a representation of a tree requires another recognizer of sorts in the brain, and thus rapidly proceeds down the slippery slope of an infinite regress. Gibson at least avoids that pitfall.

Gibson's insistence that much more information about "perceptual layout" is contained in the optic array than other theories allow was a major advance in our understanding of what the perceptual process is about. And he was no enemy of the idea that perceptual learning plays a fundamental role in the evolution of a mature perceiving organism (although he had fundamental disagreements with empiricist theorists over the nature of that learning).[1] His principle of "global psychophysics," as he first called it, the idea that observers extract and use the complex, extended information sources of the optic array to make veridical perceptual judgments, has been amply supported by experiment.[2] His theory of perception goes astray, however, when he seeks to extend what is a useful and powerful principle in one domain to cover every other aspect of perception.

Gibson's theory is a good example of what I call a monolithic perceptual theory. The force of the idea of global psychophysics derives from the fact that Gibson thought of it as, indeed, psychophysics. What does that mean? In traditional psychophysics there is a tight, one-to-one relation between physical stimulus condition and perceived event, a typical example being the relation between the frequency in hertz (cycles per second) of the air pressure wave of a simple tone and its reported pitch. There is no room for ambiguity or misinterpretation; the perception is, as it were, forced on the observer, who can do nothing to modify it. Gibson argued that the same is true of global psychophysical relations; that is, that most, if not all, perceptual judgments are of this nature, forced on the observer by the properties of the stimulating array. So, for Gibson, a perspective layout, or a gradient of texture, could have only one perceptual interpretation—except he did not think it was an interpretation. He demanded that it be considered a psychophysical judgment, pure and simple. No waffling, no intermediary events, no uncertainty.

The evidence does not fully support Gibson, but this is not the place to go into a detailed critique.[3] Gibson came more and more to see perception as a dyadic relation between observer and environment, in which stimulus events elicit responses in a tightly constrained way, as a function of the biological utility of those events. Examples abound in the fighting, mating, and feeding behavior of many bird and fish species, and even of some mammals. That theme has been beautifully exploited in the ethology of Lorenz, Tinbergen, and their followers;[4] Gibson tried to apply it consistently to human perception, and that is the theme of his last book.[5] The starkly restricted nature of the relation between eliciting stimulus and consequent response that is a *leitmotiv* of ethology fits well with Gibson's earlier insistence on the power of global psychophysics. There is no room in such a theory for cognition as this is normally understood, and Gibson had no use for hypotheses about what the brain might be up to during a perceptual episode. The theory thus appears to be excessively narrow, albeit powerful in its proper field of application.

Why was Gibson so insistent on the correctness, even the purity, of his theory? He felt a strong compulsion, almost a messianic zeal, to advance a particular epistemological view of perception; to allow compromise would be to betray that view. Why else would anyone deny such obvious facts as the importance of cognition's informing and steering of perception (as in seeing the North Star *as* the North Star), or the relevance of brain activity to understanding what's going on when we see (as in the role of photopigments in color vision)?

At the root of Gibson's epistemology is the idea that perception is an *achievement,* and one that serves very practical ends—remember the origins of his disenchantment with traditional perceptual theory, when he found it useless in helping pilots land their planes (chapter 2). That being so, the sorts of question a perceptual theory has to answer, the sorts of explanation that will be relevant to perceptual concerns, must deal with pragmatic questions like: How does the organism ensure that its perceptions are veridical (true, consonant with "reality")? What criterion is used to choose between a reliable and an unreliable perceptual cue? How does the nature of its environment control the discriminative choices that are biologically favorable to the organism? How does one determine that a line is straight? (. . . by seeing it disappear when viewed "end-on.") Talk about the brain and its analyzers is simply irrelevant to dealing with such concerns! In other words, and to take a leaf out of our earlier discussion, in Gibson's view traditional theory simply misjudges the level of discourse that is proper to the answering of genuinely perceptual questions.

Can the "one level" (of explanation) Gibson insisted on be identified in the taxonomy of table 5.1? Only with difficulty, as we shall discuss later, and it appears to be more a matter of exclusion than positive identification. In placing it at level 2 (structure, organization) and stage 3 (Where else could it go? Certainly not at stages 1 or 2; brains, and working models of brains, were misleading demons to Gibson.), some injustice is done, because it leaves out of account the utility-oriented flavor of his theory, in contrast to what categorization under stage 3 seems to require. Moreover Gibson was uninterested in, or perhaps ignorant of, many of the abstract calculi that have been used in perceptual theory, like Fourier transforms, logical networks, or Lie transformation groups.[6] In the interests of pushing a particular principle of explanation, a different epistemology, Gibson either ignored or combated the overwhelming majority of theoretical and experimental research on perception.

Gibson can be taken to task for neglecting so much that is of scientific interest in the field, but commended for attempting to change so profoundly our perspective on the nature of perception, and especially on the logical features of perceptual explanation. It is ironic that cognitive scientists have in general failed to grasp the import of Gibson's epistemological message but at the same time have accepted with enthusiasm certain other aspects of his work—but often not in ways he would have approved of.[7] Those other aspects include the profound impact his ideas have had on our understanding of what a stimulus is, and the exploitation of this influence in the field of machine vision, something referred to already in an earlier chapter.

Gibson's insistence on the careful analysis of the detailed physical features of the optic array (or any other stimulating field) resonated well with the interest of researchers in machine vision (or tactile, auditory, etc., sensing), whose primary objective is to design analyzers ("filters") in the machine to match, or extract, relevant information-bearing features in the field of stimulation. Extracting information from the array sounds pretty orthodox to a Gibsonian. The machine version then, however, tends to diverge radically from the authorized version of the theory. How so? In the machine version the outputs of these analyzers are held to be the raw material for the building up of *representations* of the external world. Not just that, but the first crude representation (as in Marr's "primal sketch") is merely one of several stages through which the information is transformed before a coherent and complete representation of the external environment is computed.[8] So it is evident that machine vision's version of perceptual theory, for all its glitz and technical wizardry (and, one has to add, a great deal of careful physical and mathematical analysis) is just another slant on the old empiricist doctrine of *constructionism*, the notion that an internal model of the world has to be built up with the aid of nonperceptual psychological (or, in this case, mechanical) elements. The point of this construction is, of course, that it is held to explain the perception of whatever is there represented. It is quite remarkable how, despite differences in detail, the various versions of machine perception hew to this line. Yet that is the very doctrine against which Gibson railed so vociferously.

Gibson was single-mindedly in pursuit of an account that does justice to logical features of the way we comprehend perception, how we talk about it and *use* perceptual information, and the achievement-oriented framework inherent in all of this. This is always implied when we claim to see (or hear, touch, taste, or smell) a *something*. The claim may be implicit, it may even be wrong—and is always subject to correction—but it is nonetheless part of what we *mean* when we say: "That's a so-and-so." That is the essence of Gibson's message, tangled though it is in a theory that looks as though it were addressing something rather different, namely the same empirical and conceptual issues that other theories address. Virtually all those other theories espouse some form of the brain representation (internal model) version of perceptual function; Gibson's is a different sort of theory, which gives us a new message about the nature of perceptual explanation.

The message is of utmost importance, even though Gibson himself was not entirely clear about its import. In his attempt to be scientifically respectable, he identified the achievement-oriented nature of perceptual theory with a particularly strong ethological stimulus-elicitation theory. There is no necessary connection between the two, and in fact mixing them together hinders the realization of what Gibsonian theory is really about. The stickleback (a small fish that inhabits freshwater streams in Europe) achieves its nest-building and procreative goals *via* the response-evoking stimuli in its environment, and does so in a more or less automatic fashion, as ethological research has elegantly demonstrated. The cognitive activity of humans is also achievement-bound, but there is nothing in the nature of things to dictate that it has to reach its goals by the same sort of automatic response elicitation systems that serve the stickleback so well. Yet that is what the thrust of Gibson's later theory amounts to. We can reject that interpretation and still accept his basic arguments on the nature of perception and the sorts of explanation to look for within it, which are his truly great contribution.

Cracking the Monolith

Can Gibson's polemics be reconciled with the vast and exciting progress that has been made in other areas, in visual neuroscience especially? Such a reconciliation is surely needed; it would be pedantic in the extreme to claim, just because most other cognitive scientists have got the theoretical side of things wrong, that their research is futile. On the contrary, the empirical findings of visual research, of neuroscience in particular, are universally recognized as among the most solid and exciting achievements of cognitive science. We cannot neglect all that table 5.1 puts before us. What is wrong—and here I side with the pedant—is that vision researchers, and neuroscientists in particular, have misconstrued the nature of their discoveries, have interpreted them as providing *explanations* of perception. That, as I argued in chapter 5, is precisely what they do not, what they *cannot* do. However, as I also argued there, those discoveries can, and do, add immeasurably to our understanding of many perceptual phenomena and their underlying physiological states.

Gibsonian theory and visual neuroscientific discoveries are complementary, informing us about perception in different ways. We can't say that nothing is going on in the brain during a perceptual episode; experiment has proved that to be false in the strongest and broadest way possible. We can't even say (as Gibson would have it) that nothing of *interest* occurs in the brain at that time. We have to phrase things differently and thereby come to a correct understanding of the matter. The way to put it, as should now be pretty clear, is to say that the brain events that are coterminous with, and often coextensive with, perception, are empirically necessary *corre-lates* of perception. They often are elicited by stimulus events, may be sufficient in a practical sense to predict what the perception will be, but do not in themselves *explain* the percept. To split hairs a bit, but in a very relevant and important way, it might be that the brain events are sufficient to explain the *occurrence* of the percept (*cause* the percept would also do) but that is not the same as explaining the percept itself. Yet it is the latter tiger that the brain scientists wrongfully suppose they have by the tail.

The schema of table 5.1 should make it abundantly clear not only that different sorts of question are tackled in the domains identified by each cell, but also that different sorts of explanation are in general appropriate to them; remember the example of symphonic music, my three levels, and Marr's example of the hand calculator, discussed in chapter 5. My criticism of Gibson's attempt at a single comprehensive theory of perception looks to be ad hominem, but in fact applies to just about every comprehensive theory of perception ever attempted. Virtually all theorists, being closet metaphysicians, attempt to capture everything in a single explanatory net. But that simply is not the nature of the beast. Diversity of action, of research tools, and modes of explanation are of the essence of what perception—and all the rest of cognitive science for that matter—is about.

There is a related, and absolutely crucial, difficulty for Gibson's theorizing. Contrary to his later position, in which the whole of cognition is subsumed under the ethological umbrella, *thinking* about perception (or any other substantial matter of fact) has to precede any progress one may hope to make in understanding or explaining it. If a Gibsonian sticks consistently to his principles, however, such ratiocination, preceding the perception-eliciting stimulation, is impossible. If not wholly a contradiction in terms in his theory, that sort of reflective thought is without doubt an activity that lies outside the bounds of what a Gibsonian organism can do! Gibson, like any other philosopher, makes his case by *plausible argument,* yet there is no place in his theoretical universe for such a thing. As we have seen in other instances, theory can, and very often does, cut itself off at the knees when applied reflexively to itself.

Gibson the philosopher thus confuses the issue of what he wants to achieve by clothing an essentially epistemological argument in the words of the psychological-empirical theory of Gibson the psychologist.

In concluding this section it should be said again that every perceptual theorist embraces, whether it is recognized or not, one epistemological stance or another. Gibson is just very much more explicit about it than most. He had important things to say; it is unfortunate that his epistemological message got mixed together with a much narrower theory about the mechanism of information pickup. In his later work this had the further unfortunate effect of leading him to defend a very implausible theory (the ethological one) of human cognition.[9] In another sense Gibson stands alone: He is the only cognitive theorist I know of to defend the thesis that cognitive science can dispense with a theory of representation, indeed that the very idea is incoherent. There is more to be said on that topic, obviously. For a start we shall see that the concept of internal representation is fraught with far greater difficulties and requires far more subtle handling than has previously been realized.

Representation and Reality: The Straight Line

Do we have to have a theory of representation? Koffka asked: "Why does a tree look like a tree?" Warren McCulloch later put the same question more simply and more forcefully: "Why does a square look like a square?" Arguing against one common interpretation of the Gestalt theory of isomorphism, he correctly pointed out that logically there is nothing to require that the brain representation of a square share any of the physical or geometrical properties of a square "out there." Nevertheless, he was convinced that some form of representation had to exist, would be central to the explanation of pattern recognition, and that it is the neuropsychologist's job to discover it. Squares can be recognized in all sorts of shapes, sizes, orientations, etc., so there must be something "inside" that corresponds to that entity, that Universal, as it used to be called, which we recognize out there in the world. This is the question of *stimulus equivalence,* or *equivalence coding,* that held a dominating position in theoretical discussions of pattern recognition in earlier times.

The thought that there must be an internal *something* that corresponds to the external stimulus class has been compelling in perceptual psychology, and even more so in neuroscience. The same is true in memory (the *engram,* as it has been called, is the neural representation of a specific memory) and in theories of thinking and language. Indeed there seems to be good evidence to support the notion, and it has been fruitful in the AI conceptions that treat cognition as a species of symbol manipulation (chapter 3). Many of those symbols are indeed the machine (internal) representations of external classes, tokens, Universals. In neuroscience the evidence for "high level" visual neurons that code for hands, faces, geometrical shapes, etc., under quite wide degrees of spatial generalization, is now thoroughly established,[10] as also for specific memory episodes. That being so, why should one question the correctness, or even the appropriateness, of any theory that allows a central explanatory role to brain representations? Yet Gibson specifically scorned the idea, denying that internal representations can have any explanatory power. How can that be? They are *there,* are they not? And they allow us to remember, elaborate, and assess information that has clear biological utility. So, how can they simply be ignored?

The answer is found in further analysis of what it means for a conception or model to have explanatory power. We have already seen that there is danger of entering an infinite regress, or of getting caught in a circular argument, when we try to identify the representation in the brain of some external pattern or object. Let us take Koffka's question about the appearance of a tree in an even more elementary and radical form than McCulloch's version about the appearance of a square. Some years later, Dennis Andrews posed the question even more simply: "Why does a straight line look straight?"[11] Actually he put it in a more general context, but the apparently simple question of straightness identifies the heart of his concern. What stimulus property could be more basic?

Surely, you will say, this is getting ridiculous. How else would you expect a straight line to appear? But there is no a priori demonstration that there is an internal representation for the property of straightness that can be put in simple one-to-many correspondence with the members of the class of entities we call straight lines. Even more serious, there is no reason to suppose that there can be simple brain representations of *single* discrete straight lines that are in on-to-one correspondence with individual straight lines out there in the world. In other words, there is no way to form the "equivalence class" of straight lines, nor any way to identify the individual members of such a putative class, if by identification we mean pointing to their corresponding ("representing") brain states. That is a very strong claim, so let us justify it.

Before doing so there is an objection to be met. The earliest result of Hubel and Wiesel, since amply confirmed by hundreds if not thousands of reports, showed that among single cells in the visual cortex of cats (and subsequently of all mammals), the cells with simple receptive field type are selective for short straight line segments. Does that not prove the internal representation of straight lines? No, and for several reasons. In the first place, that coding is not *unique*. The same cell may fire to a number of different features, such as lines in different orientations, even though its strong preference may be for lines in one particular orientation. At best it is conceivable that a population of cells have a combined output that is unique to a certain length and orientation of straight line. At this level the lengths of coded lines is very short, however, and certainly much less extended than the lines we *perceive* as straight, which may continue across the whole visual field. Low-level coding by single cells is local and by no means sharp enough to satisfy any reasonable criterion of strict cortical representation. Nor do we know whether, or how, information from individually coded line segments might be combined together to represent extended straight lines—or any other type of specific curve, for that matter.[12]

There are other, more fundamental problems. The mapping from visual field (conceived of as a plane surface perpendicular to the line of sight to simplify matters) to the retina (closely approximated by a hemisphere), for example, is not a simple affair. A straight line in the visual field will be mapped on to a variety of "lines" on the retina, none of them straight, whose curvature and extent will alter as the eye changes its direction of gaze. There is thus no easy solution to the problem of finding a unique representation for even a single straight line at the retina, let alone the problem of preserving the desired property in the mapping from retina to cortex. The *de facto* physiological local coding for straight lines is not capable of bearing the theoretical weight required for a full account of the representation of the general straight line (*any* straight line) cortically.

Even if representation for single straight lines were possible, it would be a one-many relation between any given line and the indefinitely large number of brain states (given the distortions produced by retinal projection as the direction of gaze changes) by which it is represented, so its explanatory power is suspect; how would the equivalence itself be represented? How would the brain "know" that that class of states represents a given single straight line? We are back on the slippery slope.

As if that were not difficulty enough, the knockout blow comes from consideration of another astounding property of the human visual system, its extraordinary *adaptability*. If you put on a pair of corrective spectacles, particularly one with fairly high refractive power (to correct for short sight, for example), the geometrical and perspective properties of the visual world, such as the distance, position, and shape of things, appear distorted. After a relatively short while, however, your vision adjusts—adapts, as we say—and the world again appears approximately normal. Psychologists have studied this phenomenon systematically for about a century, and have investigated some rather radical distortions, including the total inversion of the field, so things appear at first to be upside down or reversed left to right, or both.[13] One can easily imagine how disorienting and disruptive it is for the world to appear so grossly distorted. Yet, with time, valiant observers who wear these distorting devices consistently for a few days report a surprising degree of adjustment, not only in their motor coordination (they no longer bump into furniture or misreach for their coffee cups) but even in the appearance of the world.

In particular where the device has caused straight lines to appear curved, as in the wearing of wedge prisms (one of the most-studied distortions), the apparent curvature diminishes over time and eventually disappears. Another way to put this is to say: The straight lines in the environment that were artificially distorted by the prisms to appear curved, reassert their straightness! Along with this "adaptation to reality," as we may call it, distortions of position, distance, and size also disappear. How could the perceptual system embody this apparently magical property? This is not the place to go into the many attempts at explanation.[14] For present purposes it is enough to realize that the findings of adaptation to visually induced distortions pose an insuperable problem for attempts to account for unique brain representation of lines and shapes in physiological terms. Why so? Because the visual distortion is a *transformation* of the optical information supplied to the retina, so it obviously entails a change in the cortical signals corresponding to the external straight line that is under observation. Over time, however, the (externally straight) line again comes to *appear* straight, despite the systematic change in the manner of its representation in the brain. Remember that this representation is still a one-many relation, between the single external straight line and the many brain states that can correspond to different views of it.

Here's another clincher: To understand how the brain states can represent (a) the undistorted straight line, (b) the distorted line (a new equivalence class to be sure, but still the representations of a single distorted line), and (c) the distorted line adapted to by the observer so that it again appears straight, has to involve at the very least an understanding of the imposed transformation (visual distortion) and, to be consistent, how *it* is represented in the brain and controls the relations among (a), (b), and (c). It is not a logical impossibility that at some future time—probably in the very distant future, although such predictions are hazardous—there will be an understanding of how complex transformations of the type needed here can be embodied in brain processes, but it is not a certainty that this goal will ever be reached. Moreover the discovery of such a brain implementation would in no sense explain the transformation itself. If anything it has to be the other way around; knowledge of the nature of the transformation explains why such-and-such a brain process can be observed. Be that as it may, we can be certain that the representation of even something as straightforward as the straight line, in terms of brain processes, is very far from being comprehensible with the simplistic view of modeling currently in vogue.

Even more damaging to the simple view that brain representations can explain anything perceptual is the fact that, in the process of adaptation, matters are controlled by *what's out there* (e.g., straight lines), not by what is in the brain. This is fully consistent with Gibson's position: It is the features of the visual world that control the nature and extent of adaptation. The brain may oblige by adjusting its coding, but that is a consequent contingency, not an explanatory antecedent to the fact of adaptation to the "real" features of the world.

It can only make sense to investigate relevant changes in brain processes *after* some perceptual event of interest had been researched and properly characterized. To think that the brain processes *explain* the adaptation is like believing that the locomotion of a bus from New York to Boston explains John Doe's desire to visit his lady love in that fair city. It is not that. The bus journey is the means by which he implements his intention. The same goes for the transformations by which adaptation is achieved. They may be understood in terms of their ethological or mathematical characterization, for example, but those are conceptual, theoretical, logical, properties, not brain states. Similarly perception, thinking, memory, and the rest have to be understood as psychological phenomena *before* it makes any sense to search for their possible correlative brain states.

Although the representation of simple physical-geometrical features of the visual world like straight lines poses problems, it might still be argued that the discovery of such representations has a role to play in explaining how substantive shapes and objects are recognized. The discovery of a complicated set of relevant variables has not been a hindrance in other scientific endeavors; rather it has been the spur to greater effort, greater ingenuity in the pursuit of explanations. The reason why even a complex account of brain representation will not do as an explanation of perceptual occurrences is that, as we have just seen, to understand the representations themselves requires us to make use of concepts (like optical transformations) that far transcend anything we can model or understand in terms of the workings of the brain. Even if, impossible as it now seems, we were able to model those processes in the brain, that could only occur because at the conceptual level we had already made the requisite analysis of what is to be modeled. We need intact and well-functioning brains to do that, just as we need well-functioning intestines to digest food. Digging around in the brain is not going to enlighten us about perceptual processes unless we already have a firm and extensive grasp of the phenomena under study and an idea of the relevant variables (including brain function) to which attention must be paid, any more than digging around "blind" in the gut will bring enlightenment about the nature and purpose of digestion.

All very well, you might rejoin, but we *do* know a great deal about the relevant variables, so looking for brain representations makes a lot of sense. That is true; my argument was that the brain representations don't *explain* anything in a satisfactory way. What is important about the appearance of straight lines (or any other consistently perceptible features, naturally), about their distortion and reappearance after adaptation, is reported and investigated *out there* in the visual world, as Gibson so clearly argued. To understand about all of that entails an understanding of the *activity* of *perception,* involves knowing what it means to judge perceptual events, identify objects and situations, know how to interact with them to achieve desired effects and reach our intended goals. *That* is where it is relevant to have perceptual theory, and where the explanation of perception has to have its roots.

On this Gibson was right: To understand perception it is necessary to grasp the nature of a human propensity and set of activities that fit us to live in the world, from simple reflex responses to need or danger, let us say, all the way up to the most refined and complex intellectual and esthetic appreciation of nature's stupendous and benign offerings and humankind's own artifacts, from the magnificent to the trivial. That may seem a bit "highfalutin'," but it has the virtue of reminding us, once again, that perception is a many-tiered edifice.

On this Gibson was wrong: One can't comprehend, much less fully explain, everything about perception at one level, from only one theoretical point of view. He was right to banish the study of brain function to the basement when attempting to get the "logical geography" of perceptual theory clear, but wrong to insist that therefore what happens in the brain is of no interest or consequence to the understanding of perception.

A final point in Gibson's favor: It should now be abundantly clear that one cannot define the concept "visually straight" in physiological terms. Its essential nature is visual, geometrical, conceptual; straightness, one might say, is a property intrinsically foreign to the brain and its physiology. Even if it proved possible to solve all the problems of brain representation mooted above, it would still be a fact that to *understand* what it means to see, or to be, a straight line is something that could not—logically could not—be defined just in terms of what goes on in the brain. At best the brain process is a correlate of matters whose understanding entails knowledge of things outside the brain, including what we know as the reality of the physical-geometrical-biological world in which we live and the categories of thought and language by which we try to grasp it.

Representation and Reality: The General Case

That poor straight line has carried a heavy burden, but it has served to convey two vital messages. The first is that brain representation is a vastly more subtle and intricate matter than the standard model takes it to be. The second is that, should brain representation of visual categories—even humble ones like the straight line—ever be identified, it would not do the job that the standard model assigns to it. Brain representations are explained and understood in terms of the events and categories they represent, not vice versa. It is, in principle not possible to reverse the *explicans* and *explicandum*. Why not? Because to do so is to commit a simple logical error, that is—using the phrase correctly—to beg the question, to assume a priori the very principle that is to be elucidated. One can only discover the brain process of interest by first identifying what is to be sought (the property of straightness, for example) in terms that have no coinage in the brain. How then can that discovery be an explanation of the principle by which the search was motivated?

Enough of that. Let us look at the question of representation and reality in a more positive light.

A perceiving organism can, within a very wide range of biasing conditions—from changing the brightness or color of a visual display to the sorts of radical intervention described as rearrangements in the last section (turning the visual world upside down, etc.)—adapt so that the effects of the biasing are minimized and in many cases eliminated. The psychologist Harry Helson was the first to propound a general theory of adaptation level (AL) and to give it some quantitative basis.[15]

The theory asserts that whereas human perception can certainly be biased in the short run, for instance by flooding the surrounding visual scene with colored light of a single hue, the natural—and very dramatic—response of the system is to adapt to that biased ambient level and to treat the "average level of stimulation" as the *neutral point* against which other perceptual judgments (in this case of hue) are made. If the visual surroundings are flooded with pink (desaturated red) light, for instance, the world at first appears odd—pink, in fact. After a short while the pinkness appears to fade and the world regains more or less its normal appearance. Re-illuminate with "white" light, and *immediately* the world appears in green, the complementary color to pink. That, too, soon fades, and the world, yet again, gets back to its normal appearance. It seeks, one might say, a high degree of stability, simplicity, or constancy.[16]

Changes in AL have been investigated in careful psychophysical experiments, but they can be observed all the time in everyday life. For example, in the familiar dark adaptation that occurs on entering a shuttered room (although, seemingly against the case I am building, there is a good physiological explanation for this), or in the adjustment to small changes in ambient temperature of which we are typically quite unaware. AL effects are ubiquitous, often go unnoticed, but are a primary characteristic of perceiving organisms nonetheless.

Findings like these prompt the question: What is "normal"? What, indeed, is "reality"? Normality is not a rigidly fixed set of features and properties in the perceived world, nor is reality conceivable as a straightjacket that holds us so firmly in its grip that we are incapable of movement or choice. The perceived world has its labile features, as AL theory and research amply demonstrate, but this does not have to reduce our confidence in our senses as reliable guides to nature and her secrets. After all, it is only because we *do* rely on empirical observation that we have any serviceable view of what perception, including the AL phenomena that are part of it, is. Moreover, despite the short-term biasing that is evident in AL experiments, there *are* stable features of the perceived world that anchor our confidence in its solidity. The AL findings do point, however, to the need to replace the traditional stodgy, static ideas about perception and the world to which it gives access with a far more lively view of the dynamic equilibrium between the observer and his surroundings. The perceiving system responds differentially to the "diet" of incoming stimulation, adjusting its ALs appropriately, the diet itself being a function of the immediate properties of the ambient stimulating arrays.[17]

It is tempting to say that the AL phenomena are a bit of a sideshow—epiphenomena in fact—to the main business of describing and understanding perception. I shall argue, on the contrary, they are far from trivial, and in fact point the direction theory must take if it is to tackle successfully the question of veridical perception, that is to say, the matter of how we can tell perceptual "reality" from distortion, from illusion.[18] We can take as our starting point once again the position of Andrews. In an important but often neglected paper on perceptual adjustment to the external world he wrote:[19]

> We take for granted that a straight line looks straight, but this is really very surprising. The geometry of our private view of the world tallies rather well with that of the physical world revealed by measuring instruments; it also has the same number

of dimensions. It follows that straight lines are possible in both; but that a straight line in the physical world is represented by a straight line in our internal visual world is very fortunate, and demands some fine engineering in the visual nervous system. We can also locate the position of an auditory click, touch finger to toe with the eyes shut, and perceive whether two receding lines are parallel. All these performances require very fine scaling in our internal representation of the world. How does the nervous system manage these things?[20]

Andrews argues that internal representation is, by any standard, accurate and useful. Otherwise how could we perform effortlessly the sorts of task he describes? He propounds a powerful model of how the distortions and biases introduced by the "diet" of ongoing stimulation are detected and adjusted to, so that the perception of the world remains veridical. His model implements the sorts of adaptational change in sensitivity required by AL phenomena, dealt with in a more general way in Helson's AL theory. It is a matter of detecting deviations from the long-run statistical properties of the physical environment, deviations that Andrews calls "errors," and compensating for them by smart "error-correcting " devices. We shall not go into the details of the model, but consider rather the adjustment of aperceptual system to physical features of the world in a more general context.[21]

In view of my castigation of theorists who maintain that the way to explain perception is via models of brain function, it might seem surprising that I would quote with approval Andrews's portrayal of the matter, because his error-correcting devices are certainly conceived of as brain mechanisms. I did not earlier deny that internal representations may be important, but I did demolish the idea that they could be a principled way of explaining what perception is all about. They certainly can be, and very often are, useful ways of explaining certain *features* of perception and perceptual performance, as in the examples Andrews quotes (touch finger to toe, etc.). Notice, too, that he assumes the existence of internal representations of things like straight lines, but does not fully appreciate the difficulties of showing how such representation can be achieved, dismissing the matter as merely requiring some "fine engineering." There is more to it than that, as we saw. Yet our experience shows clearly enough that changes in AL occur, and it is natural to think those changes are mediated by changes of brain state, thus keeping the internal representations stable, as Andrews argued. My comments of the previous section aimed to show that the representations cannot do the job of explanation usually assigned to them. They are, however, a much greater marvel than we had realized, a heretofore unappreciated mystery of the working of the brain, accommodating its activity to the demands of its external frame of reference.

Let us adopt a slightly different point of view, and come to recognize yet another astounding property of the machinery that allows us to perceive a stable, solid world with remarkably uniform general features.

Stability and Transformation

A salient feature of Gibson's theorizing is the concept of invariance and its necessary partner, transformation. He saw clearly that it would be necessary to give some account of why, despite changes brought about in the field of view by locomotion, eye and head movements (all of which would tend to disrupt the stability of the stimulating field) the organism nonetheless *perceives* a steady, undistorted visual world of features and objects. One way to characterize the problem is in terms of distinguishing between *exafference* and *reafference,* the latter being self-produced stimulation, the former stimulation that is independent of the observer—that is, due to motion of an external "something." To put it simply: How does the visual system distinguish between the movement of the dog crossing the road and the movement of the features of the scene as I alter my line of gaze by watching the dog as it crosses the road?

This is one of the primary challenges for perceptual theory. Gibson proclaimed the theory of invariants to account for all perceptual constancy under transformations. During self-movement the whole stimulating array undergoes not just any old transformation, but one of a very limited number of possible transformations that are easy to describe. Simple side-to-side head movement or rotation of the eyes (in the case of vision) yields horizontal translation of the array, up-and- down movement yields vertical translations, oblique movements can be characterized as linear combinations of the two.[22] Movement toward an array causes optical expansion (magnification), contraction occurs on the reverse movement, and so on. According to Gibson the discrimination of these transformations permits the extraction of invariants from the array (geometrical properties of the array that remain unchanging as the transformation occurs), and this is the basis for perceiving a stable visual world.

Is this anything more than a circular argument? How are we able to perceive stability in the visual world? Because we discriminate some of its invariant (that is, stable) features! There has to be more to the matter than that. Let us approach the ideas of invariance and transformation from a different angle to see where the meat is.

In 1966 the mathematician W. C. Hoffman came to much the same conclusion as Gibson regarding the importance of visual transformations in formulating a theory of perception, but he paid far more attention to the exact characterization of the different transformations and the relations between them. That is to say, he gave them a fuller and more exact mathematical treatment.[23] And what, reduced to its most elementary terms, is that?

Hoffman noted that all the transformations of interest are *smooth* or, mathematically speaking, *continuous.* They occur in complementary pairs, a fundamental feature that Gibson failed to appreciate and exploit. What yields the key to the system is that the so-called orbits, or path-curves, of the transformations within a complementary pair intersect orthogonally (imagine superposing a grid of horizontal lines on a grid of verticals, by way of example; all the lines intersect at right angles). Transformation systems with these properties are called *Lie transformation groups,* and when "closed" together form a Lie algebra in the sense of differential geometry. This is a vastly oversimplified account of the matter, but on this basis Hoffman was able to deduce a remarkably complete and coherent account of visual pattern recognition, and from that a theory of visual space perception.

Justice cannot be done to Hoffman's ideas in a small compass, and to treat them adequately would lead much too far afield. The lessons to be learned from Hoffman's theory do not, for present purposes, require more than an indication of its general character. It goes far beyond other attempts to define the features of visual transformations, and their (mathematically) invariant properties. Most importantly, it gives a principled basis for the occurrence of recognition under transformation, and for perceptual constancy (a particular aspect of such recognition).[24] *No* appeal has to be made to brain physiology or internal representation. The concepts follow from the nature of visual transformations themselves, and their mathematical characterization.

A possible neural embodiment of the structures and operators of the transformations was also suggested by Hoffman, on the basis of the known local properties of the visual brain, and that is as it should be.[25] The transformations can't occur in a vacuum. *That* is the proper way to deal with the internal, physiological systems that implement perceptual processes: Define what it is you want to operate, and how—a matter that is not explicable in any way we can presently conceive of in terms of brain function—and *then* see if there are known brain structures that can carry out the specified operations.

Hoffman identified the elementary coding action of single visual neurons (chapter 3) as the seat of operation of the relevant transformations, and recent investigations have also brought to light physiological evidence for the "higher level" operators required in the theory.[26] That, while satisfying and satisfactory, is not the main point to be made here. The principle argument, as Gibson maintained, and from a different stance Marr also supported, is that a perceptual theory requires adequate and explicit conceptual grounding if it is to have any explanatory power. Hoffman's theory is firmly rooted in a branch of mathematics that has fruitful application to many aspects of perception.

Stability and Representation

I have touched but lightly on the Lie theory; for present purposes it is the strategical stance, rather than the details of a particular model, that is important. To give something more of the flavor and fruitfulness of the approach, here is a related idea that bears on the question of reality and representation, in the context of the experiments on optical rearrangement.

In seeking for an explanation for the findings on adaptation to optical rearrangement (turning the visual world upside-down, etc.), I discovered that all the distortion-producing transformations are, to a good approximation, *conformal,* that is, belong to a particular class of well-known mathematical transformations.[27] The visual system's task, when presented with the distorted input, is to find the *inverse transformation* to the one imposed by the distorting medium (lens or mirror) and apply it to the distorted input, thereby restoring "normality" to the visual scene. Restoring, if you like, reality. This is somewhat related to Andrews's idea of error-correcting devices, albeit more general and powerful.

The idea worked quite well,[28] but left hanging the uncomfortable question: How does the visual system "know" which inverse transformation to apply? It all seems a bit too teleological, unless one can discover an independent criterion for making the decision. It seemed that the sought-for adjustment should minimize the turbulence in visual flow fields and reduce irregularities in both its static and dynamic properties to a minimum. Subsequent work with Hoffman gave a more precise and powerful solution. The Gestalt property of *simplicity* is the well-known tendency of perceptual organization always to revert to its simplest possible form; this can be expressed in terms of the reduction to an organization in which the *smallest number* (and lowest order—but that is a topic for another day) *of Lie orbits* sufficient for full representation are present. This gives an independent criterion for the desired inverse transform, namely the one that reduces the Lie representation of the field, as we may call it, to the most basic form possible.

The concept of conformal transformation, intimately related to the Lie transformation groups with which Hoffman had worked, can be applied to *all* perceptual processing to explain the stability and reliability, the constancy, of the perceived world. In other words, we had an answer to the question of why our perceptions (with certain well-understood exceptions) are veridical, or truthful; why they remain congruent, as Andrews would have said, with the properties of the world detected by measuring instruments, with physical reality. As we wrote in 1985:

> Conformal group action stabilizes and simplifies the visual world, whether through constancy processing or cancellation of extrinsically generated distortions; the notion of conformal mapping thus fits neatly into our proposed basis for the Gestalt principle of simplicity. . . . [T]he mathematical model, with all its power and generality, determines the overall structure of visual processing; neurophysiological coding and psychophysical properties fill in the local details.[29]

Notice the order of events—it is the most important reason for describing this work here. One first seeks principles on which a perceptual system operates, and is fortunate if they can be given mathematical form. Perceptual consequences are deduced, and one looks to see whether support for them is to be found. Where does one look? In the literature of experimental psychology in the first place, and in new research designed to test the deductions; also in the workings of the brain, if the model has neuropsychological implications. First comes the work of thinking, although based on empirical knowledge of the field of the explicandum, of course, then comes the modeling from which deductions flow, and only after that the search for further empirical support. It is a "top-down" process, filled in from "below," but certainly not one that *starts* with rooting around in the brain in search of explanatory principles! What is here true of a perceptual theory must clearly apply with equal force to other branches of cognitive science. A tale of "principles first, evidence later" could be told in other fields too, such as in the levels of processing theory of memory, or the transformational grammar approach to language.

Gibson, Hoffman, and the Standard Model

The principles that today drive most research in cognitive science derive from the standard model. At first blush they do not seem to owe much to theories that aim at comprehensive treatment of a topic—in our case perception—such as the two we have been examining. Both of these urge a particular (but very different) stance as the only one possible if we want to understand correctly the nature of perception, what its function is in the daily round, as well as the theoretical concepts required to capture its fundamentals. How do Gibson's and Hoffman's theories relate to the standard model? Are they constrained by it? Do they illuminate it in a useful way?

I will briefly assess each theory in relation to the axioms of the standard model as presented in chapter 4. Gibson's position is rather straightforward. It regards the axioms of neural substrate and reducibility as wrong-headed, or at the very least irrelevant. As we saw, according to Gibson's view of perception (and a fortiori of cognition), the questions we ask and the explanations we seek are simply not addressable in terms of goings-on in the brain. He had little to say of the axiom of unlimited access (no restriction of investigation to conscious states) although he argued strenuously against the idea that ordinary perceptual experience is dependent on memory, set, inference, or other cognitive influences that act beyond our immediate awareness of the stimulating array.

Gibson certainly accepted the axioms of biological evolution and biological emergence; indeed he made them—especially the former—cornerstones of his position. This is true also of the axiom of mental emergence (emergence of mentation as a property of the brain). The axioms of machine architecture, mental architecture, and computability are, for Gibson, simply not in the appropriate universe of discourse. To invoke them as bases for explanatory principles in perception is to make, in Gilbert Ryle's terms, a category mistake. The reasons are much the same as those for rejecting the axiom of neural substrate.

Referring back to table 5.1, recall that Gibson's theory was placed in level 2, stage 3, the cell for formal theories at the perceptual level. By his own fiat Gibson restricted deliberation to stage 3; he would have nothing to do with brains, or working models of brains. Since he considered the senses *perceptual systems* (as the title of his major contribution to perceptual theory makes clear),[30] he is out of level 1 (sensory function). He claimed (wrongly, as I argued earlier in the chapter) that cognitive processes (at level 3) can all be subsumed under level 2, as aspects of perceptual activity. Gibson's theoretical tools are limited, by his own choice of territory, to a single cell of the table. And that, as I have argued from a somewhat different point of view in the past,[31] is far too restricting to allow us to accept his position as the umbrella theory of perception he intended it to be.

For Gibson the standard model is thus partly irrelevant, partly an anathema; except for the evolutionary-biological argument which came to dominate his later thinking, he is seen to be well outside the general consensus of opinion among cognitive scientists, as to both method and content.

Hoffman's ideas are closer to the standard model, yet he has attracted the interest of only a rather small group of researchers. As I argued above, his Lie transformation group theory of neuropsychology (dubbed LTG/NP; I shall call it simply the Lie theory), sets a standard of what a theory in perception should aim for. That is a strong claim, and I base it not on the particular successes of the theory, although these are not negligible, but on its structure as a framework for scientific explanation in perception.

So far as the standard model's axioms of neural substrate and reducibility are concerned, Hoffman is neutral. The Lie theory assigns a special role to brain functions, but doing so does not entail the acceptance of these particular axioms. Indeed, as the primary motivation of the theory is "top-down," and to the extent that logical and mathematical concepts are not reducible to physiological-physical processes (see above and chapter 5), the axioms can be construed as useful but subsidiary support . The theory is similarly neutral with respect to the axiom of unlimited access; it makes no claims or pronouncements regarding unconscious mental states. It certainly accepts the axiom of biological evolution, and (like Gibson) relates the emergence of the transformation groups to the interaction of organism and environment under evolutionary pressure.

The Lie theory proposes nothing that is inconsistent with the axioms of machine and mental architecture, and obviously accepts the axiom of computability; everything in the theory requires that efficient procedures be specified. It accepts the axiom of respectability, or pragmatism. On the whole, Hoffman's ideas are consistent with the standard model, much more so than Gibson's, but they do not demand strong adherence to most of its axioms. The concepts run, so to speak, parallel to those of the standard model; the aims and ideas are different, but their bases are not incompatible.

Hoffman's theory sits squarely in the third cell of level 2 in table 5.1. It is a conceptual scheme within which to order and explain perceptual phenomena, a top-down scheme, as any good theory must be. It accepts many of the tenets and techniques of traditional perceptual theory and research, shaping them to its own ends and putting them into a well-defined mathematical structure. From this flows the interpretation of a wide variety of perceptual and physiological data, in sharp contrast to the Gibsonian position.[32]

The Lie theory generates concepts that lead or steer the interpretation of the "lower" levels. There is no attempt to make physiological events like contour coding the exclusive basis for explaining pattern recognition, constancy, and the like—the typical move in neuroscience—but rather to see them as implementing certain transformational processes that explain salient features of pattern perception like transposition, invariance under transformation, and constancy. Hoffman has also suggested ways of extending his ideas to level 3, cognition proper, in terms of (the very abstract) category theory. Whether this application will have genuine empirical content, that is to say, whether any experimental outcomes can be deduced from it and verified, remains to be seen.[33]

The Lie theory exemplifies the three explanatory levels of cognitive science (see chapter 5 and table 5.1) rather well. At the conceptual level the mathematical theory of transformation groups and the function they play in perception is fundamental. From this we look to the procedures (algorithms) by means of which the specific properties of perception are mediated, the actual roles the transformation groups play in the organization of perceptual phenomena, and finally to the "wetware" of the brain that implements, in neural tissue, the algorithms of the transformation groups. Each level has its own characteristic questions and problems, each supplies a different, but relevant, species of description and explanation (recall the calculator and the Brahms symphony). All this is highly appropriate because, as we have now recognized many times, perception is a multilevel, multilayered edifice, and to comprehend it fully requires many different concepts and techniques.

The Lie theory can be called a "grand design" for perception; it has an overall conceptual sweep, it allows for the principled interpretation of phenomenological and physiological data in terms of effective procedures, and it fits into a (Gibsonian) view of the evolution of perceptual systems. One can well view the theory as a sharpening up of the ideas on transformation and invariance with which Gibson dallied, as well as a worthy successor to the Gestalt tradition of attempting to explain perceptual organization and brain function. The Gestalt psychologists mixed up their levels both factually and conceptually, as we saw; the Lie theory does a better-articulated and more sophisticated job on this front, too. It also has a better stab at answering those awkward but seminal questions about trees, squares, and straight lines in terms of conformal groups, Lie orbits, and their "prolongations", but it would lead too far afield to go into that here.[34] Where do those conformal groups come from? One may well ask. *There* an evolutionary account is entirely appropriate; they embody the constraints that the physical-biological environment imposes on any locomotary organism. They become "built in" to any motile perceptual system, because it is useful and has survival value to be able to deploy rapidly and without effort the transformation groups that ensure perceptual stability.[35]

The Lie theory thus has a principled means of meshing representation with reality; it does so by conformal group action on the immediate sensory input. From this point of view, too, it is a "top-down" theory, but one that is supplemented and complemented—completed—by the "bottom-up" action of physiological structures and functions and of psychophysical operations. Nothing less can do justice to the full panoply of perceptual phenomena; no other theory that I know of even comes close to meeting all these desiderata.

7

Mathematics and the Mind

At the age of eleven, I began Euclid, with my brother as tutor. This was one of the great events of my life, as dazzling as first love.

BERTRAND RUSSELL

On Mathematical Thinking

In chapter 6 we had an example of how a mathematical model can form the basis for a theory of perception, perhaps of more general aspects of cognition also. But the existence of mathematics and mathematical thinking has another and even more fundamental bearing on our inquiry. The existence of mathematics and mathematical thinking in fact pose prodigious problems for cognitive science, especially as this is expressed in the standard model. On the one hand mathematics can be seen as a pure product of human creativity, but on the other it gives us a uniquely powerful means of coming to grips with the natural world. It is in us, but it also binds us to what is external to our conscious mentation. So, mathematics and mathematical thinking can, and must, play a very special role in any attempt to understand cognition, not least in the business of trying to identify cognitive activity with brain processes. Hence, this whole chapter is devoted to the topic—and it will again assume a prominent place in the final chapter.

In chapter 6 we saw how problematic it is to define a straight line, a mathematical entity that looks simple enough—straightforward you might say—in terms of what goes on in the brain. The idea seems not even to be coherent, as Gibson argued so persuasively; straight lines are things in the external world, so the best we might ever hope to do is map them consistently onto their physiological "representations." Gibson thought even that was of no consequence for a theory of perception. How much more difficult and contentious, then, should be the project of attempting to identify mental abilities like the creation or understanding of mathematics as processes in the brain; yet that is precisely what the standard model sees as the overall goal of cognitive science.

There are two main problems, as there were with the straight line. The first is the logical difficulty of saying how something "out there" is to be represented in terms that are not completely circular, or that do not lead to an infinite regression of "equivalence recognizors" in the brain. The second is the sheer technical difficulty of establishing equivalence. The mappings for a straight line are complicated enough, involving as they do the concepts of transformation and adaptation to transformation (which themselves must evidently be representable in brain processes. . . . oh dear!); imagine what would be required to demonstrate the equivalence of brain states corresponding to the various ways of stating and proving, let us say, the first ten theorems of Euclid's geometry. Yet that is what the program of the standard model proclaims can be done, and it seems to find support in the success with which symbol manipulation can be implemented in traditional AI. That assumes that the question of how perceptual and cognitive elements themselves are to be represented unambiguously in real brains can, at least in principle, be answered. That is certainly an unresolved matter (think again of the straight line), but resolution is exactly what would be needed to flesh matters out; that is, to represent physiologically the thoughts and ideas of the comprehending mind.

Nowhere is this dilemma greater than in the realm of mathematics. What is mathematics? The dictionary definition says: "The abstract science of number, quantity, and space studied in its own right."[1] This is "bare bones" but tells us three important things: Mathematics is abstract, it is its own master, answerable to no one (the queen of sciences, as it has been called), and it has a wide denotation. In a public address the great geometer Arthur Cayley said: "It is difficult to give an idea of the vast extent of modern mathematics." That was in 1883! In the following century or so there has been a veritable explosion of mathematical thought and application. Far more new mathematics has been created in the past 50 years than in the rest of recorded history.

Even professional mathematicians find it impossible to keep abreast of very much outside their areas of special interest.[2] But that need not keep us from inquiring into how cognitive science can tackle the question of whether, and if so how, mathematics is to be understood in terms of the standard model. It is not a question of whether some particular branch of mathematics can be handled, it is a question of whether the very process (or processes) of doing mathematics can be accommodated. To see the problem clearly, one need think only of very elementary things, for example, this little item of arithmetic: Adding together the first two odd numbers, 1 and 3, the sum is 4. Add together the first three odd numbers, 1, 3, and 5, and the sum is nine. Add the first four, 1, 3, 5, and 7, and the sum is 16. Already a pattern emerges, which is seen clearly in the scheme:

$$1 + 3 = 4 = 2 \times 2 = 2^2$$
$$1 + 3 + 5 = 9 = 3 \times 3 = 3^2$$
$$1 + 3 + 5 + 7 = 16 = 4 \times 4 = 4^2$$

You surely now expect to find the sum of the first five odd numbers to be 5×5? And so it is; $1 + 3 + 5 + 7 + 9 = 25$. There is something appealing, even beautiful, and certainly quite compelling about such a pattern. One can formulate a general rule: The sum of the first n odd numbers is $n \times n$, or n^2. You would probably be very confident about the sum of the first six odd numbers (6×6), but how about the sum of the first 100? It is indeed 100^2, that is, 10,000. Although we certainly have not proved that fact, it could be verified by calculation, as could the same rule for any number of consecutive odd numbers we like to name. Such enumeration is not what mathematics is about; it is about things like proof of the general rule—that is, proof that the sum is $n \times n$, no matter how large n is.

The proof is not difficult, but we don't need to give it in detail. The important thing is to gain some understanding for the nature of mathematical proof itself. It consists of a logically valid argument that is based in the first instance on a set of axioms, and follows a rule (or rules) of inference to reach a conclusion. The example familiar to most people is the system of Euclidean geometry we learned about in high school. The axioms and allowable inferences have been called the rules of the game;[3] from them are deduced theorems that are true in the system. New mathematical knowledge is established by entertaining some conjecture or hypothesis within the relevant system (Euclidean geometry, for example) and demonstrating, by a sequence of allowed steps, that the hypothesis is either true or false. If it is true it is necessarily true; if it is false it is necessarily false, a self-contradiction. In the first case the hypothesis is proven, and in the second case it is disproven. Necessity follows from the fact that it would be inconsistent to accept the rules of the game but at the same time to deny the conclusions to which they lead. In this sense mathematical statements share a major feature with the "truths by convention,"[4] discussed in chapter 1—both manifest the character of necessary truth. In an older philosophical tradition they were called, as I mentioned in chapter 1, "analytic statements."

So mathematics is, fundamentally, a matter of logic, as Bertrand Russell and others surmised and were able to prove (see chapter 3). To return to our little example; the proof starts with the hypothesis that the sum of the first n odd numbers is $n \times n$. Then, with a bit of simple algebra we show that if the hypothesis is true of n, it must also be true for $n + 1$; that is, we show that the sum of the first $n + 1$ odd numbers must be $(n + 1) \times (n + 1)$. But we already know that the hypothesis is true for some particular value of n, say when $n = 3$ ($1 + 3 + 5 = 9 = 3 \times 3$), so it must be true when $n = 4$, therefore also when $n = 5, = 6, \ldots$ and so on, to any value of n we like to choose— that is, for all natural numbers. This is known as proof by induction, and it is a truly mathematical procedure, however simply exemplified here.[5] The necessity in the proof is a logical necessity; it explains why the formula for the sum of the first n odd numbers must be true. In this case, it must be true if we accept the rules of ordinary algebra, which were used in the proof.

Here is another example of a more spatial-geometrical type. It again demonstrates that property of necessity in an argument and its conclusion that is the hallmark of mathematical thinking. It also shows how a simple insight into some feature of the subject under investigation may alter the way a problem is conceived, thereby leading to a simple and elegant solution to something that at first seems to be complicated and messy.

Here is the problem: Imagine a square board, or sheet of paper, divided up into 64 equal squares, 8 rows, with 8 squares in each row ($8 \times 8 = 64$). Imagine now that you have some dominoes, rectangular in shape and of such a size that one domino will fit exactly over two squares on the board. It will not take a great effort of imagination to see that you could cover the board completely with just 32 dominoes, and you could do it in several different ways, all aligned horizontally ("east-west") or all vertically ("north-south") for example. Now comes the question: If you leave one corner square uncovered—the bottom right-hand one, let's say—is it possible to arrange the dominoes so that the opposite corner (upper left) remains uncovered when all the rest have been covered?

It is obvious (or it should be obvious—why?) that if you leave the bottom right-hand square uncovered there is going to be another single empty square somewhere when you have laid down 31 dominoes. Thirty-one? Of course, it's obvious—but again, think why this must be so. The tricky part is to decide whether the covering will allow just that one particular square at top-left to remain uncovered. Think about it for a few minutes before going to the next paragraph.

How did you proceed? Probably by imagining (or even doing, if you had a board, pencil and ruler, and dominoes handy) a few trial layouts. Your idea was probably to try to find some scheme or rule of combination that would allow you to end up with the required empty square. You probably thought the possibilities are so numerous that the solution has to be very complicated; you also may have been intrigued by the question of whether there is more than one way of achieving the result, if it can be done. No way! There is a neat and nifty proof that there is no solution; that is to say, there is of necessity no way to lay down the dominoes so as to leave that opposite corner uncovered.

The argument is disarmingly simple. Imagine, instead of the board with 64 squares drawn on it, a chessboard, with squares alternating in two colors. You might make things easier for yourself by looking at an actual chessboard, if you have one handy. Look at the bottom right-hand square, and let's say it is black. Now look at the opposite corner (top left), and it is also black. Or, perhaps, they are both white. The important thing is that they are both of the same color.[6] Now think of what happens when you lay down a domino. Because the squares of the chessboard alternate in color, a single domino will always cover one white and one black square, whether you lay it east-west or north-south. At any stage of the procedure, those remaining uncovered will therefore always consist of an equal number of black and white squares. That being so it is impossible, after all but one of the dominoes has been put in place, to have two squares of the same color left uncovered! So, it is impossible to have a covering that leaves only the opposite corner squares uncovered. The key to this elegant solution is a genuine mathematical inspiration, the realization that a previously unthought-of, or undisclosed, feature of the situation points the way to a simpler way of posing, and thus of resolving, the problem.

If these two examples leave you totally unmoved, give you no feeling at all for the esthetic appeal of the sharp but often subtle uses of mathematical argument (even in the simplest of arithmetical and geometrical examples), you will not be alone. This is sad, and perhaps largely because of the unimaginative ways that mathematics are introduced in school.[7] However, it cannot be doubted that some individuals but not others have a particular gift, a specialized aptitude, for the subject.[8] So do not despair! Although I shall appeal in various ways to the genius of mathematics and of mathematical thinking, it should be possible to follow the train of thought of this chapter without any special flair for the subject. Rather than attempting to amplify the brief dictionary definition already given, I have aimed to demonstrate something of the quality of mathematical thinking, even though in a very elementary and non-rigorous fashion. This will be quite sufficient for my present purpose, which is to introduce mathematical thinking as both a problem, and also a unique challenge, to cognitive science!

Mathematics in the World

That many sorts of mathematics are extraordinarily useful and successful in science as well as in the business of the everyday world cannot be doubted, yet mathematics has some properties that can rightly be described as unfathomable, even mysterious, if not outright magical. The first we may note is that although mathematics is evidently a product of human thought, many of its branches have a direct and illuminating bearing on our ability to grasp the nature of the world, especially in its most fundamental spatial and temporal, or generally in its physical, manifestations.[9] The argument is made that this is just because we humans have the ability to abstract; elementary mathematics at least is merely a result of the propensity to seek generality in our conceptions about objects in the world, and one of the best ways of doing this is to abstract. Numbers, for example (what we call the natural numbers, at least), are abstractions from our commerce with collections of objects like apples, people, limbs, knots, stars, and so on.[10]

There is very real doubt about whether this is an adequate description of the way young children acquire the concept of number, as Piaget and his followers have shown.[11] Moreover, the conception of mathematics as a mere tool with which to handle our models of the world, and a means to control it, has been found to be far too limiting. It was only comparatively recently that the supra-mundane character of mathematics, its drama rather than its mere grammar, was fully realized and generally accepted.

As mentioned in chapter 3, the received view of geometry well into the nineteenth century was that it (that is, specifically Euclidean geometry) gives a true and complete account of the spatial character of the world. The beauty of this account was that, in view of the rigorous derivation of theorems from Euclid's axioms, theorems that were measurably true of the physical world (e.g., that any angle inscribed on the diameter of a circle is a right angle), it was possible to ascribe a certainty to some aspects of knowledge about the world that by far transcends mere factual observation.[12]

The discovery of non-Euclidean geometries in the first half of the nineteenth century by Bolyai, Lobachewsky and Riemann gave a severe jolt to this view of the world, as we have noted in chapter 3. Not only was it possible to conceive of a geometry different from the Euclidean, in which parallel lines are not even defined, it was shown many years later, in Einstein's general theory of relativity, that the geometry that best describes our universe in the large is non-Euclidean.[13] So much for the Euclidean hegemony, which had lasted more than 2,000 years. Not only is it not unique as a geometrical system, it does not even properly describe the space of the physical world whose rock-solid reality it was supposed to guarantee.

Two very important matters confront us. The first is that the discovery of the non-Euclidean geometries—or their invention, depending on your point of view—eventually forced a huge change in the conception of what mathematics is all about, a veritable metaphysical revolution.[14] The second is that we have here an example of a discovery (or invention) in pure mathematics that only some considerable time later was to find application, in fact to become the key ingredient of, a new and revolutionary scientific theory about the nature of the physical world. That sort of application of the new geometry was the last thing in the minds of the mathematicians who created it!

This is not an isolated instance of mathematical creation preceding, sometimes by a very long time, its application in science or to some other branch of human endeavor. Things can happen the other way round too, of course, and probably much more frequently. New mathematics, even a new branch of mathematics, may arise out of the attempt to codify, simplify or otherwise formalize matters in some practical field of work or play. A well-known instance is the creation of the rudiments of mathematical probability theory by Cardano, keen to discover methods of assessing the odds in a game of chance.

Perhaps the most striking example of the first sort—the creation of a "pure" mathematics that predated its application in science—is the Greek development of the geometry of conic sections. This is spectacular, both because the mathematical development began nearly 2,000 years before the application, and also because no one could have dreamed, particularly before the requisite astronomical observations were made, that such an application could even in principle be possible.

Whitehead, writing early in the century, put it this way:

> When the Greek geometers had exhausted, as they thought, the more obvious and interesting properties of figures made up of straight lines and circles, they turned their attention to the study of other curves; and, with their almost infallible instinct for hitting upon things worth thinking about, they chiefly devoted themselves to conic sections, the curves in which planes would cut the surfaces of circular cones.[15]

Concerning the end of the Greek development with the work of Pappus of Alexandria, some 500 years after the initial discoveries, who thought the topic (conic sections) exhausted of interesting questions, Whitehead wrote:

> In truth the really fruitful ideas in connection with this branch of mathematics had not yet been even touched upon, and no one had guessed their supremely important applications in nature. No more impressive warning can be given to those who would confine knowledge and research to what is apparently useful, than the reflection that conic sections were studied for eighteen hundred years merely as an abstract science, without a thought of any utility other than to satisfy the craving for knowledge on the part of mathematicians, and that then at the end of this long period of abstract study, they were found to be the necessary key with which to attain the knowledge of one of the most important laws of nature.[16]

There are many other cases where the development of some new branch of mathematics, studied for its own intrinsic interest, was later found to be just what was needed to push ahead with scientific theory. The creation of the mathematics of complex numbers, and of group theory, are salient examples that come to mind. In recent times the work of Penrose (the Penrose we met in chapter 4) on the theory of tiling is another prime instance, to say nothing of the mathematical theories of catastrophes and of chaos.[17] The regularity with which this happens is quite uncanny.

So, it is well established that mathematics, far from being merely a sort of passive abstraction-cum-construction from experience in the physical world, can precede knowledge of the sphere to which it will eventually be applied; it has a most active characteristic in that it steers or even controls our investigation of the world, often in novel, incisive, and quite unpredictable ways. Yet, we create the mathematics, and do so often enough just for the reason that the ideas are interesting, challenging, and—as has so frequently been stated by its practitioners—beautiful, without any regard for their potential utility.[18] What lessons are to be learned from this?

Mathematical Truth

To find out, let us return to the two examples, one arithmetical, one geometrical (or at least spatial) with which this chapter began. The arithmetical example, in which an expression for the sum of the first n odd numbers was discovered, shows that there are properties of numbers, not immediately obvious, that are nevertheless there for the taking; they are true properties of numbers, and whether we happen to know them or not has no bearing whatsoever on their truth. We feel it in our bones, so to speak, that they are mathematical facts, just as much as the weights of natural objects are physical facts. Notice that in both cases it requires a certain amount of human ingenuity and codification to express the facts unambiguously.

But there is a telling difference between the two sorts of fact. The weights of objects are completely contingent and arbitrary matters; finding what the weights are involves the acquisition of additional information each time a new object is weighed.[19] Mathematical facts are not like this. They have an element of necessity about them that defies the notion of incremental information gain. Think of the rule about the sum of the first n odd numbers, which we called a mathematical fact. Each time you find the sum for a new value of n, it might be said that you acquire new information about numbers, namely the sum for that particular set of odd numbers, and in a sense you add confirmation of the rule. But, once the rule is known and proven, it would be equally true to say that counting to find the sum of a given set of n odd numbers adds no new information; the sum is already known from the rule, so finding it by enumeration is totally redundant. Moreover, that the sum of the first n odd numbers equals $n \times n$ is necessarily true. Remember? It can be proved by induction from first principles. But, as we saw in chapter 1, a necessary truth is analytic; it is true by virtue of the way words or other symbols are defined, or as a result of the axiomatic system of which it forms a part. A statement that is true under all circumstances has no factual content, no empirical means of verification. Nevertheless it is obvious that the rule about the sum of odd numbers has empirical reference, even factual content one might claim, because we can count a sum of n odd numbers to check that it agrees with the rule.

This is the heart of the matter: Mathematical truths are analytic. They are necessary truths because they are (correctly) deduced from a set of appropriate axioms, but the axioms themselves—as we now understand—are a matter of choice. How can it be that such truths then refer to states of the world that we call matters of fact, matters that are seemingly open to verification or falsification? How is it possible for both of these apparently contradictory things to be simultaneously true? The Kantian solution was to claim that mathematical truths, those of Euclidean geometry being his prime example, have a special status that governs, but also limits, our capacity to acquire knowledge of the world. They were called synthetic a priori truths. That will no longer do, and the discovery of other geometries, as valid as Euclid's from the mathematical standpoint, was responsible for the changed conception of the nature of mathematics and its place in the world. It is now recognized that whether or not some particular branch of mathematics has empirical reference is itself a matter for investigation that is quite independent of its truth or importance as mathematics (see below).

The idea of an a priori truth (one we would now call an analytic statement) that nevertheless has empirical content (which is what Kant meant by a synthetic statement) has been superseded by the distinction between statements of fact, on the one hand (synthetic), and logical/linguistic truths (analytic, or "truths by convention" as they have also been called), on the other, a distinction already made in chapters 1 and 3. The distinction was part of the positivistic program we also discussed earlier, culminating in promulgation of the principle of verification. Maintaining the distinction between analytic and synthetic statements seems so beautifully sharp, apparently clearing the way for so much progress in the understanding of how scientific truth is expressed, that it seems a pity to blur it. Yet blur it we must.

Consider again that innocent little example of number theory (to give it its grand name), the rule about the sum of the first n odd numbers which started our discussion. On the one hand, it tells us a fact about the sums of odd numbers, which quite evidently is a fact about the world, but on the other it expresses a rule that, once proved, is necessarily true and is not subject to verification within the ordinary meaning of that word. But the status of the rule is ambiguous in another sense too: Before it was proved it had the status of an empirical generalization: "The sum of the first n odd numbers is $n \times n$? Extraordinary! Let's count up and see." After it was proved it had the status of a necessary truth: "The sum is $n \times n$? Of course, a little algebra shows that it must be so." How we categorize the statement thus depends entirely on the state of relevant mathematical analysis and proof.[20] If that is true in this fairly trivial example, it must be true in many another more substantial instance; in fact, in every other instance. Hence, there is no absolute criterion for assigning statements about numbers and number theory to one category or the other.[21]

What is true of numbers and number theory is true of mathematical "facts" in general. Indeed the creation of new mathematics proceeds largely on the basis of starting from hypotheses about what might be the case, or ought to be the case, to surmises about how one might go about demonstrating their truth, to the search for adequate and logically watertight proof that a particular hypothesis is correct.[22] The hypotheses can be of the most varied types, but are essentially different from conjectures about the application of mathematical models to the natural world, from cosmology to the dynamics of population biology to the network properties of neural tissue. The latter are verified by interpretation and observation, often of the most complicated and difficult sorts. But speculation about purely abstract mathematical entities like n-dimensional matrices, strange attractors, and Riemann surfaces is conceptual and demands a very different form of verification—that achieved by logical argument; in other words, by derivation within an appropriate axiomatic system. This is perhaps the ultimate in what is known as "curiosity-driven" research; that is, research that expresses in its purest form the human urge to extend the frontiers of knowledge. From this point of view one could describe the goal of mathematics to be the reduction of as much knowledge as possible (logically possible, no less) to forms that are explicit, no longer conjectural, but fully grasped and accounted for within the framework of an axiomatic, proof-dependent scheme for comprehending reality—in other words, everything!

Mathematics of the World

From Galileo to Kant to Einstein to Hawking, the belief that mathematics is the royal road to true scientific knowledge has been loudly proclaimed. In antiquity Pythagoras and his followers held that the secrets of the universe, of existence itself, are revealed in number. Small wonder that mathematics has been called the queen of sciences. And yet there is the awkward fact that mathematical truths are said to be merely analytic, just tautological consequences of the axiomatic system in which they happen to have been proved. If that is so, we could be forgiven for toying with the opposite notion, namely, that mathematics is nothing but a barren and vaporous construction of the human mind; barren, that is, of any significance for the world of human culture, including its scientific achievements. But this has clearly to be wrong, too; we do not need to argue over the central role mathematics plays in modern science.

So, perhaps this is the correct way to view things: Mathematics is truly a creation of the human mind, sufficient unto itself, and with criteria of validity that have no dependence on "facts of the matter," including numerical and other such facts, like verifying by calculation the sum of the first n odd numbers. If we take the abstractness of mathematics in full seriousness, we see that this is how things do stand. A branch of mathematics can be developed—many have been—that has no physical realization, but that nonetheless qualifies in the fullest sense as mathematics. This is what Campbell called the "uninterpreted calculus."[23] The question of whether it has application to anything else, such as a physical, biological or cultural entity, whether it provides a model of that entity, is a very different matter. How is that decided?

The answer is: It is decided on pragmatic, but basically still-conceptual grounds. This is most evident in the requirement that a genuine theory must yield deductions that can be verified by some form of empirical observation. But in the history of scientific inquiry the cart has often been put before the horse, because the discovery of mathematical truths has often followed on the acute examination of physical systems. The early discovery of simple truths to do with the geometry of triangles originated in the first crude attempts at surveying land plots in ancient Egypt (*geometry* after all means "earth measurement").[24] All of Euclidean geometry "fits" with the properties of the physical space of the near environment, so its discoverers and codifiers could be forgiven for mistakenly concluding that their mathematics dispensed a magical new knowledge of that space. Similarly the mathematics of the later Greek classical period are derived from the desire to understand music, astronomy, properties of material bodies, shape, quantity, and number, all securely grounded in the character of the perceptible environment.[25] Nevertheless they laid the foundations for trigonometry, algebra, and mechanics, as well as an astoundingly sophisticated geometry of curves and surfaces, all of them abstractly mathematical in the best sense, and all the more remarkable for the fact that some of the technical devices employed in their discovery and analysis were cumbersome and primitive in the extreme. The Greek way of representing numbers, of counting, for instance, was even less accommodating than the Roman system of numeration we find so awkward. Did you ever consider trying to work with fractions or negative numbers using Roman numerals?[26] The Greek mathematicians were even worse off, which renders truly astounding the triumphs of mathematical insight they achieved.

It is time for us to recognize that those achievements stem from the human propensity to wonder and speculate; the fact that the first things about which conjectures were made (so far as we know) were rather mundane should not blind us concerning what is the cart, what the horse. The driving force, the inspiration if you like, for this early mathematics was the human intellect, finding freedom to roam and create its own problems, conjectures, and solutions. That came first. The material on which those (apparently) newfound powers were let loose seems from this point of view to be of a decidedly subsidiary, contingent nature.[27]

What is true of the Greeks is true of the mathematicians of all time, a theme we shall take up presently. First, let us return to our second elementary example, the question of covering the chessboard with dominoes.

Mathematical Imagination

Notice that a verbal description of the situation is enough to trigger what may be called a spatial "picture," an imaginary chessboard with its attendant features of alternating black and white squares, etc. Even if you happened to set up a real board to help solve the puzzle I posed, you can scarcely doubt the capacity of most normal people to imagine the board with many of its features, even if the picture is a bit fuzzy. Likewise with the placement of the dominoes. It is not difficult to imagine the actions of placing them on the board, or the consequences; for example, the fact that after each domino is put down there will be an equal number of black and white squares remaining uncovered (until the 32nd piece is put in place).

One could certainly argue that these abilities depend on familiarity with the materials, chessboards, and dominoes, but what of a blind or paralyzed participant? Such persons can display spatial imagination, which may be different, less complete, less articulated than that of people without those handicaps, but it is not absent. It would seem unlikely that the development of spatial concepts, spatial imagination, is totally dependent on some specific sensory input for its appearance, although such experience no doubt facilitates its maturation.[28] To be behavioristic one could call the missing element *epistemic drive,* to use Berlyne's term (chapter 2), but that is too dry and academic a term to cover all that is involved here. In recent times there have been numerous attempts within cognitive science to understand images, assess their properties, exploit their vicissitudes and underscore their potential as the currency of mental life.[29] Without in any way belittling that work, one can say that it does not go nearly far enough in providing insight into what cries out for better understanding. One thing lacking, as we shall presently discuss, is attention to the driving, compelling force that motivates mathematical thinking.

There can be no doubt that images are real and play an important role in mental life, and nowhere more so than in mathematics. It seems to me, however, that the more fundamental concept, as well as the more enigmatic, is the concept of imagination. Back to the chessboard again: To imagine it does not entail that you entertain some specific image or images; I called the imagined chessboard a "picture," but that is only partially helpful. It is not—for most people at any rate—even a partially faithful copy of the original, a "something" in the head like a poorly developed photograph. There is also no doubt that different people have images that vary in a number of ways, particularly in vividness and "liveliness"; their reportable characteristics (introspections) do not seem to play as important a role in the exercise of imagination as one might suppose. In the celebrated experiments of Shepard and Metzler on the mental rotation of images,[30] it was not that the subjects rotated some stage prop in the (internal) Cartesian theater, as Ryle might put it, rather they imagined rotating a real object—"out there," as it were. The same is true of our chessboard, or indeed of the manipulation of anything presented, in a manner of speaking, as "food for thought." And that is what brings us back to the topic of mathematics.

We can be sure that individuals have very different capacities to imagine objects, events, and abstract entities, but this is not just a matter of differences in image quality, such as vividness or speed of appearance. When I said that the posing and solution of the chessboard problem displayed the features of something genuinely mathematical I had in mind that it calls into operation a capacity to actively imagine that seems to lie at the root of so much mathematical understanding, and particularly of the creation of new mathematics. The fact that we applied it to something as familiar and mundane as a chessboard is scarcely pivotal; we could have looked at more complicated, more technical, more abstruse examples on which to exercise our imaginations, such as a problem involving a three-dimensional array, or one needing familiarity with differential calculus, or posing a paradox of symbolic logic. The essence of the matter would have been the same, but fewer readers (one supposes) would have had the time, technical knowledge, patience, or disciplined imagination to follow the exposition and to formulate a solution.

My claim is that to do mathematics involves a capacity not only to abstract, but also to look with a compelling urge, a particularly dynamic sense of inquiry, and an active but well-controlled capacity to imagine a wide variety of problems and situations. Mathematicians have that capacity far more than is the norm, and among mathematicians the gift varies greatly, but that does seem to be the key ingredient. Imagination can be elicited, as in the chessboard problem, but it can also "well up" in a creative urge, without apparent external stimulus.[31] What has cognitive science to say about imagination in this sense? Virtually nothing. Is that important? Most certainly!

The chessboard problem calls into play the imagination, conjecture *in abstracto,* the search for putative solutions. That is why it is fundamentally a mathematical problem, but it is scarcely the only consideration. Not every situation in the world is amenable to mathematical analysis. A definition that allows us to circumscribe the valid fields of activity would be nice, but the danger is that it would be too restricting. Who is to issue a mandate on what mathematicians may concern themselves with? Maybe the whole world and all its furniture is their oyster! Later I shall present examples to illustrate the character of original mathematical thought, even where seemingly unpromising fields have yielded their secrets to mathematical analysis. For now it is sufficient to make the rather obvious point that mathematical inquiry often starts with questions that involve quantity, perceptible entities, tangible things, the world of extension in the Cartesian sense. Where it goes from there is limited only by, of course, human imagination. The greater the mathematician, the greater the range and depth of that imagination, and often the more obscure, or surprising, or even entertaining, the field to which it is applied.

Invention or Discovery?

We started off with examples from the two fields in which mathematics first flourished, arithmetic and geometry. You might wonder: How can such simple things teach us anything about the arcane mysteries of this august Platonic topic? Surely its secrets must be shrouded in the far reaches of the intellectual stratosphere? Can a couple of almost paltry applications to numbers and figures reveal anything of significance? The answer most certainly is yes, and to show that, another comparison with music may be helpful.

If you want to learn about the fundamentals of music (classical Western variety, to keep matters from getting out of hand) a simple tune with basic harmonization will give you most of what you want: say, "Twinkle, Twinkle Little Star." Even better would be one of those delectable little minuets written by Mozart at the age of six, which, incredibly enough, already manifest something of the pure genius that was later to blossom in the fullness of his mature compositions.[32] One could learn about melody, meter, rhythm, form, key, and time signatures, harmony, modulation, and cadence—the elements required for the proper understanding and appreciation of music. It is just so with mathematics. You don't need to get technical, complicated, or abstruse, to gain an appreciation of its fundamental character.

We have already seen that mathematical thought calls forth the exercise of imagination, that it demands abstraction, that it tends to be focused (to start with anyway) on things in the world around us. Mathematical thought is geared to seeking generalization, simplification, pattern, and, yes, beauty in its conceptualization of everything of which it treats, no less in the humble spatial rules that govern the chessboard than in the most sophisticated cosmological theory. In that sense we can get a true idea of the role mathematics plays in mental life even on the first rungs of its mighty ladder.

Returning to the rule for summing the first n odd numbers: It required a mind (or several) to "think it up," but the rule is certainly true independently of that fact and of those minds. As I said earlier, it is a fact about the world. Here is an important question: Was the rule invented, or discovered? You may have noticed that I hedged earlier on this, and wrote of the "creation" of new mathematics, even of the most elementary sort. The question has divided mathematicians sharply into two camps (formalists and intuitionists) and the differences really do hinge on this question of invention versus discovery. If your inclination is to think of mathematics as purely man-made, a form of intellectual creation that happens to be applicable to the external physical world in some (but not all) of its manifestations, you will tend to the invention side, and say that it is just good fortune, a matter of serendipity, to find that this intellectual game has useful work to do in the world. Not a few great mathematicians have held this view. If, however, you see mathematics in the Platonic sense as a world of sublime truths that transcends our time and space-limited existence, to which humanity is vouchsafed occasional and incomplete access, you will prefer the metaphor—but surely it is much more than a mere metaphor—of discovery. That position, too, has had its most distinguished protagonists.

Recalling the work of the early Greek geometers on conic sections might incline one to the discovery paradigm. Arguing on the side of invention leads one to stress the aspect of abstracting in the first instance. The world presents us with plenty of examples of single items, and of pairs (ears, eyes, arms, pairs of apples, oranges, persons, reproductive mates, etc.). What we abstract as their common feature is their pairness, no mean intellectual feat when it first occurred, no doubt, but still one might argue a human invention that imposes itself on the world. It would be no less true to say that the world imposes its own constraints on the form the abstraction takes, but still, the human element has to be there to do the abstracting.

What makes this argument less than compelling is the seeming impossibility of constructing, imagining, inventing, a world where number is not present in any form whatsoever. That we can name entities, distinguish one object from another, contrast one attribute with another requires that we can say (with Bertrand Russell, in *Principia Mathematica* [1910]) *this* and not *that*. Integers seem so profoundly embedded in the way we cognize the world that to think them "away" is really impossible. Given the natural numbers (the positive integers), however, it seems that a stronger case can be made for subsequent human invention—of negative numbers, fractions, decimals, trigonometric ratios, and so on. The great nineteenth-century German mathematician Kronecker put it this way: "God made the integers, all else is the work of Man."

Now we seem to be getting to more solid ground. Think, for example, of the decimal system. You might argue that fractions are, like the integers, too much a feature of the environment to be totally man-made. We experience division of single entities into equal parts, which we call halves, into threes (thirds), or fours (quarters), etc., and share the apple between two, three, n people. Expressing fractions in the way we do is man-made, but that can be thought of (like counting itself, and in particular systems of counting to different bases) as simply a choice of symbolization, a matter of convenience, rather than something that gives any insight into the way mathematics comes about. Fractions, one might say, occur in nature, without human intervention. The decimal system, however, is a pure human invention, as is the Arabic system of nu-meration that it exploits. (But, to qualify the point yet again, one can argue that a num-ber system based on ten must have arisen from the quantification of the number of digits on two hands—but then, why not a system based on five?) With the decimal system we start to leave the here and now, in a manner of speaking, and strike out into the great unknown.[33] There the possibilities are boundless, including, as many would insist, discoveries that appear to foreshadow the Platonic world.

The distinction that mathematicians and mathematically inclined philosophers have made between the two accounts of the nature of mathematics is too sharp; it poses a dichotomy in which neither account does the topic anything like full justice. A more moderate position can claim that both discovery and invention play essential roles in the creation of mathematics; there is no need to hold that it has to be exclu-sively one or the other. Indeed once stated, that seems rather obvious. The theories of Piaget, and the account he gives of the development of mathematical thought in young children, are consistent with this view.

According to Piaget the development of concepts of number, space, and time, as well as ideas about more specific mathematical-geometrical properties such as rela-tive position, proximity, continuity, similarity, straightness, and curvature have a distinct natural history.[34] They are conceived of as part of a general process of grow-ing into, adapting to, the vicissitudes of the given environment, that any biologically successful organism undergoes. Piaget writes of two main processes that are needed to accomplish this feat. He calls them *assimilation* and *accommodation,* technical terms in his lexicon, but ones having a connotation very similar to their normal use.

Development proceeds, Piaget says, by a constant interaction between what the organism has, and what the environment offers. What the organism has are *schemas,* action patterns in the first instance into which environmental events feed; the lowest of these, the first to appear after birth, are innate sensory-motor schemas having to do with obtaining nourishment and avoiding danger. The schemas are not rigid, however, they are unlike the fixed-action patterns in lower vertebrates described by ethologists. They assimilate the properties of the stimuli to which they respond, and accommodate to them; that is, they change their action patterns to deal efficiently with the (at first merely biological) tasks at hand. But this change also implies a real change within the organism. Piaget argues that this concept of flexible and adaptive action patterns is the basis of all learning, of all problem-solving behavior, and, at a higher, "self-reflexive" level, of all understanding.

This is not the place to go further into Piaget's theories, nor do I wish to give the impression that they contain all (or even any) complete answers to the problems of cognition.[35] The concept of a developing schema, that, on the one hand, assimilates something of the domain to which it responds, and, on the other, accommodates its own structure and action in an adaptive way does seem to be helpful. What is said to happen in every child as it matures very likely is what happened over the centuries when coherent thought, mathematics included, was developing.

Back to the question of invention versus discovery in the creation of new mathe-matics, or even the rediscovery of old mathematics, if you like. The important ques-tion has to do with the creation of something original, without known precedent. The very first action-based counting schemas surely occurred in practical situations.

Piaget's way of describing abstraction from a variety of events would be to say that the action schema assimilates the features of objects and accommodates itself to their properties, one of which is numerosity. It adapts, one might say, to be able to deal successfully with that property on future occasions. It formalizes the relations.

Is this mere wordplay? I think not, because it promotes just that conception of interaction between agent and operand that is needed to identify the beginnings of mathematics. It cannot have arrived out of nowhere, have had nothing to do with the physical environment, as a pure invention theorist would have to claim. But equally it is not possible to conceive of its discovery without having some account of the primitive steps in cognitive development that preceded it. How much more likely it seems to be that the structure of the environment feeds into the information-seeking organism (as Gibson might have put it), which in turn molds the cognitive apparatus of the mind to prepare it for further adventure (as Gibson certainly would not have said).

That may be at least a plausible account of the origins of mathematical thinking, but what of its subsequent blossoming? The invention protagonist would have to say that only a small amount of environmental help was needed to get the subject "off the ground," just the discovery of the integers, let us say, the rest being invented (formalized) without any outside promotion or interference. One inclined to emphasize the discovery side of the coin (and it is certainly possible to think of them as two sides of the same coin) would, by contrast, point to the more mysterious (intuitive) aspects of mathematical creation that seem to transcend the prosaic perspective of the opposing viewpoint.

Let us look at some of the wonders of mathematics, and see which point of view best fits the bill. Actually we will look at what seems at first to be but a tiny and elementary part of mathematics, the question of what we mean by a number. We shall find that it leads far afield indeed.

What's in a Number?

The Pythagoreans held that number,[36] that is to say, the set of positive whole numbers (integers), rules supreme in nature and in thought. If that is so, then any two numbers are commensurable; that means that each contains so-and-so many units of the same type, so that the ratio of the two can be expressed as the ratio of two integers, say p and q. This new number, the fraction p/q is called a *rational number*. The Pythagorean claim, then, was that all ratios occurring in the natural world are commensurable and can be expressed as rational numbers. It was a nasty surprise for one of them—perhaps even the master himself—to discover that there are naturally occurring quantities that are *incommensurable*. Two line lengths are commensurable if their ratio can be expressed as a rational number, p/q. Geometrically speaking this means the lines can be divided into exact numbers of (perhaps very small) equal segments; the ratio of the numbers of segments in each line is the ratio of their lengths. In a tidy Pythagorean world this is how things should be. As I remarked earlier, fractions do seem to be a part of the natural world, and if all quantities could be expressed in this way we might be content with a very limited discovery component in our view of mathematics; what there is in the way of quantity in the world depends in principle only on the discovery of whole numbers and ratios of whole numbers. We might then think of these rational numbers as the natural categories of the world (chapter 2) as far as quantity is concerned.

It was known to the early Greek mathematicians that certain "abstract" quantities, such as the square root of 2 ($\sqrt{2}$), are not rational, cannot be expressed as p/q, where p and q are integers. The Pythagoreans wanted to hold that quantities of this sort are not part of the real world of natural objects and events. Unfortunately for them, it turned out that a simple application of their famous theorem (the square on the hypotenuse is equal to the sum of the squares on the other two sides of a right-angled triangle) to a very solid and familiar geometrical figure showed that the side and diagonal of a square are incommensurable! This is easy to see if we take a square with side equal to 1— draw a diagonal, and we have two right triangles, each consisting of two adjacent sides of the square and the diagonal (figure 7.1). Application of the theorem of Pythagoras to either triangle tells us that the length of the diagonal is $\sqrt{1+1}$, that is, $\sqrt{2}$. Disaster! The diagonal is a perfectly respectable geometrical object, as is the side of the square, yet between them they imply something shocking but fundamental. There are quantities that are real in the world but, in a genuine sense, are unmeasurable. If we can measure the side of a square exactly in terms of some measuring rod, we cannot measure its diagonal precisely with the same rod, no matter how fine the divisions on it. No proper fraction, the ratio of two integers, nor any finite decimal number can express the ratio between the two lengths perfectly. We call such beasts irrational numbers.[37]

Together, the rational and irrational numbers constitute the *real* numbers. One

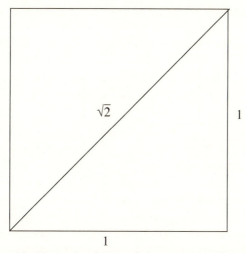

FIGURE 7.1. A square with side equal to 1 (the unit does not matter; it could be one inch, one centimeter, or one mile.) The diagonal divides the square into two right-angled triangles; so by the Pythagorean theorem, its length is $\sqrt{2}$ (= the square root of $1^2 + 1^2$, which is $\sqrt{2}$). The ratio of side to diagonal for *any* square will likewise be $1:\sqrt{2}$, for by Pythagoras the diagonal of a square of side a will be $\sqrt{a^2 + a^2} = a\sqrt{2}$.

can picture them on the number line (the real number line, as a mathematician would say), as "points" that fill up all the available positions on the line. But not quite all positions, as we shall soon see.

Is the appearance of the irrationals a discovery, or an invention? So far, one might still be inclined to say it is a discovery, both as to the proof that there are quantities like $\sqrt{2}$ that cannot be expressed as p/q, where p and q are integers (the usual proof incidentally proceeds by assuming the opposite—that $\sqrt{2}$ can be expressed as p/q—and showing that the assumption leads to a contradiction), and as to the natural occurrence of incommensurables. When one comes, many centuries later, to the question of how to handle irrationals properly, or *rationally*, one might say, within the general concept of what a number is, the matter takes on a rather different complexion. It turns out, for example, that between any pair of rationals, no matter how close together they may be (think of them as adjacent points on the real number line), there is an infinite set of irrationals!

Transcendental Numbers

To conceive how the irrational numbers "fit in" between pairs of adjacent rational numbers is far from straightforward and involves new (apparently arbitrary) definitions with their accompanying formalism. To make a watertight, logically correct case here requires the application of human ingenuity that seems to steer us toward the invention side of the issue. Imagination is involved, but of course it is disciplined imagination. The decisions involved are arbitrary only in the sense that conjectures about what will lead to a consistent and satisfactory theory of the real numbers are entertained, their consequences evaluated, and a choice of what will best fit the bill then made. That is where the job of strict proof comes into play. Discovery of an anomaly, a problem, leads to the invention of a foolproof procedure for solving, taming, the monster.

So far so good, but the matter does not rest there. We have expanded the idea of what number is, to include the irrationals. It turns out that the sorts of numbers we have so far discussed, both rationals and irrationals, are all expressible as the solutions to a certain class of algebraic equation (e.g., $x = \sqrt{2}$ is the solution to the equation $x^2 = 2$; $x = 3\sqrt{(1 + \sqrt{5})}$ satisfies $x^6 - 2x^3 - 4 = 0$, etc.). For this reason they are called *algebraic* numbers. Are there real numbers other than the algebraic ones? It might be expected that the rational and irrational numbers together would fill up all the possible positions on that number line, without "gaps." There is another class of numbers that are "genuine," in that they can be expressed in (nonterminating) decimal form, but they are not algebraic. That is to say, they are not expressible as the solutions to algebraic equations. They are called *transcendental*.[38] Such numbers lead us far beyond the more familiar ground of the algebraic numbers, yet they are indeed real numbers. One of the most important of them is also very familiar; it is π, the ratio of the circumference to the diameter of a circle.

The concept of π is simple to comprehend, and it is surely a common feature of the natural world.[39] It has been recognized as of supreme mathematical significance at least since Archimedes in the third century B.C. started to analyze its properties—and also, by the way, obtained a remarkably good estimate of its value. Only toward the end of the nineteenth century, however, was it proven that π is transcendental. It is not rational, expressible as the ratio of two integers, so it is (at least) irrational; yet it is not algebraic. Nonetheless it is real; an approximation to it can be written down as a decimal number—to the first few decimal places, it is 3.14159—but it has no terminus, it goes on forever.[40] However far one takes the decimal expression (and it has been calculated to millions of places—perhaps billions by now), the obtained number is not (logically cannot be) the exact value of π. So the circumference and diameter of the circle are not merely incommensurable in the way the side and diagonal of a square are; at least for that ratio we have a succinct expression with an algebraic interpretation. To grasp something of the nature of π, and of transcendental numbers in general, leads us far out of the province of mere invention, which is accommodated to the immediately perceptible, where the creation of a new tool, a new definition, is adequate to fit the situation. It takes us into a realm where imagination and intuition rule, where mathematical truths that (literally) transcend the everyday world invite discovery.

Let us start the journey with the transcendental numbers. They are more difficult to handle, far more slippery mathematically speaking than the algebraic numbers, and when first discovered (1844) it was reasonable to conjecture that they would be a rare breed. Imagine the astonishment in the mathematical establishment, not to say outrage, when it was demonstrated that, on the contrary, they are infinitely more numerous than the algebraic numbers! This was at a time (1874) when no transcendental numbers had actually been found, and well before it was proven that the familiar π is transcendental (1882). The man who discovered this remarkable fact about the "numerosity" of the transcendentals was Georg Cantor, the first mathematician to find satisfactory ways of dealing with the infinite—indeed with more than one type of infinity. Did he just invent methods of handling infinite sets, or did he really discover (some of) their properties?

The answer is that he hit upon ways of enumerating the members of a set that proved to be extremely fruitful in comparing the "size" of sets (strictly speaking, their cardinality), even of infinite sets. It would be a fair description to say that his intuition told him that this method would be promising, his imaginative application of the method led to extraordinary and counterintuitive results, and his logical rigor allowed him to prove that the results are, nonetheless, consistent and mathematically fruitful. Formalism was thus given its due, after the fact, as it were, but Cantor's work has far more the flavor of discovery by intuitive application of appropriate methods than of the routine invention of novel tools. Those infinite sets certainly exist "out there," independently of any mathematician's recognition of them; examples are the points on a line, the points on a two-dimensional plane (both of which by the way have the same "number" or cardinality—just one of the many counterintuitive results that stem from Cantor's theory), the natural numbers, the fractions, etc. Their ontological status is not altered by the meddlesome inquiry and incredible findings of a mathematical genius. Even Cantor himself had great difficulty believing some of his own results!

Back to the transcendentals: Despite the fact that Cantor proved them to be vastly more numerous than the algebraic numbers, not many truly independent transcendentals have actually been discovered. Apart from π, there is only one other that plays a similarly fundamental role in modern mathematics, and that is e, the base of the so-called Naperian, or natural, logarithms. Logarithms are immensely useful mathematical tools, and as such can be considered as inventions; but their uses, and especially the wonders to be uncovered by inquiry into the nature of e, far transcend (again, literally) the question of mere utility.

What is e? One definition is that it is the sum of the infinite series:

$$1 + \frac{1}{1!} + \frac{1}{2!} + \frac{1}{3!} + \frac{1}{4!} + \ldots + \frac{1}{n!} + \ldots ,[41]$$

This expression certainly looks like a number, but how do we know that the series has a finite sum and that it is unique? To give a convincing answer to that question is well beyond the scope of this book. We shall have to accept that a unique sum exists and is a transcendental number, thus having no exactly discoverable numerical value. To the first few decimal places, its value is 2.71828 . . .

What are the properties of e that make it so important? They are legion, and to indicate many of them requires at least a nodding familiarity with calculus; others are more accessible. It can be shown, for example, that e is intimately associated with the trigonometric ratios, sine(x) and cosine(x) that state the relations between the sides of a right-angled triangle, something that is familiar enough in the high school mathematics class, as well as in the ordinary environment.[42] But to fulfill my promise not to get too technical and still give some of the flavor of what is involved, let us first take a look at yet another broadening of the concept of number, and then come back to e.

Imaginary Numbers

We have outlined the expansion of the concept of number from rational (fractional) to irrational, to transcendental. This certainly enlarges our understanding of what a number can be, but there is more to consider: Irrational numbers involve things like the square root of a number m, when there is no rational number n such that $n^2 = m$ (i.e., the root does not exist as an integer or a fraction). What about the square root of a negative number? Can there be such a thing as a number s, where $s^2 = -t$, where, for the sake of argument, t is rational? If there be such a thing as s, how does it fit into the established conception of what number is? Is it in any sense a number? Leading mathematicians at the time the question was first seriously debated, including both Descartes and Newton, were of the opinion that the idea is absurd; s for them was a logical impossibility. Descartes went so far as to call s *imaginary,* a name that has—perhaps unfortunately—stuck.[43] Now we recognize that imaginary numbers are not mere oddities but play a fundamental role in what Stewart calls the "flaming pit" of analysis[44] (as contrasted with the "quagmire" of algebra); his point is of course that progress in mathematics continually throws up puzzles and problems that at first seem insoluble but challenge the researcher to achieve ever newer and more powerful methods for solving them.

It is customary to express all imaginary numbers in a format that uses i, which is the square root of -1 (by definition $i^2 = -1$). Any other negative root can be expressed as the product of a "normal" root and i ($\sqrt{-8}$ is, for example, $i\sqrt{8}$) by the usual algebraic rule for the product of radicals. The whole topic of imaginary numbers is thus developed in terms of the properties of i. What can we make of i? Not much on our own, but with the help of Bernoulli, Leibniz, and especially Euler, mathematical geniuses of the early eighteenth century, a great deal. Euler for example produced in 1748 the miraculous formula

$$e^{ix} = \cos(x) + i\sin(x).^{45}$$

We can't go into how he did it, but rest assured that his method was impeccable.

Why is the formula miraculous? Because it ties together three mathematical entities that appear to be not merely different, but of profoundly unlike natures. Here we have e, a transcendental number, linked in a formula to i, the mysterious imaginary number, which appears both in the exponent of e and as a coefficient of a trigonometric ratio on the right-hand side of the formula; trigonometric ratios, one might think, are entirely different creatures than transcendental and imaginary numbers. On top of that we have x, a quantity (a real number, let's say) that can vary freely; the formula tells us that the relation between these unlikely bedfellows holds for all values of x.[46] One step further; let us substitute π for x, so that the right-hand side becomes $\cos(\pi) + i\sin(\pi)$. $\cos(\pi)$ is -1 and $\sin(\pi)$ is 0, so the formula becomes:

$$e^{i\pi} = -1$$

which appears even more extraordinary, and has had magical appeal to the mathematical imagination ever since Euler produced it two and a half centuries ago. We now have a transcendental number (whose exact numerical value cannot be written down), raised to the power of an imaginary number (which cannot even be assigned any ordinary numerical value), multiplied by a second transcendental, and the result is -1, the most humdrum, basic, simple and (neglecting the minus sign) unspectacular arithmetical unit one can think of. Talk about intuition, talk about discovery! What are we to make of it? Where does it all lead? It leads, believe it or not, to an outburst of mathematical insight and creativity of boundless promise. As Stewart puts it, in reference to i: "The jungle creature was no longer breaking the odd twig, it was laying waste to great swathes of forest; more a rhino than a squirrel. But could it be trapped?"[47] Put it another way: It is beyond the wit of man to *invent* such a marvel!

The troublesome and pesky i began to look like a fabulous monster grabbed by the tail, but what possible use could it be? However remarkable Euler's formula might appear, would it yield any further results in mathematics, and could it by any stretch of the imagination be thought to have practical significance? In both cases the answer is a resounding yes.

It has been remarked that mathematicians "blundered into" imaginary numbers. They only started to do useful work when it was found (discovered?) that complex numbers of the form $(x + iy)$, where x and y are themselves real numbers, have a

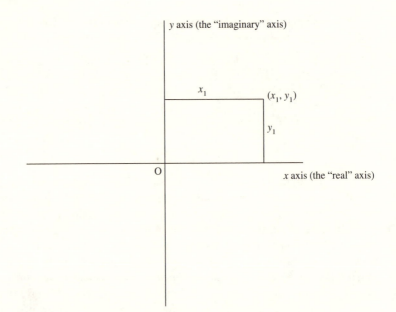

FIGURE 7.2. The "complex plane," also known as the Argand diagram. Each point on the plane (x, y) represents a single complex number, $x + iy$. The rules for addition, subtraction, multiplication, and division for complex numbers are not the same as for real numbers, and this gives complex numbers, and their representation on the Argand diagram, many special and unusual properties.

novel geometrical interpretation. We can readily see that such a complex number has a "real" part, x, and an "imaginary" part, y. These can be interpreted as the abscissa and ordinate (horizontal and vertical coordinates) of a single point on the complex plane, as in ordinary coordinate geometry (figure 7.2). Here we have a species of two-dimensional number, but one that has a perfectly definite geometrical interpretation as a point on the complex plane, which is called the Argand diagram.

We've got to two dimensions, but why stop there? Why not a three-dimensional analog of the complex number? Why even stop at three? How about four, or five, or n dimensions? The details are technical and tricky, but there you have it. Once started on his wondrous voyage, there's no stopping the creative mathematician. He both discovers and invents as he goes along, and marvelous indeed are some of the things that come to light on the way. That is getting off our main topic, however, which is to ask whether these new beasts (complex numbers) are fruitful as mathematics, first of all, and, second, to inquire whether they have any useful application.

Here is what Stewart says about those questions:

> From the mid-nineteenth century onwards the progress of complex analysis has been strong and steady with many far reaching developments. . . . The abstruse invention of complex numbers, once described by our forbears as "impossible" and "useless," has become the backbone of mathematics, with practical applications to

aerodynamics, quantum theory, and electrical engineering.[48] What more could one ask for?

Incidentally, Euler's formula has a beautiful realization on the Argand diagram (see below), and there are many other startling and important connections between π, e, and the trigonometric ratios. Some indication of how they are connected can be gleaned from the fact that they can all be expressed as power series, that is, as infinite series of terms in rising powers of x. In general such a power series can be written:

$$a_0 + a_1 x + a_2 x^2 + a_3 x^3 + \ldots$$

where the as remain to be defined. For example:

$$e^x = 1 + \frac{x}{1!} + \frac{x^2}{2!} + \frac{x^3}{3!} + \ldots$$

where $a_0 = 1$, $a_1 = 1/1!$, $a_2 = 1/2!$ . . . etc.,

$$\sin(x) = \frac{x}{1!} - \frac{x^3}{3!} + \frac{x^5}{5!} - \frac{x^7}{7!} \ldots$$

where $a_0 = 0$, $a_1 = 1/1!$, $a_2 = 0$, $a_3 = -1/3!$ . . . . etc., and so on.

We know that e is a number, so what about e^x? And if e^x were admitted, what about $\sin(x)$? Euler's miraculous formula tells us that $e^{i\pi}$ has a numerical value (-1), but does that mean it is a "mere" number? Consider again that formula with both sides multiplied by the (real) number r:

$$re^{ix} = r\{\cos(x) + i\sin(x)\}$$

and notice that the right-hand side, written out as $r\cos(x) + ir\sin(x)$ is a complex number: $r\cos(x)$ is the real part, $r\sin(x)$ is the imaginary part. It therefore represents a point on the Argand diagram (the complex plane). Which point? Recalling a bit of high school coordinate geometry (the only time I will ask you to do so), $\{r\cos(x),\ r\sin(x)\}$ represent a point on a circle with center $\{0,0\}$ and radius r: $r\sin(x)$ is the ordinate, $r\cos(x)$ the abscissa. If you happen to be familiar with polar coordinates, you will recognize the expression re^x: It is the formula for a circle centered at the origin with radius r. The form re^{ix} simply puts the circle on the complex plane. So, here we have an interpretation of Euler's formula; figure 7.3 will help. x is the angle between the line from a given point on the circle and the abscissa, and as x increases from 0 to 360°, or 0 to 2π in radian measure, the values of $r\sin(x)$ and $r\cos(x)$ vary periodically between $-r$ and r, and are "separated" by the fact that one of them is the real part of the complex number, the other its imaginary part. The same is true— although less obvious—of re^{ix}; it too varies with periodicity 2π. Again the basic ideas are illustrated in figure 7.3.

So much for a small peek at the mysteries of the complex plane and of the numbers that inhabit it—a far cry indeed from the notion of the simple counting of objects. Lack of space precludes our taking the next step, which would be to consider further the questions of infinity and the summation of infinite series, topics of great depth and subtlety, that have played a prominent, indeed a vital, role in the development of mathematics. The message for cognitive science has, however, been sufficiently established.

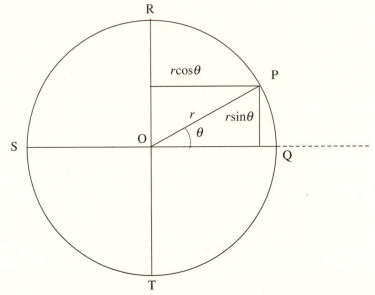

FIGURE 7.3. The circle of radius r, centered at the origin O, on the complex plane. The radial line from O to P on the circle makes an angle θ with the horizontal axis. (It is customary to use Greek letters for angles in a geometrical or trigonometric context; the change from $[x, y]$ to $[r, \theta]$, going from figure 7.2 to figure 7.3, is just a change from Cartesian to Polar coordinates.) As the point P moves around the circle from Q to R, θ goes from $0°$ to a right angle—or to $\pi/2$ in the preferred radian notation; $r\sin\theta$ goes from 0 to r, and $r\cos\theta$ goes from r to 0, changing smoothly as the point P moves. Likewise, as P moves from R to S, the values go from r to 0, and 0 to $-r$, respectively. Notice that in this quadrant cosine values are negative, as will the sine values be in the third and fourth quadrants (as P moves from S to T to Q.) If these sine and cosine values are plotted along the horizontal axis as a function of θ, starting say at Q, the well-known undulating sine and cosine curves are generated (hence those names.)

The Nature of Mathematics:
Discovery, Beauty, Imagination

So, what is the message? Insights like Euler's, results of the sort I have little more than hinted at, are the lifeblood of mathematics. And mathematics in turn is the lifeblood of science! Remember too that we have looked at only one small thread in a rich skein of intellectual endeavor. What is meant by *number*, how the concept has emerged and grown, what the consequences are for the development of mathematics, are vital and enthralling matters, but still leave virtually untouched the vast fields of geometry, algebra and analysis. To get some feel for these, and if you have the stomach for a greater (but still mild) dose of the more technical side of things, you cannot do better than to consult two of the books on which I have drawn for some of this chapter: Dunham's *Journey through Genius: The Great Theorems of Mathematics* and Stewart's *The Problems of Mathematics*.

The true character of mathematics is bound up with its sense of discovery, with the realization that the human mind has boundless freedom to create new mathematics, that this process of creation has elements of discovery as well as invention, and that its products can be immensely useful and beautiful. It is also basically cumulative: new ideas, discoveries, and techniques continually throw up new problems and questions, as well as answering old ones. As Piaget would have put it, new states of equilibrium are continually being established and then transcended, the processes of assimilation and accommodation ensuring that the new knowledge is both solidified in the present and ready to steer the way of future development. There is no end in sight, nor will there ever be. No wonder many great mathematicians are drawn to the idea that there is a Platonic world "out there" to which their creative insights give them access. As to the usefulness of mathematics, it has often been remarked that there is an uncanny, almost unreasonable air about the success with which it can be applied to the physical world;[49] I already quoted Einstein's dictum to the effect that the ultimate mystery of the universe is its comprehensibility, which is to say its willingness to yield its secrets to mathematical analysis. As to its beauty, again many a leading figure has waxed eloquent in its praise. Here is Bertrand Russell, a down-to-earth practitioner if ever there was one, not given to poetic flights of fancy:

> Mathematics, rightly viewed, possesses not only truth, but supreme beauty—a beauty cold and austere, like that of sculpture, without appeal to our weaker nature, without the gorgeous trappings of painting or music, yet sublimely pure, and capable of a stern perfection such as only the greatest art can show.[50]

What has cognitive science to say in response to such an idealistic paean of praise? The answer is—not much. In fact the whole of mathematical thinking, especially its more imaginative and innovative aspects, pose a genuine problem for the standard model. It is not just that cognitive psychologists have little useful to say about the form and flow of imaginative thought, about genuine creativity and originality; they also have little stomach for the sorts of experience mathematicians not infrequently describe when attempting to characterize their most creative moments. Jacques Hadamard, himself no mean practitioner, documented in considerable detail the stages through which the birth process of new mathematics typically goes. He called them intuition, incubation, illumination, and verification. Whether or not one subscribes to this as an adequate description of the typical case, there can be no doubt that unusual states of consciousness often accompany mathematical creation. Here is what Henri Poincaré, one of the greatest mathematicians of the century, had to say about incubation: "the role of this unconscious work in mathematical invention appears to be incontestable"; and further on, "One is present at his unconscious work, made partially perceptible to the over-excited consciousness, yet without having changed its nature. Then we vaguely comprehend what distinguishes the mechanisms or, if you wish, the working methods of the two egos."[51]

This is how Einstein expressed his experience:

> The words of the language, as they are written or spoken, do not seem to play any role in my mechanism of thought. The psychical entities which seem to serve as elements in thought are certain signs and more or less clear images which can be "voluntarily" reproduced and combined.

The above-mentioned elements are, in my case, of visual and some of muscular type. Conventional words or other signs have to be sought for laboriously only in a secondary stage, when the mentioned associative play is sufficiently established and can be reproduced at will.[52]

And again, rather in support of Russell: "The most beautiful experience we can have is the mysterious. It is the fundamental emotion that stands at the cradle of all true art and all true science."[53]

The response of cognitive science to such revelations is a shrug of the shoulders. They are at best intriguing but (like introspectionism a century ago) without relevance to a serious scientific theory of thinking, and at worst hold the possibility of leading us badly astray. However that may be, it should be noted that descriptions of unusual states of awareness are actually ubiquitous and can be very compelling when made by an exceptionally creative individual, whether artist, poet, musician, philosopher, or mathematician.[54] What stands out in the case of the mathematician is the fact that this "creative turmoil" can lead to results of utmost importance for understanding the world, for science, even for the materialistic version of science that propounds the gospel of the clockwork universe.

To return to the thought with which the chapter started: There are seemingly insurmountable obstacles in the way of giving a coherent account of representation in the brain of external things as simple as straight lines. In particular it is impossible (logically impossible) to define externally perceptible features in terms of a brain process. To attempt to do so is to put the cart before the horse; until we know what a straight line is, there is no sense to be made of an attempt to identify it with a brain state. The same goes for everything else of a perceptible-cognitive nature, including the concepts, procedures, and activities that we recognize as mathematical. Their true character is to be sought elsewhere, in the very activity of mind itself, in imaginative, forceful, insightful thinking, and not in the firing of an agglomeration of neurons, no matter how large or complicated it may happen to be.

In writing this chapter I have sought to give substance to this view, in part by stealth. On purpose I provided few figures or diagrams and tried to leave a good deal to the imagination. In thinking about the simple rule about the sum of n odd numbers, and even more so in the chessboard-domino problem, I tried to fire up that spirit of inquiry, of controlled conjecture, of rational insight, that is the heart of mathematical thinking. It was the same with our exploration of the growth of the concept of number. If you followed, your powers of imaginative thinking were certainly engaged. If you got lost, you still must have savored some of the sense of wonder, order, beauty, that informs all of mathematics, from the humblest to the most exalted. Either way, you will have experienced the fact that knowing what brain processes are involved is wholly irrelevant to the understanding and enjoyment of mathematics.

Finding out something of what goes on in the brain as one thinks mathematically, as is now happening, will tell us a lot about the brain,[55] but nothing, or nothing of any note, about mathematics and how it is done. To reiterate one of my principal themes: You have to know about mathematics before you can begin to study how it might be represented in the brain, or embodied in any other physical system such as a computer.

In conclusion: As I said at the beginning of this chapter, the existence of mathematics and the nature of mathematical thinking pose prodigious problems for cognitive science. I have concentrated on this one type of thinking, because its characteristics are so clear, so open—on the surface at least—to detailed scrutiny. Its products are so reliable as to seem invincible, and yet so important to our project of getting to grips with the nature of our world. But what has been said of mathematical thinking is true in some measure of all rational thought, indeed all forms of deliberate mentation. To understand the latter it seems therefore that we could do worse than take our cue from what mathematics has to teach us about cognition. That is one reason why I have devoted what might seem an inordinate amount of space to discussion of mathematics and mathematical thinking. Another reason is that cognitive science really has not paid sufficient attention to the matter, despite its inherent appeal and importance. It has vital lessons to teach us about the mind, as I have attempted to demonstrate, and in subsequent chapters I will show how these lessons can lead us to new and striking perspectives on the nature of cognition.

8

Explanation in Cognitive Science

It is not certain that everything is uncertain.

BLAISE PASCAL

Seven Questions about Explanation

Chapter 1 presented seven questions about explanation in psychology, questions about how cognitive science can contribute to the understanding of mind. Here they are again in summary form:

(1) What is the nature of psychological explanation?
(2) What is the relation between "commonsense" psychological explanations (as in folk psychology) and their scientific counterparts?
(3) If the relation in question 2 is ill-defined, can one demarcate more satisfactorily the field of scientific explanation of mind?
(4) Is knowledge of the physiological substrate for a psychological process necessarily involved in its explanation?
(5) What is the relation between prediction and explanation?
(6) Has the field of artificial intelligence (AI) anything new to offer the science of mind?
(7) Is it useful to explore the common territory, or indeed the border disputes, between literary and artistic insight—even the views of scientific thinkers outside the conventional realm of cognitive science—on the one hand, and on the other the approach to psychological explanation favored in cognitive science?

By chapter 4 we had gained a fairly distinct idea of the consensus view in cognitive science about the nature of mind and how to go about explaining it. I expressed this in terms of ten widely held axioms, statements that are taken as defining the standard model of the mind in cognitive science. Briefly, they are the axioms of:

(a) *Neural substrate.* Mental activity is a function only of brain processes.
(b) *Reducibility.* The physiology of the brain will eventually be fully understood in terms of physical laws.
(c) *Unlimited access.* Cognitive science is not limited to investigation of conscious states.
(d) *Biological evolution.* The brain is a product of biological evolution, and will eventually be understood completely in these terms.
(e) *Biological emergence.* When brains achieve a certain size, mental activity (including consciousness) emerges.
(f) *Mental emergence.* Mental activity can be understood solely as a product of the natural history of this development.

The recent computational trend in cognitive science supports the additional axioms of:

(g) *Machine architecture.* The goal of cognitive science is to determine what sort of machine the brain is (its functional architecture).
(h) *Mental architecture.* This is revealed by the success of axiom (g).
(i) *Computability.* Theory must be precise and computational.
(j) *Respectability* (or pragmatism or orthodoxy). Results must be public, reliable, and jibe with accepted canons of research and theory in the field.

Does the standard model embodied in these axioms allow us to meet and answer satisfactorily the seven questions?

To the first question, concerning the nature of psychological explanation, the standard model's answer would likely be on two levels. Consider first the concept of a *model:* a behavior can be explained if one has a model from which particular empirical results can be deduced, and experimental findings support the predictions.[1] The more fully a model describes the detailed experimental outcomes that will confirm (or disconfirm) it, the stronger is its explanatory power. It should be explicit, quantitative, computational (chapter 2). If its mode of operation can be tied to known sorts of neural function, so much the better. The remarkable success of neuroscience in unraveling the coding functions of the brain, of AI in modeling a large range of "cognitive" activities, and of computational theory in solving difficult problems in neural networks[2] (chapter 3) might lead one to suppose that there's an end of the matter. At the level of "small-scale" modeling of cognitive function the standard model seems to be on the right track.

At a more comprehensive level explanations are related to the general *theories* one holds about the nature of humankind and its world, and here again the standard model has a definite position: Mind is a product of natural evolution; present cognitive capacities have developed in accordance with the demands of biological imperatives, accelerated for sure by cultural and technological progress, but still within the bounds of what can be expressed in, and accommodated within, the world as a physical system (Popper's *w1*). Explanations, therefore, will be essentially reductionistic, aimed at proving that everything in cognitive science that is truly characteristic of mind, including consciousness, can be reduced to, exhaustively described in terms of, the workings of physical laws. At this level—which is metaphysical, as I have several times insisted—one is talking about epistemological principles, about a system of beliefs about the correct way of establishing knowledge and justifying it. To that extent the question of explanation is no longer just a scientific question. The standard model is content with the picture of mind complete within *w1;* we shall come back to the question of how well that fits the facts. For ready reference, let us call "mind within *w1*" problem (1).

Our second question concerns the relation of psychological explanation in cognitive science to commonsense, workaday explanations. We have a well-developed and remarkably sophisticated system of concepts, beliefs, and traditions that are used to explain our social, personal, and cognitive activities, namely *folk psychology.* Many characteristics of folk psychology are very much the same ones attributed to language by Chomsky: universality, spontaneity, generativity, diversity within a basic motivational and cognitive framework, rapid acquisition at a young age, and competence that is not always adequately reflected in performance.[3]

Psychologists can study folk psychology, just as linguists study language, as a phenomenon of nature, but cognitive science demands more from psychological explanations of mentation than folk psychology can supply. Again the comparison to linguistics is instructive. It is expected that we can get at the mechanisms of the mind, at the very root of what constitutes mentation, of consciousness, memory, thinking, and the rest. The standard model does actually accept, if reluctantly, the general framework of folk psychology, its beliefs, its talk of intentions etc., and the existence of other minds like our own, but looks *elsewhere* for the mechanisms that will give us a more "scientific" account of how they operate. Such accounts we expect to find by studying the action of the brain, by simulating cognitive activity on a computer, by formalizing in other ways the processing of information. This satisfies the criterion of producing deductions testable by experiment, but does it constitute an alternative *theory* of mind? This question is very open to debate, and I shall call it problem (2).

The third question concerns the relation of folk psychological explanation to more scientific forms of explanation, which falls naturally within the same province as problem (2), but to keep things orderly I will discuss it separately in the guise of attempting to answer the question: Can the standard model *dispense with* the conceptions and language of folk psychology? This is problem (3).

The fourth question asks whether knowledge of the physiological substrate (generally in the brain) is a necessary part of a scientifically valid explanation in psychology. We saw, particularly when discussing Gibson's views in chapter 6, that there can be strong disagreement on this point. In the standard model, however, there is little argument about the importance of brain mechanisms; but that they are a *necessary* part of every psychological explanation does not follow; that requires further discussion, and is problem (4).

The fifth question, on the relation of prediction to explanation, was aired quite extensively in chapter 5. The standard model has little to say about it, but it is central to my thesis. I shall raise it again, especially in relation to the "self-reflexive" nature of psychological explanation, about which the standard model says nothing. This is problem (5).

The sixth question asks what artificial intelligence has to offer in terms of explanations of mind. We saw in chapter 3 that its practitioners claim that the answer is: Quite a bit. We need not dispute it but still need to be sure that not too much is conceded. The AI approach to mind is evidence of seduction by the dream of the clockwork universe par excellence, and the difficulties that it poses need further deliberation. Is the fascination with mechanical "minds"—certainly a dominating feature of current cognitive science—drawing us into a fertile vale of discovery or into a blind alley? That is problem (6).

Finally, what of the relations of cognitive science to other, no less sincere, attempts to grapple with mind, as in religious faith, "depth" psychology, drama, poetry, fiction, historical, anthropological, and sociological analysis? The orthodox approach in cognitive science has virtually nothing to say on this topic and would, I suppose, bundle all attempts at dealing with mind in these other ways under the rubric of folk psychology, that is, as matters scarcely worthy of serious scientific debate (which takes us back to problem (2)). The fact remains, however, that these other ways of contemplating mind are, to the vast majority of thinking people, more attractive, more interesting, more comprehensive and compelling than anything the standard model has to offer. So our last problem, problem (7), is: Why does contemporary life, the great cultural sweep of scientific and humanistic endeavor that we recognize as modern civilization, pass cognitive science by with barely a sidelong glance, scarcely any glimmer of recognition or interest?

The Stance of Cognitive Science

We have, therefore, a number of compelling issues on which the standard model has little to say, or where its edicts are open to serious debate. We shall examine them, and attempt to see what is fruitful, what barren, in its concept of the mind. In chapter 9 I shall offer suggestions about what can be done to revive, or reinvent, a more vivid appreciation, and indeed a more realistic picture, of mind. Before doing so let us take the problems in the order in which they are raised here, with the exception of problem (3), which is postponed to the penultimate spot.

Problem (1): Can Mind Be Restricted to w1?

The first of Popper's three worlds is $w1$, the world of material objects and processes, where physical law holds sway. It is accessible to measurement, quantification, mathematical modeling; it is in this sense open to inspection, but seems to share none of the qualitative features of his other two worlds, $w2$ and $w3$. Popper's first major question was: Is $w1$ closed? That is, would a complete description of $w1$ contain everything that can be known, specifically including facts pertaining to the mind and its explanation? His answer was no, for reasons outlined in chapter 4. To summarize the argument: The cultural products of humanity ($w3$) can, and do, exist independently of any particular conscious or material manifestation. They can, and do, react back on $w1$. They are accessible to—and are captured by—human conscious effort and inquiry, which are defined as the province of $w2$. That being so, there can be no justification for restricting our scientific attention to $w1$; it is not closed, it interacts continually and powerfully with $w2$ and $w3$, so there is no a priori argument for granting it a superior or more basic status than theirs.

Many practitioners of cognitive science are not drawn to the substance of such debates; nonetheless it is meet for us to inquire further into the consequences of attempting to restrict attention to *w1*. In the first place, the defining characteristics of *w1* are not as clear as one might like to think. Second, occurrences in *w2* may be predictable from events in *w1,* but that is not to say that they are explainable in terms of it, as we saw in chapters 5 and 6. Third, confining attention to *w1* excludes from consideration certain of those cultural products that define what it is to be human: language, art, religion, science itself, insofar as these transcend the here and now, even the particular material objects (books, journals, computer memory, CDs, etc.) in which they are physically realized and preserved.[4]

The substance of the material world is not as solid as classical science would have it. Matter, as nineteenth-century science conceived it, is a myth.[5] The comfortable idea that goings-on in the brain can be described and understood in terms of cellular and molecular processes has been supplemented, even supplanted, by the conception of quantum events as the arbiters of brain function. We saw an attempt to develop a model of brain-mind interaction on this basis in chapter 4, and a proposal about how future developments in quantum theory may provide explanations of mental phenomena—consciousness, creative thinking, and the like.

There have been several other conjectures about how quantum-level processes in the brain might lead to a better understanding of mind/body relations, somewhat outside the mainstream of cognitive science.[6] They are certainly very relevant to our theme, but I shall not consider them further, because, as should by now be evident, any extension of physical law or theory, however important and intriguing in its own right, does not "leap the barrier" from *w1* to *w2*. This is not an arbitrary or empirical barrier, it is a *logical* constraint, and does not prejudge the issue of whether or not there may be powerful and intimate relations (correlations) between quantum events in the brain and mental events. If there are, they cannot be the relations of *explicans* to *explicandum.* Why not? Because as physical theory quantum theory is in the same logical box as classical theory. The arguments of chapter 5 showed that physiological processes—in principle reducible to classical physical events—do not ever entail mental events, so do not explain them. Physiological processes that might in principle be reducible to quantum events are no different unless, as still seems possible under one interpretation, it turns out that the observation of quantum events themselves requires the action of a conscious observer.[7] In that case the question of mind confined to *w1* takes on a very different flavor, but hardly one that gives comfort to the materialist doctrine of the standard model.

The appeal of the "quantum brain" stems from the fact that events in the quantum world are mysterious, and certainly not in accordance with the determinism of the clockwork universe, and the standard model as we have come to know them. The mystery of the quantum world is due to the incongruity between what common sense (folk physics?) and classical physics view as real, and what quantum theory and experiment tell us is the true state of affairs.[8] The relation of mind to brain is also mysterious, so perhaps it is not unreasonable to hope that the former mystery may help to solve the latter. At present, however, that is no more than an unfulfilled promise.

So far we have found no persuasive argument for restricting the study of mind to *w1*. If we accept Popper's argument about the lack of closure of *w1,* there is no reason to suppose that explanations of mind will have to be, or be reducible to, statements about *w1.* This is equally true of mental (cultural) products. Hence the standard model is flawed in its implicit restriction of mind, and the study of mind and its products, to *w1.*

Problem (2): The Standard Model as a Theory of Mind

As suggested earlier, there is a fundamental difference between a *model* and a *theory,* something that will bear further discussion. A model is an abstract representation of an event, object, or set of facts. It does no more than formalize the facts and their relations in accordance with some (generally noncontroversial) schema, paradigm, or generalization. This can be achieved at differing levels of abstraction. We talked in chapter 5 about working models, and abstract models, of the brain. Both were based on an understanding of what the relevant structures and variables are that affect the brain's operation. Usually a model is quite circumscribed and modest in its demands on the imagination, beliefs, or credibility of its originator and users. It is typically constructed and invoked to do a particular job, to refine a concept or sharpen the predictions to be made within an already established theoretical or empirical domain.

A theory, in sharp contrast, is much more ambitious. It lays out the groundwork for what there is in a particular domain (its *ontogeny*) and how it is to be studied and explained (its science—indeed its *epistemology*). Whereas a model can appeal to a theoretical perspective or position for justification, this is not possible for a theory, which is itself the very core of the relevant perspective and position. How then is a theory to be justified? One is tempted to say: On first principles. One should yield to the temptation, because not to do so is to fall into the more egregious error of denying one's principles. As we have discussed several times, to hold a theory is to commit oneself to a metaphysical position, even if it be the (untenable) metaphysical position that metaphysics is nonsense. Such commitment is a necessary component of any scientific enterprise. It is the first principle to which we adhere. The other principles are less likely to make a working scientist nervous, such as: The theory works; it is parsimonious; it succeeds where its rivals fall down; it is in harmony with the temper of the times.

That last criterion is important. One of the great triumphs of modern science is to have created a rather unified view of what there is in the world and how to study it. Natural science in the past 500 years, and particularly since the seventeenth century, has come to dominate the Western world's view of cosmos, nature, and man. Despite the twentieth-century revolutions in physics, it is a view still very much in evidence, probably more so in the life and social sciences than anywhere else. The standard model, insofar as it falls under the aegis of any theoretical perspective, is pretty solidly committed to the clockwork universe. It does not *provide* an explicit theory of mind, rather it acquiesces in one that has been around since Darwin's day. To knock it out of its complacency requires more than just the assertion that *w1* is not closed; it will need a more thorough analysis of what is left out of account in such a theory and a demonstration that the omissions are of vital importance. That I shall have to leave to later (together with problem [3]), merely concluding for now that the standard model does endorse a particular theoretical view of mind, that this view is traditional, not to say hidebound, and that we can expect to do substantially better.

Problem (4): Explanation and the Physiological Substrate

Most cognitive scientists hold that the full understanding of a psychological phenomenon must include knowledge of what the brain processes are that support it, but there are two important exceptions. Computer scientists who simulate mental functions generally claim that it is the *program* they devise that is crucial; its principles and mode of operation are what determine whether, and if so in what manner, the simulation is successful. The hardware and the operating system on which they run are, of course, necessary conditions of the simulation but of no theoretical importance in the sense that many different types of system could be made to run the same simulation, including, for one of this persuasion, the "wetware" of the brain. This indifference to the physical method of implementation led Bunge to describe such AI researchers as mentalists![9] (A *mentalist* is one who denies that the brain has anything to do with consciousness, with cognitive activity.) That should give one pause for thought, although there *is* a big difference between claiming that there is no physical substrate and acknowledging that any of several different substrates could adequately do the job. The important distinction is between those who believe that the structure of the brain and how it functions *determines* mentation, and those who regard it as merely a necessary adjunct. Bunge, along with most cognitive scientists from the Gestalt psychologists to Searle with his talk of "powers of the brain," belong in the former group.

The more radical dissenter from this orthodoxy is Gibson, as we discussed in chapter 6. Although even he would not have denied that there are goings-on in the brain when mentation occurs, he strenuously denied that they in any way constitute *explanations* of cognition, including specifically perception. This tends to give us pain, because we know a very great deal about the brain processes that underlie—that are correlated with—perception; but that is not all that's required for an explanation. Gibson's great merit was to realize that explanations always commit one to a conceptual stance; they are never theory-neutral. He always proceeded from that principle. His stance was that the perceiver has biological and (perhaps derivative) cognitive goals to achieve; talk of "how perception operates" should therefore always be a matter of how those goals can be reached. Explanation in perception is no more nor less than the explication of how information in the environment is discriminated and used to help achieve those goals. According to Gibson, this holds for all types of cognition. Explicit reference to brain activity is no more relevant than it is to the understanding and enjoyment of mathematics (as we saw in chapter 7). But one might also add: No less relevant either! In both cases brains are needed; they are a necessary concomitant of cognition.

Gibson is a rare exception in cognitive science, but an important one. He demonstrates not only that valid psychological explanations, even in perception, do not have to invoke the physiological substrate, but he teaches us two even more cogent lessons. The first is that we need to be ever watchful of the *purpose* an explanation is to serve, what goal its invocation is to further. The second is that explanation only makes sense within an established conceptual domain. As we said earlier, genuine scientific explanation has an air of inevitability about it because it accepts the assumptions of that domain (made explicit if possible as axioms) and *deduces* the to-be-explained result from them as a necessary consequence. Rather against the current tide, we conclude that the concept of explanation needs to be handled with care, not bandied about loosely as a catch-all for reconciling one research finding with another.[10]

To conclude this section we may say: Not only is it unnecessary to know or invoke the physiological substrate to give a valid psychological explanation, in many cases it is misguided to try to do so.

Problem (5): Prediction, Explanation, and Self-reference

In chapter 5 the distinction between prediction and explanation was aired extensively, particularly in relation to the three levels of function: sensory coding, perceptual organization, and cognitive use. As a reminder, and taking a couple of points from the discussion of the last two sections, we can say that predicting, *forecasting,* from events at one level to those at another is possible, but *explaining* events at one level in terms of those at another is not. Prediction as forecasting, an empirical matter, is subject to few logical constraints, whereas explanation is—or should be— firmly controlled by its conceptual pedigree. That is what permits the tight deduction of testable consequences from a model or theory.

The standard model takes little account of such niceties, but we cannot dispense with them. Consider the matter of producing a theory (or model) in cognitive science. How can one go about explaining such activity, which is itself cognitive? Empirical correlations between various cognitive behaviors (sitting down and thinking hard) and the outcome (the theory produced) might be of interest but would scarcely be relevant to an evaluation of the theory's correctness or importance. What excites interest is the extent to which the theory affords insight into its field of application, provides deductions about novel phenomena, reconciles previously inconsistent findings, yields a better perspective on what is of fundamental importance for the field; we bring our own cognitive powers to bear in assessing the new theory. The theory itself has a life of its own that is independent of our interest in it or ability to evaluate it. There is even independence from its own creator, once the theory has been fashioned. In Popper's terms, one could say the theory is now in *w3*.

For a theory in archaeology, physics or literary criticism, the matter is unproblematical; one can to a greater or lesser degree *stand back* from the arena to which the theory makes reference, which is the potential and actual strength of impartial scholarship, including science.[11] What about a theory in cognitive science? In particular: What about a theory of thinking? It, unlike other scientific theories, does *not* have that same independence from its author, because the theory should, if it is self-consistent and complete, be able to account for whatever it is in its author that brought it into existence. A theory of thinking has to be, in a very radical way, *self-referential.* In its present form the standard model has no way of dealing with this problem, nor I think any loopholes through which it might try to slip. One gambit which will not work is to say that there are plenty of theories in cognitive science that are not self-reflexive in this manner, theories of memory, object recognition, language acquisition, for example. But one cannot avoid the problem for a theory of thinking, unless one were prepared to argue that thinking is not an essential part of developing such a theory. Moreover thinking is used in the production of *all* cognitive theories, even though it may receive no explicit mention in the exposition of many of them. The problem exists for any general cognitive theory, and even to some extent for models of more limited scope.

The standard model almost totally fudges the difference between (empirical) prediction and explanation, between cause and reason. It has not generally, despite Marr's admonitions, taken any account of the principled distinctions between levels of function and their attendant explanatory desiderata (chapter 5). It provides no explanation for the creativity of thinking (chapter 7), and has especial difficulty when confronted with the fact that presumption of the ability to think has to precede the production of *any* cognitive theory, which should be able to account for the manner of its own conception and birth, courtesy of the mind. Finding correlations between behavior or brain states and the production of cognitive theory would not help. It would not relieve us of the need to account for—to explain—original cognitive production. Something more is called for, and that something has to include consideration of the problem of self-reference.

Problem (6): Minds, Brains, and Computers

Computers have no insurmountable difficulties providing simulation of brain processes, and this is particularly true of the parallel distributed processing (PDP) simulation of the "classical" brain.[12] Whether quantum computers will do as well with the putative quantum brain remains an open question, as far as I know,[13] but not one that need affect our discussion. As physical systems quantum computers and brains are in the same logical space as their classical counterparts vis-a-vis the mind (see above). The question we have to address is what AI, in any of its forms, has to offer that is helpful to our understanding of *mind.*

Remembering the distinction between model and theory made above, it is evident that AI offers much that is useful at the level of modeling and simulation; this has been claimed and acknowledged since the early days of computer science.[14] What of theory?

Some leading cognitive scientists have made a case for disposing of the concept of mind and replacing it with mechanical "equivalents." Perhaps the most perceptive and thoughtful of these essays—and one not contaminated with the missionary zeal often attendant on such efforts—is Richard Gregory's *Mind in Science.*[15] As a matter of fact this title is a total misnomer; it should be *Mind out of Science,* because that is the burden of his message. According to Gregory, and this is a commonly accepted point, the concept of mind originated in the prescientific era of human attempts to understand the world, including our place in it; these attempts were replete with accounts of supernatural beings as the instigators and controllers of natural phenomena as well as human destiny. Science's program has always been to opt for *efficient causes* over *final causes,* in fact to replace the latter with the former. These are the Aristotelian names for the difference between a proximal, mechanical "push the billiard ball" type of cause that is the ideal of the clockwork universe (something more than a Humean cause, be it noted), and the forward-looking, intentional, "in order to" type of cause that seeks the source of change in a belief, a motive, a plan of action. The former is impersonal, objective; the latter tends to the personal, the subjective, to equate everything in the world with the desires or plans of an active, purposeful agent. Hence, according to Gregory, the gods, heroes, monsters, and magicians of myth and saga, the movers and shakers in prescientific attempts to make sense of the world.

Science has had brilliant success, as Gregory documents, in its program of exorcism and replacement as far as the mineral kingdom is concerned, and has done nearly as well for the plant and animal kingdoms since Darwin entered on the scene. For consistency's sake, and to achieve closure, it is only to be expected that the same program should be applied to that last frontier, as the saying goes, where final causes are still accorded a certain scientific respectability, namely the human mind itself. In folk psychology, as will be obvious, the local currency is still mainly backed with final causes. Most of the attempts to be "more scientific" in cognitive science have aimed to replace this with the hard currency of efficient causes, whether in physiological, algorithmic, machine architectural, or some other terms. So, as Gregory puts it, the final step in reaching a scientific conception of mind is to replace it fully with the mechanical analogs of artificial intelligence. This constitutes a full-fledged *theory* of mind, because it does far more than merely present models formulated to give computational solutions to particular problems; it makes a claim as to the very *nature* of mind. Mind, on this view, is a machine; it is computational in action, and fully determined by the material of which it is constructed and the programs it is designed to implement. The claim is one that many cognitive philosophers have wrestled with, Searle perhaps foremost among them in recent years (cf. chapter 3). One might even characterize it as the most important claim, the severest challenge, that cognitive science offers to commonsense (folk) conceptions of what the mind is all about.

So we can say that AI offers a very great deal at the theoretical level. The question is: Should we buy what is offered? To answer that question let us turn back to:

Problem (3): The Concept of Mind in Folk Psychology

Can the standard model dispense with the concepts and language of folk psychology? With all due respect to Gregory, and practically the whole of the AI community, the answer is quite evidently a resounding no. Hodgson, in his beautifully measured survey of matters of the mind,[16] points out that "the best description of the events *as mental events* (that is, in their *subjective* character) must use the language and concepts of folk psychology, which can, of course, be improved and refined" (p. 381). This is true, but does not go nearly far enough; it is not just that folk psychology offers the best description; there is an important sense in which it gives the *only* description. As things stand, if we were bold enough, we might even go so far as to claim: It is the only *possible* description.

Hold on, you may say: How can that possibly be? First of all, to claim exclusivity in that way is hazardous, not to say foolhardy; remember the fate of the verification principle? Second, such a claim runs counter to the whole thrust of cognitive science of the last 50 years or more, which has been to insist that folk psychology is essentially prescientific. Is all that to be thrown out as a misguided attempt to import scientific values into an inherently nonscientific field? Rest assured, that is not my intention; rather it is to throw light on the boundary where the murky waters of final causes (intentionality) still obstruct the attempt to let flow in clear channels the efficient causes of the clockwork universe. There is also constructive work to be done— but later, in chapter 9.

The AI assault on mind has had many distinguished protagonists, as well as committed opponents.[17] Many of the latter have pointed out that the attempt to explain mental acts in terms of machines is wrong-headed; it puts the cart before the horse, because machines are imbued with "intelligence" only to the extent that humans design it to be so. Kolers and Smythe[18] argue that the problem is even more radical; the language of machine intelligence is heavily infected with a penumbra of mentalistic plausibility imported by the wholesale use of the terms of common parlance that describe (natural) mental processes and activities. A very straightforward case is the use of the word "memory" to refer to the storage of information in a machine. Storage and retrieval are machine operations to be sure, but to think that one can understand human memory better because machines can be designed to have those functions is an egregious error. To ascribe "memory" to the machine is in the first instance a harmless bit of shorthand; to then claim that anything of cognitive significance follows from the fact that the machine has memory is simply to confuse the metaphorical use of a term with a metaphysical claim. It is to impute to the machine something far weightier than the adroit use of a label warrants.[19]

So, we are seduced into the idea that machines can have a sort of mind because of the way we talk about them. But, however true that may be, the fact of the matter is that machines *can* do extraordinary things like learn to prove theorems and translate between natural languages. If we can understand how the machine does those complicated things, and to a large extent we can, surely that should help us understand how minds do them? Very well, but we are back to the point, already made several times, that getting a helping hand (or handle) to solve a problem does not necessarily give an explanation of the nexus out of which the problem arose. As far as explaining mental occurrences is concerned, it seems obvious enough that before one can even pose a question, or consider what might constitute an adequate explanation, one has to be able to identify and describe what one is talking about. *For that, the language and concepts of folk psychology are required!*

As Chomsky showed in his classical demolition of the case for radical behaviorism,[20] you need the concepts of stimulus and response as instruments of analysis a priori to set up Skinner's behavioristic system, however atheoretical the system itself was claimed to be. It is therefore illogical to suppose that the concepts can be derived as consequences from the system that purports to explain them. Just so, we cannot even conceive of, or talk about, whatever it is we think cognitive science claims to be studying, in the absence of the manner of thought, and the linguistic categories and conventions, of folk psychology. Doubtless these can be sharpened and refined, as Hodgson says, but to think that they can be dispensed with, or supplanted by some other supposedly more "scientific" set of terms, is wrong. But it lends a gloss to some accounts of neuropsychology, for example, a gloss that is usually quite illusory and thoroughly misleading.[21]

Can the standard model get on without the folk-psychological language and concepts of mind, can it redefine or refine them out of a useful existence? The answer is: The question cannot even be posed, let alone answered or alluded to *without* those concepts and that language (suitably improved, perhaps). No meaningful dialogue can even get *started* in their absence! That is the reason why, at the beginning of this section, I claimed that folk psychology gives the only possible foundation for an account of mind.[22] So the short but sufficient answer to our question about the necessity of the concepts of folk psychology is actually: No, we most certainly cannot dispense with them. From this we shall, in due course, draw out some radical consequences.

Problem (7): Why Is the Standard Model Ignored by Contemporary Culture?

Orthodox cognitive science is, in one important respect, in tune with the tenor of the times. The prevailing opinion in the science-oriented segment of our culture is that human bodies, brains, and with them minds, are just products of natural processes (biological evolution), and that we can discover all we need to know about them, indeed all there is to know, by studying them as such products. In many ways this is hugely successful, as only a brief inspection of the literature of popular (and not-so-popular) science, even a casual glance at the medical and science pages of a newspaper, will show. Talk of things such as the ability of biochemical agents to bend the mind, of putative new gene therapies for mental as well as physical dysfunction, of the discovery of physiological anomalies that cause dementia, etc. are commonplace. All speak to the powerful effects of applying biological and medical research findings to mind and body, but little thought is given to the question of how well we can *understand* minds, and selves, on this basis.

That is where one might look to cognitive science to supply answers. In some respects it tries to do so, but in general it merely reinforces the prevailing climate of ideas.[23] Certainly in providing processing models of attention, memory, skilled performance, verbal learning, and the like it adds to the store of scientific knowledge, but these provide no startling insights to engender change in the accepted picture of mind as natural biological phenomenon.

The standard model is thus cocooned, so to speak, within an already existing conception of what man, and mind, are. Cognitive science may not enjoy (if that's the right word) the status of total irrelevance in contemporary culture, but there are not too many ways in which it can compete for attention in the marketplace of persuasive ideas and images. What a dramatist, a novelist, a culturally orientated explorer, or an adventurous and imaginative journalist has to say about human life, about society and its attendant hopes, fears and follies, is simply more arresting, more insightful, more *telling* than what the cognitive scientist has to offer. What, for instance, has the standard model to contribute to an understanding of the ubiquitous tensions, dangers, and atrocities that plague the modern world? No comfort, no insight, no hope of resolution or relief come from that quarter.

One might argue that it is not the job of science to offer palliative care, or solutions to the world's practical problems. Nevertheless, science does have something to offer in most situations where dilemmas obtrude and disaster threatens. Cognitive scientists, by contrast, seem with rare exceptions to sit it out on the sidelines. Does that mean that they are really irrelevant, just playing games? Surely this cannot be, should not be. We should be to able lead, not merely follow, in the enterprise of ridding the world of its humanly engendered problems; getting clear on what we know about mind, and what we can know, should be a major part of their amelioration.

Can anything be done about this? At least one can suggest how the standard model needs to be supplemented, in certain respects supplanted, by a more vibrant, vivid, but still realistic appreciation of the truly great qualities of mind and of how we can study and come to understand them. An important first move in this direction is to look again very carefully, and in detail, at what it means to say that the phenomenon of mind can be *explained.* The practical consequences of this inquiry may not be immediately evident, but in terms of understanding what sort of journey we are on, that first move is fundamental. As Chairman Mao said: "Even the longest journey starts with a single step."

Explanation in Cognitive Science: Taking Stock

We need to reconsider the question of explanation, but also a number of other topics where the ability of the standard model to capture the essence of mind was found to be suspect, and where it seems possible to give a more positive, more realistic, vital, and dynamic account. These will follow quite naturally once the question of explanation has been fully examined.

We have discussed already the fact that any psychological theory of cognition has a unique self-referential property that sets it apart from other scientific theories. Such a theory purports to explain how knowledge, or some branch of knowledge, is acquired, systematized, and validated. Even if its domain is restricted, say to memory, the theory cannot escape the fact that it is necessarily grounded on cognitive capabilities, including in this case the memory, of its author.[24] He or she has to manifest superior cognitive performance, which must include a general understanding of the nature of cognition, and to do that she or he has to "use her (his) head." Cognitive theories, particularly theories of thinking, inherently carry this self-reflexive epistemological burden.

Most researchers in cognition, including experimental psychologists, turn a blind eye to such matters. They ignore the fact that they, as cognizing beings, are part of the equation they are trying to solve. They are content, with few exceptions,[25] to formulate their models and theories without examining or stating explicitly the broader assumptions on which they are based. Such a stance is not uncommon in science, although philosophers of science are wont to point out the likely dangers of such unexamined theorizing.[26] Scientific knowledge, as is well recognized, advances by the critical examination and acceptance or rejection of new ideas and findings under a rigorous system of both formal and informal peer review.[27] The ground rules are very occasionally revolutionized (Kuhn's "paradigm shift") as in the advance from classical to relativistic physics, or from behaviorism to cognitive psychology, but by far the more usual situation is the one in which the rules do not change, or do so only very gradually. A strongly pragmatic element prevails as far as scientific explanation is concerned, given that there is normally a strongly consensual climate of opinion on what constitutes adequacy of explanation in a given field.

There is such a prevailing climate of opinion in cognitive science, as we have seen amply demonstrated, and even where there are dissensions from it, three of the basic epistemological assumptions seem to be universally accepted without question. These are, in the terms introduced in chapter 4, the axioms of unlimited access (cognitive science is not limited to investigation of conscious states) and of biological evolution and biological emergence (brains are products of natural evolution, and when they get big enough mental activity emerges). Of these, the latter two are by far the most important for the present discussion. Even the radical dissenters in other respects, such as Eccles, Popper, and Penrose, accept them.

The idea that the human brain has arrived by any other route than that of natural evolution in the biological world is not questioned. I am not going to question it either, but I am going to show that there is an important sense in which that account fails to yield a full and adequate *explanation* of mind. The same goes for the assertion that consciousness, and therefore mind, will somehow become more comprehensible as physical theory advances.

What have these matters to do with understanding mind? The answer is: Everything. A sharp distinction must again be drawn between (Humean) prediction and explanation (chapter 5); the paradigm or ideal of scientific explanation involves far more than the mere provision of a causal circumstance, or context. It is often said that psychology should not ape physics in its explanatory ambitions, yet there is a core feature of explanation in the natural sciences that we should attend to more carefully. In physics the paradigm theory is mathematical, and the most successful of these are called *superb* theories by Penrose, because they have never failed. They involve the strict deduction of consequences from a (mathematical) model, so that the consequents are *entailed* by the antecedents. The experimental tests of those deductions have always been positive for the superb theories.[28] The relationship of entailment does not have to be formulated mathematically, but it does need to have the same logical force as a mathematical deduction (see the discussion in chapter 5).

Cognitive science needs models in this sense, models in which mental acts (level 3 phenomena) are deducible as necessary consequents of the antecedent conditions. In that case, however, the antecedents cannot be purely in $w1$ as physical, neurophysiological, or mechanical events. Why not? As was established many years ago,[29] and as was argued in chapter 5 and again earlier in this one, no finite string of statements about physical, physiological, or mechanical events ever *entails* a statement about a mental event. So, in the stricter sense of explanation here employed, no such string can ever explain a mental event. This point, about the impossibility of deriving psychological statements from purely "natural" (physical, physiological) ones, was first discussed by the English philosopher Richard Peters,[30] and is closely related to the "naturalistic fallacy"—making the same point in regard to ethics—

which goes back to Hume. I will call it the *Peters principle*. It is a crucial principle, and has been thoroughly obscured, first by the fact that there demonstrably are intimate and extremely regular correlations between physiological events and mental happenings and, second, by the near-obsession most cognitive scientists show for "explaining" the latter by the former. What purports to be an explanation here is nothing of the sort; it is an assertion of causal context. I note once more, and this will be taken up again later, that even the causal context of a theory of thinking (quite apart from the question of explanation) evidently must involve thinking (that of its author). This all appears to be approaching vicious circularity, but in any case grants the case that thinking cannot be explained on premises, or within a milieu, that exclude the occurrence of thinking.

The Peters principle applies with full force to attempts to account for consciousness, freedom of the will, mental creativity, etc., as resultants of quantum-physical events in the brain. They may be *consequences* of such activity allright, but they do not *follow logically* from them. Therefore, to repeat my old refrain, they are not explained by them. The argument applies equally at both the classical and quantum levels; it only seems less plausible at the latter because the stranglehold of deterministic laws of classical physics seems to be abated, and the mysteries of the quantum world seduce us into the hope that something substantial about the mental world can be jiggered[31] out of it.

The Peters principle applies just as strongly to the opinion, probably more widely held than any other in cognitive science, that minds emerge in brains when they become large enough and complex enough, and that happens, naturally, in the course of biological evolution. There have been many fine attempts to chronicle the course of this development by using evidence from the fossil record, general biological, linguistic, and psychological principles, and, of necessity, a healthy dose of speculation.[32] This is not the place to enter that fascinating field, except to insist that such chronicles do nothing to explain anything of mentation and consciousness according to the principle of explanation here set forth. Again it is a simple matter; no finite set of statements about evolutionary pressures, response to such pressures, or adaptations to them *entail* any statement whatsoever about mentation. Until we get used to the idea that a close set of correlations, even of efficient causes, is not logically sufficient in itself to explain any consequent event, there will be an almost perverse insistence that mind and its genesis are open to a complete and exhaustive explanation in terms of biological-evolutionary events.[33] The reason for this blinkered view is nothing other than a mere habit of thought. We have been so persuaded by the materialist dogma, so dazzled by the successes of the doctrine of the clockwork universe and its sequelae, that we long ago gave up the thought that they may not have the final words to say about everything, including the nature of mind.

To summarize the discussion of the last two sections concerning the weakness of the standard model's take on explanation, we have the following: (1) a failure to distinguish between prediction and explanation; (2) an inadequate conception of what explanation is all about; (3) an inability to dispense with the categories of folk psychology (or some conceptual equivalent) while at the same time believing that they must be discarded as "prescientific"; (4) the inability to even name or describe the relevant domain of discourse of cognitive science without the concepts and language of folk psychology; (5) the mistaken belief that some refinement of physical theory can overcome the problems of understanding and explaining cognitive states and activities in materialist terms; (6) a similarly mistaken doctrine that mind can be explained as an emergent property of brains that grow to a certain size and complexity as a natural response to evolutionary pressures.

All that remains now is to suggest how to put matters right, and that is a fairly tall and controversial order!

Explanation in Cognitive Science: Moving Ahead

A great deal of weight has been placed on a conception of explanation that will appear to some to be excessively strict, not to say narrow. Here is an example of the sort of argument that might be marshaled against it, followed by discussion of why the argument is misguided.

> When we observe symptoms of disease in a person (high temperature, abnormal pulse, various pains, etc.) we are apt to say that they are caused by an infection, and that may constitute a perfectly good explanation of the symptoms. In saying that we are doing far more than identifying a sequence of observables (the Humean interpretation of "cause"), and we are pointing to a well established and understood relationship between invasion of the body by bacteria and certain changes in physiological function. There is no relation of *entailment* between the antecedent (infection) and consequent (fever), yet this is a perfectly good example of a *causal explanation*.

Granted, that is the way we use the words, but there is a world of difference between, on the one hand, establishing the antecedent-consequent factual relation of infection to the appearance of disease by recording a series of simple observations and, on the other, gaining a detailed understanding of the processes that lead from invasion to the bodily responses we call sickness. If those bodily responses are understood in terms of how the immune system and its many components counter the invasion and thereby provoke the observed symptoms, we do in fact have a model of immune system activity from which the occurrence of symptoms can be deduced. That is the force behind the argument that saying the infection caused the sickness is an explanation of it. The same can be said of explaining the passage of the sun across the sky. It can be explained as a (necessary) consequence of the earth's rotation, and that in turn can be explained in terms of a model of planetary dynamics, which in turn brings us to Newton's law of gravitation, which yields finally (but perhaps not *finally,* that is too big a promise) to general relativity. In every case, however, the explanation invokes a model of physical action from which the consequent observations are *deduced.* The fact that different explanations are available, that they are contingent on time and the present state of knowledge, does not vitiate the major point, which is the logical requirement that there be a deductive relation from an accepted model (set of explicit assumptions) at the root of any valid scientific explanation.

It is always so; we may often use a loose form of speech that seems to give a broader denotation to the word *explanation,* but on closer scrutiny it inevitably transpires that the meat of the matter hinges on the relation of necessary consequence, of entailment, at some level of detailed modeling, as I have so often—pardon me— explained. It is certainly true that we frequently talk "above the level" so to speak, at which the detailed model operates, but that is no reason to abandon the principle that determines whether or not a valid explanation is at hand. We shall find this point to be very apposite to the discussion, later in the chapter, of the "emergence" of mind, whether from its physical substrate, or as a consequence of biological evolution.

There is another way to look at the claim that no set of *w1* statements is ever equivalent to a *w2* statement, so never can furnish an explanation of the latter. It is the argument, which has already been hinted at, that no *w2* statement can be reduced without remainder to a set of statements about *w1*. In a splendid and justly famous article entitled "What Is It Like to Be a Bat?" Thomas Nagel explicitly and eloquently argued the point:

> The recent wave of reductionist euphoria has produced several analyses of mental phenomena and mental concepts designed to explain the possibility of some variety of materialism, psychophysical identification, or reduction. But the problems dealt with are those common to this type of reduction and other types, and what makes the mind-body problem unique, and unlike the water-H_2O problem . . . or the oak tree-hydrocarbon problem, is ignored.
>
> It is most unlikely that any of these unrelated examples of successful reduction will shed light on the relation of mind to brain. But philosophers share the general human weakness for explanations of what is incomprehensible in terms suited for what is familiar and well understood, though entirely different . . . indeed, we have at present no conception of what an explanation of the physical nature of a mental phenomenon would be. Without consciousness the mind-body problem would be much less interesting. With consciousness it seems hopeless.[34]

Nagel goes on to highlight some of the essential properties of mental phenomena not captured in a physicalist, mechanical, or similar reduction, the central concept being that a "point of view"; what it is like to *be* you or me (or a bat) defies such a resolution. The argument appears to have been first made by Sprigge in 1971 (see chapter 3). Other philosophers have tackled the problem from somewhat different perspectives; Honderich points out that, rather than face it head-on, philosophers (and cognitive scientists generally, if they even recognize the difficulty) have a strong tendency to look *elsewhere* for solutions,[35] or, as Putnam says: "intentionality won't be reduced, and it won't go away."[36] Such philosophers, together with some other like-minded thinkers, while sensitive to many of the difficulties of the position, find it impossible to envisage that alternative accounts of mind might be had without recourse to, or reduction to, some aspect of *w1*.

Nagel's arguments, and indeed my own as an extension of the Peters principle— which are really just the converse of Nagel's—undermine the contention that a reductionist program will do the trick. I prefer my way of posing the matter because it puts things in a more clearcut and forceful way. According to Nagel you can't get rid of mental states by attempting to reduce them without remainder to physical states, but I assert that you cannot even pose any meaningful question about mental states if you restrict your dialogue to what's available in *w1*. That puts the onus squarely on the materialist to justify his position. You might take the lack of reducibility to be a sort of unfortunate accident in the ontology and epistemology accepted by modern thought, something one might still be able to circumvent with a bit of fast footwork (indeed this has been attempted),[37] but the point that nothing about mentation can even be articulated, much less explained, by means of statements expressed exclusively in terms of *w1* cannot be sidestepped in that fashion.

If you want to talk about the mind in any meaningful way, you have to have a language for doing so, and that means you have to accept, initially without conditions, as it were, a bunch of mental concepts and the words in which they are expressed. That is the prior fact; attempting then to get rid of the "mental penumbra" by reduction, simple denial, or ridicule (all of which have been tried) is only then possible as a consequent activity. Such attempts have never been successful. The fact of the matter is that a *w1* account can never bridge to *w2* in the sense of explaining properties of the latter in a rigorous way.

Yet, the materialist bias persists. Turner[38] remarks insightfully that when a Weltanschauung is a religion its assumptions are simply not questioned; it describes the way things are. Old-fashioned materialism is the way things are in cognitive science; surely we can acknowledge at least the chance that this is too severe a constraint on the possible ways of understanding mind.

To return to the related, and very basic, problem of self-reference: A cognitive theory results from human thinking. Such creative thought has to be accounted for in any comprehensive theory of thinking, a sort of "bootstrapping" that might make us feel uncomfortable, but does it pose any insurmountable problem? It certainly does if one hopes to derive the power of thought from principles of brain action and the like. That avenue is closed, as we have seen, so what other alternatives are available? There is only one, so far as I can see, and that is to acknowledge that any model that will yield an adequate explanation of mental activity, whether of thinking, consciousness, or some other facet of mentation, must itself *assume* in its premises, be they described as axioms, initial principles, or shall we say more generally as the model's *logical territory,* the existence of certain features of mental life ab initio.

Surely, you will say, that is going too far, that is giving the game away? It is one thing to claim that we must accept some mental concepts and language as "given" to identify whatever it is we are trying to get at with talk of the mind; one might think that successive refinement and extension of such concepts will eventually lead to a better, more scientific understanding of mind, the tack taken by orthodox cognitive philosophy and science. It is quite another to claim that *any* explanation, in my strict sense, requires that the mental qualities must preexist in the principles from which explanations of mental phenomena are to be deduced. That, surely, makes the explanation circular: What is to be explained is already *assumed* in the premises of the argument. How can that be useful or lead to better understanding of mind?

It is in the nature of deductive argument that the premises in a certain sense do already contain the conclusions they imply. It is the eduction, the elucidation, of the consequences by using the accepted rules of the game that defines what is meant by entailment. From this point of view one could assert that the whole of mathematics (ignoring for the moment problems raised by Gödel's work; see chapter 4) is but a bunch of analytic statements, little more than tautologies; accept the axioms, and the proven theorems *must* be true, because they are already contained implicitly in the axioms (see chapter 7). That, however, does not render mathematics a trivial enterprise! Even in the statement of a simple Aristotelian syllogism of the "All men are mortal . . ." variety, it is clear that the conclusion is likewise there, hidden in the premises, waiting to be drawn out.[39] But here too we do not deny that useful new knowledge is obtained from syllogistic (or other logically tight) reasoning. Despite the apparent circularity, deductive reasoning is at the heart of the way we systematize and codify mathematical and scientific knowledge; it should be as true of cognition as of any other discipline.

So, it appears necessary that the logical territory in which our models of mind are embedded contain—presuppose—mental concepts, and it ought to strike us as absurd to have thought otherwise. In the seventeenth century, orthodox scientific theory held that worms and other simple creatures arise spontaneously from river mud. In terms of strict (but not too careful or detailed) observation of antecedent-consequent conditions, that seemed to be the way things are; you might come to the same conclusion about the spontaneous generation of fruit flies on a bowl of ripe fruit on your kitchen table! It took an innovative and courageous scientist to contest the orthodox theory, and it is interesting to note that in this instance the refutation was not on the basis of more careful observation, but on a question of principle. Francesco Redi[40] argued that life could only arise from life, and not be generated from mud, or any other lifeless substrate. Today this seems too obvious to be worth discussion, indeed we can laugh at the alternative. Yet, not much more than three hundred years ago it caused such serious scientific strife that the good doctor only narrowly escaped the fate of Giordano Bruno, burnt at the stake in 1600 for promulgating the Copernican heresy.[41]

Why do we dismiss so easily the orthodox seventeenth-century opinion on the origin of lower forms of life? It is because our standards of observation and theory have advanced enormously since that time. Of course it's absurd to impute life-generating powers to mud. Our general knowledge of biology and biochemistry simply tell us that the notion can be dismissed out of hand. And yet let us be careful not to practice too brash a variety of cultural snobbery; one generation's cherished theory is another's idol of absurdity. What we prize today as orthodox doctrine on the origins of mentality will as surely be laughed at 300 years hence as the ideas Redi fought against 300 years ago are food for present merriment.

There is more to be learned from this example. The mud-to-mudpuppy-in-one-step theory is absurd because (among many other factors) we know that the propagation of life requires the handing on of genetic material from similar life forms, the synthesis of very complicated amino acids and proteins, their ordering according to complex laws of embryogenesis, and so on. Many of the processes are known in detail, so much so that the concept of mud-to-mudpuppy-in-*many*-steps is not absurd at all. In fact it is the orthodox doctrine of the origins of life. Synthesis of the building blocks of living forms from inorganic materials is seen as the major step in evolving artificial life, and it has been solved.[42] Aha! you will say, it is also just so with the origins of mind. We may grant that a "one-step" explanation of mind in terms of current brain processes poses difficulties, but just as the story of the origin of life becomes plausible when spread over a great many small steps, so it may be also with the account of how mind originated.

This is not the place to go into the question of whether artificial life is in all respects the same as natural life; for primitive life forms the argument in favor is pretty strong. There is one telling point to be made, however. At any given stage of evolutionary development, it is not possible to say *prior to the event* what the next step will produce by way of novel forms of life. Certainly one expects that the adjustment to some particular ecological niche (adaptive radiation) will have advantages for survival, but that is far too general a statement to be convincing as an explanation of the exact features some particular species happens to display. If the features had been different, *the explanation would still have remained the same,* seemingly impervious to the matter of detailed factual support. Put another way: If no particular piece of empirical evidence can count against the theory, it must then surely appear to be of questionable value as an explanation. That is an attack on the most revered of all sacred cows in the Halls of Science—belief in the explanation of the origin of species by natural selection—so we had better have a strong argument to support it.

The New Razor of Occam

We provide that support with the help of no less a figure than Karl Popper. His greatest contribution to the philosophy of science is enshrined in his principle of falsifiability.[43] This is in many respects the complement of the verification principle (chapter 1), and was used by him as a sword to cut away the tangle of pseudoscientific parables and myths that so easily can be paraded in the guise of true science. What distinguishes, or demarcates, to use his term, the genuinely scientific from other unworthy pretenders to that estate? It is the fact that a scientific theory (or model) lays itself open to the possibility of falsification. In other words, the theory must be able to specify conditions for an *experimentum crucis*—or more than one. If the experiment(s) should turn out to support the theory, all fine and dandy, but that is not a definitive result, because by the nature of things, further empirical tests of the theory are always possible and might still lead to its rejection. That is the so-called problem of induction; an indefinitely long string of verifications does not amount to logical proof. A single falsification, however, a result that refutes the theory, is a different matter. It alone *is* decisive for the theory's rejection (although scientists are good at salvage operations, at modifying theory to accommodate unexpected—unwanted—findings). Popper pushed the falsification principle as the criterion of true science to extreme lengths, and has been criticized both moderately[44] and radically[45] for doing so. Nevertheless it stands as the single most effective tool for discriminating between what is genuine empirical science from complexes of ideas that serve some other purpose even while parading in scientific garb.

As a young man in Vienna, Popper was especially troubled by the claims of psychoanalysis and communism to be scientific theories of human personal and social-economic behavior, respectively. Most disconcerting was the fact that no reasoned argument, and in particular no piece of evidence, regardless of its strength, could shake the structure, much less the foundations, of these systems. As Popper finally concluded, there was no set of circumstance in which their proponents could be persuaded that an empirical test might lead them to abandon those theories. That is, they were in principle not open to falsification. This led him to two major conclusions. The first is that neither Marxist communism nor psychoanalysis (at least in the forms then prevalent) enjoyed the status of genuine science. The second, and the one of primary concern to us, was the discovery of the importance of the principle of falsification, as described above, and its subsequent elevation into a touchstone of scientific methodology.

To return to the question of evolution: Painful as it may be to say it, by the criterion of falsifiability the theory of evolution by natural selection is not a scientific theory! The reason is straightforward enough. For its proponents there is no piece of empirical evidence that would lead them to abandon the theory; it is thus unfalsifiable.[46]

There have been many attempts to show that the development of certain forms of life, especially some that live in symbiotic relationships, are impossible to understand in evolutionary terms,[47] but such arguments disturb the evolutionist as little as the water running off the proverbial duck's back. I am not concerned here to evaluate the quality of the arguments against natural selection (in any of its many variations) or of the evidence adduced in support of them. The only point to be made is that the theory of evolution by natural selection is as unassailable as communism or psychoanalysis, and for precisely the same reason; its proponents would not accept any evidence as refuting it. The fact that communism and psychoanalysis have fallen on hard times is beside the point; evolutionary theory is far better supported by empirical evidence than they ever were, and it is true that different models falling under its rubric are from time to time proposed and discarded (Popper's paradigm scientific procedure of *conjecture and refutation*), but the core principle never comes up for serious questioning. I am far from saying that it is therefore wrong, only that it now enjoys a status different from that of any ordinary scientific theory. It, more than any other statement of established knowledge, represents the very core of the metaphysical principle of materialism, or as it is sometimes called, materialistic monism. If it is not a scientific theory in Popper's sense, what is it? Like communism and psychoanalysis, in this respect at least, it is an ideology.

This detour into philosophy of science was needed in order to defend the claim that the theory of natural selection is incapable of explaining the emergence of any particular species (with such-and-such characteristics) at a particular place and time. It is too general for that, and can accommodate post hoc to anything that happens to be the case; it is therefore not a very sharp instrument for making predictions either. One can deduce from the theory that when ecological conditions alter there will sooner or later be responsive changes in the organisms concerned. Most of these changes will be nonadaptive;[48] but whether adaptive or not, all modifications will be attributed to chance—the home, like Oxford, of lost causes. Unlike that great and lovely city, however, you cannot visit "chance" to make sure it is doing the job you assign to it. So there is a sense in which appeal to chance is merely "saving the appearances," to use a term much in vogue at the time when the Ptolemaic system of cosmology held sway.[49] Saving the appearances becomes important when current orthodoxy about evolution demands that an underlying belief be unchallenged.

Please note again that I am not claiming that the theory is wrong, only that its gaps are often filled as much by leaps of faith as by evidence, and that genuine explanatory power is one such gap.

It is thus not possible to say at any given point in the process, and *prior to the event,* what the next step in evolutionary development will produce. This is as true of the appearance of mind and mind-like phenomena as it is of anything else, including new plant and animal forms. To say that evolution, or evolutionary pressure, can give an explanation of such events is therefore true only in a very weak sense. In fact, staying with the distinctions made in chapter 5, we can say that biological conditions provide the context, or causal circumstance, within which a particular form of life (including mental life) may emerge; that is very much not an explanation of the *particulars* of what emerges.

The idea of mind as an "emergent property" of brains has certainly been popular. The phrase has, like "cognitive dissonance," a certain convincing ring about it. In neither case does the coining of a neat or suggestive phrase, however, establish the scientific *bona fides* or utility of the idea or thing referred to. In fact the whole argument of this section and the preceding one has been leading up to the plain and simple assertion that what emerges is not *in any way* explained by the context, the causal circumstance, of its emergence. The mud-to-mudpuppy-in-many-steps theory is made plausible, not by the fact that there are many steps between initial and final states (so that there is lots of room for gradual change, for distancing the final product from its first generators, thereby decreasing the wonder at the apparent anomaly between origin and destination), but by the fact that the factors producing and controlling those steps are to a high degree understood. The analogous account of mud-to-bowl-of-porridge-(brain)-to-mind is, in contrast, fraught with problems. I will just mention again the main one: It is that of leaping the barrier from $w1$ to $w2$. The barrier is a conceptual one and—as we now know, courtesy of the Peters principle— a series of moves in $w1,$ however long and intricate, cannot surmount it. Even if, as in the mudpuppy example, many of the intermediate steps were known (which they are not), the problem will not go away, despite the efforts of many of the brightest and best minds in cognitive philosophy. (What's that? You may well ask; it is the awkward specter of mental self-reference intruding yet again in the debate.) One is strongly tempted to assert, taking a leaf from Francesco Redi's book: Mind can only arise from mind! If that seems like too strong a dose of metaphysics, we can perhaps agree on a less dramatic version. Keeping our sights firmly on the character of deductive argument, we can assert: Mind can only be explained by mind. The *double entendre* here is deliberate. The premises of the explanatory model must contain mental terms, and the author of the model must himself evince and deploy mental capacities.

The two most widely held conjectures about the origins of mentation, that it arises from the physiological action of the brain and that it emerges "naturally" in the course of biological evolution, are well supported by empirical evidence, on the one hand, and by the scientific tenor of the times, the widely held metaphysical stance of materialism, on the other. Having put to rest the mistaken notions that mind can be explained in terms of current brain activity and/or as an emergent property of brains, it is now time to be much more positive. It is time to ask what it *is* possible to say about the nature of mind from a scientific perspective, from the point of view that acknowledges the preeminence of an observational, phenomenalistic stance and the need to look toward the possibility of a comprehensive theory of mind, but one that nonetheless questions the adequacy of materialistic natural science to provide all the answers. It is time also to widen the investigation to encompass aspects of mind that have suffered neglect—to put it mildly—at the hands of the standard model; to inquire whether we can or should reinstate aspects of Popper's other worlds, $w2$ and $w3$, that have been relegated more or less to oblivion in the standard account of what the mind is all about.

9

The Sacred River

The most important task for philosophy in the modern world is to resurrect the human person, to rescue it from trivializing science, and to replace the sarcasm which knows that we are merely animals, with the irony which sees that we are not.

ROGER SCRUTON

Some 200 years ago Samuel Taylor Coleridge wrote the following immortal lines:

> In Xanadu did Kubla Khan
> A stately pleasure-dome decree:
> Where Alph, the sacred river, ran
> Through caverns measureless to man,
> Down to a sunless sea.

Who would deny the marvelous sonority of the language, the poetic inspiration, that informs these lines, even if—as seems likely—they were composed under the influence of opium? So he wrote on, for some 50 more lines, until "a man from Porlock" (a nearby village) arrived "to settle some business," breaking the reverie, which was thus lost forever. We are reminded of Emerson's essay "The Oversoul," where he depicts the mind, man himself, as the stream whose source is unknown:

> The philosophy of six thousand years has not searched the chambers and magazines of the soul. In its experiments there has always remained, in the last analysis, a residuum it could not resolve. Man is a stream whose source is hidden. The most exact calculator has no prescience that somewhat incalculable may not balk the very next moment.

Here is another poetic image of the mysteries of the waters of life: Ariel's song from *The Tempest:*

> Full fathom five thy father lies;
> Of his bones are coral made;
> Those are pearls that were his eyes;
> Nothing of him that doth fade
> But doth suffer a sea-change
> Into something rich and strange.

The river, as metaphor for life, has been used often in literature, even in music, where Smetana's invocation of the river Moldau, from the orchestral suite *Má Vlast* (My Country) being perhaps the best-known example. The metaphor can be extended to the river of conscious life, to the stream of consciousness itself, another literary device: Think of Molly Bloom's soliloquy in *Ulysses*. A most insightful image in drama is provided by the English writer Charles Morgan. Shortly before World War II he wrote a play, prefaced by an essay on singleness of mind, entitled *The Flashing Stream*. Many aspects of consciousness fit congruently with this metaphor, as we shall soon see. What has all this to do with cognitive science? We'll come to that question, but first let us remind ourselves of what that science currently has to offer.

The Reach of the Mind

Chomsky revolutionized linguistics by pointing to certain essential features of language that had escaped the attention of traditional cognitive science. These included its universality, generativity, and innateness (chapter 3). His revolution gave a totally new slant to empirical research on language, and went some way toward achieving his goal of reaching a fresh understanding of mind. Of permanent value in the Chomskian revolution is both the theory, in its aspect of searching for the ideals of language, and the fresh impetus given to seeking out what's actually there to be discovered about language as a vital and vibrant attribute of human life—perhaps the most compelling one of all. Questioning the older doctrines of linguistic theory resulted in a whole cornucopia of novel ideas and findings; it provided a motive for reexamining the nature and details of language in the real world.

That has been true of most of the great revolutions in scientific thought. It was true of Copernicus and the heliocentric theory of planetary motion, of Redi and the question of the origins of life, of Goethe's insistence on the evolutionary continuity of species and the metamorphosis of plants (special creation and preformism were the accepted theories of his times),[1] of Wallace and Darwin and paleontology (catastrophism was the order of the day, and the assumed time scale of orthodox geology was wildly different from current thought; the theory of special creation still held sway),[2] of Lorenz and the establishment of ethology.[3] In each case insistent curiosity, certainty that the old ideas were inadequate, and renewed respect for the wonders of the natural world, smashed the favored icons and opened the way for new and better science. In every case the key to progress was the conviction that what's actually out there in nature, awaiting discovery, is vastly more significant than the theories currently held by orthodox science. Perhaps it is time for us to adopt something of that stance.

Cognitive science has developed far too restricted an image of humankind, a truly pusillanimous concept of mind. We need to reassess our subject of study, view it in a broader context, look again at salient features of cognition that have escaped our close attention. Can we follow in the steps of those great pioneers of science, take a fresh look at cognition's characteristics and capacities, and so inject new life into our comprehension of mind? Is there a new metaphor for mind that will set us on the right path?

Let us take the literary metaphor seriously, and think of it this way: Mind is a sacred river, a flashing stream.[4] We have already encountered many aspects of mental life that fit this picture. Mind has a continuity in time, at least in the waking state; it flows and changes but still maintains a certain integrity. It also comprises many things that are "beneath the surface"—not in our immediate consciousness. Those things are not absent, however. Some can be recovered at will, but many cannot. In that submerged state they are seldom, if ever, inactive. They may surface without warning or personal effort to determine much that goes on at the surface, in our conscious lives, for instance in the vicissitudes and idiosyncrasies of memory. They may flash up, with dramatic inspiration, or well up with a gentle but sure gesture; they are immediately recognized as partaking of the stream's essence, whether their content be brilliant or banal, sharp or degraded, clearly recognized or misapprehended. They are part of ourselves. Shear puts it this way:

> . . . identification of pure consciousness with the self . . . offers a simple explanation for the otherwise very problematical fact that common sense continues to insist that the self is somehow present in all experience, even when unable to isolate it, and even when intellectual analysis convinces us that it cannot be given in experience by any empirical quality. . . . For the self is present in all experience, there to be noticed, more or less clearly, as qualityless pure experience.[5]

Much of the time we can survey the surface of the stream with equanimity, contemplating its contents, or what is reflected in it, but sometimes there is less sureness, less clarity. What is experienced can be tinged with doubt, anxiety, euphoria, without our knowing what the source of those feelings may be. The river is in one sense who we are, as Shear says, yet we can stand back from it, ruminate on it, ride it, to a degree control it. Perhaps the most telling aspect of the metaphor, and the most difficult to comprehend, is that a river is capable of carrying and containing within itself items whose nature is unlike itself. What floats upon it may be flotsam, it may be profound wealth, it may alter the very nature and scope of the stream.[6] Below the surface there is also valuable treasure to be found, perhaps transformed treasure like the coral and pearls of Ariel's song. The stream is the vehicle for communication of love, of truth, of the will to serve science, commerce, of artistic expression and achievement; for growth, for capacities, events, and activities seemingly foreign to its own nature.

This may all seem rather fanciful, some of it has been heard before, and above all it has to be taken as metaphor, not too literally, not with obsessive concern for the (no doubt many) ways in which it does not fully capture the gesture and flavor of mind. The metaphor is not far from the "stream of thought" described and discussed so elegantly by William James and others. He noted, too, that the "self . . . opposed (to changing experiences) . . . as the permanent is opposed the changing and inconstant . . . is felt by all men."[7] It carries overtones of the unconscious made familiar by Freud and further expounded in the annals of dynamic psychology.[8] The fact that mind is so clearly identified with the self; is something that endures through time, develops; is dynamic, changeable, in many ways mysterious but at the same time challenging in its immediacy and comprehensibility, surely should invite us to reassess our methods of studying it, to inquire what neglected characteristics and capabilities need to be reexamined. Are those "caverns measureless to man" empty? Can we in any way discover their treasures, casting new light on the source of our ideas, ideals, and inspirations?

My answer is a positive yes! I do not suggest new paradigms for research, although such may be a good idea. I simply urge that we follow in the footsteps of Redi, Goethe, Darwin, Lorentz, and Chomsky, taking a fresh and unprejudiced look at the subject matter before us, as it exists, strives, and creates in the common round of everyday civilized life, as well as in the talents of creative geniuses—representative men, as Emerson called them.

The standard model in cognitive science concentrates attention on what is regular, predictable, average, ordinary, in mental activity. It exploits the fact that cognitive functions in the vast majority of educated individuals with intact brains follow well-prescribed routines.[9] Perception, memory, problem-solving, and the like show few major deviations from established norms. That is nothing to be concerned about in itself, but it engenders a fixity of interest that can be stultifying. Consider another primary property of mind that is widespread but less easily captured with our standard tools of analysis; consider creativity, whether intellectual, artistic, or in practical life. How is it handled? The usual way is to describe it as clearly as possible in terms of the concepts already accepted within the standard model, then attempt to measure it with psychometric tests; to inquire whether it has a structure, a set of "dimensions" that can be identified, quantified, and named.[10] This is like pinning a butterfly to the board, examining its special morphological features, classifying it, and giving it a name. All these are useful and important matters, but they do not come anywhere close to the heart of what it is to be a butterfly. That is better done by a field naturalist. I am suggesting that we need to retrace our steps and become naturalists again, to follow the observational route with open minds in the search for enlightenment.

Where should we look if we want to get to the essence of cognitive creativity? We should look to the work of creative individuals, surely, and to the fruits of their labors. F. W. Turner has made a bold attempt to find common ground between literary culture and science. His description of modes of understanding that transcend simple behavioral or materialistic formulations are quite compelling, especially his concept of "performative acts," whether in drama, dance, music, or fiction. A great part of his argument hinges on the fact that creative context is all-important; what the author conceives and intends to convey is of the essence of performance, and is left out of consideration in a purely behavioristic account of the matter. From the artist's point of view that is like mistaking the medium for the message. The words, notes, gestures, etc. are the vehicles by means of which the artistic achievement is conveyed, it is not itself the achievement.[11] We can learn an important lesson from this distinction, however little cognitive scientists have been inclined to take their cue from literary sources. What is true in the world of the arts described by Turner is surely no less true of the creative thought of scientists and mathematicians.

For Turner, the flashing up of new ideas out of the sacred river, their expression in novel artistic forms, is paramount. Something very similar is to be found in the way Michael Polanyi, a physical chemist, describes the progress of science in the passionate commitment of scientists to the discovery of the "hidden world" of ideas and phenomena (the contents of those measureless caverns) that are immanent, however vaguely formulated to start with, in their conception of the arena of their research.[12] How much better he captures the mood and action of the working scientist than the dry "conjectures and refutations" of Popper.[13] Both have their place as valid descriptions of the scientific enterprise, but neither one is complete without the other, and together they bracket the range of activities and experiences of creative researchers. It is noteworthy that both deny, with varying degrees of commitment and explicitness, the simple materialist account of human thought and scientific discovery. Popper's cautious way describes the grammar of scientific progress and knowledge, Polanyi's fiery path the drama. I suggest that in these terms cognitive science has fashioned much of the grammar of the mind but has left its drama largely out of account. It is imperative to know about the grammar of intellectual creativity, but that is hardly a complete reckoning. What it lacks—obviously enough once the point is made—is attention to the highlights: the flights of imagination and inspiration of which great minds are capable, the drama.

That drama is nowhere so evident in science as in the creativity of mathematical invention and discovery, and in the ways that mathematics can be applied to the solution of problems both in science and in practical life. There, if you like, the metaphor of the flashing stream proves its mettle, and it is the reason (not the cause, please note) for devoting a whole chapter—chapter 7—to mathematics and mathematical creativity. We discussed in chapter 4 Penrose's refutation of the algorithmic concept of mind (its grammar), which was based largely on his immediate experience as a creative mathematician (its drama). Remarkably enough—but perhaps not so surprisingly, if one takes the view that they are describing a fundamental and inescapable ground of our reality—Penrose finds the basis for his later philosophy of mathematics and mind in Popper's three worlds (chapter 4), albeit in a fashion that transcends Popper's formulation in important ways.[14] He introduces this theme only at the very end of *Shadows of the Mind*, and quite briefly, although as more than a mere afterthought. But the matter bears closer scrutiny and fuller development; it is of utmost importance to our understanding of the drama of mind. Holding to it consistently may, however, lead us to positions considerably beyond what Penrose had in mind.

One Universe, Three Worlds

Figure 9.1 is reproduced from Penrose's book, showing his variation on Popper's basic theme. He points to three great mysteries, contained within the overall enigma of why there should be just these three worlds, three that appear to encompass the extant universe and all that we can know about it. Popper's first world $w1$, as was described in chapter 4, is the world of material furniture and fact, from tables and chairs to stars and the fundamental particles of which physics tells us. The second, $w2$, is the world of conscious awareness, of sensation, emotion, hopes and fears, of

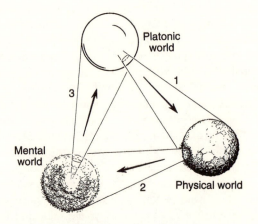

FIGURE 9.1. Roger Penrose's elaboration on Popper's three worlds: Each world emerges mysteriously from a small portion of another world in a cyclical fashion. From *Shadows of the Mind: A Search for the Missing Science of Consciousness* (Oxford University Press, 1994), p. 414. Reproduced by permission.

thinking and belief. It is, as Penrose notes, of necessity the one with which we are first and most intimately in touch, yet also the one about which we know least in precise scientific terms. It is the world which, as Russell says, gives us knowledge by acquaintance. The mystery mediating between the two is pictured by the second arrow in figure 9.1, suggesting that from a small part of *w1* (principally the brain) the whole of *w2* somehow emerges. Notice that *emerges* is here used not to label a scientific hypothesis, as in the postulate that mind is an emergent property of large and complex brains, but to point to what it truly is: a recognizable but still mysterious feature of our universe.

The second mystery (the third arrow of figure 9.1) is concerned with the undeniable fact that activity in *w2* gives ready access to a world of ideal forms and ideas, traditionally called by mathematicians the Platonic world. Moreover it is only a small part of *w2* that mediates this access—in most of us it is a vanishingly small part. By far the greater part of our mental life is not concerned with mathematics or other idealizations, but the part that is gives access (in principle anyway, or as far as Penrose conceives it) to the whole of *w3*. Again, the arrow does not indicate an hypothesis aimed at explaining why the two worlds have this relation, it is the expression of a genuine mystery in the way our universe is put together. Notice that Penrose's characterization of *w3* is much narrower than Popper's in one sense (it is concerned principally with mathematical ideas) but much broader in another (it is seen not merely as a world of "cultural products," but as something beyond us, independent of us and our cognitive activities—the "caverns measureless to man"—a world underlying the very structure of the universe). It also has more powerful epistemological clout, as we shall now discuss.

The third mystery (the first arrow in figure 9.1) joins a small part of *w3* to the whole of *w1,* thereby expressing the fact that some part of mathematics (perhaps only a very small part) plays a decisive role in our ways of understanding the physical world, and especially its most fundamental properties. We earlier discussed what has been called "The unreasonable effectiveness of mathematics in the physical sciences."[15] Although this arrow expresses the primary direction of the influence, it is not the only means of interaction between these worlds. As Penrose states: "There is a very remarkable depth, subtlety, and mathematical fruitfulness in the concepts that lie latent within physical processes."[16] That is, contemplation of the physical world is itself at times the engine that drives mathematical advance.

Penrose lays out the case for the three worlds and their mysteries in a delicate and insightful way. Not wishing to suggest that this picture of three worlds is a definitive or final exposition of the way things are, Penrose sums up as follows:

> There is a seemingly paradoxical aspect of these correspondences, where each world seems to "emerge" from but a tiny part of the one which precedes it. I have drawn . . . [our figure 9.1] so as to emphasize this paradox. However, by regarding the arrows merely as expressing the various correspondences, rather than asserting any actual "emergence," I am trying not to prejudge the question as to which, if any, of the worlds are to be regarded as primary, secondary, or tertiary.
>
> Yet, even so, . . . [figure 9.1] reflects another of my opinions or prejudices. I have depicted things as though it is to be assumed that each entire world is indeed reflected within a (small) portion of its predecessor. Perhaps my prejudices are wrong. Perhaps there are aspects of the behavior of the physical world that cannot be described in precise mathematical terms; perhaps there is mental life that is not rooted in physical structures (such as brains); perhaps there are mathematical truths that remain, in principle, inaccessible to human reason and insight. To encompass any of these alternative possibilities, . . . [figure 9.1] would have to be redrawn, so as to allow for some or all of these worlds to extend beyond the compass of its preceding arrow.[17]

Let us grant that any prudent student of science, aware as they must be of the distinction between what is logically possible and what is in fact the case, or discoverable, would have to agree with these remarks. Yet for most cognitive scientists, the assumptions and prejudgements of current scientific doctrine will tend to render Penrose's sentiments suspect. That, however, is not a rational attitude. The only position that makes sense is to keep an open mind, and examine any claim on its merits. For many the assertion of the reality of imaginations surfacing in the flashing stream may be disconcerting, to take a striking—we might even say a scintillating—example, but in the case of mathematics at least those sparks of insight cannot be dismissed as vaporous will-o'-the-wisps. They can perhaps be accommodated by some version of the three worlds view but still challenge us to look more closely at the mystery of how one world feeds into and affects another.

Where Popper assigns to $w3$ a somewhat austere and distant role, for Penrose it is far more interactive and cogent in the generation of human knowledge and understanding. But there is a sense in which Penrose, too, does not go far enough in characterizing $w3$ and the role it plays in the unfolding scientific picture of the universe. He allows that there will be thinkers who attribute more than just mathematical principles and truths to $w3$, for instance the other Platonic ideals of beauty and goodness. But there is another way in which his conception is not bold enough; why should the influence of his mathematical-Platonic version of *w3* be limited to its intimate involvement with physical laws, with only that aspect of nature? There it has undeniably been extraordinarily effective, but that is no reason to deny it further scope. Here are a couple of instances of what I have in mind.

In discussing how the purpose and workings of a machine are to be understood, Michael Polanyi takes what we may call the engineer's stance.[18] In trying to understand a (novel) machine the engineer does not just correlate input with output, take it apart and examine the components, or drive the machine to destruction; he looks for the ideas behind the machine's design, tries to understand how features conceived by the designer are embodied in the machine's parts in a manner that allows it to do its job. Machines have, by definition, a purpose, and to understand a machine means to recognize its purpose and how it is implemented. This Polanyi contrasts with investigation of the laws of physics and chemistry; he points out that no amount of investigation of those topics can yield explanations of what a machine is for in the designated sense.[19] Yet a paradox is at hand: To the extent that the ideas behind the machine's design are expressible logically or mathematically, in a control diagram, flow chart, or a set of equations, they have their origin in *w3*. But they are as intimately embedded in the structure of the machine as the mathematics of relativity or quantum mechanics are inherently "in" the processes of physical reality, and this seems to destroy, or at least blur, the distinction between teleology (in technology) and the impersonality of scientific law that Polanyi is at pains to make.

My point is not to try to reintroduce the concept of teleology to science, at least not in any simple way, but to show that the purity of the ideals of the Platonic world are not so easily separated from the artifacts and goals of practical human activity and invention as one might think, and as Penrose would have us believe.[20] The interactions of *w3* with *w1* and *w2* appear to be even stronger and broader than he imagined.

Another conclusion is inescapable if we are to be consistent, and it takes us well beyond Polanyi's distinction between the understanding of machines, on the one hand, and of physical law that can be expressed mathematically, on the other; there is no intrinsic reason to limit our investigation to these two alone, just because mathematics has been found to have useful application to them. Perhaps *w3* plays a role in other constituents of the universe in ways of which we so far have little conception. Consider another fundamental natural phenomenon for which there is no profound mathematical treatment, namely, the growth and metamorphosis of plants. By this I do not mean the mere description of growth rates, the cataloguing of morphological character, or even mathematical models of population dynamics, diffusion, and the like. I am thinking of a mathematics that captures the deep properties of biological form and growth in the same way this happens in physics. There is a power and subtlety in the mathematical characterization of the physical world that can be, and has been, successfully apprehended. Contemplation of the physical world can be mathematically fruitful, as well as vice versa. The process started in the modern era with Galileo, has been going strong ever since, and shows no sign of reaching a terminus. There is no reason at all to suppose that similar mathematical qualities may not reside in the biological world, of which the morphology, dynamics, and metamorphoses of plant growth is but one example, qualities that reveal the intimate realities presently there hidden. Some progress in this direction has been attempted, but the fundamental properties have not been laid bare.[21] Perhaps the requisite mathematics has not yet been discovered—or invented (chapter 7).

So we must allow the logical possibility that *w3* has that very same intimate relation to biological reality that it has to the physical; it is just that the former has as yet not been uncovered. Moreover, there is no reason to limit the relation to the plant kingdom; the same possibility exists for all of biology and, startling as the thought may be on first acquaintance, to mental life as well. That introduces something which is in principle new and different because, as we have observed (chapter 8), the mental cannot be *reduced to* (Nagel) or *derived from* (Dodwell) *w1*. As we shall soon see, there are some aspects of mind that do seem to have their natural habitat in *w3*. Is a "mathematics of the mind" out of the question, or is there perhaps some other treasure trove awaiting exploitation?

I am not here referring to the application of mathematics to psychological processes in what is known as *mathematical psychology,* most of which is quite superficial, but to what one may call the deep structure of the mind. If this is reminiscent of Chomsky's talk of the deep structure of language, that is as it should be, although he had in mind something more technical, less compelling, metaphysically speaking, than many of his interpreters have inferred (chapter 3). Even the application of Lie group theory to perception (chapter 6) and similar essays[22] do not take us very far in the desired direction. One has to conclude that a mathematical treatment approaching the level of insight into mentation that is standard fare in physics and cosmology simply does not exist. The topic is a closed book at present, but it is important not to forget that it may one day be opened. After all, flashes from the depths of the stream are usually unpredictable, and the less predictable, the more dramatic their effects tend to be. And who would deny that this flashing up, should it occur, will be more dramatic than anything in the history of cognitive science! It may occur as the mathematical analysis of physical law proceeds, which is where Penrose places his bet, but perhaps it awaits some other unsuspected novel development, even the creation of a brand new branch of mathematics. Maybe the answer will not lie in mathematics after all. What if there are coral and pearls of a different sort to be brought to light? Could *w3* have other denizens that will point the way?

It boils down to this: If one accepts the conception of three worlds and grants *w3* the independence and permanence conferred on it as the repository of mathematical and other imperishable wisdom, one is also bound to accept that the exploration of the relations of *w3* to the other worlds cannot be artificially restricted by our current knowledge and prejudices. Such other relations may indeed seem mysterious and at present incomprehensible, but that is not a valid reason for attempting to deny their reality and importance. Accepting them does not betray a mystical streak, as some skeptics will want to argue, but a rational-observational one. Superstition is the faulty belief that there is mystery where none exists. Equally grave is the opposite fault of negative superstition, the insistence that there is no mystery when one is truly extant. Science has done a great job of exorcising superstition; we need to have the courage not to fall into the opposite trap of failing to identify negative superstition when it occurs, of denying mystery when it is plainly in view, as it is when we contemplate the relations of the three worlds to each other. Consistent adherence to the three worlds doctrine leads us into unfamiliar territory, maybe to places where we feel uneasy ("at sea" I would have said, but perhaps that is stretching our liquid metaphor a little too far) but not necessarily into a morass. (The "Sargasso sea" perhaps? Not such a bad metaphor that—to be in the doldrums and gyrated slowly in circles by a giant vortex!) To acknowledge the mysteries is not to deny the possibility that they may one day be resolved. Discomfort is no excuse. As Confucius said: "The scholar who cherishes the love of comfort is not fit to be deemed a scholar."

Let us see what else is to be found in *w3* to help us on our way.

Ideals

Perhaps, to return to our original metaphor, we simply need the confidence to navigate the sacred river with a clear head and a steady hand on the tiller. As any sailor knows, it is far better to steer by observation of the natural hazards and opportunities proffered by local conditions than to rely on information furnished by a time-worn chart. We also need to do a little fishing in the stream; in reexamining the sorts of evidence we should pay attention to we would, after all, merely be following in the footsteps of the great innovative masters—Copernicus, Kepler, Newton, Darwin, and the rest. What additional sorts of evidence might there be?

One of the most powerful shapers of the cognitions of the growing child, as well as of the mature adult, is the presence of ideals. In an important but little-noticed paper, John Macnamara argues that there is no possibility of understanding broad areas of cognitive psychology unless the role of such ideals is taken very seriously.[23] Incredibly enough, ideals have been largely ignored in psychological theory for over 300 years, and this is no doubt because psychologists (following Hobbes, who based his system on analogy with Galileo's kinematics of physical bodies)[24] embraced enthusiastically the metaphysics of the clockwork universe. Although ideals certainly play their part in that universe, or at least in its understanding as a physico-mathematical system, they are excluded from the psychologist's lexicon by the accident of its birth in empiricist philosophy, because for Hobbes, Locke, and Hume the idea (the ideal) is derived, in all cases, from the sensible. Ideas are "conveyed to the mind" by the senses, so cannot transcend them.

What is meant by an ideal? We have already discussed one sort extensively, namely those that are at the heart of mathematics. We know that the geometer's point and straight line, for example, are idealizations that no physical instance can reproduce, although we understand quite well what it means to approximate to the ideals.[25] Ideals, or idealizations, are at the heart of physical theory too. One such is the concept of a body not acted on by an external force, another is absolute zero temperature. Physically unrealizable states like these are idealizations that yield the fundamental laws of physics. No physicist thinks of them as properties of the material world; they are, as Macnamara says, in the mind of the physicist rather than in the matter they study. Nonetheless, they are essential components of the models by which he seeks to comprehend that matter.

Does the standard model incorporate ideals in this sense? Implicitly, and in certain limited respects, the answer is yes. The ray model of light propagation is used in describing the optical properties of the eye, for example, and "perfect memory" is a standard against which actual performance can be judged. We have seen how in certain respects the Chomskian theory seeks to lay out the ideal properties of language, and—most clearly—the canons of logical argument set the stage for rational debate. In few cases, however, do ideals play an explicit role in theorizing. Where they do, the results can be arresting. The most obvious examples in recent decades have been in the Chomskian theory of language, as we have discussed already, and in the Piagetian theory of intellectual development. There have been few cases that have captured the general attention of psychologists so obviously as these. And yet as they matured these theories tended to fall back on the idea that all the competence of which they treat is just a biological gift, something to be accounted for by evolutionary exegesis. Such a theoretical move poses problems, as we have seen.

Other places where ideals surface are the fields of AI, robotics, and information theory. In all these cases we are talking of ideals that express themselves primarily in *w1*. Nothing wrong with that, you might say, so do the ideals of physical theory. There is, however, one very great difference. As we have repeatedly seen, what occurs in *w1,* be it in terms of machines or evolutionary change, does not entail logically anything about mentation, and therefore is of limited explanatory value. We shall have to search further to discover more about the nature of ideals and the deeper role they should play in the explanation of mental life.

One can make a distinction between clear and obscure ideals. The former are best exemplified by mathematical entities that have precisely defined properties, like the point and line. Examples of the latter are truth, fairness, and justice. We understand rather well what these ideals are, how they function to regulate our lives, but they have no formally watertight definition. Although to debate the nature of a geometric line and settle the matter by democratic vote would be nonsense (all right, it is not inconceivable for that to happen, but it would be stretching the concept to absurd lengths), it would not at all be out of line for such debate to occur, and be fruitful, for bringing obscure ideals into sharper focus. Indeed, that is what a major part of philosophy, law and politics—to say nothing of theoretical science—is all about.

Whereas there is no doubt that the clear ideals, or many of them, are indigenous to *w3,* one might be less sure about the obscure ones. In both cases, however, there is the common characteristic that an ideal is something to which an object, action, or property in *w1,* or in fact in *w2,* may approximate, without ever realizing it perfectly. In both cases ideals play a compelling if not a determining role, whether in theory or practice. A number of insightful but informal examples are presented by Macnamara, although he does not discuss them within the three-worlds framework. Imagine what we would think of a teacher who disdained the notion of fairness in grading his students' work, or the scientist who professed no interest in establishing the truth of his research. There is nothing in principle to limit the ideals to mathematical or purely logical concepts; the ideals of well-considered conduct, belief, and motivation are just as central to the civilized human condition, a point of view at least as old and venerable as Socrates himself. They are, in a very important sense, what we live by.

The distinction between the ideal and the mundane[26] is much like the distinction Chomsky makes between linguistic competence and performance; the linguistic intuition that tells us when a string of words is a grammatical unity has the flavor of measurement against an ideal standard. Similarly when we tell a lie, fail to keep a promise, or do something unjust, intuition tells us that the action departs from the ideal. Sometimes we can make the matter explicit, sometimes it is the subject of heated argument (as in legal debate), and sometimes matters are not to be decided with finality (as in one version of Wittgenstein's brand of philosophy). In each case, however, it is the ideal that supplies the criterion against which we assess conduct, accept judgment, or suspend belief, a very different core involvement of ideals in psychological activity than was described above for the standard model.

Here is Polanyi again on the scientist at work:

> Yet personal knowledge in science is not made but discovered, and as such it claims to establish contact with reality beyond the clues on which it relies. It commits us, passionately and far beyond our comprehension, to a vision of reality. Of this responsibility we cannot divest ourselves by setting up criteria of verifiability—or falsifiability or testability, or what you will. For we live in it as in the garment of our own skin. Like love, to which it is akin, this commitment is a "shirt of flame," blazing with passion and, also like love, consumed by a devotion to a universal demand. Such is the true sense of objectivity in science . . . the discovery of rationality in nature, a name which was meant to say that the kind of order which the discoverer claims to see in nature goes far beyond his understanding; so that his triumph lies precisely in his foreknowledge of a host of yet hidden implications which his discoveries will reveal in later days to other eyes.[27]

That is idealism for sure, and it is not given to many to taste its fruits to the full. Nonetheless the passage expresses well the fact that ideals in both senses, as moral canons or intuitions and as logico-mathematical prescriptions, play a prominent, indeed an indispensable part, in the progress of science. They are alive, too, in all other branches of human culture.[28] I find it impossible to give a principled (idealized) account of which ideals belong, without question, in *w3,* or which, if any, can be excluded from it with certainty. It is beyond question, however, that many of our most powerful ideals, both clear and obscure, do belong there and are among the fundamental arbiters of human cognition.

One cannot study the mind and its creative potential without acknowledging the pivotal role ideals play in its functioning. The mysteries of how ideals are apprehended and of how they steer and monitor the human enterprise stand, no matter how anxious we might be to minimize their presence and influence in the interests of scientific pragmatism and parsimony.

States of Consciousness

Cognitive science tends toward the study of what we think of as "normal" states of consciousness, everyday awake experience, from attentive to preattentive to unattentive, dreaming, and less clearly identifiable states like social and self-consciousness. There have been many investigations and reports of unusual and abnormal states, but these are thought of as fringe topics, at best, so far as cognitive science is concerned.[29]

But just as it is misguided to look exclusively to the everyday, the mundane, the average, in seeking to understand creativity, so it is a mistake to look only at what is "normal" when attempting to grapple with the facts of consciousness. I do not mean that one has to delve into the shadows of the paranormal, although there may yet be rich treasure to be garnered there.[30]

Just as it was fruitful, when trying to come to terms with creativity, to look at one of the purest and most powerful examples, namely mathematical creativity, so too in considering states of consciousness an important perspective is gained by approaching brilliant if untypical examples, examples that manifest an unusually heightened or dramatic character. Interestingly enough these are very often, although not always, associated with episodes of high creativity, whether in musical composition, mathematical discovery, poetic fantasy, or scientific insight. Such unusual episodes of altered consciousness can be a signal of the flashing up of treasure from the depths of the stream. Indeed, if one likes the metaphor, one might even say that the heightened consciousness *is* the flashing up, conveying from the depths new knowledge, new insight, new artistic endeavor and artifact. The notion that the products of human genius are gems thrown up from the unconscious is, after all, an old one.

A recent investigation of the experience of consciousness (in both senses) by Jonathan Shear makes the case strongly that philosophers, and cognitive scientists generally, have been negligent, if not narrow-minded in their treatment of the topic.[31] Here's how he introduces the matter:

> Throughout history there have been recurring reports of a group of remarkable experiences of what we can call the deep structures of consciousness. . . . The major intellectual, aesthetic and spiritual traditions of Asia have for centuries held them to be central to the attainment of full intellectual, aesthetic, and moral maturity. The same experiences played a central role in the philosophical traditions of ancient Greece. They have also . . . been reported, often in great detail, by creative geniuses from Plato to Einstein.
>
> Despite their occurrence throughout the history of civilization, these experiences have by all reports been quite rare. . . . Consequently our modern Western intellectual tradition, with its emphasis on scientific method and free, repeatable access to data, has until recently not paid much attention to them.[32]

Shear proceeds to examine in some detail Plato's description of transcendental experiences, their relation to other traditions, to the treatment of self and consciousness in a modern perspective by Western philosophers, from Descartes on. At all times and in all places, as he notes, there have been witnesses to such salient but unusual experiences, and in large measure (given their cultural diversity), they have been in good agreement. Those who have described them in the Western world have most often been poets (Thomas Traherne, Wordsworth, Rilke), musicians (Mozart, Brahms), and mathematicians (Poincaré, Einstein), to quote only a few of the most outstanding examples—obviously creative geniuses all. There are also witnesses among common folk, however. Other peculiar states have often been described, such as near death experiences (NDEs), lucid dreams, and the like.[33] With the progress of medical science in prolonging life artificially it would hardly be surprising if such reports were to occur with increasing salience and frequency. I will not detail these matters further; for our purposes it is enough to realize that there is a whole world of phenomena of consciousness that has been almost wholly neglected by cognitive science.

The neglect has not, however, been total. Two sorts of response to the acknowledged existence of these states have been offered. The first is that such rare and untypical reports do not merit the attention of serious science. The second is that they can be dismissed as the result of unusual biochemical conditions in the brain such as would be induced by extreme stress, toxicity, anoxia, or some such anomaly, which has been advanced particularly as an explanation of NDEs. Biochemical change no doubt occurs, but to attribute the full significance of NDEs to changes in brain chemistry is on a par with attempting to explain veridical perception, or the following of a complex argument, in terms of what's happening to the neurotransmitters in the brain (see next section). I do not offer an alternative explanation, but merely wish to point out that this one won't do. It is an example of that mistaking of a causal context for an explanation with which we are already familiar (chapter 5). It as little explains the phenomena as the chemical events in the photoreceptors of the retina explain visual perception. They are relevant certainly, but are far from telling the complete story.

As to the argument that we need have no truck with the rare and untypical, it will be sufficient to observe that such an attitude has never served science well. The only reasonable attitude to assume is one of caution but at the same time open-mindedness.[34] Let's not be afraid to look at what observation of unusual mental phenomena, such as altered states of consciousness, has to offer. "Observation" here means the untrammeled study of consciousness in all its richness and variety.

Shear describes in some detail common elements in the accounts of unusual and exalted states of consciousness given at different times and places, and within different cultural traditions. We know there is communality in the more mundane aspects of conscious experience, so it should not come as too much of a surprise that it holds for unusual states too. The interested reader should sip at Shear's cup; it is anything but poisoned.

Good Things Come in Threes

We have discussed Popper's three worlds, and earlier the conception of three levels of psychological function, with three corresponding levels of explanation. We also had Marr's distinction between three levels of function and explanation in computational science. Are these threes purely coincidental? I think not. Marr's levels, exemplified in his description of the operations and use of a handheld calculator (physical, algorithmic, and conceptual) are very close to my scheme for psychology (sensory-physiological, organizational-perceptual, and cognitive-operational), although the mapping from one scheme to the other is not perfect. Rather than give a detailed analysis of the differences, it seems more fruitful to consider these threefold frames in relation to Popper's worlds.

Taking the lowest level first, it is obvious that the physiological and physical belong in *w1* without question. No problems there. At the top end, the conceptual level of Marr (mis-represented by him, it may be recalled, as the computational level) and the cognitive level in my scheme represent *w3*, the world of ideals and idealizations, logical and mathematical entities, formal theory and conceptualization (see table 5.1). What of *w2*? Here the fit is not so clear, but remember that a prominent role of *w2* is to mediate between the other two worlds, as in the assertion of conscious effort in gaining access to the mathematical verities of *w3* and applying them to the understanding of *w1* (see figure 9.1). In similar vein one can see the middle algorithmic level of Marr as the one that operationalizes the conceptions (idealizations) from above, organizing and controlling the implementation at the lowest level. Likewise with the organizational-perceptual level of my scheme. So the three-level schemes take on a far wider and more powerful role in our metaphysics than was evident on first acquaintance. Speaking personally, the three-level taxonomy for cognitive science evolved over several years (roughly, the early 1970s), nearly a decade before Popper's three worlds set me thinking on broader epistemological lines. The discovery of the harmony between them then gave me confidence to assert that the taxonomy is appropriate for all of cognitive science, not just its perceptual aspect.

The Priority of Concepts

What has all this to do with the meat and potatoes of cognitive science? Are we not getting a little too fanciful, rather far from the serious business of understanding the mind? Not at all. Comprehensive schemes of this sort are necessary to keep our ideas about how to study and understand the mind on track, and this is just one part of the task of ordering (with Popper, or Bunge, or many another systematizer, whether of the Right or Left, politically correct or not) our general ontology and epistemology—our metaphysics.

What consequences, if any, follow for the study of mind? By far the most telling is this: We need to achieve conceptual clarification before psychological (or other cognitive) research begins. The first fruit of such analysis should be the recognition that contemporary research hews to a quite narrow line, focusing on a set of behaviors and problems that are amenable to experimental investigation, computer simulation, or both. It is, as we say, paradigm driven. Even so, some of the protagonists of this line argue that it can deal with most of the great issues of human achievement.[35] Narrowness is not in itself a fatal flaw, all science limits itself to "manageable" problems; but to be unaware of the narrowness, which appears to be the situation in cognitive science, is troublesome. An example used earlier illustrates the problem.

Finding out to what extent chimpanzees can learn to understand and use language has been a favorite topic of psychological research, linguistic controversy, and philosophical speculation for some years. Lost in all of this flurry of activity is the question of whether such research is on language, that is, whether it will reveal anything of interest or importance about language itself. The implicit assumption has been that it will; otherwise, why go to all the trouble and expense of doing it? That, as we also discussed, is a blunder. One has to know what language is before undertaking the investigation. At best it will yield new information about the capabilities of chimpanzees, and that may be worth having, but one should not be deluded into imputing much more to the findings than that. Such research could sharpen the linguistic debate, bearing on topics like the optimal conditions for language learning, teaching techniques, the role of reinforcement, ordering of item difficulty, even refining some of the concepts of linguistic theory. None of this, however, affects the main point, that some considerable basic understanding of language has to precede the factual investigations.

To be more general: All psychological, and specifically cognitive, research shares the implicit assumption that the logical and linguistic territory has already been surveyed. To do research on memory, to take another typical example, only makes sense once one has a good conceptual grasp of the subject. Such research investigates the character of short and long-term memory, the conditions of encoding and retrieval, the "depth" of processing (superficial, syntactic, semantic), the acquisition of skills versus the attainment of new conceptual knowledge, and so on.[36] All of this can be characterized as level 2 work, aimed at elucidating the routines of memory, the processes and procedures that affect the efficiency of memorization and recall; to the extent that it is more than merely descriptive it is algorithmic in intention, even if this is not explicitly named or recognized. Make no mistake, I am not therefore belittling experimental memory research. I am trying to make clear what it is, and what it is not. It certainly increases our understanding of the way memory operates; it does not challenge our intuitions (ideals, natural categories, folk conceptions) of what memory is. All that, as I said, has to come first, before there is any discernible point to doing the experimental research.

Contemporary research in cognitive science is based primarily, indeed almost exclusively, on the uses and metaphors of the algorithmic, level 2, variety. Cognitive scientists have been remarkably obtuse (although in one sense very successful) in their attempts to reduce cognition to the workings of algorithmic, computational, process models. This, even though one of their leaders, Marr, was clear that a level of explanation is required that is above the algorithmic, and not reducible to it. My goal, especially in chapters 6 and 8, has been to give a careful account of the limitations of process models, and especially of where they fail as explanatory ideals. There is a distinct gap between what is logically required for an explanation to do its intended job, and what current practice provides and thinks of as sufficient for the task.

To raise again a case made in the last chapter, we cannot even start to identify the nature of what it is we hope to investigate in cognitive research without the language and concepts bequeathed us by the cultural tradition of folk psychology. This is of course much more than the simple peasant-centered hodge-podge of nostrums and beliefs the name implies; it is the grand legacy of Plato and Aristotle (ignoring, for brevity's sake, the vast arena of even earlier civilizations); of the Church Fathers and the scholastics; of Shakespeare, Schiller, and Dickens; of Molière, Hegel, and Emerson—all of whom helped set the stage before Wundt, James, and Freud started to exploit it in the name of science.[37]

Absolutely no psychological (or, as we may also say, intentional) consequence follows from a model couched in exclusively algorithmic, physical, or physiological terms, which is the way contemporary cognitive science proceeds. Psychological explanation requires mental, intentional antecedents, as we have already established;

the point was first argued by the philosopher Richard Peters many years ago, and I earlier called it the Peters principle.[38] Explicitly, it is the principle that no statement of psychological import can be deduced from premises that themselves have no psychological reference whatever. The fact that it, and other related philosophical arguments of the same era, have been lost or ignored for so long simply attests to the fact that psychology (cognitive science) is not a completely rational enterprise.

Science limits itself to manageable problems, and change in what is recognized as manageable is itself a major factor in scientific progress, whether it be driven by technology (neuroscience is a prime example), the power of thought (of which theoretical physics is the clearest instance), or practical exigencies like the need to navigate the high seas. The majority of advances in cognitive science have been very much in the first category, in neuroscience as noted, but equally in the powerful techniques employed by AI. We need to become more aware of this, to be far more self-conscious about the inherent limitation in the goals that can be achieved in a discipline driven primarily by technology. We are strong in our investigations of $w1$, and even in some respects of $w2$, but, bearing in mind Macnamara's message, we certainly need to pay much more attention to $w3$. We have seen a number of ways in which this can be achieved: by giving much more thought to the pivotal role played by ideals, to the variety and subtlety of intellectual (and other) creativity, to the flashing stream of consciousness and the treasures it yields up. Above all we have absolutely to pay due respect to the Peters principle when attempting to give explanations of cognitive phenomena.

Some protagonists of a three worlds view will no doubt dislike the vista I have opened up, seeing it like the work of the Sorcerer's Apprentice, who conjured up a magical process he could not control or stop. The prospect of such unease no doubt explains why Popper limits the power of his $w3$ by confining it to human artifacts, as Penrose circumscribes his by considering only mathematical truths. The fact is, however, that all ideals, all idealizations, have the right to be considered for the status of denizens of $w3$. To make principled distinctions between those that do and those that do not belong is, as I remarked earlier, very difficult, and perhaps impossible. Macnamara rightly insisted that ideals are the very stuff of which the comprehension of mind stands most in need. We should go ahead without prejudice to examine where that path leads us.

An immediate and obvious possibility is to look to $w3$ for the principles of explanation otherwise lacking in cognitive science. Models in other branches of science have the property that from them observable consequences can be deduced; the consequences have the character of inevitability once the model is accepted. Although this is especially true of mathematical models of physical processes, it is not confined to them. Explanatory models for mental phenomena as incisive as this are lacking in psychology, but if we had them, among the axioms, assumptions, or antecedents there would have to be intentional statements—the Peters principle; the logic of entailment requires it to be so. Whether or not a new sort of mathematics were to be devised to meet this requirement (something seemingly beyond our present powers of comprehension, although complexity and category theory may be on the right road), we can say with assurance that the statement of such a model would need to incorporate entities from $w3$; ideas, idealizations of one form or another. In view of the Peters principle, we can be certain that some of these would be intentional concepts or ideals. In this way we can catch a glimpse of how Macnamara's concerns might start to be met, and what this would imply for our metaphysics.[39] It is in stark contrast to the habits of thought of the cognitive science community.

Realizations of Self and Mind

All genuine psychological explanation thus seems to require us to enter, to draw our ideas from, w3. A startling new thought now emerges: If we would understand ourselves, we also have to plunge into the sacred stream, to enter w3. We discussed earlier a limitation on theory that is unique to cognition, namely that any theory of thinking, being the product of a thinking person, a mind, is necessarily also about itself. But we also saw that the theory must incorporate ideals of intentionality (the Peters principle), ideals that are in the provenance of w3, so understanding ourselves means, inter alia, recognizing ourselves under the aegis of that world, as the bearers or embodiment of ideals contained in it. This even points the way to resolution of that central dilemma, raised early on in our inquiry, namely the question whether psychology is to be pursued as a purely natural, as opposed to a moral, science.[40] The answer now is clear: Psychology is not, cannot be, a purely natural science. It is, at least in major part, a science of the ideal, an ideal science—what in German is called a *Geisteswissenschaft*.

This thought about the role of w3 is startling because it stands both Popper's ontology and his epistemology on their respective heads. It reverses his ontology because, rather than w3 being just a world of intellectual and other cultural products, it is seen to be the progenitor (as Plato also would have it) of all that is culturally powerful and precious in humankind. We thus come to see ourselves as the vehicles for the expression of the entities of w3, not—or not only—as their creators. If that seems to be too strong medicine, it is because of our ingrained prejudices and habits of thought, not because the argument is wildly implausible or tendentious. Popper's epistemology is stood on its head, too, because, rather than needing to find openings to w3 through the strivings of human intellect, activities that are in w2, we come to realize that those strivings themselves can also flow to us under the influence of ideals that are in w3, as is indeed implied by the earlier quotation from Polanyi (note 27). Again, we get the picture of the human mind as the bearer of, as the vehicle of, ideas and ideals that are gestated in w3 but are brought to birth out of the flashing stream.

All this follows quite naturally and straightforwardly from the realization that in trying to account for thinking we cannot neglect the way our own thought processes are necessarily and intimately engaged. Our thoughts don't appear out of nowhere, but their origins are a mystery yet. We have the choice, accepted by the standard model, to claim that they are no more than a function of brain processes, but we have found ample reason to deny the force of that as an explanation of thinking. Or, we can accept some version of the "w3 origins" view, thereby acknowledging an explanatory principle that denies the basic tenets of the materialist ontogeny. If you *think* about it, the latter has to be the choice to make.

Vehicles and Ideals

The distinction between performance and what the performance is designed to impart, made by Turner in the first instance with regard to dramatic and other artistic fare, illustrates nicely the general distinction between vehicle and what is conveyed, between carrier and signal, that starts to emerge from our deliberations. To adopt the negation of McLuhan's well-worn slogan: The medium is not the message! To think otherwise is to be snagged—rather than raised—by our own bootstraps, and modern cognitive theory is indeed something of a bootstrapping undertaking. Our own cognitive activity is the precondition for everything else; we can't get outside our own intellectual skins. A minimal way of putting this is to say with MacKay (and many others) that an information system cannot completely comprehend its own activities.[41] This does not mean that we have to fall back solely on prescientific or "commonsense" conceptions of the mind, although such common understanding is the ground of the conceptual analysis needed before process models can throw light on cognitive behavior. As I said before, we are fundamentally constrained by the very cognitive capacities that are themselves part of what we seek to explain. That limitation need not be destructive, as an example from perception will make clear.

It has frequently been argued (and is a favorite theme of introductory textbooks in perception) that knowledge gained from the senses—for example, vision—is unreliable, because we know from experimental investigation that the senses transduce, filter, or even distort, information from the world. What we "perceive" is not what's there; exact empirical knowledge is thus impossible. That argument, which looks at first to be impregnable, fails to take account of the fact that our knowledge of the sensory transducers themselves (and indeed of the physical instruments used to measure their activity) is itself empirical knowledge derived from sensory experience. But if we cannot rely on that knowledge, the first argument loses all its force. Why? Because the original argument assumed something that, by its own insistence, should not and cannot be assumed, the reliability of knowledge derived from the senses.[42] Yet all empirical knowledge, and in particular all scientific understanding, is based on knowledge derived from the senses.

How, then, do we save our respectability, even our sanity? We do so by realizing that we have concepts of the action of the sense organs—ideals, the "clear and distinct ideas" of Descartes—including how this relates to the activity of perceiving. With the aid of these concepts, "thought models of perceptual processes" as we may call them, we are able to achieve coherent accounts of how empirical knowledge is acquired. It must be emphasized that the insight achieved through contemplative reflection, through thinking, is a necessary part of achieving the desired coherence, as Descartes showed us long ago. Just so, our ideas about cognition are derived not merely from fallible observation and technological analogy, but from the working of the conceptual apparatus by means of which we label, characterize, and distinguish one psychological capacity from another. That is why thinking, the vehicle of analysis, has to have priority in our attempts to get a handle on cognition, rather than consciousness, self, or any other putative "mental contents." Without the former, we can make nothing of the latter; without the ideals of *w3* we cannot enter and understand *w2*, to say nothing of *w1*.

The limitation of self-reflexivity we have identified as an aspect of cognitive theory is thus not confining. It is a limitation only in the sense that we cannot go outside cognition to explain cognition; we do not need to look elsewhere, as Ted Honderich puts it (chapter 8). Rather than being destructive, the limitation of reflexivity should "keep our feet to the fire," force us to face a core feature of cognitive activity and our attempts to explain it. Denying the role of reflexivity certainly has been destructive, to the extent that cognitive science has looked elsewhere for its explanatory principles—to brain mechanisms, computer simulations, biological exigencies, and the like. The problems generated by that misdirected search has been the theme of much of this book. My argument does nothing to belittle the relevance and importance of neuroscience, or the material basis of thought and action, but it does lead to the conclusion that identifying the material substrate is not what it has been taken to be. It is not the beginning of an explanation of mind, but the end of a search for the biological correlates of mentation, itself a thoroughly satisfying intellectual pursuit. But you can't explain thinking without acknowledging the active role thought itself plays in the creation of your, or anyone else's, theories of cognition.

Conceptual clarity, analysis, and understanding of mental acts and attributes are needed before psychological science can begin. Algorithmic models alone do not yield sufficient explanations, despite their obvious value in other respects. To return again to one of my favored examples, language: Before any insightful research can be undertaken there has to be a prior understanding of the nature of language, its role in communication, the basis of speech acts like promising and commanding, its emotive function; in general the way language games, in Wittgenstein's sense, are at the heart of—are the vehicles of—mental life and social intercourse. To have a good grasp of all this does not require us to do experiments or construct elaborate models, although it does require familiarity with the ways we conduct our daily lives. It only makes sense to have a theory of language in cognitive science after these preliminaries have been—explicitly or, more likely, implicitly—correctly apprehended. A psychological theory of language is then something that clarifies the processes that make verbal (and possibly other) communication effective; it treats of development and learning, biological substrate, rules and tools, useful cognitive strategies, social and environmental factors, etc.—it treats of the necessary empirical conditions for language to flourish. It does not work to reveal the essence of language, whatever that may be. It identifies the processes, many of them algorithmic, that make language possible, make it a vehicle for expression of other things.

What of the Chomskian theory of language? Surely that goes beyond the restrictive role I have assigned to cognitive models? It does so in the sense that it redirects our attention away from an excessively peripheral, conditioning-based account toward a more innate, centralist, biologically grounded conception of language competence. To make more of Chomskian theory than this is to grant my case, to court the idea that language competence, the idealized standard to which we have some access, is derived from $w3$, which is a different matter.[43] That, however, goes well beyond what most cognitive scientists have been willing to contemplate or concede. In other respects, Chomskian theory, as generally received, does little to change the general conception of language that common sense, folk psychology, and philosophy all commend to us.

Modern cognitive theory is virtually all at the algorithmic level, level 2 as we called it, or seeks to relate level 2 occurrences to action at level 1. Typically a computational model is elaborated with some neurological embodiment in mind; alternatively, a model couched in neural terms aims to be computationally adequate.[44] Either way the psychology of the situation, as mental phenomenon, is not addressed directly, it is assumed. The computational model provides the vehicle (the medium) but not the substance (the message) of cognition. That is the reason why cognitive models and theories in their current form do not and cannot displace, or replace, our understanding of the nature of mental events, including thinking and consciousness. That is the reason why the materialism of contemporary cognitive science, a doctrine arrived at through our capacity to think, will not do as the sole basis for explaining or understanding the capacity to think.

Stephen Toulmin, in an acute analysis of reasons and causes, makes the following wry comment:

> Finally, in the neurophysiology of higher mental functions, the problem of reasons and causes reaches—depending on your viewpoint—the ultimate point of acuteness, or of absurdity. Many neuroscientists believe that we are at last within sight of explaining, in neurophysiological terms, all the basic causal interconnections and influences involved in the operation of the brain and central nervous system. And when that day finally arrives—as Charles Townes likes to remind us—the scientists concerned will certainly wish to *take credit* for their intellectual feat. "Take credit for what intellectual feat?" we may ask: "For the scientific discovery that strictly causal brain-mechanisms underlie all rational thought-processes—*including* the scientific discovery that strictly causal brain-mechanisms underlie all rational thought-processes."[45]

Enough said. Toulmin calls this Townes's paradox, which it surely is. It neatly encapsulates several of the major weaknesses of cognitive (and, most obviously, neuropsychological) theory which we have been at pains to expose.

Marking Out the Territory

The general outcome of our investigation is in certain respects a fresh paradigm for cognitive theory and research, a new tool for unraveling the problems of explaining mental acts, consciousness, and self, in scientific terms. It does not seek to undermine the achievements of cognitive science, only to put them in proper perspective. It proposes acknowledgment of the legitimate range of, and the proper preconditions for, cognitive theory. This is a matter of *demarcation,* to use Popper's serendipitous word. He used it to draw a line between true science and other thought systems— equally powerful in their own way, although not as durable—that seem to have the style and trappings of science but do not live up to its standard of empirical challenge, what Popper called the criterion of falsifiability. The term *demarcation* is used here in a different sense, to distinguish between level 2, algorithmic process models, the standard fare of cognitive science, and the more general level 3 theory that is needed if we are to grasp the full nature of cognition. Another demarcation is also to be observed, between what we study, and what we make of it. There is no way, for example, that cognitive research could falsify the properties of mental life or natural language, or alter them to any but a trivial extent by prescription, any more than the biologist can falsify or fundamentally alter the general nature of cell growth, or the physicist the fall of an apple—to say nothing of reordering the might and majesty of cosmological events. These are simply the phenomena the scientist works with.[46] Cognitive science, however, has to accept a constraint that is unique to it: Its subject matter is also part of the toolbox to be deployed in trying to understand its phenomena. So the demarcation between the two is not quite the "observer-observed" relation we are used to in the rest of science. We do not have, to use Nagel's insightful phrase, the luxury of "the view from nowhere." Cognitive science has yet to come to grips with that fact.

Does that paralyze us? It should not do so. To continue with the favored example: Cognitive research, given language as phenomenon, can make contributions to understanding how language is generated, acquired, and transmitted, what its biological basis might be. This is indeed what contemporary cognitive theorists aim for. They go beyond their designated domain if they attempt more, if they fail to recognize our first demarcation, between process model and genuine theory of mind. For that, as the arguments of this chapter have demonstrated, a far deeper appreciation of the sources of mental life, including the role that the ideals of $w3$ play in it, a greater humility in the face of the manifest mysteries of the three worlds and their interactions, is needed. Swimming in the sacred river, afloat on the flashing stream, we have to find new bearings and be prepared to reassess the limitations as well as the genuine achievements of cognitive science, to navigate prudently as well as dive for treasure.

Once again, the positive outcome to be hoped for from our inquiry is much greater clarity in the definition of territory, in the line of demarcation between the object of study and the models we devise to capture its processes, as well as the distinction between process models and theory of mind. We need to cultivate a proper modesty in our claims for the genius of modern cognitive science. To reiterate a point, we cannot lose sight of the fact that what we need in order to be able to study the mind is already part of the object of study, and a very important part of that stems from $w3$. Theories are devised by minds, not brains! Did anyone ever really believe it possible to explain thinking without thinking? Can the delicious ambiguity in that question be captured in any current cognitive model of the mind?

Finale: Coda 1

Let me summarize the results of our inquiry so far by first returning to the seven questions about psychological explanation raised in chapter 1. How near have we come to finding answers to them? And, of at least equal importance, to what extent have we gained insight into why proper analysis of the questions is fundamental to healthy and rational progress in cognitive science?

(1) Can we give a useful but still general definition of psychological explanation? The answer is yes, but the explanations provided by cognitive science are almost always of a very restricted kind. They involve algorithmic, process models. Such models only have force and substance within an al-

ready defined context of psychological concepts justified by the "intentional landscape" of folk-psychological (commonsense) language.

(2) Is there a schism between folk-psychological and scientific explanations in cognitive science? The answer is again yes, for reasons given in the previous paragraph. The difference is real, and is captured in the observation that we can't even talk about psychological matters, let alone explain them scientifically, without first invoking and using intentional language—the Peters principle.

(3) Is it possible to give an adequate meaning to the notion of psychological explanation in the scientific sense? Again, yes, but it is limited in current cognitive science in the way stated in (1), above. There is no reason, in principle, to abide by this limitation. In fact there is every reason not to (see below).

(4) Is identification and understanding of the physiological substrate a necessary condition for explaining cognitive activity? Here the answer is an emphatic no, most clearly illustrated in Gibson's arguments about explanation in perception. Too obsessive a concern about that substrate may indeed obscure the nature of the to-be-desired explanation.

(5) Does knowledge of the physiological substrate ever yield true explanations of psychological phenomena? The answer is again no. Cognitive scientists have all too often confused close, even near-perfect, correlations between events at one level and phenomena at another, with explanations. This is to confuse (Humean) causal circumstance with (theoretical) sufficiency.

(6) What has AI to offer? Much in the way of rigorous process models, simulations, and helpful analogy: Nothing in the way of genuine theory of mind. AI, together with neuroscience, provides the prime example of looking *away* from cognition to obtain explanations of cognition, a fundamentally flawed mode of theoretical investigation. Cognition has to be explained and understood on its own terms: Cognitive explanations are produced by minds, not brains or machines. Such explanations in particular are necessarily self-reflexive.

(7) Is there a common core to the various forms of psychological explanation espoused by different branches of cognitive science? There undoubtedly is: It is the common core of the machine-like process models idealized in the clockwork universe. But the precision and clarity of these models is bought at the expense of glossing over a fundamental difficulty, as far as the intentional concepts at the heart of psychology are concerned. How is this common core related to other cultural traditions concerned with the explanation of the human mind? The answer to that question is: By a rather tenuous thread!

To reconcile the doctrines of the standard model with what folk psychology has to offer, the latter now seen in its grand embodiment—the flower of civilization—requires some thought, but the reconciliation should be done in a constructive way. The two approaches are complementary, rather than opposed. We need only look again at the phenomena to be explained, including the great cultural achievements of the past three thousand years (at least), to realize that further investigation of the nature of ideals, of *w3,* is the path to follow. Ideals play a seminal role in human life, not least in our cognitive pursuits. Following this path leads to new conceptions of the nature of mind, or perhaps to the reanimation of older extant images, to a stronger and more vibrant appreciation for the genius of the human species and to more positive expectations for the understanding of our own creativity. This does not oppose the scientific work on models and algorithms, but rather complements it. The metaphysical stance of cognitive science, however, is a different matter. It is diametrically opposed to what I called right at the beginning the idealistic view. As a result of our deliberations, we now have even stronger grounds for thinking that is the right term to use, as well as the right avenue to pursue.

Finale: Coda 2

Let us look again at some of the phenomena of human cultural achievement, contemplate some of the lessons they can teach us about self and mind. In particular, what does the evolution of consciousness, something for which there is ample evidence, suggest about the human condition, where we stand, and where we might be going? As a cautionary note to guided us, we might remember one of Warren McCulloch's favorite remarks: "Don't bite my finger; look where it's pointing!"

The intellectual leaders in any age, whether they be priests, poets, philosophers, politicians, seers, scientists, or social activists, share this in common: They believe that the metaphysics they advocate are the one and only right thing. We have discussed several examples of this, and described how new science often breaks the mold of established orthodoxy. But this is not the only way in which new conceptions of the nature of human and cosmic reality come into being. One can make the generalization that, whatever the engine that drives it, evolution into new forms is a major characteristic, perhaps the only constant one, in the process leading civilization from one epoch to another. To be sure, that process sometimes seems to be stalled; Aristotle and Plato to a great extent ruled the examined life for close to two thousand years. But change is the general rule, and change has been accelerating since the appearance of modern science, as I outlined in chapter 1. Once again the image of Alph, the sacred river, moving at times swiftly, at others slowly, seems apposite, as well as the picture of the flashing stream out of which we draw our inspirations, novel insights, and other gifts.

In presenting my thesis I have used evidence and analogies, especially from music, mathematics, and language. Other disciplines could have supplied ammunition, but these three are salient, and close to my heart, so I shall use them again to illustrate this last theme, the nature and importance of the evolution of consciousness, of our cognitive powers, and what they tell us about the human condition.

Language—myths and poetry, in particular—are among the oldest manifestations of culture. Even the ancient forms have immediate appeal in the modern world; the *Aeneid* and *Odyssey,* for example, still hold great interest, and are continually being retranslated and reissued. Yet, how different they are, compared to modern literary canons, and the multitude of intermediate forms that were created between them. Studying those heroic sagas can tell us something of how the ancient Greeks experienced their world, of how the appearance and development of new ideas is heralded in the introduction and use of new words.[47] As Shear describes,[48] Plato even gave explicit recognition to the "secret doctrines" from which he drew his wisdom, and Socrates acknowledged his "Daemon," certainly things that seem rather removed from modern intellectual life. But the main point is that, throughout the history of culture we find an uninterrupted flow of new concepts, images, thought forms, worldviews, that drive civilization forward.[49] Most of them promulgate new ideals, of artistic expression, religious observance, justice, social organization, scientific knowledge, educational philosophy, or whatever. Generally speaking, they expound new metaphysical conceptions of the way things are—or should be. Where did Shakespeare's inspirations come from, or Goethe's, Kafka's, or Whitman's? You might say that in the modern literary world such visionary work has been displaced by realism and deconstruction, but the history of consciousness should give us assurance that there will yet again be change. The new new will displace the old new, and proclaim itself the one and only truth. The only real surprise would be if all this dried up totally, and cultural time stood still.

Music teaches us something a little different. Whereas the poetry and drama of Greece can still hold us enthralled, the music of those times, insofar as we can guess what it was like, was simple and crude, unlikely to appeal to the modern ear. There is quite a bit of guesswork here, because the written form of music, its permanent record, came on the scene but lately, scarcely a millennium ago. Listening to Renaissance music (two or three hundred years on), although it has many of the elements associated with the Western classical tradition—meter, rhythm, melody, and harmony—strikes one as lightweight, lacking the emotional and esthetic appeal of the Baroque era that followed it. Where did the new inspirations come from? They were, of course, fashioned by the minds of great innovators like Allesandro Scarlatti, Bach, and Vivaldi, ushering in new forms, harmonies, and instrumental and orchestral effects. For them, it was a form of worship, something that may strike the modern mind as quite peculiar, but nonetheless attesting to the fact that culture—consciousness—changes and evolves.

The development from one musical style to the next was not, and is not, always revolutionary. It can be smooth and direct. Bach's sons composed in a manner that anticipated and led easily into the classical elegance of Haydn and Mozart. But Beethoven followed, and broke new ground that *was* revolutionary, ushering in the Romantic era. Up until this time music, when not explicitly ecclesiastical, had been, basically, entertainment. With Beethoven the image of music as the expression of individuality, the vehicle of pain, grief, joy, freedom, and other ideals, came to a full flowering. Did he just think that up? One has to wonder.

And so it goes, through many changes of style, technique, and fashion, right up to the modern era. Musical culture has always evolved, and continues to do so. A remarkably constant feature within this ever-changing stream is the fact that, at least since Beethoven's day, what is felt to be innovative, and of primary importance to the composers, is most often not appreciated by the audiences for which it was written. Yet, within a comparatively short space, some of it at least is recognized as the work of genius and wholeheartedly embraced. It is difficult for us to realize that this was true of Beethoven, even of some of his early work, which sounds concordant, even mellifluous to us. When first performed, it provoked outrage. Perhaps the most notorious case is Stravinsky's *Rite of Spring,* which caused near riots in Paris when first heard. To us it is powerful, suggestive, even thrilling, but hardly the stuff of revolution. I will confess that quite a bit of what passes for modern classical music leaves me cold; I call it experimentation with sound. But, I have to admit, too, that young people find it more accessible, and some of it no doubt will achieve permanent status within the domain of serious music. Awareness of what is of value simply changes. The stream flows on: What is flotsam for some is, or becomes, treasure from the deep for others. Here, too, one has to see the hand of an evolving consciousness, something of which the only completely surprising aspect would be its total cessation.

And what of mathematics? We have already treated it a good deal more thoroughly than any other cognitive achievement, so I will be brief. Like poetry and drama, it first finds recognizable modern guise in classical Greece, especially after the fourth century b.c., with an amazing flowering in the third century, the time of Euclid and Archimedes. The latter is widely acknowledged to be one of the greatest mathematicians of all time.[50] The achievements of Greek mathematics are still the foundation of much that is current, useful, and insightful in the modern field. Mathematics is, in contrast to many artistic fashions, almost wholly cumulative. What is at the forefront of modern work builds in every case on what went before. What is most important, deep, as mathematicians like to say, just like the classics in literature, holds more permanent sway, and affects its future far more than less substantial ideas. Progress in mathematics, as in music, depends on technical innovations in notational and other formal elements, as in the development of calculus, matrix notation, and coordinate systems, as well as mechanical aids like the computer. Important as these are, they most certainly do not give anything like the full flavor of mathematical innovation. In fact they occur, are invented or discovered, in the course of truly innovative and insightful research. That is something brought into being by human effort and creativity, just like great literature and music. All are hallmarks of the wonders of human achievement. Like those others, mathematics is in a state of continuous development. Nobody can say where that will lead, and, again, the only really stunning surprise would be if it came to a sudden halt.

So, we are carried along on the sacred river, whether we will it or not. Of course the achievements that make it so are realized in the efforts and accomplishments of individual human lives. Taken as a whole they present a picture of the future of human civilization that has two outstanding, and at the same time humbling, characteristics. First, the evolution of civilization, of consciousness, will not come to a standstill, and second, the river will take us on a journey that will offer up many a new blinding insight and unanticipated delight. We can see no terminus, at least as long as physical conditions can support life on the planet. That is another reason, and a very hopeful one, to convince ourselves that cognitive science can be, and must be, brought to a realization of the dignity and potential of humankind far beyond what its current principles—and principals—are able to admit.

Give Hamlet the last word, hackneyed though it be through overexposure:

There are more things in heaven and earth, Horatio,
Than are dreamt on in your philosophy.

Notes

Chapter 1

1. We shall have to use a number of familiar words in possibly novel ways. The word *mentation* will identify any type of mind-like activity, whether conscious or not. This is hardly a watertight definition, even somewhat circular, but the proper connotation will emerge in due course.

2. Bronowski (1973).

3. Russell (1945). An intriguing slant on this development is given in Koestler (1959).

4. Barfield (1988), Bronowski (1973), Clarke (1969), Russell (1945), Tarnas (1993). See also Snow (1945/1993).

5. Boring (1929/1950), Polyani (1962, corrected edition). Wittgenstein was one of the first to challenge Cartesian dualism. See Wittgenstein (1975, posthumous).

6. See, for example, Hodgson (1991), Lockwood (1989). More detailed consideration of both this and related material covered here and in the following two chapters, is provided in Dodwell (in preparation).

7. Dennett (1988), Fodor (1983), Searle (1995). For further elaboration, see Dahblom (1993), Lepore and von Gulick (1992), and issues of *Behavioral and Brain Sciences,* passim.

8. The doctrine of positivism was strong in science around the turn of the century, followed by philosophical doctrine in the ensuing decades.

9. For a fuller discussion of this important matter see Ayer (1936/1946), Urmson (1966), von Wright (1971); also note 6.

10. Bronowski (1973).

11. Russell (1945).

12. Armstrong (1968). See also Bunge (1980).

13. Capra (1982).

14. Whitehead (1927). Some modern philosophers stake out similar positions, as, for example Rorty (1979), Rorty (1991).

15. In Heisenberg (1952). See also Heisenberg (1958). English-speaking readers will probably miss the literary reference here to the devil's work in Goethe's *Faust.*

16. For further elaboration, see note 6; also Eddington (1935) and Carrel (1935).

17. The philosopher Thomas Nagel has discussed this matter in a somewhat different guise in his important book *The View from Nowhere* (1986). We shall take a look at his ideas in chapter 9.

18. Penrose (1989).

19. E.g., Hawking (1988), Davies (1983), among many others.

20. Corballis (1991).

21. Morris (1967).

22. Speculation among biologists, which we will discuss later, tends also to be cast in a relentlessly materialist mold. See, for example, Dawkins (1995).

23. E.g., Dennett (1991), Gregory (1981), Newell (1991).

24. Dreyfus and Dreyfus (1986), Searle (1990), Turner (1985).

25. E.g., Koestler (1966), Koestler (1967).

26. Dodwell (1970a), Dodwell (1970b), Dodwell (1983), Dodwell (1990), Dodwell (1994).

27. Nagel (1961); see also Miller (1990).

28. Polyani (1962, corrected edition), Popper (1934/1959), Popper (1969).

29. Hadamard (1945), Penrose (1989), Whitehead (1927).

Chapter 2

1. The history of the early laboratories is well described in Boring (1929/1950); for a later assessment see Murray (1988).

2. Stevens's *Handbook of Experimental Psychology* (revised): Atkinson et al. (1988).

3. Dennett (1991), Ryle (1949).

4. Humphrey (1951).

5. Galton, (1883); see also the references given in note 1 for this and for the historical material in the rest of this chapter.

6. Binet (1903).

7. Minton and Schneider (1980).

8. Craik (1947).

9. This is described quite fully in Wozniak (1995).

10. Thorndike (1932).

11. Hull (1943).

12. One of the earliest and most incisive critics was J. A. Deutsch (1960). See also Koch (1954).

13. Berlyne (1960).

14. Lorenz (1970/1971); Tinbergen (1951). For a modern assessment of ethology and its role in behavioral science, see Ingle, Mansfield, and Goodale (1982).

15. Roitblatt et al. (1995).

16. Bartlett (1932). This book is a genuine classic in the field.

17. As an undergraduate I heard Bartlett give a rather positive assessment of American psychology. This was in the very early 1950s, when the yoke of behaviorism was still strong; Bartlett had just completed an extended visit to some of the major centers of experimental psychology in the United States. A nod to the scientific rigor of the behaviorist tradition was the then-current form of political correctness, even from so eminent a dissenter as Bartlett.

18. This has been called the Ebbinghaus tradition, after its founder. See Boring (1929/1950).

19. This approach is well represented by Neisser (1982). See also Baddeley (1993).

20. See Murray (1993) for an in-depth discussion of the origins of contemporary psychophysics and the responses thereto in *Behavioral and Brain Sciences*.

21. Koffka (1935) and Köhler (1929), both classics of the Gestalt literature.

22. Lashley (1942), Sperry, Miner, and Myers (1955).

23. This has recently been discussed in detail by Murray (1995).

24. This idea was first put forward in Gibson (1950) and subsequently developed in Gibson (1966).

25. Hebb (1949), another classic in the field.

26. All this historical material is treated in more detail, but essentially from the same point of view, in Dodwell (in preparation). See also Solso and Massaro (1995).

27. J. A. Deutsch (1955). For more general treatment, J. A. Deutsch (1960) is relevant. For more on this topic, see Dodwell (1970b) and Dodwell (in preparation).

28. See note 27; also Dodwell (1992a) for further elaboration on this theme.

29. Miller (1956).

30. Broadbent (1958).

31. Craik (1947).

32. The major work here so far as psychology is concerned is Wiener (1948). Other important work on machine-robotic simulations of human behavior are Ashby (1952) and Walter (1953), which contain many of the original ideas that bore fruit in later research. See also Anderson and Rosenfeld (1988).

33. Holst and Mittelstaedt (1950).

34. Cannon (1932).

35. Neisser (1982).

36. Neisser (1967).

37. The original work was described in the 1970s. Subsequently this has become a flourishing field of theory and research. See, for example, Kosslyn (1981), Kosslyn (1987), Paivio (1986), and Pinker (1997).

38. Shepard and Metzler (1971).

39. Cooper and Shepard (1973).

40. Personal communication, circa 1970, S. S. Stevens, sometime preeminent professor of psychophysics at Harvard University and mentor to many younger scholars, myself included.

41. E.g., Berman (1981), Dreyfus and Dreyfus (1986), Koestler (1967), Searle (1995).

Chapter 3

1. See Dodwell (in preparation).

2. Excellent descriptions of the achievements of modern neuroscience are to be found in a special issue of *Scientific American* (1992) and more specifically on neuroscience of the visual system in *Scientific American* (1988), which was also published as a book. Description of the early history of neuroscience of the visual system is to be found in Dodwell (1970b), which also contains a discussion of the theoretical importance of this type of research. Schiffman (1982) is a good standard textbook that explains much of the background material. A more recent account, but with less detail on neural action, is Bruce and Green (1990).

3. For more details see Schiffman (1982) or Hubel (1988). I am concentrating here on inter-neural communication; specialized neurons can also can have connections with muscles and sense organs. The coding of stimulus intensity by rate of firing is well established, but other possible properties of the temporal Morse-like code are less well understood.

4. *Scientific American* (1988), Edelman (1992), Kimble (1994).

5. Bagnoli and Hodos (1991), Blakemore (1978), Hubel and Wiesel (1985).

6. See Perrett et al. (1989) and Ono et al. (1993).

7. Goldman-Rakic (1992), also several other papers in *Scientific American* (1992).

8. See discussion of this point in Dodwell (1970b).

9. Spillman and Werner (1990), Adelman (1987), Luria (1973), Ono et al. (1993).

10. Boden (1987), Boden (1988), Gregory (1981).

11. Anderson (1964), Anderson and Rosenfeld (1988), Bolter (1984), Hofstaedter (1979), Pickover (1991), Sloman (1978).

12. I use the word *mentation* to cover everything we customarily recognize as mental activity—both conscious and unconscious. A denotation like this is, at present, more helpful than the attempt to make a watertight definition.

13. Urmson (1966), Hunter (1990).

14. For instance, Suppes (1957), or Hofstaedter (1979).

15. Gardner (1958), Gregory (1981).

16. See Hostfaedter (1979) for a splendid range of ideas and discussion on this topic.

17. Pitts and McCulloch (1947).

18. A field strongly promoted by the seminal book of Grossberg (1987).

19. Grimsdale et al. (1959).

20. Feldman (1985).

21. Marr (1976), Marr (1982).

22. For a general defense of this position, see Marr (1982).

23. Uhr (1966).

24. Newell and Simon (1972), Newell and Simon (1976).

25. Austin (1962), Koestler (1966), Polyani (1962, corrected edition), Turner (1985).

26. Winograd (1972), Hofstaedter (1979). A thoughtful if tendentious discussion of the problems and their attempted solutions is given by Pinker (1994).

27. An early champion of this view was Uhr (1966).

28. See Dodwell (in preparation), and also remarks on Ryle later in the chapter.

29. One of the more recent, and certainly quite entertaining essays in this genre is Dennett (1991).

30. Searle (1980); see also later work that expands his major themes: Searle (1990), Searle (1995).

31. See note 12 above. Mentation may include conscious thought and decision making, reasoning, daydreaming, recalling, reminiscing, believing, etc. Some people ask for a watertight definition, as they do for "consciousness." That is not a particularly profitable enterprise, in my view, although it has been attempted often enough.

32. See Dodwell (in preparation), note 30.

33. See Searle (1980), Searle (1990), and associated *Behavioral and Brain Sciences* commentary.

34. Searle (1994).

35. Newell (1991).

36. See Newell (1992), and associated *Behavioral and Brain Sciences* commentary, especially Dodwell (1992).

37. See, for example, Clark (1989), Fodor and Pylyshyn (1988), and, from a somewhat different approach, Grossberg (1987), Rumelhart and McClelland (1986); also Fodor (1985).

38. Buchanan (1948). This volume, containing the most famous of the Dialogues in Jowett's inimitable translation, is the best introduction to this source.

39. This was the learning mechanism proposed by Thorndike (1932), and kept alive in modern times by Skinner (1938), Skinner (1978), and Skinner's followers.

40. See Corballis (1991), chapters 5, 6, and 7, for a very good review of the development of human language.

41. Harris (1993), chapter 2, gives a succinct but excellent history of the development of linguistic science. For an earlier view, see Bloomfield (1933).

42. A distinction is made in linguistics between a transformation—the action of transforming—and a transform, which is the resultant when a transformation has been applied. In many other applications—for example, in geometry—the one word transformation covers both meanings.

43. There have been many other attempts to analyze meaning, one of the best-known being Ogden and Richards (1923). Chomsky's was the first to marry the analysis to such a dramatically wide-ranging theory of the formal elements of a grammar.

44. Lenneberg (1967).

45. Gibson (1966); Chomsky (1980), with associated *Behavioral and Brain Sciences* commentary.

46. Harris (1993) chapters 5 and 6. See also Corballis (1991), chapters 5 and 6.

47. Chomsky (1957).

48. Lenneberg (1967), Brown (1973), Gardner (1985), Miller (1977).

49. Pinker (1994).

50. Keller (1908). For more recent accounts and experimental research, see Kosslyn (1981), Paivio (1986).

51. A balanced assessment is to be found in Harris (1993).

52. See Harris (1993), chapter 10.

53. White (1983). This is a good introduction to the twentieth century analytic tradition in philosophy.

54. Dodwell (in preparation), Urmson (1966), Hunter (1990).

55. Ryle (1949). For recent sympathetic assessment of Ryle's contribution to the understanding of mind, see Priest (1991).

56. Bunge (1985), Bunge and Ardila (1987), Bunge (1990).

57. See, for example, Madsen (1985), with contributions by Bunge, Dodwell, and others.

58. E.g., Dennett (1991), Dennett (1979), Dennett (1987), Madsen (1985).

59. See, for example, Dennett (1991) and Dennett (1995).

60. See Dodwell (in preparation). For a very different and powerful account of the philosopher's role in cognitive science, see Rorty (1979).

61. See Austin (1962), Hunter (1990), and Kenny (1984).

62. Koestler (1967, xiii).

Chapter 4

1. Lockwood (1989), p. 1. There is an excellent discussion of this whole topic in his chapter 1. See also Sprigge (1971), pp. 167–68.

2. Popper and Eccles (1977).

3. See Parfit's paper in Blakemore and Greenfield (1987), p. 20; also Parfit (1984) and Wiggins (1967).

4. Sperry, the first major researcher in this area, became decidedly skeptical on the question of whether self can be identified simply as a function of brain integrity; Sperry (1983), but also Gazzaniga (1985).

5. See discussion by Nagel (1979), and also the discussion in Lockwood (1989). Brain integrity and the unity and continuity of the "stream of consciousness" is certainly a complicated and confusing field of investigation.

6. Hofstaedter and Dennett (1981), Dennett (1991), Dennett (1978).

7. Popper and Eccles (1977). Sir Karl Popper is widely acknowledged to be the most in-

fluential philosopher of science since Bertrand Russell; Sir John Eccles, Nobel laureate, a foremost neuroscientist of the twentieth century.

8. Dennett (1979).

9. Frege (1893/1964).

10. Popper and Eccles (1977), p. 61.

11. See van Rooijen (1987), and for further discussion see chapter 8.

12. Popper and Eccles (1977), p. 96.

13. Modern clinical neuropsychology has a different perspective on brain dysfunction and mathematics: see Dehaeme (1998).

14. See Stewart (1992) for discussion of recent developments in this field.

15. Not so long ago a fault in a widely used computer chip was announced, with serious consequences for some users. How was it discovered? By a mathematician at his desk, using a computer to facilitate his work!

16. Popper and Eccles (1977), p. 176.

17. For an especially sharp attack along these lines, see Bunge and Ardila (1987), chapter 1.

18. Bunge and Ardila (1987), Eccles (1987), Eccles (1993).

19. Henry Margenau, quoted by Eccles, in Blakemore and Greenfield (1987), p. 301.

20. To be sure, neuroscientists have identified units in monkey cortex that seem to fire as correlates of "intention" (Hietanen and Perrett, 1993) but for some reason that is not really obvious, this has not been seen as supporting evidence for the Eccles model.

21. Penrose (1989), Penrose (1994). See also Penrose (1990) and the associated *Behavioral and Brain Sciences* commentary.

22. See Wason and Johnson-Laird (1972) on the factors that affect "logical" thinking and decision making.

23. Piaget (1952), Piaget (1954), Piaget (1971).

24. Piatelli-Palmarini (1980). See also Karmiloff-Smith (1994).

25. There has been a great deal of research on this topic. See, for example, Siegler and Robinson (1982). Recent experimental work is described by Dehaeme (1997).

26. Goodman (1976).

27. This very important matter is dealt with fully in chapter 9.

28. Gleick (1987), Peitgen et al. (1993). Penrose (1994) has a nice discussion and illustration with the game of snooker to demonstrate the same point. The sensitivity to initial conditions is simply too great to allow for accurate prediction. This is also known as the "butterfly effect," the notion that a butterfly stirring the air in Peking can transform storm systems next month in New York. All the more remarkable, you might rejoin, as there is now no such place as Peking—at least in China!

29. Reyes et al. (1991), Macnamara and Reyes (1994).

30. See arguments in Dodwell (1992a) in response to Newell's views on the scope of AI modeling.

31. In a thoughtful review of *The Emperor's New Mind*, Aaron Sloman (1992) identifies no less than eight versions of the strong AI claim.

32. Hadamard (1945), Hardy (1967), Westfall (1980), among many others.

33. The nature of mathematical thinking is discussed further in chapter 7.

34. See, for example, Bell (1946), also Hardy (1967), Dunham (1990), and Wertheimer (1978).

35. Russell (1945), p. 28.

36. Penrose (1989). chapters 3, 4, and 5, and especially Penrose (1994), chapter 8. Also Penrose (1997).

37. Penrose (1994), pp. 64–65.

38. E.g., by Hofstaedter (1979), Stewart (1992), and Arbib (1964), among others.

39. An extensive debate among philosophers started with a controversial paper by Lucas (1961). See Hofstaedter (1979), p. 751.

40. Ryle (1949).

41. Bertrand Russell calls the passage in which our world is likened to a cave, whose denizens (i.e., us) see only shadows of the bright world outside (the world of "reality"), the most famous in Plato's writings.

42. Lockwood (1989), p. 8.

43. Zajonc (1993).

44. Penrose (1994), p. 350.

45. The idea of quantum computation is discussed by D. Deutsch (1985), D. Deutsch (1997), Lockwood (1989), as well as Penrose (1994).

46. To be fair to Penrose, he seems to be well aware of this point. In the very last pages of *Shadows of the Mind,* there are passages in which he sheds his mantle of Serious Scientist and admits with passion—almost with poetry—some of the self-imposed limitations of the physicist's view of reality. In this he is certainly not alone. To name only the most prominent, Einstein, Eddington, Jeans, Schroedinger, Heisenberg—even Newton, from a rather different perspective—have voiced similar sentiments. Polanyi's magnum opus sounds the same theme.

47. This would be disputed by those who claim to give a detailed natural history of the emergence of mind. We shall consider the ideas of the leading proponents of this theme in chapter 8.

Chapter 5

1. E.g., Dodwell (1975) and Dodwell (1977). The germ of the concept came to me much earlier; see Dodwell (1960).

2. Historically the background to these questions goes back especially to the Gestalt movement of the 1930s. There has been a strong revival of interest in more recent times. See for instance Beck (1982), Dodwell and Caelli (1984), Kubovy and Pomerantz (1981), Murray (1995).

3. The theoretical importance of reafference in animal perceptual systems was first described by Holst and Mittelstaedt (1950) in their work on stabilization of the perceptual field and its importance for motor control. The further distinction between reafference and exafference has played a leading role in subsequent perceptual theory; see, for example, Howard (1966).

4. Others have proposed different numbers of levels, from four to seven that I know of, on one basis or another; see, for example, Feldman (1985), Uttal (1981). I shall argue that, from the point of view of the logic of explanation, three suffice.

5. See, for example, Spillman and Werner (1990), one among many possibilities.

6. Gibson (1966) presents the best-argued position here; polemical to be sure, and often persuasive, if not always 100 percent convincing.

7. See, for example, Gardner (1985) or, to get the flavor from a classical source, Neisser (1967).

8. E.g., Dodwell (1975).

9. Helmholtz (1856–66/1962). This is made possible by the mathematical-physical theory of Fourier analysis that permits the resolution of a complex periodic repeating waveform into a series of sinewave components that differ in frequency and amplitude. Moore (1989).

10. Pickles (1988).

11. This may seem paradoxical because the whole science of acoustics arose from consideration of the nature of sensed tones. The psychical thus *preceded* the physical investigations. Nonetheless, considered purely as physical phenomena, acoustic signals do not entail or force on us the recognition of something we call tonal sensations. In that sense, it is correct to claim that, however tight the observed relation between the two may be, the one type of event does not explain the other. Of course there are physiological theories that purport to explain the transduction from physical signals to sensations, but that is another matter, which we shall address in due course.

12. The differences between a model and a theory will come up for consideration in chapter 9.

13. For example, chosen from a vast array of possibilities: Heil and Mele (1993), Mach (1883/1960), Nagel (1961), Polyani (1962, corrected edition), Popper (1934/1959), von Wright (1971).

14. See Dodwell (1960) for a full account of this.

15. Boring (1929/1950) gives an excellent summary of Hume's views, as of so much else in the history of psychology.

16. Von Wright (1971), for example, but the instances could be multiplied almost indefinitely.

17. We could relax this by accepting that the result could follow with a certain probability less than one, but that does not alter the fundamental tenor of the argument.

18. Psychophysics is a vast and active area of research and theory that we can barely touch on. See for instance Murray (1993).

19. I have changed my thinking on the way the levels should be defined and carved up. I used to base the taxonomy on the threefold division: sensation, perception, cognition. See Dodwell (1975), Dodwell (1993). Now, mainly for epistemological reasons but also in deference to the huge advances that have been made in sensory physiology these last few years, the proper division seems to me to be sensory physiology, sensory awareness and perceptual organization, cognition.

20. Such demonstrations are to be found in any textbook on perception, and often enough in introductory texts too. See, for example, relevant chapters in Grusec et al. (1990).

21. Those studies are outlined in chapter 3, but are described in any reasonably current book on vision, for example, Spillman and Werner (1990). Ono et al. (1993) is an advanced treatment and quite technical; for a more relaxed account see *Scientific American* (1988), *Scientific American* (1992).

22. Some theorists might want to call this sensation, but I prefer another term. Sensation has too much the flavor of simple elements, like the sense data or qualia dear to the hearts of philosophers. I am thinking of the organized wholes that are "presented" to us, in a manner of speaking, by our perceptual level 2 apparatus.

23. Some fascinating research has compared differences between chess masters and novices in the perception of, and memory for, pieces on a chessboard. Masters were enormously much better at remembering or reconstructing a game position than novices. When the pieces were placed randomly about the board, in contrast, both groups were equally poor at recalling the positions of the pieces. A nice demonstration, surely, of the difference between perception (a) and perception (b)! See Holding (1985); also, for a more recent treatment, Saarilouma (1995).

24. I don't want to press too far with this example, even though there are some fascinating avenues worth exploring. To hint at just one: Is it possible to define the empirical conditions at level 2 that make the game possible? After all, it can be played from memory, there are blind people who excel at it, computers can do it, and so on. None of this affects or distracts from the argument that we have to proceed to level 3 to get anywhere with compre-

hending what the game is, and that before that can happen sensory events (level 2) of one sort or another must occur.

25. See Macnamara and Reyes (1994), Reyes et al. (1991).

26. This aspect of Gestalt psychology has been largely forgotten, although it was a mainstay of its theoretical position. A recent book by David Murray (1995) will, one hopes, rekindle interest in a neglected but important aspect of the Gestalt school. Wertheimer's work on problem solving is a classic in the field, and makes great use of the idea that the perceptual form in which a problem is posed is integral to the ease of its solution.

27. One might question the assertion that there is such a thing as "pure" cognition, which can occur in the absence of any perceptual activity whatsoever. The point is a good one, but I shall defer it to chapter 8.

28. Research on cognition, specifically on reasoning, is replete with examples of this sort. See, for example, the classical work of Wason and Johnson-Laird (1972) referred to earlier.

29. A *teleological* explanation is one that involves the Aristotelian "final cause": that is, it is an explanation that invokes the purpose for which the activity is engendered, as opposed to the "efficient cause," which identifies the immediate antecedent to an action, as in the setting in motion of the proverbial billiard ball.

30. A particularly thoughtful and incisive account of these matters is given by von Wright (1971), whose monograph is very clear, wide-ranging, and quite a bit less Anglocentric than most other treatises on scientific explanation written in English.

31. Campbell (1920/1957). This is an old but insightful account of the place of theory in science. See also Frank (1957) for an immensely learned and erudite account of theory in science and of science in the general culture.

32. It could be argued that development requires another dimension of the taxonomy, itself orthogonal to the two dimensions of the present array. It would be an interesting exercise to work this out, but it lies beyond the scope of this chapter.

33. See, for example, Geschwind (1974), Milner and Goodale (1993), Mishkin et al. (1983), Ono et al. (1993), and Penfield (1977).

34. Many of the original ideas in this field were proposed by Uttley (1954), Uttley (1959). For modern treatment, see Carpenter (1989).

35. Further consideration of these matters is to be found in Abraham and Shaw (1992), Boden (1987), Boden (1988), Dennett (1991), Hofstaedter (1979), Hofstaedter and Dennett (1981), and Macnamara (1986).

Chapter 6.

1. This theme is ubiquitous in Gibson's writing. For its earliest, and perhaps clearest, statement, see Gibson (1950).

2. See, for example, Cutting (1986).

3. See Dodwell (1970b); Fodor and Pylyshyn (1988).

4. Ingle, Mansfield, and Goodale (1982), Lorenz (1970/1971), Tinbergen (1951).

5. Gibson (1979).

6. It was pointed out by Zusne (1970) that Gibson's theorizing would have benefited if he had had a greater familiarity with the mathematical modeling of perception being explored in his day.

7. Including myself at an earlier time! This is especially evident in Dodwell (1970b).

8. See, for example, Feldman (1985) and Marr (1982).

9. For more detailed criticism of Gibson's various positions, see Dodwell (1970b) and Dodwell (1994).

10. E.g., Caelli and Dodwell (1982), Gallant et al. (1993), Perrett et al. (1989).

11. Andrews (1964).

12. There have been attempts to model the process, but they are speculative, for example, Andrews (1967). Subsequent attempts have aimed more at the matter of texture perception than the representation of extended contours. See, for example, Zucker (1984).

13. This work, as so much in perception, originates with Helmholtz, but the first systematic studies were done by Stratton (1897). The heyday of investigation into adaptation to *rearrangement,* as it came to be called, occurred in the 1950s and 1960s. See, for example, Dolezal (1982).

14. See, for example, Dodwell (1970a), Dodwell (1992a) for the history and recent trends in this field.

15. The major work is Helson (1964). His ideas were originally propounded in 1938, and have subsequently been refined and further quantified, but the basic concept still stands.

16. The term *constancy* also has another more technical meaning, to be discussed shortly.

17. It is remarkable that Gibson made some distinguished contributions to the study of adaptational phenomena as a young man, but that seemed to play no part in the rather fixed conception he later championed of the relations between a perceiving system and its stimulating array. The AL phenomena seem to contradict very directly the later Gibsonian theory.

18. I am not talking here of the traditional illusions like the Müller-Lyer, although these are indeed special instances of the problem we are addressing. See Dodwell (1990).

19. Andrews (1964).

20. Andrews (1964), p. 104.

21. But see, for example, Dodwell and Humphrey (1990) for a general discussion, and the application of Andrews's model to an interesting and unusual set of adaptational phenomena.

22. In the accepted language of geometry, a translation is a uniform displacement in a single direction.

23. The primary references are Hoffman (1966), Hoffman (1970), Hoffman (1980). A fairly nontechnical introduction is given in Dodwell (1983). The relation to Gestalt psychology, which from one point of view Hoffman's theory completes and elaborates, is given in Hoffman and Dodwell (1985). For recent assessments of the theory's strengths in application, see Dodwell (1992a) and Dodwell (1994).

24. *Perceptual constancy* is a technical term, and refers to the fact, ubiquitous in perception, that the perceived properties of things (their shapes, sizes and colors, for instance) vary much less than the properties of a fluctuating stimulus array alone predict, or would lead one to expect.

25. Hoffman (1970).

26. Gallant et al. (1993).

27. A conformal transformation, or mapping, is expressed in terms of complex numbers. It takes points, lines, and other features from one complex plane to another, preserving some properties such as the angle at which pairs of contours intersect, but allowing great freedom in others, for example, line orientation, curvature, and position. See Dodwell (1970b), chapter 8, for a brief review of these mappings.

28. For details see Dodwell (1967), Dodwell (1970b).

29. Hoffman and Dodwell (1985) p. 521.

30. Gibson (1966).

31. Dodwell (1970b), chapter 10.

32. Hoffman (1984), Hoffman (1994).

33. On this, see Hoffman (1985) and note 28.

34. The most relevant papers are Hoffman (1970), Hoffman (1984), and Hoffman (1985).

35. More on this important matter can be found in Dodwell (1983). Similar ideas have been expressed by Carlton and Shepard (1990).

Chapter 7

1. *The Concise Oxford Dictionary* (1990).

2. See Stewart (1992) for an engaging and not-too-demanding quick tour of some of the highlights of modern mathematics; one of several attractive possibilities.

3. Stewart (1975). Like other definitions, the axioms and rules of inference of an axiomatic system are not open to question or verification; the only question of importance is whether they are consistent and relevant to the matter under investigation. See also the discussion in chapters 4 and 5.

4. See Rennie and Girle (1973), p. 106, for a discussion of this point.

5. The actual proof involves a double use of the inductive method, first to show that the nth odd number has the form $2(n - 1) + 1$, and from that to establish that the sum of the first n odd numbers is $n \times n$, or n^2. There are other ways of demonstrating this truth about odd numbers, but our example is a simple way of getting a feel for how mathematical proof works.

6. If you are imagining it, you may have trouble establishing that opposite corners are the same color. Think of it this way; if the bottom right-hand square is black, the upper right-hand square must be white, because the colors alternate within the right-hand column of eight squares. Now go across the top row, right to left. The colors still alternate, so if the top right-hand one is white, the top left-hand one must be black: that is, the same color as the bottom right-hand square.

7. There have been many attempts to present mathematics and its teaching to young children in interesting ways. One of the very best, and my favorite, is Liebeck (1984).

8. If, once you saw the solution to the chessboard problem, you immediately started to wonder whether the rule holds for "chessboards" of other sizes—4×4 or 9×9, say—or boards with three colors of squares (can there be such a thing?) or in three or more(!) dimensions, then you certainly have a bent for mathematical inquiry, or at least an appreciation of what makes for fascination in such inquiry.

9. There are many fine expositions of this important matter. Some recent essays include Davies (1983), Davies and Brown (1986), Hawking (1988), Hodgson (1991), Lockwood (1989), Penrose (1989).

10. Bertrand Russell was one of the first, but by no means the only, proponent of this view. In fact he sought to establish the logical basis of mathematics on the most elementary distinction between *this* and *that,* or *not this.* What simpler abstraction could there be?.

11. In a long and very influential series of monographs the Swiss child psychologist Jean Piaget described and analyzed children's ability to understand concepts of number, space, causality, and similar ideas: for example, Piaget (1952), Piaget (1953), Piaget (1954), Piaget (1971). Subsequent research has by no means supported all of his claims, but his general approach to intelligence as a dynamic, interactive, biologically based capacity of the growing young mind to adapt to its increasingly complex *Umwelt* has had a deep impact on cognitive science, not dissimilar from the Chomskyan revolution in its account of the child's acquisition of language. See Karmiloff-Smith (1994).

12. As propounded most famously in the philosophy of Immanuel Kant (1724–1804). He wrote, in his *Prolegomena to Any Future Metaphysics:* "It happens, that though we cannot

assume metaphysics to be an actual science, we can say with confidence that certain pure a priori synthetical cognitions, pure mathematics and pure physics, are actual and given; for both contain propositions which are thoroughly recognized as absolutely certain, and yet as independent of experience. We have therefore some at least uncontested synthetical knowledge a priori, and need not ask whether it be possible for it is actual." Quoted by Frank (1957), pp. 50–51. See also Popper (1969), chapter 2.

13. This dramatic turn of events has been often described. A good account of the matter, including much of the historical background, is given in Dunham (1990).

14. See, for example, Polyani (1962, corrected edition), chapter 1.

15. The conic sections are ellipses (of which circles are a special case), parabolas, and hyperbolas.

16. Whitehead (undated, circa 1912), chapter 10. The reference here is to Kepler's discovery that the orbits of the planets are ellipses—conic sections!—with the sun at one focus, a model of the solar system that fits with Newton's inverse square law of gravitational attraction.

17. See Stewart (1992), passim, but especially chapter 9.

18. Bell (1937), Hardy (1967).

19. In general this is true, and we can ignore the special case, as in a set of weights and measures, in which there is a preordained rule relating one weight to another—generally a mathematically expressed rule, be it noted.

20. It also depends, as we now understand, on the interpretation of the mathematical signs and symbols as having reference to what common sense calls numbers.

21. Fermat's last theorem is a splendid example. It states that for all integer values of n greater than 2, there is no solution to the equation $x^n + y^n = z^n$. For a couple of hundred years this seemingly innocent and simple conjecture defied proof, despite the best efforts of many leading mathematicians. Fermat claimed to have a simple proof that he didn't bother to write down! As I understand it, the extremely complicated proof recently found has not satisfied all of the cognoscenti, so evidently the theorem still rests in limbo—for the moment.

22. It would be instructive to pursue this theme but would lead too far afield. An excellent introduction to this aspect of mathematical creation and discovery is given in Dunham (1990).

23. Campbell (1920/1957).

24. Some remarks on the origins of arithmetic and geometry can be found in the first chapter of Dunham (1990), another splendid introduction to mathematics, especially in its historical and creative contexts.

25. Heath (1921).

26. This is well described by Dunham (1990). See also Heath (1921).

27. Vitruvius, quoted by Heath, thus remarked about great men who possessed an equally profound knowledge of all branches of science, geometry, astronomy, music, etc.: "Men of this type are rare, men such as were, in times past, Aristarchus of Samos . . . Appolonius of Perga . . . Archimedes and Scopinas of Syracuse, who left to posterity many mechanical and gnomonic appliances which they invented and explained on mathematical [lit. "numerical"] principles" (Heath (1921), vol. 2, p. 1).

28. Piaget and his followers have made much of the fact that, important as environmental stimulation is, the drive to represent, organize, and use the fruits of cognitive effort cannot be explained thereby. The human mind in its developmental aspects is simply too virtuosic, too focused and too subtle to be captured by the notion of a passive processor of environmental inputs. See especially Piaget (1952), Piaget (1954), Bruner (1986), Halford (1982).

29. The study of imagery in the modern era was initiated by D. O. Hebb, as we have discussed. Much important work, both theoretical and experimental, has appeared subsequently.

For instance, Kosslyn (1981), Kosslyn (1987), Neisser (1967), Paivio (1986) among many others. Pinker (1985) has a good selection of relevant papers.

30. Shepard and Metzler (1971).

31. This quality is found in other highly creative individuals too, of course. Perhaps the preeminent example in modern times is found in the compulsive outpouring of poetry and poetic images in the young Goethe (Fairley, 1947).

32. Hinson (1990).

33. There are many books on the history of numbers and mathematics, and their role in the unfolding of our culture and the development of science. Three very different perspectives are given by Bell (1946), Hofstaedter (1979), Schimmel (1993).

34. These ideas are laid out in a series of monographs by Piaget, including those already cited (note 11). The empirical support for Piaget's theories is not exactly solid, but the conception of how rational thinking develops in the child is nevertheless insightful, and helpful. See Siegler and Robinson (1982).

35. Some neuropsychologists dispute Piaget's account. See, for example, Dehaeme (1998).

36. This and the following section owe much to the discussion in Dunham (1990).

37. The nomenclature of mathematics is often odd, even bizarre, but sanctioned by tradition. There is nothing nonrational about the irrational numbers, for instance! Incidentally there are rational numbers, too, that have decimal equivalents that do not terminate, but in those cases the decimal number displays a repeating pattern; for example, $\frac{1}{7} = 0.142857142857$ . . . ad infinitum. The decimal expression of an irrational number never has a repeating pattern of this sort.

38. See note 37.

39. Not quite, of course. We should more properly say that it is an ideal that is frequently, but never perfectly, reflected in nature. See chapter 9 for discussion of the place of ideals in human cognition.

40. Note that this is not in itself the defining characteristic of a transcendental number, as many other numbers share the property. See note 37.

41. The expression $n!$ is $1 \times 2 \times 3$ . . . $\times n$, and is called "n factorial."

42. See note 39, however.

43. See note 37.

44. Stewart (1992), p. 157. Chapter 12 of this book gives an excellent review of the discovery and exploitation of imaginary numbers. Analysis is the branch of mathematics that explores, usually with the tools of set theory and calculus, the nature of "functions." These can be thought of, generally, as expressions relating variables like x to its powers, $\sin x$, $\log x$, and so on.

45. *Cos* and *sin* are the universally used abbreviations for the cosine and sine trigonometric ratios.

46. Somewhat simplified for the sake of exposition, I'm afraid, but the essentials are correct. In what follows the radian measure of angle is used, so π radians = 180°; by ordinary trigonometry $\cos 180 = -1$, and $\sin 180 = 0$.

47. Stewart (1992), p. 157.

48. Stewart (1992), p. 161.

49. See note 16.

50. Quoted by Dunham (1990), p. 286, from Russell (1951).

51. Quoted by Shear (1990), from Poincaré (1908/1968).

52. Quoted from correspondence in Hadamard (1945), reprinted in Einstein (1979), pp. 35–36, and quoted by Shear (1990), p. 130.

53. From Einstein (1979), quoted by Shear (1990), p. 131.

54. This point is well documented and discussed in a level-headed way by Shear (1990), especially his chapter 6; also chapter 8, this volume.

55. See Dehaeme (1998) for a good recent account of this.

Chapter 8

1. *Prediction* is here used in the somewhat loose way unfortunately sanctioned by tradition, not in the strict sense defined in chapter 5. We are considering *deductions* from the model.

2. Ballard et al. (1983), Ballard (1986), Grossberg (1987).

3. There is now an extensive literature on children's attribution of memory, motive, and intention to others, that is, on their discovery of "other minds"—for example, Carey and Gelman (1991).

4. The argument is as old as Socrates himself. See Hofstaedter (1979) and Hawking (1988) for some intriguing variations on this theme.

5. Davies (1983), Davies and Brown (1986), and Hawking (1988) present concepts of modern physics for the nonspecialist; also Capra (1982), who gives a more apocalyptic view. See also note 6.

6. The most prominent and fully thought out of these are Hodgson (1991), Jahn and Dunne (1987), Lockwood (1989). All of them are excellent, and well worth study. Lockwood is a philosopher, Hodgson a high court judge, Jahn an engineer. Each work in its own way is an intellectual tour de force.

7. I am referring to the so-called Copenhagen interpretation; see Hodgson (1991), p. 321, also Lockwood (1989), especially chapter 13.

8. These incongruities and anomalies are well described in the references of notes 5 and 6. A delightful book devoted exclusively to this theme, with an intriguing title, derived from one of the most famous of the quantum "thought experiments" that lead to startling paradoxes about the nature of the world, is *Schroedinger's Kittens* (Gribbin, 1995).

9. Bunge and Ardila (1987).

10. Typical of the latter is Newell's remark in his *Unified Theories of Cognition:* "All along, I keep referring to predictions. This is simply shorthand for all the various uses of descriptions, such as explaining behavior, controlling behavior, or constructing something that behaves to specifications. Although there are differences in these activities and some descriptions are more suited to one than another, it became tiresome to be explicit each and every time. 'Prediction' will cover them all" (1991, p. 48). Such remarks obviously are directly counter to my position, and in fact serve to obscure some of the most vital distinctions that need to be made in cognitive science. See Dodwell (1992a).

11. It is the very pinnacle of objectivity identified by T. Nagel (1986) in *The View from Nowhere*. That, however, as he so persuasively argues, is only one stance from which to attempt to come to grips with reality; there must be others.

12. E.g., Morris (1989).

13. See, for example, Penrose (1994), chapter 7.

14. A good early discussion is to be found in Uhr (1966). See also Ashby (1952), Uttley (1954), and Uttley (1959).

15. Gregory (1981).

16. Hodgson (1991), especially in regard to the present question: see his chapter 16.

17. Examples of the first type are Edelman (1992), Newell (1991), Shank (1982); of the latter, Dreyfus and Dreyfus (1986), Polanyi (1966), Polyani (1962, corrected edition), Popper and Eccles (1977).

18. Kolers and Smythe (1984).

19. I have given only the bare outline of one part of Kolers and Smythe's case against the computational view of mind, which rests principally on the distinction between dense and articulated symbol systems propounded by Goodman (1976).

20. Chomsky (1957); cf. chapter 3.

21. On this point, see Lockwood's remarks on Churchland's account of color vision; Lockwood (1989), chapter 8, this volume.

22. It is true that this claim to some extent begs the question of the priority of folk psychological concepts and language. Logically it is conceivable that someone could come up with an alternative system that dispenses with them. No one who really understands the problem has the faintest idea how this might be done. Earlier attempts never came anywhere near an approximation of a satisfactory substitute. Most consistent attempts, such as those of Hull and Skinner, have been dismal failures. They did, however, at least acknowledge their ambition to replace folk psychology radically without borrowing from it. The AI and similar programs aim to replace it by sleight-of-hand, importing its magic by the back door.

23. This is true even of students of language, the very attribute that is held to distinguish us humans from other creatures. You can look in vain in Jackendoff (1987) and Pinker (1994), for example, for anything that denies, extends, or otherwise rejuvenates or replaces the image of humankind promulgated in the standard model.

24. I am considering general theories here, such as a theory of the nature of memory, rather than restricted models for particular abilities such as episodic memory. Notice that the latter always occur in the context of some more general (if still implicit) theory, so do not escape the point I am making about self-reference.

25. See, for example, MacKay (1967).

26. E.g., Popper (1959/1934) among many others.

27. This point is eloquently and elegantly set out by Polanyi (1962).

28. The power of theory in physics is epitomized in the aphorism attributed, I believe, to the great theoretician Louis de Broglie: "If the facts don't fit the theory, so much the worse for the facts!".

29. Dodwell (1960).

30. Peters (1960).

31. *Jiggering:* A way of fishing in a brook. The angler (likely a young boy), lying on the bank, slips his hand stealthily under the unsuspecting victim's belly and tickles it into repose. Then, with a flick of the wrist, the dirty deed is done, and the fish lies expiring on the bank. A similar mortal end awaits any mental event haplessly lured into the delicate clutches of a quantum theorist!.

32. Some recent examples of note are Corballis (1991), Donald (1991), and Humphrey (1992). Young (1987) also gives a well-reasoned account of the genesis of mind from a biologist's perspective.

33. There have been very many attempts to establish this, including those noted in the previous footnote. A fierce defender of this faith is Dawkins (1986), Dawkins (1995), whose arguments are very persuasive. Other thoughtful essays include Thorpe (1978), Young (1987), and various authors in Blakemore and Greenfield (1987).

34. Nagel (1974), p. 1.

35. Honderich (1988).

36. Putnam (1988).

37. See, for example, Hofstaedter and Dennett (1981).

38. Turner (1985).

39. The identification of the logical and linguistic subtleties underlying the theory of

syllogistic reasoning have been identified and analyzed by Reyes et al. (1991) and by Macna-mara and Reyes (1994). These matters are far from straightforward, but this is not the place to enter into them.

40. Francesco Redi (1626–1698), Italian doctor, scientist, and poet. The new doctrine is given in his major work, *Osservazioni Intorno agli Animali Viventi* (1684).

41. These days we like to think of ourselves as far too civilized and sophisticated to con-template such drastic remedies. Yet the orthodox defense of science against novel and heretical ideas is still just as angry and ready to fight as in the seventeenth century. The only difference is that today we talk of burning the heretic's books, not his body. If you don't believe me, see Sheldrake (1987). In the later editions of this book the appallingly narrow-minded response of the scientific establishment to his views is outlined, including the recommendation of at least one reviewer that the book was worthy only of consignment to the flames.

42. This is a favorite theme of many biologists, and is an oft-told tale. One very convincing account is give by Dawkins (1986).

43. Popper (1934/1959), Popper (1969).

44. Ackerman (1976).

45. Stove (1982).

46. See Esterson (1993) on Freud, for example. The question of verifiability is some-thing else. The great strength of Darwin's theory and its modern derivatives is the enormous weight of evidence that is consistent with the concept of natural selection, including recent observation of the selection within a few generations of features favorable to survival. My point is not to deny any of this—it is empirical science at its best. But the fact remains that evolutionary *theory* is not in any ordinary sense falsifiable as far as its adherents are concerned.

47. See, for example, Watson (1951).

48. There will be many intermediate forms between one successful species and a new form derived from it that has survival value. These "drop out" and leave no trace, yet they are a vital part of the evolutionary process.

49. See Barfield (1988).

Chapter 9

1. Fairley (1947), especially chapter 9.

2. This is an oft-told tale. See, for example, Bernal (1969), volume 2.

3. Lorenz (1970/1971).

4. Some might object to the term *sacred* (also equated with *inviolate* in my thesaurus); at least it serves to remind us of Coleridge's rich image.

5. Shear (1990), p. 106.

6. To take a leaf from Donald (1991).

7. James (1890), pp. 297–298. See also Priest (1991), p. 152.

8. There is of course a huge literature on dynamic psychology. One recent source book is Shamdanasi and Munchow (1994).

9. For excellent examples of the best research in this tradition, see Grusec et al. (1990).

10. Guilford (1967), Sternberg and Detterman (1986), Sternberg (1990). A perhaps more enterprising approach has been taken in AI. See, for example, Hofstaedter (1997).

11. Turner (1985). The concept of vehicle is not developed expressly by Turner, but it conveys the essence of his message. A fascinating glimpse of what this can mean in the world of modern theater is provided by commentary on Samuel Beckett as producer of his own plays (Gontarski, 1985).

12. Polanyi (1962, corrected edition). Michael Polanyi took a decade out of his research

career to bring to fruition his thoughts on epistemology, scientific creativity, and personal knowledge in general. His work, which has been sadly neglected, is chock full of interesting ideas, compelling descriptions of the nature of deep research creativity, and commentary on the human condition.

13. Popper (1969).

14. Penrose says that his conception of the three worlds is only "somewhat related" to Popper's; despite a difference in emphasis, the basic idea seems to be very much the same, as we shall discuss.

15. See Wigner (1967).

16. Penrose (1994), p. 416.

17. Penrose (1994), p. 418.

18. Polanyi (1962, corrected edition), especially chapter 11.

19. Polanyi (1962, corrected edition); he would undoubtedly have approved of Marr's later account of the three levels of description and analysis of a calculating machine (see chapter 6, this volume). Notice that the recent thread we have identified that seeks for understanding of mental phenomena precisely in some advance in the laws of physics is diametrically opposed to Polanyi's distinction between technological and scientific understanding.

20. A somewhat related point is made from the viewpoint of an experimental physicist by P. W. Anderson (1994) in his review of *Shadows of the Mind*.

21. Leyton (1992). In this regard the work of D'Arcy Thompson (1917) was pioneering. New and often surprising applications of mathematics, and indeed new mathematics per se, are continually being discovered and developed. Recent examples are found in chaos theory, fractal geometry, and applications of group theory to concepts of causal sequence. See, for example, Gleick (1987), Peitgen et al. (1993), and Waldrop (1992) on the former, Leyton (1992) on the latter. On the need for a new understanding of the laws of morphogenesis, see Sheldrake (1987).

22. For example, Carlton and Shepard (1990). See also the extensive and often elaborate analyses of visual and other sensory functions, in research journals such as *Spatial Vision, Vision Research,* and the journals of the Optical and Acoustical Societies of America.

23. Macnamara (1990). See also his related earlier discussions in Macnamara (1986).

24. Hobbes (1651/1958).

25. Robert Hooke (1635–1703), one of the first scientists to make systematic use of the microscope in his investigations, demonstrated how far the perceived nature of point and line are from the ideals of geometric objects. What appears to the naked eye as a "perfect" line, for example, the edge of a very sharp knife, is seen under the microscope to be quite flawed. From this he did not draw the conclusion, as we now do, that the ideals transcend their physical exemplars, only that the apparent congruence between the two is based on an optical limitation! As we have seen, the teasing apart of the formal, ideal nature of geometry from the realization of a particular geometry in its application to terrestrial circumstances was anything but a simple intellectual achievement, and only occurred in the nineteenth century.

26. The distinction is the same as that between the sacred and the profane (in the original meaning of that word). Why is the river of our metaphor sacred? Because it is the carrier of ideals!

27. Polanyi (1962, corrected edition), p. 64.

28. Examples abound, of course. One very salient example in the field of visual art is Arnheim (1982).

29. Crook (1980), Davies and Humphreys (1993). The latter has been described as the best anthology on consciousness to date.

30. There is lively debate about this matter. One of the most impressive experimental and theoretical programs is the PEAR initiative. See Jahn and Dunne (1987). As I mentioned

earlier, the recent appearance of two new journals concerned with the study of consciousness is a hopeful sign that the topic is resurfacing as an object of serious scientific investigation (see the preface to this volume).

31. Shear (1990).

32. Shear (1990), p. 1.

33. Becker (1993), Green and McCreery (1995), Grey (1985), Moody (1981), Tart (1975). These authors all emphasize the coherence and consistency across cultures, etc., of such accounts. See also note 30.

34. It is undeniably true that unusual states of consciousness and similar matters have attracted the attention of the lunatic fringe, as well as the unwary, but this is not reason to dismiss them out of hand. Science has always required its practitioners to be capable of sorting the seed from the chaff. See Colman (1995), Wilson (1998).

35. A fine example is Hofstaedter (1979).

36. Baddeley (1990). For a broad look at memory, see Butler (1989).

37. A great survey of this legacy is Kenneth Clarke's *Civilization* (1969), far more searching and worthwhile than the TV series of that name from which it originated. It should be required reading for any aspirant to a well-rounded appreciation of our cultural heritage, and especially for one who intends to study cognitive science. The same might be said of the more recent, and also excellent, *The Passion of the Western Mind* by Richard Tarnas (1993) and *The Gifts of the Jews* by Thomas Cahill (1998).

38. The earliest version was couched in terms of motives and justification (see Peters [1960]), and later it was made more general. See also Hamlyn (1957) and Dodwell (1960).

39. Macnamara made some progress in this direction in linguistics, and in the relation of logic to psychology. See Macnamara (1986).

40. A question of immense import to an earlier generation—see, for example, Lyall (1855)—but seldom raised in contemporary debate. See, however, Harré and Gillett (1994), Shotter (1975), and Shotter (1993).

41. MacKay (1967). As the American scientist Lyall Watson put it: "If the brain were so simple we could understand it, we would be so simple we couldn't."

42. One form of this argument was I believe given by Edmund Husserl (1890/1982). A closely related one goes back to the philosophy of Democritus; see Lockwood (1989).

43. Expressed in terms of ideals, Macnamara would want to do so too. He has argued for the close similarity in relation that holds between mathematics and physics, on the one hand, and logic and psychology, on the other. In both cases the role of $w3$ enters into the discussion in an essential way, obviously enough. See Macnamara (1990).

44. Some good examples of both types are to be found in various chapters of *Mindwaves* (Blakemore and Greenfield, 1987), and are the staple fare of most contemporary experimental (including cognitive) psychology.

45. Toulmin (1970), p. 3.

46. I did not say that intervention and control are not possible; but they are or should be in the province of technological application, rather than the science of pure discovery.

47. Especially insightful here is the work of Barfield (1952).

48. Shear (1990).

49. Clarke (1969).

50. For a splendid tour through the history of mathematics, see Dunham's *Journey through Genius* (1990), mentioned already in chapter 7.

References

Abraham, R. H., and Shaw, C. D. (1992). *Dynamics, the Geometry of Behavior.* (2nd ed.). Reading, MA: Addison-Wesley.

Ackerman, R. J. (1976). *The Philosophy of Karl Popper.* Amherst: University of Massachusetts Press.

Adelman, G. (Ed.). (1987). *Encyclopedia of Neuroscience.* 2 vols. Boston: Birkhaeuser.

Anderson, A. R. (Ed.). (1964). *Minds and Machines.* Englewood Cliffs, NJ: Prentice-Hall.

Anderson, J. A., and Rosenfeld, E. (Eds.). (1988). *Neurocomputing: Foundations of Research.* Cambridge, MA: MIT Press.

Anderson, J. R. (1987). Methodologies for studying human knowledge. *The Behavioral and Brain Sciences, 10,* 467–505.

Anderson, P. W. (1994). Shadows of doubt. [Review of Penrose (1994)]. *Nature, 372,* 288–289.

Andrews, D. P. (1964). Error-correcting perceptual mechanisms. *Quarterly Journal of Experimental Psychology 16,* 104–115.

Andrews, D. P. (1967). Perception of contour orientation in the central fovea, part 2: Spatial integration. *Vision Research, 7,* 999–1013.

Arbib, M. A. (1964). *Brains, Machines, and Mathematics.* New York: McGraw-Hill.

Armstrong, D. M. (1968). *A Materialist Theory of the Mind.* London: Routledge and Kegan Paul.

Arnheim, R. (1982). *The Power of the Center.* Berkeley: University of California Press.

Ashby, W. R. (1952). *Design for a Brain: The Origin of Adaptive Behavior.* New York: Wiley.

Atkinson, R. C., Herrnstein, R. J., Lindzey, G., and Luce, R. D. (Eds.). (1988). *Stevens' Handbook of Experimental Psychology.* New York: Wiley.

Austin, J. L. (1962). *How to Do Things with Words.* Oxford: Clarendon Press.

Ayer, A. J. (1936/1946). *Language, Truth, and Logic.* London: Gollancz.

Backus, J. (1969). *The Acoustical Foundations of Music.* New York: Norton.

Baddeley, A. (1990). *Human Memory: Theory and Practice.* Hove, U.K.: Erlbaum.

Baddeley, A. D. (1993). *Your Memory: A User's Guide.* 2nd ed. Harmondsworth, U.K.: Penguin.

Bagnoli, P., and Hodos W. (Eds.). (1991). *The Changing Visual System: Maturation and Aging in the Central Nervous System.* New York: Plenum.

Ballard, D. H. (1986). Cortical connections and parallel processing: Structure and function. *The Behavioral and Brain Sciences, 9,* 67–120.

Ballard, D. H., Hinton, G. E., and Sejnowski, T. J. (1983). Parallel visual computation. *Nature, 306,* 21–26.

Barfield, O. (1952). *Poetic Diction: A Study in Meaning.* Orig. pub., 1928. London: Faber and Faber.

Barfield, O. (1988). *Saving the Appearances.* 2nd ed.; orig. pub., 1957. Middleton, CT: Wesleyan University Press.

Bartlett, F. C. (1932). *Remembering.* Cambridge: Cambridge University Press.

Beck, J. (Ed.). (1982). *Organization and Representation in Perception.* Hillsdale, NJ: Erlbaum.

Becker, C. B. (1993). *Paranormal Experience and Survival of Death.* Albany: State University of New York Press.

Bell, E. T. (1937). *Men of Mathematics.* New York: Simon and Schuster.

Bell, E. T. (1946). *The Magic of Numbers.* New York: McGraw-Hill (Whittelsey House).

Berlyne, D. E. (1960). *Conflict, Arousal, and Curiosity.* New York: McGraw-Hill.

Berman, M. (1981). *The Reenchantment of the World.* Ithaca, NY: Cornell University Press.

Bernal, J. D. (1969). *Science in History.* London: C. A. Watts/Pelican Books.

Binet, A. (1903). *L'Etude Experimentale de l'Intelligence.* Paris: Schleicher.

Blakemore, C. (1978). Maturation and modification in the developing visual system. In R. Held, H. Leibowitz, and H. Teuber (Eds.), *Handbook of Sensory Physiology.* New York: Springer.

Blakemore, C., and Greenfield, S. (Eds.). (1987). *Mindwaves.* Oxford: Blackwell.

Bloomfield, L. (1933). *Language.* New York: Holt, Reinhart and Winston.

Bode, C. (1946). *The Portable Emerson.* New York: Viking Penguin.

Boden, M. A. (1987). *Artificial Intelligence and Natural Man.* 2nd ed. New York: Basic Books.

Boden, M. A. (1988). *Computer Models of Mind: Computational Approaches in Theoretical Psychology.* Cambridge: Cambridge University Press.

Bolter, J. D. (1984). *Turing's Man: Western Culture in the Computer Age.* London: Duckworth.

Boring, E. G. (1929/1950). *A History of Experimental Psychology.* New York: Appleton-Century-Crofts.

Broadbent, D. E. (1958). *Perception and Communication.* New York: Pergamon.

Bronowski, J. (1973). *The Ascent of Man.* New York: Little, Brown.

Brown, R. (1973). *A First Language: The Early Stages.* Cambridge, MA: Harvard University Press.

Bruce, V., and Green, P. (1990). *Visual Perception: Physiology, Psychology, and Ecology.* 2nd ed. London: Erlbaum.

Bruner, J. (1986). *Actual Minds, Possible Worlds.* Cambridge, MA: Harvard University Press.

Buchanan, S. (Ed.). (1948). *The Portable Plato.* New York: Viking.

Bunge, M. (1980). *The Mind-Body Problem: A Psychobiological Approach.* Oxford: Pergamon.

Bunge, M. (1985). From mindless neuroscience and brainless psychology to neuropsychology. *Annals of Theoretical Psychology, 3,* 115–133.

Bunge, M. (1990). What kind of discipline is psychology: Autonomous or dependent, humanistic or scientific, biological or sociological? *New Ideas in Psychology*, 8(2), 121–137.

Bunge, M., and Ardila, R. (1987). *Philosophy of Psychology*. New York: Springer.

Butler, T. (Ed.). (1989). *Memory: History, Culture and Mind*. Oxford: Blackwell.

Caelli, T. M. and Dodwell, P. C. (1982). The discrimination of structure in vectorgraphs: Local and global effects. *Perception and Psychophysics, 32*, 314–326.

Cahill, Thomas. (1998). *The Gifts of the Jews: How a Tribe of Desert Nomads Changed the Way Everyone Thinks and Feels*. New York: Nan A. Talese.

Campbell, N. R. (1920/1957). *Foundations of Science: The Philosophy of Theory and Experiment*. [Formerly titled: *Physics, the Elements*]. New York: Dover.

Cannon, W. B. (1932). *The Wisdom of the Body*. New York: Norton.

Capra, F. (1982). *The Turning Point*. New York: Simon and Schuster.

Carey, S., and Gelman, R. (Eds.). (1991). *The Epigenesis of Mind*. Hove, U.K.: Erlbaum.

Carlton, E. H., and Shepard, R. N. (1990). Psychologically simple motions as geodesic paths: 1. Asymmetric objects. *Journal of Mathematical Psychology, 34*, 189–228.

Carpenter, G. (1989). Neural network models for pattern recognition and associative memory. *Neural Networks, 2*, 243–257.

Carrel, A. (1935). *Man the Unknown*. New York: Harper.

Chomsky, N. (1957). *Syntactic Structures*. The Hague: Mouton.

Chomsky, N. (1959). Review of Skinner's "Verbal Behavior." *Language, 35*, 26–58.

Chomsky, N. (1980). Rules and representations. *The Behavioral and Brain Sciences, 3*, 1–61.

Clark, A. (1989). Microcognition: Philosophy, Cognitive Science, and Parallel Distributed Processing. Cambridge, MA: MIT Press.

Clarke, K. (1969). *Civilization*. New York: Harper and Row.

Cohen, G. (1989). *Memory in the Real World*. Hillsdale, NJ: Erlbaum.

Colman, A. (Ed.) (1995). *Controversies in Psychology*. London: Longman.

Cooper, L. A., and Shepard, R. N. (1973). Chronometric studies of the rotation of mental images. In W. G. Chase (Ed.), *Visual Information Processing*. New York: Academic Press.

Corballis, M. C. (1991). *The Lopsided Ape*. Oxford: Oxford University Press.

Craik, K. J. W. (1947). Theory of the human operator in control systems. *British Journal of Psychology, 38*, 56–61.

Crook, J. (1980). *The Evolution of Consciousness*. Oxford: Oxford University Press (Clarendon).

Cutting, J. E. (1986). *Perception with an Eye for Motion*. Cambridge, MA: MIT Press.

Dahblom, B. (Ed.). (1993). *Dennett and His Critics*. Oxford: Blackwell.

Davies, M., and Humphreys, G. W. (Eds.). (1993). *Consciousness: Psychological and Philosophical Essays*. Oxford: Blackwell.

Davies, P. C. W. (1983). *God and the New Physics*. London: Dent.

Davies, P. C. W., and Brown, J. R. (1986). *The Ghost in the Atom*. Cambridge: Cambridge University Press.

Dawkins, R. (1986). *The Blind Watchmaker*. London: Penguin.

Dawkins, R. (1995). *River out of Eden: The Darwinian View of Life*. London: Weidenfeld and Nicholson.

Dehaeme, S. (1997). *The Number Sense: How the Mind Creates Mathematics*. New York: Oxford University Press.

Dennett, D. C. (1978). *Brainstorms: Philosophical Essays on Mind and Psychology*. Montgomery, VT: Bradford Books.

Dennett, D. C. (1979). Review of Popper and Eccles, *The Self and Its Brain. Journal of Philosophy, 76*, 91–97.

Dennett, D. C. (1987). *The Intentional Stance*. Cambridge, MA: MIT Press/Bradford Books.

Dennett, D. C. (1988). Precis of the intentional stance. *The Behavioral and Brain Sciences, 11*, 495–546.

Dennett, D. C. (1991). *Consciousness Explained*. Boston, MA: Little, Brown.

Dennett, D. C. (1995). *Darwin's Dangerous Dream*. New York: Simon and Schuster.

Deutsch, D. (1985). Quantum Theory, the Church-Turing principle and the universal quantum computer. *Proceedings of the Royal Society of London, A 400*, 97–117.

Deutsch, D. (1997). *The Fabric of Reality*. London: Penguin.

Deutsch, J. A. (1955). A theory of shape recognition. *British Journal of Psychology, 46*, 30–37.

Deutsch, J. A. (1960). *The Structural Basis of Behavior*. Chicago: Chicago University Press.

Dodwell, P. C. (1960). Causes of behaviour and explanation in psychology. *Mind, 69*, 1–13.

Dodwell, P. C. (1967). A model for adaptation to distortions of the visual field. In W. Wathen-Dunn (Ed.), *Models for the Perception of Speech and Visual Form*. Cambridge, MA: MIT Press.

Dodwell, P. C. (1970a). Space perception and the neurophysiology of vision. *Psychonomic Monographs, 36*(13), 205–212.

Dodwell, P. C. (1970b). *Visual Pattern Recognition*. New York: Holt, Rinehart, and Winston.

Dodwell, P. C. (1975). Contemporary theoretical problems in seeing. In E. C. Carterette and M. P. Friedman (Eds.), *Handbook of Perception*, vol. 5. New York: Academic Press.

Dodwell, P. C. (1977). Criteria for a neuropsychological theory of perception. *Cahiers de Psychologie, 20*, 175–182.

Dodwell, P. C. (1983). The Lie transformation group model of visual perception. *Perception and Psychophysics, 34*, 1–16.

Dodwell, P. C. (1985). Is neuropsychology something new? *Annals of Theoretical Psychology, 3*, 143–150.

Dodwell, P. C. (1990). Perception. In J. Grusec, R. Lockhart, and J. Waller, (Eds.), *Foundations of Psychology*. Toronto: Copp Clark Pitman.

Dodwell, P. C. (1992a). Unified cognitive theory is not comprehensive. *Behavioral and Brain Sciences, 15*, 443–445.

Dodwell, P. C. (1992b). Perspectives and transformations. *Canadian Journal of Psychology, 46*, 511–537.

Dodwell, P. C. (1993). From the top down. *Canadian Psychology, 34*(2), 137–151.

Dodwell, P. C. (1994). On raising our sights. *Spatial Vision, 8*(1), 9–17.

Dodwell, P. C. (in preparation). "The Roots of Cognitive Science."

Dodwell, P. C., and Caelli, T. M. (Eds.). (1984). *Figural Synthesis*. Hillsdale, NJ: Erlbaum.

Dodwell, P. C., and Humphrey, G. K. (1990). A functional theory of the McCullough effect. *Psychological Review, 97*, 78–89.

Dolezal, H. (1982). Living in a World Transformed. New York: Academic Press.

Donald, M. (1991). *Origins of the Modern Mind*. Cambridge, MA: Harvard University Press.

Dreyfus, H. L., and Dreyfus, S. E. (1986). *Mind over Machine: The Power of Human Intuition and Expertise in the Era of the Computer*. New York: The Free Press.

Duffy, C. J., and Wurtz, R. H. (1991). Sensitivity in MS neurons to optic flow stimuli, 2. *Journal of Neurophysiology, 65*, 1346–1359.

Dunham, W. (1990). *Journey through Genius*. New York: Wiley.

Eccles, J. C. (1970). *Facing Reality*. New York: Springer.

Eccles, J. C. (1987). Brain and mind, two or one? In C. Blakemore and S. Greenfield (Eds.), *Mindwaves*. Oxford: Blackwell.

Eccles, J. C. (1993). Evolution and consciousness. In T. Ono, L. R. Squire, M. R. Raichle, D. I. Perrett, and M. Fukuda. (Eds.), *Brain Mechanisms of Perception and Memory*. New York: Oxford University Press.

Eddington, A. (1935). *The Nature of the Physical World*. London: Dent.

Edelman, G. M. (1987). *Neural Darwinism*. New York: Bantam Books.

Edelman, G. M. (1992). *Bright Air, Brilliant Fire.* New York: Basic Books.

Egner, R. E., and Dennon, L. E. (Eds.). (1961). *The Basic Writings of Bertrand Russell.* New York: Simon and Schuster.

Einstein, A. (1979). *Ideas and Opinions.* New York: Dell.

Emerson, R. W. (1849/1946). The Oversoul. In C. Bode (Ed.), *The Portable Emerson.* New York: Penguin Books.

Esterson, A. (1993). *Seductive Mirage: An Exploration of the Work of Sigmund Freud.* Chicago: Open Court.

Fairley, B. (1947). *A Study of Goethe.* Oxford: Oxford University Press (Clarendon).

Feldman, J. A. (1985). Four frames suffice: A provisional model of vision and space. *Behavioral and Brain Sciences, 8,* 265–289.

Fodor, J. A. (1983). *The Modularity of Mind: An Essay on Faculty Psychology.* Cambridge, MA: MIT Press.

Fodor, J. A. (1985). Precis of the modularity of mind. *The Behavioral and Brain Sciences, 8*(1), 1–42.

Fodor, J. A., and Pylyshyn, Z. (1988). Connectionism and cognitive architecture. *Cognition, 28,* 3–71.

Frank, P. (1957). *Philosophy of Science.* Englewood Cliffs, NJ: Prentice-Hall.

Frege, G. (1893/1964). *The Basic Laws of Arithmetic.* Berkeley: University of California Press.

Frye, N. (1957). *Anatomy of Criticism.* Princeton, NJ: Princeton University Press.

Gallant, J. L., Braun, J., and Van Essen, D. C. (1993). Selectivity for polar, hyperbolic, and cartesian gratings of macaque visual cortex. *Science, 259,* 100–103.

Galton, F. (1883). *Inquiries into Human Faculty and Its Development.* London: Dent.

Gardner, H. (1985). *The Mind's New Science: A History of the Cognitive Revolution.* New York: Oxford University Press.

Gardner, M. (1958). *Logic Machines and Diagrams.* Chicago: University of Chicago Press.

Gazzaniga, M. (1985). *The Social Brain: Discovering the Networks of the Mind.* New York: Basic Books.

Geschwind, N. (1974). *Selected Papers on Language and the Brain.* Dordrecht/Boston: Reidel.

Gibson, J. J. (1950). *The Perception of the Visual World.* Boston: Houghton-Mifflin.

Gibson, J. J. (1966). *The Senses Considered as Perceptual Systems.* Boston: Houghton-Mifflin.

Gibson, J. J. (1979). *The Ecological Approach to Visual Perception.* Boston: Houghton-Mifflin.

Gleick, J. (1987). *Chaos: Making a New Science.* New York: Penguin Books.

Goldman-Rakic, P. S. (1992). Working memory and the mind. *Scientific America, 267*(3), 110–117.

Gontarski, S.E. (1985). *The Intent of Undoing in Samuel Beckett's Dramatic Texts.* Bloomington: University of Indiana Press.

Goodman, N. (1976). *Languages of Art: An Approach to a Theory of Symbols.* Cambridge, MA: Hackett.

Green, C., and McCreery, C. (1995). *Lucid Dreaming.* New York: Routledge.

Gregory, R. L. (1981). *Mind in Science: A History of Explanations in Psychology and Physics.* London: Weidenfeld and Nicholson.

Grey, M. (1985). *Return from Death: An Exploration of the Near-Death Experience.* London: Routledge and Kegan Paul.

Gribbin, J. (1995). *Schroedinger's Kittens and the Search for Reality.* New York: Little.

Grimsdale, R. L., Sumner, F. H., Tunis, C. J., and Kilburn, T. (1959). A system for automatic recognition of patterns. *Proceedings of the Institute of Electrical Engineeers (U.K.)*, *106*, 210–226.

Grossberg, S. (1987). *The Adaptive Brain*. Amsterdam: Elsevier.

Grusec, J., Lockhart, R., and Waller, G. (1990). *Foundations of Psychology*. Toronto: Copp Clark Pitman.

Guilford, J. P. (1967). *The Nature of Human Intelligence*. New York: McGraw-Hill.

Hadamard, J. (1945). *The Psychology of Invention in the Mathematical Field*. Princeton, NJ: Princeton University Press.

Halford, G. S. (1982). *The Development of Thought*. Hillsdale NJ: Erlbaum.

Hamlyn, D. W. (1957). *The Psychology of Perception*. London: Routledge and Kegan Paul.

Hardy, G. H. (1967). *A Mathematician's Apology*. Cambridge: Cambridge University Press.

Harré, R., and Gillett, G. (1994). *The Discursive Mind*. London: Sage.

Harris, R. A. (1993). *The Language Wars*. Oxford: Oxford University Press.

Hawking, S. (1988). *A Brief History of Time*. New York: Bantam.

Heath, T. L. (1921). *Greek Mathematics*. 2 vols. Oxford: Clarendon.

Hebb, D. O. (1949). *The Organization of Behavior*. New York: Wiley.

Heil, J., and Mele, A. (Eds.). (1993). *Mental Causation*. Oxford: Oxford University Press.

Heisenberg, W. (1952). *Zur Geschichte der physikalischen Naturerklärung*. English translation, *Philosophic Problems of Nuclear Science*, by F. C. Hamer. London: Faber and Faber.

Heisenberg, W. (1958). The representaion of nature in contemporary physics. *Daedelus, 87*, 95–108.

Helmholtz, H. V. (1856–66/1962). *Treatise on Physiological Optics*. New York: Dover.

Helson, H. (1964). *Adaptation Level Theory: An Experimental and Systematic Approach to Behavior*. New York: Harper and Row.

Hietanen, J. K., and Perrett, D. I. (1993). The role of expectation in visual and tactile processing within the temporal cortex. In T. Ono, L. R. Squire, M. E. Raichle, D. I. Perrett, and M. Fukuda (Eds.), *Brain Mechanisms of Perception and Memory: From Neuron to Behavior.* New York: Oxford University Press.

Hinson, M. (Ed.) (1990). *Mozart: Piano Music from His Early Years*. Van Nuys, CA: Alfred Publishing.

Hobbes (1651/1958). *Leviathan*. New York (original ed., Paris): Library of Liberal Arts.

Hodgson, D. (1991). *The Mind Matters*. Oxford: Oxford University Press.

Hoffman, W. C. (1966). The Lie algebra of visual perception. *Journal of Mathematical Psychology, 3*, 65–98.

Hoffman, W. C. (1970). Higher visual perception as prolongations of the basic Lie transformation group. *Mathematical Biosciences, 6*, 65–98.

Hoffman, W. C. (1980). Subjective geometry and geometric psychology. *International Journal of Mathematical Modeling, 1*, 349–367.

Hoffman, W. C. (1984). Figural synthesis by vector fields. In P. C. Dodwell and T. M. Caelli (Eds.), *Figural Synthesis* Hillsdale, NJ: Erlbaum.

Hoffman, W. C. (1985). Some reasons why algebraic topology is important in neuropsychology: Perceptual and cognitive systems as fibrations. *International Journal of Man-Machine Studies, 22*, 613–650.

Hoffman, W. C. (1994). Equivalent dynamical systems: A formal model for the generation of arbitrary shapes. In O. Ving-Lie, A. Toet, D. Foster, J. A. M. Heijman, and P. Meer (Eds.), *Shape in Picture*. Berlin: Springer Verlag.

Hoffman, W. C., and Dodwell, P. C. (1985). Geometric psychology generates the visual Gestalt. *Canadian Journal of Psychology, 39*, 491–528.

Hofstaedter, D. R. (1979). *Goedel, Escher, Bach: An Eternal Golden Braid*. New York: Basic Books.

Hofstaedter, D. R. (1997). *Le Ton Beau de Marot: In Praise of the Music of Language*. New York: Basic Books.

Hofstaedter, D. R., and Dennett, D. C. (1981). *The Mind's I*. New York: Basic Books.

Holding, D. R. (1985). *The Psychology of Chess Skill*. Hillsdale, NJ: Erlbaum.

Holst, E. von, and Mittelstaedt, H. (1950). Das Reafferenzprinzip. *Die Naturwissenschaften, 37*, 464–476. Translated as: The principle of reafference: Interactions between the central nervous system and the peripheral organs. In P. C. Dodwell (Ed.), *Perceptual Processing*. New York: Appleton-Century-Crofts.

Honderich, T. H. (1988). *A Theory of Determinism*. Oxford: Clarendon Press.

Howard, J. (1966) *Spatial Orientation*. New York: Wiley.

Hubel, D. H. (1988). *Eye, Brain and Vision*. San Francisco: Freeman.

Hubel, D. H., and Wiesel, T. N. (1962). Receptive fields, binocular interaction and functional architecture in the cat's visual cortex. *Journal of Physiology, 160*, 106–154.

Hubel, D. H., and Wiesel, T. N. (1968). Receptive fields and functional architecture in monkey striate cortex. *Journal of Physiology, 195*, 215–243.

Hull, C. L. (1943). *Principles of Behaviour*. New York: Appleton-Century-Crofts.

Humphrey, G. (1951). *Thinking: An Introduction to Its Experimental Psychology*. London: Methuen.

Humphrey, N. K. (1992). *A History of the Mind*. New York: Simon and Schuster.

Hunter, J. F. M. (1990). *Wittgenstein on Words as Instruments*. Edinburgh: University of Edinburgh Press.

Husserl, E. (1890/1982). *Ideas Pertaining to a Pure Phenomenology and to a Phenomenological Philosophy*. Trans. F. Kersten. The Hague: Nijhof.

Ingle, D., Mansfield, R., and Goodale, M. (Eds.). (1982). *Recent Advances in the Analysis of Visual Behavior*. Cambridge, MA: MIT Press.

Jackendoff, R. S. (1987). *Consciousness and the Computational Mind*. Cambridge, MA: MIT Press.

Jahn, R. G., and Dunne, B. J. (1987). *Margins of Reality*. New York: Harcourt Brace.

James, W. (1890). *Principles of Psychology*. New York: Holt, Rinehart and Winston. Repr. New York: Dover, 1950.

Kant, I. (1724/1902). *Prolegomena to Any Future Metaphysics*. Trans. P. Carus. Chicago: Open Court.

Karmiloff-Smith, A. (1994). *Beyond Modularity: A Developmental Perspective on Cognitive Science*. Cambridge: Cambridge University Press.

Keller, H. (1908). *The World I Live In*. New York: Century.

Kenny, A. (1984). *The Legacy of Wittgenstein*. Oxford: Blackwell.

Kimble, D. (1994). The nervous system and the brain. In A. M. Colman (Ed.), *Companion Encyclopedia of Psychology*. London: Routledge.

Koch, S. (1954). *Modern Learning Theory*. New York: Appleton-Century-Crofts.

Koestler, A. (1959). *The Sleepwalkers: A History of Man's Changing Vision of the Universe*. London: Penguin.

Koestler, A. (1966). *The Act of Creation*. New York: Dell.

Koestler, A. (1967). *The Ghost in the Machine*. London: Hutchinson.

Koffka, K. (1935). *Principles of Gestalt Psychology*. New York: Harcourt, Brace and World.

Köhler, W. (1929). *Gestalt Psychology*. New York: Liveright.

Kolers, P. A., and Smythe, W. E. (1984). Symbol manipulation: Alternatives to the computational view of mind. *Journal of Verbal Learning and Verbal Behavior, 23*, 328–330.

Kosslyn, S. M. (1981). *Image and Mind*. Cambridge, MA: Harvard University Press.

Kosslyn, S. M. (1987). Seeing and imagining in the cerebral hemispheres: A computational approach. *Psychological Review, 94*, 148–175.

Kubovy, M., and Pomerantz, J. R. (Eds.). (1981). *Perceptual Organization*. Hillsdale, NJ: Erlbaum.

Lashley, K. S. (1942). The problem of cerebral organization in vision. *Biological Symposia, 7,* 301–322.

Lenneberg, E. (1967). *Biological Foundations of Language*. New York: Wiley.

Lepore, E., and von Gulick, R. (Eds.). (1992). *John Searle and His Critics*. Oxford: Blackwell.

Leyton, M. (1992). *Symmetry, Causality, Mind*. Cambridge, MA: MIT Press.

Liebeck, P. (1984). *How Children Learn Mathematics*. Harmondsworth, U.K.: Penguin Books.

Lockwood, M. (1989). *Mind, Brain and the Quantum*. Oxford: Blackwell.

Lorenz, K. (1970/1971). *Studies in Animal and Human Behaviour*. Vols. 1 and 2. London: Methuen.

Lucas, J. R. (1961). Minds, machines, and Goedel. *Philosophy, 36,* 120–124.

Luria, A. R. (1973). *The Working Brain*. Harmondsorth, U.K.: Penguin.

Lyall, W. (1855). *Intellect, the Emotions, and the Moral Nature*. Edinburgh: Constable.

Mach, E. (1883/1960). *The Analysis of Sensations and the Relation of the Physical to the Psychical*. Trans. C. M. Williams and S. Waterlow. New York: Open Court.

MacKay, D. M. (1967). *Freedom of Action in a Mechanistic Universe*. Cambridge: Cambridge University Press.

Macnamara, J. (1986). *A Border Dispute: The Place of Logic in Psychology*. Cambridge, MA: MIT Press/Bradford Books.

Macnamara, J. (1990). Ideals and psychology. *Canadian Psychology, 31*(1), 14–25.

Mcnamara, J., and Reyes, G. (Eds.) (1994). *The Logical Foundations of Cognition*. New York: Oxford University Press.

Madsen, J. (1985). *Annals of Theoretical Psychology, 3* (whole issue).

Marr, D. (1976). Early processing of visual information. *Philosophical Transactions of the Royal Society (London), B 197,* 441–475.

Marr, D. (1982). *Vision: A Computational Investigation of the Human Representation of Visual Information*. San Francisco: Freeman.

McCulloch, W. S., and Pitts, W. (1943). A logical calculus of the ideas immanent in nervous activity. *Bulletin of Mathematical Biophysics, 5,* 115–133.

Miller, G. A. (1956). The magical number seven, plus or minus two: Some limits on our capacity for processing information. *Psychological Review, 63,* 81–96.

Miller, G. A. (1990). On explanation. *Annals of Theoretical Psychology, 6,* 7–37.

Milner, A. D., and Goodale, M. A. (1993). Visual pathways to perception and action. In T. P. Hicks, S. Molotchnikoff, and T. Ono (Eds.), *Progress in Brain Research*. Amsterdam: Elsevier.

Minton, H. L., and Schneider, F. W. (1980). *Differential Psychology*. Monterey, CA: Brooks/Cole.

Mishkin, M., Ungerleider, L. G., and Macko, K. A. (1983). Object vision and spatial vision: Two cortical pathways. *Trends in Neuroscience, 6,* 414–417.

Moody, R. A. (1981). *Life after Life*. New York: Bantam Books.

Moore, B. C. J. (1989). *An Introduction to the Psychology of Hearing*. 3rd ed. London: Academic Press.

Morris, D. (1967). *The Naked Ape*. London: Cape.

Morris, R. G. M. (Ed.). (1989). *Parallel Distributed Processing: Implications for Psychology and Neurobiology*. New York: Oxford University Press.

Murray, D. J. (1988). *A History of Western Psychology*. 2nd ed. New York: Prentice Hall.

Murray, D. J. (1993). A Perspective for viewing the history of psychophysics. *Behavioral and Brain Sciences, 16*, 115–186.

Murray, D. J. (1994). What are the "goals" of the human memory system? *Behavioral and Brain Sciences, 17*(4), 676–677.

Murray, D. J. (1995). *Gestalt Psychology and the Cognitive Revolution.* New York: Hawthorn Wheatsheaf.

Nagel, E. (1961). *The Structure of Science: Problems in the Logic of Scientific Explanation.* New York: Harcourt, Brace and World.

Nagel, T. (1974). What is it like to be a bat? *Philosophical Review, 83*, 435–450.

Nagel, T. (1979). Brain bisection and the unity of consciousness. In T. Nagel (Ed.), *Mortal Questions.* Cambridge: Cambridge University Press.

Nagel, T. (1986). *The View from Nowhere.* Oxford: Oxford University Press.

Neisser, U. (1967). *Cognitive Psychology.* New York: Appleton-Century-Crofts.

Neisser, U. (1976). *Cognition and Reality.* San Francisco: Freeman.

Neisser, U. (Ed.). (1982). *Memory Observed: Remembering in Natural Contexts.* San Francisco: Freeman.

Neisser, U. (1988). Five kinds of self-knowledge. *Philosophical Psychology, 1*, 35–59.

Newell, A. (1991). *Unified Theories of Cognition.* Cambridge, MA: Harvard University Press.

Newell, A. (1992). Precis of *Unified Theories of Cognition. Behavioral and Brain Sciences, 15*, 425–492.

Newell, A., and Simon, H. A. (1972). *Human Problem Solving.* Engelwood Cliffs, NJ: Prentice-Hall.

Newell, A., and Simon, H. A. (1976). Computer science as empirical enquiry: Symbols and search. *Communications of the ACM, 19*, 113–126.

Ogden, C. K., and Richards, I. A. (1923). *The Meaning of Meaning.* London: Kegan Paul.

Ono, T., Squire, L. R., Raichle, M. E., Perrett, D. E., and Fukuda, M. (Eds.). (1993). *Brain Mechanisms of Perception and Memory: From Neuron to Behavior.* New York: Oxford University Press.

Paivio, A. (1986). *Mental Representations: A Dual Coding Approach.* New York: Oxford University Press.

Parfit, D. (1984). *Reasons and Persons.* Oxford: Oxford University Press.

Peitgen, H.-O., Jurgens, H., and Saupe, D. (1993). *Chaos and Fractals: New Frontiers in Science.* New York: Springer.

Penfield, W. (1977). *The Mystery of the Mind.* Princeton, NJ: Princeton University Press.

Penrose, R. (1989). *The Emperor's New Mind: Concerning Computers, Minds, and the Laws of Physics.* Oxford: Oxford University Press.

Penrose, R. (1990). Precis of *Emperor's New Mind: Concerning Computers, Minds, and the Laws of Physics. Behavioral and Brain Sciences, 13*, 643–705.

Penrose, R. (1994). *Shadows of the Mind.* Oxford: Oxford University Press.

Penrose, R. (1997). *The Large, the Small, and the Human Mind.* Cambridge: Cambridge University Press.

Perrett, D. I., Harries, M. H., Bevan, R., Thomas, S., Benson, P. J., Mistlin, A. J., Chitty, A. J., Hietanen, J. K., and Ortega, J. E. (1989). Frameworks of analysis for the neural representation of animate objects and actions. *Journal of Experimental Biology, 146*, 87–113.

Peters, R. S. (1960). *The Concept of Motivation.* London: Routledge and Kegan Paul.

Piaget, J. (1952). *The Child's Conception of Number.* New York: Humanities Press.

Piaget, J. (1953). *The Origin of Intelligence in the Child.* London: Routledge and Kegan Paul.

Piaget, J. (1954). *The Child's Construction of Reality.* New York: Basic Books.

Piaget, J. (1971). *Biology and Knowledge.* Chicago: University of Chicago Press.

Piatelli-Palmarini, M. (Ed.). (1980). *Language and Learning: The Debate between Jean Piaget and Noam Chomsky.* Cambridge, MA: Harvard University Press.

Pickles, J. O. (1988). *An Introduction to the Physiology of Hearing.* 2nd ed. London: Academic Press.

Pickover, C. A. (1991). *Computers and the Imagination.* New York: St. Martin's Press.

Pinker, S. (Ed.). (1985). *Visual Cognition.* Cambridge, MA: MIT Press.

Pinker, S. (1994). *The Language Instinct.* New York: William Morrow.

Pinker, S. (1997). *How the Mind Works.* New York: Norton.

Pitts, W. H., and McCulloch, W. S. (1947). How we know the universals: The perception of auditory and visual forms. *Bulletin of Mathematical Biophysics, 9,* 127–147.

Poincaré, J. H. (1908/1968). Mathematical creation. In M. Kline (Ed.), *Mathematics in the Modern World: Readings from Scientific American.* San Francisco: Freeman.

Polyani, M. (1962, corrected edition). *Personal Knowledge.* London: Routledge and Kegan Paul.

Polanyi, M. (1966). *The Tacit Dimension.* London: Routledge and Kegan Paul.

Popper, K. (1934/1959). *The Logic of Scientific Discovery.* London: Hutchinson.

Popper, K. (1969). *Conjectures and Refutations.* 3rd ed. London: Routledge and Kegan Paul.

Popper, K., and Eccles, J. C. (1977). *The Self and Its Brain: The Argument for Interactionism.* New York: Springer.

Premack, D. (1985). "Gavagai!" or the future history of the animal language controversy. *Cognition, 19,* 207–296.

Priest, S. (1991). *Theories of the Mind.* London: Penguin.

Putnam, H. (1988). *Representation and Reality.* Cambridge, MA: MIT Press.

Redi, F. (1684). *Osservazioni Intorno agli Animali Viventi che si Trovano negli Animali Viventi.* (N.P.). See also Redi, F. (1688). *Esperienze Intorno alla Generazione degli Insetti.* Firenze: Martini.

Rennie, M. K., and Girle, R. A. (1973). *Logic: Theory and Practice.* Brisbane: University of Queensland Press.

Reyes, G. E., Reyes, M., and Macnamara, J. (1991). Functoriality and grammatical role in syllogisms. *Report #91–6, Departement de Mathematiques et de Statisitique, Universite de Montreal,* 1–58.

Roitblatt, H. L., Bever, T. G. and Terrace, H. S. (Eds.) (1995). *Animal Cognition.* Hillsdale, NJ: Erlbaum.

Rorty, R. (1979). *Philosophy and the Mirror of Nature.* Princeton, NJ: Princeton University Press.

Rorty, R. (1991). *Objectivity, Relativism, and Truth.* Cambridge: Cambridge University Press.

Rosch, E. (1973). Natural categories. *Cognitive Psychology, 4,* 328–350.

Rumelhart, D. E., and McClelland, J. L., (1986). *Parallel Distributed Processing: Explorations in the Microstructure of Cognition. Vol. 1: Foundations.* Cambridge, MA: MIT Press/Bradford Books.

Russell, B. (1919). *An Introduction to Mathematical Philosophy.* London: Allen and Unwin.

Russell, B. (1940). *An Inquiry into Meaning and Truth.* New York: Norton.

Russell, B. (1945). *A History of Western Philosophy.* New York: Simon and Schuster.

Russell, B. (1951). *The Autobiography of Bertrand Russell.* Boston: Little, Brown.

Russell, B., and Whitehead, A. N. (1910). *Principia Mathematica.* Vol. 1. Cambridge: Cambridge University Press.

Ryle, G. (1949). *The Concept of Mind.* London: Hutchinson.

Saarilouma, P. (1995). *Chess Players' Thinking.* New York: Routledge.

Savage-Rumbaugh, E. S. (1984). Acquisition of functional symbol usage in apes and children. In H. L. Roitblatt, T. G. Bever, and H. S. Terrace (Eds.), *Animal Cognition* Hillsdale, NJ: Erlbaum.

Schiffman, H. R. (1982). *Sensation and Perception: An Integrated Approach.* New York: Wiley.

Schimmel, A. (1993). *The Mystery of Numbers.* New York: Oxford University Press.

Scientific American. (1988). The brain. Ed. D. H. Hubel. *Scientific American, 260.* (special issue).

Scientific American. (1992). Mind and brain. Ed. D. H. Hubel. *Scientific American, 267*(3) (special issue).

Searle, J. (1980). Minds, Brains, and Programs. *Behavioral and Brain Sciences, 3,* 417–458.

Searle, J. (1990). Consciousness, explanatory inversion, and cognitive science. *Behavioral and Brain Sciences, 13,* 585–642.

Searle, J. (1994). *The Rediscovery of the Mind.* Cambridge, MA: MIT Press/Bradford Books.

Shamdanasi, S., and Munchow, M. (Eds.). (1994). *Speculations after Freud: Psychoanalysis, Philosophy, and Culture.* New York: Routledge.

Shank, R. C. (1982). *Dynamic Memory: A Theory of Reminding and Learning in Computers and People.* Cambridge: Cambridge University Press.

Shear, J. (1990). *The Inner Dimension.* New York: Peter Lang.

Sheldrake, R. (1987). *A New Science of Life.* 2nd ed. London: Collins (Paladin Books)

Shepard, R. N., and Metzler, J. (1971). Mental rotation of three-dimensional objects. *Science, 171,* 701–703.

Shotter, J. (1975). *Images of Man in Psychological Research.* London: Methuen.

Shotter, J. (1993). *Conversational Realities: Constructing Life through Language.* London: Sage.

Siegler, R. S., and Robinson, M. (1982). The development of numerical understanding. In H. W. Reese and L. P. Lipsett (Eds.), *Advances in Child Development,* vol 16. New York: Academic.

Skinner, B. F. (1938). *The Behavior of Organisms.* New York: Appleton-Century-Crofts.

Skinner, B. F. (1978). *Reflexions on Behaviorism and Society.* Engelwood Cliffs, NJ: Prentice-Hall.

Sloman, A. (1978). *The Computer Revolution in Philosophy: Science and Models of Mind.* Brighton, U.K.: Harvester.

Sloman, A. (1992). The emperor's real mind: Review of Roger Penrose's *The Emperor's New Mind: Concerning Computers, Minds, and the Laws of Physics. Artificial Intelligence, 56,* 355–396.

Snow, C. P. (1993). *The Two Cultures.* Orig. pub., 1957. Cambridge: Cambridge University Press.

Solso, R. L., and Massaro, D. W. (1995). *The Science of Mind.* New York: Oxford University Press.

Sperry, R. (1983). *Science and Moral Priority.* Oxford: Blackwell.

Sperry, R. W., Miner, C., and Myers, R. E. (1955). Visual pattern perception following subpial slicing and tantalum wire implantations in the visual cortex. *Journal of Comparative and Physiological Psychology, 48,* 50–58.

Spillman, L., and Werner, J. S. (Eds.). (1990). *Visual Perception: The Neurophysiological Foundations.* New York: Academic.

Sprigge, T. L. S. (1971). Final causes, 1. *Proceedings of the Aristotelian Society, supplementary vol. 45,* 149–170.

Sternberg, R. G., and Detterman, D. K. (Eds.). (1986). *What Is Intelligence? Contemporary Viewpoints on its Nature and Definition.* Norwood, NJ: Ablex.

Sternberg, R. J. (1990). *Metaphors of Mind: Conceptions of the Nature of Intelligence.* New York: Cambridge University Press.

Stewart, I. (1975). *Concepts of Modern Mathematics.* London: Penguin.

Stewart, I. (1992). *The Problems of Mathematics.* 2nd ed. Oxford: Oxford University Press.

Stove, D. C. (1982). *Popper and After: Four Modern Irrationalists.* Oxford: Pergamon.

Stratton, G. M. (1897). Vision without inversion of the retinal image. *Psychological Review, 4,* 341–360, 463–481.

Suppes, P. (1957). *Introduction to Logic.* New York: Van Nostrand Reinhold.

Tarnas, R. (1993). *The Passion of the Western Mind: Understanding the Ideas That Have Shaped Our World View.* New York: Random House/Ballantine.

Tart, C. T. (Ed.). (1975). *Transpersonal Psychologies.* New York: Harper and Row.

Thompson, D. W. (1917). *On Growth and Form.* Cambridge: Cambridge University Press.

Thorndike, E. L. (1932). *The Fundamentals of Learning.* New York: Columbia University Teacher's College.

Thorpe, W. H. (1978). *Purpose in a World of Chance: A Biologist's View.* Oxford: Oxford University Press.

Tinbergen, N. (1951). *The Study of Instinct.* Oxford: Oxford University Press.

Toulmin, S. (1970). Reasons and causes. In R. Borger and F. Cioffi (Eds.), *Explanation in the Behavioral Sciences.* Cambridge: Cambridge University Press.

Turner, F. W. (1985). *Natural Classicism: Essays on Literature and Science.* New York: Paragon.

Uhr, L. (1966). *Pattern Recognition.* New York: Wiley.

Urmson, J. (1966). *Philosophical Analysis: Development between the Two World Wars.* Oxford: Oxford University Press.

Uttal, W. R. (1981). *A Taxonomy of Visual Processes.* Hillsdale, NJ: Erlbaum.

Uttley, A. M. (1954). The classification of signals in the nervous system. *EEG and Clinical Neurophysiology, 6,* 479–494.

Uttley, A. M. (1959). The design of conditional probability computers. *Information and Control, 2,* 1–24.

van Rooijen, J. (1987). Interactionism and evolution: A critique of Popper. *British Journal for the Philosophy of Science, 38,* 87–92.

von Wright, G. H. (1971). *Explanation and Understanding.* Ithaca, NY: Cornell University Press.

Waldrop, M. M. (1992). *Complexity.* New York: Simon and Schuster.

Walter, W. G. (1953). *The Living Brain.* London: Duckworth.

Wason, P. C., and Johnson-Laird, P. N. (1972). *Psychology of Reasoning: Structure and Content.* Cambridge, MA: Harvard University Press.

Watson, E. L. G. (1951). Evolution and creation. *The Golden Blade, 3,* 43–56.

Wertheimer, M. (1978). *Productive Thinking.* Orig. ed., 1945. Westport, CN: Greenwood Press.

Westfall, R. S. (1980). *Never at Rest: A Biography of Isaac Newton.* Cambridge: Cambridge University Press.

White, M. (1983). *The Age of Analysis.* New York: Meridian.

Whitehead, A. N. (1927). *Science and the Modern World.* Cambridge: Cambridge University Press.

Whitehead, A. N. (undated, circa 1912). *Introduction to Mathematics.* London: Williams and Norgate (Home University Library).

Williams, C. (1938). *The Flashing Stream.* London: Macmillan.

Wilson, E. O. (1998). *Consilience: The Unity of Knowledge.* New York: Knopf.

Wiener, N. (1948). *Cybernetics: Control and Communication in the Animal and the Machine.* Cambridge, MA: MIT Press.

Wiggins, D. (1967). *Identity and Spatio-Temporal Continuity.* Oxford: Blackwell.

Wigner, E. (1967). *Symmetries and Reflections.* Bloomington: Indiana University Press.

Winograd, T. (1972). *Understanding Natural Languages.* New York: Academic.

Wisdom, J. (1936). Metaphysics and verification. *Proceedings of the Aristotelian Society, London, 37.*

Wittgenstein, L. (1975, posthumous). *The Blue and Brown Books.* Oxford: Blackwell.

Wozniak, R. (Ed.). (1995). *Behaviorism: The Early Years.* New York: Routledge.

Young, J. Z. (1987). *Philosophy and the Brain.* Oxford: Oxford University Press.

Zajonc, A. (1993). *Catching the Light.* New York: Bantam.

Zucker, S. (1984). Early orientation selection in dot patterns. In P. C. Dodwell and T. M Caelli (Eds.), *Figural Synthesis.* Hillsdale, NJ: Erlbaum.

Zusne, N. (1970). *Visual Perception of Form.* New York: Academic.

Index

rearrangement. *See* adaptation (rearrangement)
reason, 55, 74, 89–93
recall, 21, 26. *See also* memory
receptive field, 33
Redi, F., 170, 173, 176, 178, 216n
reducibility, axiom of, 58
reductionism, 36, 168
redundancy, 35. *See also* Information Theory
reflex, conditioned, 19
reinforcement, 21, 52
Relativity, General Theory of, 11, 78, 130
Rennie, M. K., 211n
representation
  by machine, 67
  neural, 33, 36
  place in perceptual theory, 119
  of psychological function, 34, 37
  and reality 107–125
    the general case 117–119
    the straight line, 113–117
res cogitans, 6
res extensa, 6
retina, 33, 34
retinal receptive fields. *See* receptive field
Reyes, G. E., 206n, 209n, 216n
Reyes, M., 206n, 209n, 216n
Richards, I. A., 205n
Riemann, B.130, 134
Rilke, R. M., 187
Rite of Spring (Stravinsky), 200
river, as metaphor, 176. *See also* flashing stream
Robinson, M., 206n, 213n
robotics, 28, 39, 203n
Rock, I., 96, 97
Roitblatt, H. L., 202n
Romantic era, 199
Rorty, R., 201n, 204n
Rosenblith, W., 83
Rosch, E., 55
rotation, mental, 29
rule, of entailment, 97
Rumelhart, D. B., 204n
Russell, B., ix, 4, 20, 40, 43, 53, 62, 63–65, 76, 126, 128, 138, 149, 150, 180, 201n, 206n, 207n, 211n, 213n
Ryle, G., 54, 55, 78, 123, 202n, 204n, 205n, 207n

Saarilouma, P., 208n
sacred river, 175–200. *See also* flashing stream
Saupe, D., 206n, 217n
saving the appearances. *See* Barfield, O.
Scarlatti, A., 199
schema, 21, 72. *See also* memory; thinking
Schiffman, H. R., 203n
Schiller, G., 190
Schimmel, A., 213n
Schlick, M., 67, 68
Schneider, F. W., 202n
Schroedinger, E., 10, 79, 207n
science, 62
  abuses of, 9, 216n
  and epistemology, 171, 172
  goals of, 14
  idealism in, 186
  and metaphysics, 7, 9, 10, 209n, 216n
  and mind, , 10–11, 58–81
  and the modern world, 9–11
  and the understanding of mind, 10, 11, 161
  and understanding the world, 7–10
Scientific American (journal), 203n, 204n, 208n
scientific explanation, 3, 164, 167, 168, 196–198
  and folk psychology, 197
  observation and renewal, 176
scientific research
  its drama, 179 (*see also* Polanyi, M.)
  its grammar, 179 (*see also* Popper, K.)
Scruton, R., 175
Searle, J., viii, 44, 201n–204n
self, 60, 61, 75
  and brain, 62
  and mind, 192–195
self-produced stimulation, 120
self-reference, and cognitive theory, 159, 160, 193, 194
self-reflexive stance, in cognitive science, 74
semantics, 47
sensation, 22. *See also* psychophysics
sense organs, 22, 33
sensory physiology, 83, 84
sensory qualities, 17, 86, 88, 208n
sensory-motor schemas. *See* Piaget, J.
sentences, 26, 53